Paths to the
Middle East

Paths to the Middle East

Ten Scholars Look Back

Edited and compiled by Thomas Naff

State University of New York Press

Published by
State University of New York Press, Albany

Printed in the United States of America

For information, address State University of New York Press, State University
Plaza, Albany, N.Y. 12246

Production by Marilyn Semerad
Marketing by Nancy Farrell
Text composition and design by Osage Associates

Library of Congress Cataloging-in-Publication Data

Paths to the Middle East : ten scholars look back / edited and
    compiled by Thomas Naff.
        p.   cm.
    Includes index.
    ISBN 0-7914-1883-9 (HC : acid free paper). — ISBN 0-7914-1884-7
(PB : acid free paper)
        1.Orientalists—Biography. 2. Middle East—Study and teaching-
-History—20th century.   I. Naff. Thomas.
DS61.7.A1P38   1993
956' .0072—dc20   93-14597
                                                          CIP

To R. Bayly Winder and Albert Hourani, two who led the way

Table of Contents

Preface

For most of the first half of this century, the academic field of Islamic or Near and Middle Eastern studies was defined for the most part by European scholars who were archeologists, philologists, historians, and theologians, not infrequently combining all of these roles in themselves. Some of them were men—together with a smattering of women—of considerable breadth of mind, vision, and experience, who perceived themselves as maintaining an honorable tradition of service to God, country, and learning, profoundly dedicated to exploring and interpreting the Islamic world to their fellow westerners. Modern social science had not as yet made its impact on non-western scholarship.

As intelligent as their vision was, their mentality remained, with a few notable exceptions, Eurocentric. They acknowledged themselves as Orientalists and, subsequently, we too labeled them as such. While mediating the cultures and religions of the Near and Middle East to their countrymen, they simultaneously endeavored to carry what they considered to be superior forms and standards of western erudition to the learned classes of the region. Meanwhile, if their fellow Western countrymen, on whom they had little impact, thought about the region at all, most embraced a stereotypical, often cheap, romantic view of decadence, heathenism, mystery, and danger, popularized by the penny (sou, pfennig) press and reinforced by travelogues and popular art. In their endeavors, these Orientalists sometimes became, in a variety of ways, the partners—and sometimes the witting or unwitting instruments—of their governments, which, for motives of national self-interest and religious ideology, sought to westernize the "oriental" nations over which they had become colonial rulers.

It is the wont of each generation to refract the historical and social past through the prism of its own values and to make judgments accordingly. Thus have many of the current generation assessed the Orientalists and, in recent years, given to their Eurocentricity and identity with the colonial policies of their governments an *ex post facto* pejorative spin. This perception is in many respects justified but, at the same time, like most sweeping condemnations, it has not been consistently on the mark nor altogether fair. The Orientalists were, after all, creatures of their times shaped by the ethos of their day, as were the missions they set for themselves. If they are to be viewed objectively, they must first be taken on their own terms. Some of them, by the breadth and depth of their intellects, by their generosity of spirit—of which several of the authors in this volume claim to be beneficiaries—were too large to be encapsulated by a label like "Orientalist."

Through whatever contemporary prism their lives and work may now be perceived, however they may be judged, their overall scholarly accomplishments cannot be denied. With few of the research and analytical tools we possess today, they broke new scholarly ground and laid a firm basis for the modern study of the region and its cultures. Perhaps of equal importance, they trained the generation whose representatives are included in this volume and who are among the great names and pioneers of post-World War II modern Middle East studies. (These authors were the students of some of the great teachers and scholars of their day, now dubbed "Orientalists"—H. A. R. Gibb, Phillip Hitti, Louis Massignon, et al.)

However, the generation represented in this volume began to split away from the traditional pattern of Orientalism for a combination of reasons. Among them were their direct personal experiences with the region, the changed ideological and intellectual milieu of the 1930s and 1940s, in which they grew up, and because the Orientalist tradition was not as strong in the U.S. as in Europe. From their altered perspectives they cut new paths to the Middle East, paths which provided direction for the generation that followed.

◆ ◆ ◆

At the present time, the field of Middle East studies is undergoing yet another generational change. The generation that succeeded the "Orientalists"—and who constitute our link with them—trained the present generation of Middle East scholars and, in many cases, also had a hand in shaping government and corporate policies toward the region after World War II. They have now begun to retire. To preserve their insights into the past and their visions of the future for those who have not had the privilege to study with them directly, a number of major Islamic and Middle East scholars were asked to provide their perspectives and views in a short, personal "summing-up" of their careers.

This book is a compilation of their responses. It provides a unique evaluation of the last thirty or forty years by ten of the most distinguished pioneers representing key branches of the field. They have provided their perspectives on the past and present, their vision of future paths to be explored, and their wisdom drawn from decades of experience and scholarship. The contributors are all exemplars among our senior colleagues. Despite various backgrounds and professional pursuits, all these specialists possess a unique asset—a long perspective on the Middle East (and on the profession of being a "Middle East specialist") molded by their individual professional and personal experiences.

The eminence of these authors, earned through their contributions as scholars and teachers, should in itself draw our attention to their personal development and aspirations. However, their stories are important also because their work and writings mark a turning point in the study of the Middle East. Collectively they reveal the slow and difficult evolution of Middle East studies in the United States—a process which is, as it should be, still in process. Separately each author shows us a discrete contribution to the modern incarnation of the field.

Whatever didacticism is offered in this book is neither formal nor does it stand alone. Lessons, insights, wisdom, and inspiration are almost invisibly woven into the fabric of fascinating biographical narrative told with wit, style, self-effacement, and candor. The authors have taken us into their confidence, speaking openly about their formative experiences and observations. Their stories provide a human face to the profession.

♦ ♦ ♦

Because of the varied experiences and paths taken by the contributors, a single unifying theme for the book proved to be impossible. Therefore, it was decided not to try to structure the contributions too closely but rather to let a variety of approaches be used as a way of reflecting more truly the individual perceptions of the contributors. They come from a broad range of backgrounds. Albert Hourani was born to Lebanese parents and grew up in Manchester, England. Charles Issawi and Pierre Cachia were born in Egypt. Issawi's parents were Syrian and Cachia's were Maltese and Russian. Halil Inalcik was born in Turkey and Farhat Ziadeh in Palestine. Dankwart Rustow was born in Germany but spent his later youth in Turkey, where his father had gone as a political exile from Nazi Germany. J.C. Hurewitz was born in the U.S., where his father, an Orthodox Rabbi from Poland, and his Lithuanian mother came (like the parents of other of our authors) so that their children could live in a democracy. Don Peretz was also born in the U.S., but his father came from Palestine, and members of his family served in early Israeli governments. George Makdisi and Ernest McCarus were born in the U.S. as well, but their parents were Lebanese. For most of the authors in this volume, living in a mixture of cultures and languages was a normal part of their lives.

Their lives also encompassed a broad array of educational experiences—Azhari and American missionary schooling in Cairo and Beirut in the 1930s; Oxford in the 1930s and 1940s; the University of Ankara during and after World War II; Jesuit schools in Lebanon before and after the war; Hebrew University in Jerusalem during the Israeli struggle for independence; the Sorbonne in post-war Paris; and a variety of American universities, principally Columbia and Princeton. Many were involved in the development of the early centers for Middle East studies, most notably at Princeton (Ziadeh, Rustow, and Issawi), Columbia (Hurewitz, Issawi, and Rustow), and St. Antony's College, Oxford (Hourani). Hourani also contributed to the development of centers at Harvard and Chicago. Peretz went on to establish a center at SUNY Binghamton, and Ziadeh established a center at the University of Washington in Seattle. (Our late colleague, Bayly Winder, who died before his contribution to this volume was completed, established a center at New York University.)

Other commonalities emerge. All led interesting lives *before* they turned their minds to scholarship. They were well traveled, broadly educated, and linguistically sophisticated. (All speak several languages, some being fluent in six or more. Charles Issawi, for example, mentions his knowledge of French, Arabic, English, Italian, German, Spanish, Polish, Russian, Persian, and some Turkish—and his field is economic history!) They are also intellectually curious, avid readers, ambitious, and disciplined. Not surprisingly, they supplemented their formal education with a considerable amount of self-training. Most of them served in the military during WW II or held sensitive wartime government posts. As they contemplated careers, only one of them (J. C. Hurewitz) set out to become a Middle East scholar. Serendipity, coincidence, life's little accidents, and war-time service all helped focus their final career choices on the Middle East.

These authors, having determined to undertake careers that centered on the Middle East and Islam and trained for the most part in an older tradition of scholarship, emerged in 1945 into a new political and social order that included enormous new intellectual challenges. The received tradition of scholarship that shaped their minds—a tradition which had already been on the threshold of change when the war broke out—was rapidly being displaced. Novel techniques of teaching (most conspicuously in language training), new ways of organizing and conducting research, fresh analytical approaches, and the development of new tools of analysis were all part of this change.

But these novelties were only concomitants of the shattering of the old order in a process of change that was breathtaking in its complexity, scale, and pace. The rapid post-war achievement of independence by former mandates and colonies was accompanied by the universal, sometimes violent, rejection of the ethos and ideologies of imperialism just as the evolving post-war era was shaping itself into something of a gigantic paradox—the world was fragmented into an unprecedented number of self-governing, often fractious nation-states while at the same time, on a macrocosmic strategic level, it coalesced roughly into the two opposing ideological camps of communism and democracy. Emblematic of the two blocks were their superpower leaders, who locked into a deadly nuclear competition. The emergence of two "superpowers" capable of imposing their preserve over or destroying vast portions of the earth was in itself unexampled and a defining force of the new order. Later a third bloc, formed of the non-aligned nations representing a variety of political systems, tended to play one superpower off against the other. Finally, two other unprecedented realities of the post-war world had an impact on all nations: the threat of nuclear annihilation on the one hand and global interdependence (economic, scientific, technological, and cultural) on the other. Both were intensified by a revolution in communications.

For scholars and other regional specialists such as the contributors to this volume, the intellectual challenge of the transformed world lay in the need to develop new perspectives, concepts, theories, and techniques of scholarship—no less than a new sociology of knowledge and learning—if they were to cope with the swirl of change in which their generation was caught up; they had somehow to manage the vast flow of new information, data, and, above all, ideas which forced them to reassess the historical past, view the present with a different set of critical eyes, and, in the end, to make sense of and explain it all. They and their peers met the challenge and in the course of so doing, helped to redefine and strengthen their fields as part of the general burgeoning of new academic disciplines and area studies. This achievement, perhaps more than any other, distinguishes them from those of us who came later.

How did these scholars and their peers reshape the fields of Islamic and Middle Eastern studies? Foremost, they responded by accepting and encouraging change; by opening their minds to new ideas, perspectives, disciplines, and techniques and then absorbing them critically; and by producing new analyses, interpretations, and syntheses. They implanted these values in their students. They pioneered in opening new branches of Middle Eastern studies, particularly in the social sciences (especially anthropology, sociology, and modern economics), linguistics, folk literature, and Islamic art and architecture. They gave these disciplines as much standing as more traditional focuses of study on the Middle East, such as philology, history, and religion, by emphasizing the necessity and importance of interdisciplinary studies.

Reflecting the need for innovation in adapting to new conditions in higher education, they embraced the idea of organizing non-western studies into interdisciplinary language and area studies centers where students would be required to learn the substance and tools of more than one field of specialization and, most importantly, to learn at least one major language of the region. They contributed significantly to the internationalization of education by helping to create and direct the first wave of area studies centers not only at the few universities where the field already existed (usually as an adjunct to religious studies or archeology) but also at others in locales spread around the country (where the introduction of a stand-alone Middle East program was truly a novelty); by awakening their colleagues in the established disciplines to the importance and interconnections of Middle East studies (and of all nonwestern studies) to their own; by modernizing and diversifying Middle East studies curricula and in so doing introducing significant changes in the breadth, depth, and organization of the field; by stimulating the interest and support of governments, foundations, and the corporate community in the revamped anatomy of Middle East studies; and by creating professional organizations, such as the Middle East Studies Association (MESA), for the promotion of the field.

Integral to these developments was the building of important research libraries on the Middle East, some at institutions where such collections never existed before, thereby ensuring the future presence of the field in some form or other at a greater number of universities than at any time in history. With the larger number of programs came an unprecedented number of students who chose to specialize in the region, and, because of new cross-disciplinary offerings (which not infrequently included professional schools), had career options opened to them that only a generation ago were not even contemplated.

These changes were necessitated by and reflect the radical alterations in the way the generations who are succeeding these authors were socialized and educated in an era of revolutionary advances in communications and computer technology. The ubiquity of television brought the world into their homes and schools in previously unimagined coverage and delivery; they grew up more visually oriented in their reception of information. For those who paid attention, the world became a little smaller, more immediate, perhaps a little more familiar and less 'foreign' as they grew into maturity. Along with these developments, jet propulsion transformed air transportation, linking the regions of the globe even closer and making travel more affordable and comfortable. At the same time, opportunities for student travel increased dramatically. Those young sojourners who seized the chance for travel were exposed to other cultures and languages and offered new perspectives. So too were their peers who found themselves overseas by virtue of serving in the military or Peace Corps. The usual result of such travel for most of them was that old stereotypes broke down and their experiences often had a formative impact on the shaping of their minds and values, particularly those who served in the Peace Corps.

In some respects, the generation of students taught by our contributors were as well or even better traveled and experienced than our authors at a comparable age. Moreover, they have had more opportunities while still students for conducting thesis research in the region itself. Our authors not only helped to create the new order within their professional realm, but they have inspired their students to emulate them in taking the field in a forward direction and have instilled a willingness to experiment and change course as events and opportunities demand.

◆ ◆ ◆

With this general context in hand, this may be the appropriate juncture to address the reader's curiosity about such questions as how the particular contributors to this volume were chosen, why women are not represented, and what the authors were asked to do?

We began with a loose set of criteria for whom to approach as potential contributors—each must have had at least twenty-five years of academic experience or an equivalent professional experience in, for example, the foreign service, have earned a generally recognized high standing in the field by virtue of the significance of their publications and teaching, and, as far as possible, have played in some fashion a pioneering role in modernizing the field.

At the outset we were prepared, if necessary, to produce two volumes of biography in order to be inclusive. However, a number of factors militated against our original intentions—among them the problem of obtaining sufficient foundation support for a project of such size and duration, and the reluctance of various presses to gamble on a very large single volume, let alone two volumes of the same nature. But the most difficult obstacle proved to be the prospective authors themselves. All of those whom we hoped would participate —whether or not technically "retired"—are still intellectually vital and working hard, with a full slate of professional obligations, a schedule of deadlines for publications, and an agenda for polishing off unfinished projects postponed until retirement.

For all but a few of those we approached, the notion of writing a brief autobiography for publication was a novel one and was not accorded a very high priority even if the inclination were there. Thus the task of persuading them to add our project to their list of deadlines proved very difficult for those who agreed and impossible for others. Some, who agreed initially, withdrew later because of time constraints, and one died before he wrote his contribution. However, there is a glimmer of hope that those who declined might, if they are approached again on a future occasion, be willing to contribute to such a volume at a later date. Despite their reluctance to do so now, upon reflection most admitted that the idea has a certain attraction. (Who among us does not have even a trace of immortal longing?)

Virtually all of the women who met the criteria were approached. Unfortunately, this number was small since relatively few women of that generation had been active in the field. It is only relatively recently that significant numbers of women have joined the ranks of Middle East specialists, having had the way paved by that earlier generation of women. During the post-war period academia, government service, and the corporate communities were almost the exclusive hegemony of men. It was precisely because those women had to be exceptionally committed and have strong personalities in order to be undaunted by such a barrier and able to enter the profession against heavy odds that we especially wanted their contributions. As talented as their male peers, their gender alone made them pioneers. To our extreme disappointment, none of the women scholars we asked to contribute agreed to do so. They demurred primarily for the same reasons as their male counterparts, but, (and unlike many of the men), they uniformly insisted that few would be interested in their lives!

There is another group of women who should probably be more clearly represented in this volume. These intelligent, perceptive, talented, and generous women played a difficult amalgamation of roles that were crucial to our authors—as colleagues, confidants, editors, typists, hostesses, guardians of access and time, mediators, and more. We refer, of course, to wives, several of whom abandoned their own careers to raise children and lend support to the careers of their husbands. Their contributions to the histories that follow are hereby gladly, warmly, and respectfully acknowledged.

♦ ♦ ♦

Like the criteria for selection, the frame of reference suggested to our authors was also fairly accommodating. They were invited to choose any point of departure they wished, such as the earlier parts of their lives or the time at which they began their training, and to consider from the perspective of their individual experiences and ideas what and where the field was then, where we have come, and how we have got here and to weave into the narrative their own roles and what it has all meant to them in an amalgam that combined in some kind of balance the personal and professional. In so doing, they were encouraged to discuss teachers, colleagues, students, and other individuals who played a significant role in their lives, to analyze successes and failures, to discuss what they think needs to be changed, and to provide a few words about future directions.

In sum, it was decided that the best summing up would be what each contributor wanted it to be and that each chapter should be, above all, a task of enjoyment and satisfaction to the writer. The authors were asked to use the guidelines to the extent they wished but to write what gave them pleasure, and thereby we would all be the beneficiaries.

Finally, it may be appropriate to summon up the words of two early readers of this volume. Nowhere else, one of them observed, have the intellectual and personal experiences of such a group of distinguished Middle East specialists been captured in a single volume. "Accounts of their personal experiences," the other stated, "and the expression of their personal views make up a document for historiographical studies that are yet to come...taken together, they [the authors] are among the founding members of the distinctive field of Middle East studies." It should be borne in mind that this volume is intended not as an ending but, rather, as an experimental beginning in the hope that it may inspire future imitators.

Spelling and Transliteration

Because each chapter represents its contributor's unique personal experiences and perceptions, editing was kept to a minimum in order to preserve each distinctive voice. The individual authors' preferences in spelling, grammar, and language usage were respected, as were their use of diacritical markings and conventions of transliteration. Some authors provided footnotes and complete bibliographical references; others mentioned works casually in passing. No effort was made to force authors to conform to a specific style.

Acknowledgments

This book would not have been possible without the generous support of the Ford Foundation and the Andrew W. Mellon Foundation to whom we extend our sincere appreciation. But we owe most particular thanks to Dr. Gary Sick, former program officer of the Ford Foundation, who provided us with crucial start-up funds; to Neil S. Rudenstine, the Executive Vice President of the Mellon Foundation at the time we made our appeal and now president of Harvard University, who shared our belief in the value of this volume and gave his support generously; and to Harriet Zuckerman, his successor, for continuing the Mellon Foundation's generous and patient support.

In addition, it is not only fitting but an utter necessity to avow the vital role of another woman in the production of this volume—Shirley Smith, my associate editor. She is a consummate professional, a gentle editor who possesses the skills of a polished diplomat—an essential editorial skill since it is rare to encounter authors who do not brood over their words like hens over chicks. She has an unusual critical eye and great patience. She is also fearless and unflappable in the face of computer and software obstructions. It is doubtful that this book would have appeared in as good shape or timely a fashion had Shirley Smith not been on hand.

CHAPTER 1

A Road-Map of Opportunities Made and Missed

Pierre Cachia

Approach Road

I was born in an Egyptian provincial town, of a Maltese father and a Russian mother. British law as it was then took account only of descent through the father, so I was a "British subject by birth." The language of the home, however, was French, for no other reason than that it was the only language my parents had in common; fortunately, it was also the *lingua franca* of virtually all the foreign communities in Egypt. At the same time, anyone who came to the door spoke Arabic. I therefore grew up bilingual. For some reason I have never fathomed, however, I never let one language "run" into the other as many other Levantines do, and I have remained something of a purist in all the languages I later had to acquire. (I remember being irritated by the intrusion of French into Thackeray's novels, and even more by the way George Eliot larded hers with incorrect Italian!)

No less relevant to my career is that in 1931, after I had completed my primary schooling in French, my father decided that, since we lived in an Arab country, my brother and I ought to learn Arabic. This was a most unorthodox step to take in days when the mastery of European languages was the gateway to employment and to social acceptance, and my father was roundly condemned by his friends and colleagues for jeopardizing our future, especially as we now had to repeat the primary stage of education, starting with the alphabet. My father held firm nevertheless, and for the next seven years my brother and I attended schools where we were the only non-Egyptians and where Arabic was the medium of teaching for all subjects.

There can be no doubt that this gave me a better grounding in Arabic than I have been able to impart to my students, who had no choice but to acquire the language in concentrated doses at university level. But I also deem it my good fortune that in those days the graduates of the ancient Islamic Seminary of al-Azhar had a virtual monopoly on the teaching of Arabic, if only because they commanded lower salaries than the product of the modern universities. Schoolboys being the same the world over, we used to make merciless fun of our Azhari teachers, for their social comportment, even their habits of speech, and above all their uneasiness when they took to European dress stood out against the Westernized behavior that was becoming the norm. And—perhaps because of the way they themselves were trained—most of them were eccentric; but their command of the language was phenomenal.

To fellow Arabists I need not say that the distinctive feature of their training was their reliance on memory work, starting with the memorization of the entire Qur'an. The whole of Arabic grammar also had been codified in nearly a thousand lines of doggerel, and this too—along with a voluminous commentary—they learned by heart, so that they had an authoritative pronouncement on every linguistic problem literally at the tip of their tongue.

The converse of their achievement was that memorization was the only scholastic achievement that they valued, and despite pious directives from the Ministry of Education that the emphasis in all our courses was to be on understanding and independent thought, what they expected of us was what they had been taught themselves. To learn something was to learn it by heart, and that included a number of "prescribed" poems. At the end of our secondary schooling, we all sat a national examination, which included orals. At mine, I found myself sitting across a table from two teachers, one of whom would start a line from the middle of a poem and this I had to pick up, but before I completed it the other would start a line from the middle of another poem, and so it went on. I was also grilled about the meaning of individual words in the poems, but not a question was asked that drew on my appreciation of the poetry, or that reflected theirs.

The teachers' and program designers' background was such that even in other subjects the emphasis on memorization was only comparatively less intense. And the pressure to do well was enormous, for at the end of the secondary school stage tens of thousands of children throughout the country sat to identical papers in thirteen subjects, all compulsory, and the successful candidates were not only graded but ranked on a national scale. As for the unsuccessful ones, their prospects of employment were so blighted that there was a crop of suicides each year when the results were announced. The nature of the effort required is indicated by the fact that, although French was my mother-tongue, I could not have passed the examination in it without reading the prescribed text because all the questions bore directly on its contents. For the history paper too, I dutifully listed in an exercise book all the dates we were expected to remember, and I recall that there were 962, although the dates themselves have gone the way of all trivia. I was so caught up in the system that I thought it unfair that drawing should be one of the compulsory subjects, for this I could not "mug up," and my ham-fistedness at it cost me top ranking!

One of the evils of the emphasis placed on memory work was that it discouraged steady work throughout the school year. It was only during the six to eight weeks immediately preceding the final examination that one buckled down to serious preparation, and for many that meant night-long sessions of reading and recitation in the company of a friend. As many of my classmates had no electricity at home, I could through May and June look out of my window and see under each street light a column of gnats twirling above a boy crouched on the pavement, an open book propped between his knees, and at his right hand a pot of strong, black, stewed tea to keep him awake.

However, educational practices must not be judged by their misapplication. Literate people greatly underestimate the wealth that memory can hoard, or its usefulness. If not cultivated for its own sake and divorced from other faculties, a memory well-trained and well-exercised can be a great factor in efficiency. It is probably true that nothing we learn is ever entirely lost, only mislaid. When she was in her fifties, for no reason that she could identify, my mother suddenly remembered from first word to last an insignificant poem she had recited at school before she was ten. Friends tell me that I, too, have a strong associative memory, and it is true that a single word casually dropped in conversation can transport me as if on a magic carpet to a realm of experience long outlived, or to a store of information long unused.

Yet I cannot claim to be able to emulate my Azhari teachers on the plane that might have been most useful to me professionally. Among dictionaries, one of my favorite hunting grounds is the *Lisan al-'Arab* with its rambling articles on all the derivatives that a root can generate. Most editions do not mark out the key words typographically, so in my copy I have taken to underlining these in red as I go—and I am chastened to discover how often I have looked up the same word. The trick I have not learned is how to summon at will a specific item of information out of the mental recess in which it is skulking in idleness.

It must be added that the commitment of the Azharis to their language went beyond the mechanical. They treasured it in a way that stands in sharp contrast to the functional approach of Westerners. One of my teachers used to open his dictionary at random every morning and learn one word that he had never encountered before, whether or not he was likely to have a use for it. He had the same priorities, and no doubt the same rewards, as collectors of fine china.

The life of foreign communities in Egypt at the time deserves a more serious and fuller study than can be attempted here. Even in a provincial town where there were seldom more than twenty or thirty families of European extraction, these formed little islands of Westernism, of privilege (and self-delusion), scarcely conscious of the sea of Egyptian reality bathing their shores and at times sending waves of resentment crashing against them. My father's inclinations and his choice of schooling for me ensured that I grew up less aloof from, and less ignorant of, our Egyptian surroundings than were most of our fellow interlopers. Even so, the language of the home, our tastes in music and in other forms of entertainment, our styles of dress, our table manners, and a measure of prejudice that I do not believe can ever be entirely eradicated militated against free social intercourse. Virtually all my friends of like age were Egyptian, but our friendship seldom extended beyond the confines of the school. There we dressed alike, sat side by side in the classroom and the refectory, vied with one another at identical occupations. But on the one occasion when I visited one of them in his home, I was so devastated by the poverty and the squalor that I had not the heart to expose him to the comparative luxury of the apartment we occupied.

All the same, immersion in an Arab environment was bound to penetrate me if only by osmosis. And two specific incidents stand out in my memory as contributing directly to later insights.

One occurred when, at the age of fifteen, I went with some thirty schoolboys on a visit to Aswan in the far South of Egypt. Two of the boys were natives of that city, and their fathers invited the entire group—which had to be split into two for the purpose—to dinner in their homes. Such acts of hospitality even from people of modest circumstances were not new to me, but more testing instruction was to follow, for at the end of the meal, without any warning, the teacher in charge called upon me to make a speech thanking and praising our host. Slowly and awkwardly I got up to my feet, and after a century of tongue-tied agony just as awkwardly I sat down again, without having uttered as much as the vocative "Gentlemen!" For years afterwards, I never attended a function without having a speech ready, no matter how unlikely I was to be called upon to deliver it. What gems of rhetoric were thus lost to the world I cannot count, but I gained my first inkling of the importance given to ready wit and eloquence in traditional Arab culture, and in later years it was with ripples of sympathy that I read how an al-Hariri or an al-Juwayni was shamed for failing to rise instantly to far more demanding literary or theological challenges.

The other incident took place even earlier, when I was eleven. A numerous party, including my family, had spent a pleasant day at an out-of-the-way estate in the Fayyum province. As we headed back on foot to the nearest town, the column stretched out along the road. Finding myself among the stragglers and eager to rejoin the leaders, I veered into what seemed to be a short cut, but the road soon faded into a patch of desert. I did not know then that on featureless terrain one tends to trudge in circles, and this is what I must have done for the next two-and-a-half hours, until darkness fell and I could detect in the distance the light of an electricity-generating plant. I made straight for this, arduously climbing the highest dunes rather than lose sight of it by staying on low ground. And when I found a cemetery obstructing me, I dared not go round it but scaled the wall and threaded my way between the tombs. Suddenly I was challenged by a gruff voice—that of the cemetery guardian, who must have taken me for a grave-robber; but when he realized that the intruder was only a small boy, he grabbed me firmly by the wrist and led me on to safety.

Years later, I read a study by a colleague criticizing a pre-Islamic poet for comparing his lady-love to the light in a hermit's cave. This he deemed an artificial image since there was no trace of a religious feeling in the poem. It struck me that the critic was off course in seeking devotional overtones in the poetry. Egyptian-born but city-bred, he had no experience of how comforting the faintest light can be in desert wastes.

By contrast to Arabic, English was taught in State schools at a very modest level, and French at a pitifully low one. So the time came when my father came round to the view that, since we were British, my brother and I ought also to acquire some facility in English. For this purpose, he sent us to the now defunct Lincoln School, a subsidiary of what was then called the American University *at* Cairo, which (perhaps sensing that it was no longer merely passing through) has since changed the preposition in its title to "in." Lincoln School used to issue its own diplomas, but it also prepared us for the London University Matriculation Certificate, a widely recognized and therefore very desirable qualification.

The man I credit with teaching me English was Dr. Worth C. Howard. He also had a deep love of language, and his way of nurturing mine was to return my essays with only a tiny red check mark under any word that was not quite right. I would then spend hours working out just what the objection was, and how it was to be met. Later on, I applied a more merciful variation of his method to my language students: I devised a number of one-letter symbols to hint at whether it was diction or syntax or vocalization or sense that they had slipped on. They sometimes complained that their papers came back with more red than blue on them, but I believe the bloodletting did some good! And when editing Eutychius of Alexandria's *Kitab al-Burhan,* I discovered that two of the manuscripts I was collating differed only in tiny but recurring details, so I again used superscript letters to mark the variations, sparing myself and the reader dozens of footnotes per page.

It will surprise some that, although I have never had any leaning towards the sciences, I was much impressed with the science teacher, Mr. Herbert Vandersall, whose uncompromising intellectual honesty I greatly admired. A peppery man who yet had the grace to apologize handsomely and publicly minutes after he had lost his temper with a student, he was particularly impatient with any of us who tried to round off a science paper with some rhetorical flourish. "Say what you have to say and then stop," he would sputter. Inasmuch as I have come to believe that this is a cardinal rule for literary writing as well as for the exercises he set us, I credit him with having had almost as much of a hand in my formation as had Dr. Howard.

It was also Dr. Howard who put it into my head that I might go on to higher education. The possibility had never loomed above the family's horizon, and even then my brother had no hesitation in seeking paid employment instead. After my father died, I found among his papers evidence that he had had to borrow money to see me through my B.A., and his first application for a loan had been turned down by the bank that employed him with the comment that he was being "too ambitious" for me.

Yet all along I had been that oddest of oddities among schoolboys: a child who loved learning. Not that my school days were without tension—on the contrary, my earliest years were washed with floods of tears over every difficulty encountered, and there was an occasion when at the age of eight I remained in school long after classes had been dismissed not because I had incurred some punishment, but because I had come up against a problem in arithmetic that I could not solve, and I would not yield to the entreaties of the kindly nun who taught me as she urged me to go home and tackle the knot again in a less frantic frame of mind.

Indeed from the time I was four I had been fascinated by writing—not authorship, of course, but the mere process of linking a few loops and dents together on a piece of paper to make sense. Every particle of knowledge subsequently laid across my path was received with wide-eyed wonder. Random thumbing of a dictionary has long been a favorite pastime of mine, and it was with a thrill of delight that I chanced across the information that the word "glamour" is a variant of "grammar!"

It is not surprising, therefore, that by the age of thirteen I was quite set on the path my life was to follow: I was going to be a teacher, and my subject would be literature. The very first books other than school texts that I ever owned were two collections of French nineteenth-century poetry that my father gave me. I have them still. The only change that took place over the years was that my love veered from French to Arabic literature, especially the modern. And—as if prefiguring much later developments in my life—the first book in English to come into my possession was a collection of English and

Scottish ballads. I came to know "The Twa Sisters" long before I trod Scottish soil, or had mastered standard English!

I was—as every teenager ought to be, especially one brought up on such Romantic fare—highly idealistic at the time. My sense of vocation I explained to myself as a desire to give as much joy as I had received. In my undergraduate days, however, I was given a different interpretation by my psychology professor, who said that people went into teaching basically because they were exhibitionists who enjoyed standing before a class with all eyes upon them, so that when I became senile I was likely to take my clothes off in public. I was chastened, but not deflected from my course.

The Primrose Path

The American University also introduced me to the very term "co-ed." In my earliest schooling, before I was ten, I had been one of three boys admitted— exceptionally, and not without misgivings—to a girls' school run by French-speaking Franciscan sisters. But on the whole the attitude of the educational establishment towards sex was severely repressive. Burnt into my memory is a day in the primary school where I first learnt Arabic when all of us boys were summoned to the yard and made to form three sides of a square. Then the headmaster appeared carrying a bundle of canes, and two boys not yet in their teens were marched in. We were told that they had been "teasing girls," and the headmaster proceeded to beat them and beat them and beat them, first on the hands, then on the feet, then on the buttocks, until all the canes were broken. Looking back, I realize that "teasing" was no doubt a euphemism for some more serious offence, but at the age of eleven I was left wondering why boys could tease each other with impunity but girls had to be treated as if they belonged to a different species altogether.

It was also borne in on me that both the supposed effectiveness of corporal punishment and the psychological scars it reputedly leaves have to be calibrated according to the norms of the society to which one belongs. A successful and well-balanced Egyptian professor once told me that, as a child, whenever he was naughty his father used to hang him by the feet "like a bat" and beat him with a leaded cord. Most of the boys I knew were accustomed to harsh treatment from parents and from teachers, and they were neither particularly well-behaved nor maladjusted as a result. My conviction is that such procedures are not only offensive in every sense of the word but also wasteful at best. They certainly did not extinguish our interest in girls.

And at AUC there was—especially in the Arts courses—a fairly large proportion of girls. Curiously it was not there but much later, at Columbia University, that I heard a colleague, an American through and through, decry co-education. His argument was that girls mature more quickly than boys, so that precisely at the time when most young people enroll in universities the co-eds appear to be brighter, and this saps the confidence of the men!

In point of fact, most of the girls in AUC ranked near the top of the class, but this was due at least in part to selectivity, for they usually came from wealthier and better homes and boasted parents uncommonly open to modernistic ideas. Furthermore, whereas the male students had to give thought to the material rewards that a degree would earn them, the girls were motivated mainly by love of learning. They also provided me with a prime illustration of the lame steps by which a society lurches forward when exposed to a new culture, for when they had completed their training and were eager to put it to use, the very fathers who had defied the prejudices of their contemporaries by allowing them to attend a co-educational institution objected to their going into employment. The concern was not to shelter them, for several that I knew were allowed to do social work among prostitutes provided it was unpaid, for the greater threat to the family's reputation was that it should be said they sent out their daughters to bring in pennies.

Among my classmates was the first Muslim girl to enroll in AUC. This was Aziza Shukri, the daughter of a titled doctor and a person of sterling qualities and firm character. She eventually married Ahmad Husayn, who occupied a succession of ministerial and ambassadorial posts, including a spell at the United Nations, where social functions brought Aziza into piquant encounters with a near contemporary of ours at AUC, Mrs. Abba Eban. Aziza later played a vigorous part on her own in Egypt's family planning endeavors, and both she and two younger sisters of hers, differently talented but equally positive and enterprising, have remained firm friends of mine to this day.

Most of the co-eds, however, were Christian or Jewish and, having had the very solid schooling offered by the Lycée Français, were more at home in French than in Arab culture, even if of Arab blood. One of the most engaging was Andrée Saab, the daughter of a Lebanese count. Wealthy but unspoiled, she had what the Arabs call "wisdom of the heart," manifested in acts of sensitive and impulsive generosity. Once, when in a fruiterer's shop, she saw the face of a small ragamuffin stuck to the window from the outside, wide-eyed at the sight of the luscious wares displayed. On the spur of the moment she bought a kilogram of apples and gave them to him. Apples were something of a luxury in Egypt then, and some of our friends were quick to point out that the money she had spent would have kept the lad's family for a week, but I sensed that the gesture was comparable to the bathing of Jesus's feet with costly perfume, and true to the limpidity of Andrée's nature. It is no surprise to me that under her married name of Andrée Chédid she has made her mark as a poetess and novelist, although still in French and not in Arabic or English.

Wasteland Trails

My studies were interrupted by war service in the British Eighth Army (when the Americanisms planted into me by my teachers were vigorously hoed out). With the "desert rats," I marched westward along the northern coast of Africa. The Libyans were pleased to see us displace the Italians, and indeed a contingent of Sanusis fought alongside us. But our reception in Tunisia was different. The Germans had been drumming into the population that we were coming to champion the French and the local Jews against them. It so happens that to minimize the very common war hazard now grotesquely termed "friendly fire," we had adopted the same markings visible from the air as the Americans, so our vehicles featured a five-pointed star, and this in a yellow paint that was supposed to turn red if there was poison gas in the air. The association of yellow stars with the Jews seemed to confirm the Tunisians' worst fears, and their first reaction to our appearance was to stay out of sight. It was in Medenine that I first had a chance to approach some, and as soon as it was discovered that I spoke Arabic I was feted and escorted from one café to another, where I was plied to saturation with a succession of drinks all heavily flavored with mint.

In one of these cafés, I was surprised to see a large portrait of King Fuad. As he had been dead for some six years and the royal family was none too popular with Egyptian nationalists, I asked why he was so honored and was told that if only their leaders could wrest from the French concessions similar to those he had obtained from the British, the Tunisians would be happy indeed! I thus had an early glimpse of the nature of Egypt's prestige in the Arab world. I also learned that distance does lend enchantment even to political personalities.

Alas, two days later I was detailed to witness and report on the execution in the town square of two Tunisians found to have cut our telephone lines, and both the fund of goodwill I had started and my zest for adding to it were drained. I moved on.

As an interpreter, it also fell to my lot at one time to inspect Tunisian brothels. Needless to say, our concern was not with public morality, or even with the spread of venereal disease, but with the possibility of leakage of military information, for not a few of the women there were Italian. That was where I discovered how varied and powerful local customs can be if only in response to economic pressures, for I repeatedly came across evidence that—despite the stringency of Islamic sex laws and the no less fierce code of honor celebrated in folk literature—there were Muslim communities where it was accepted that a woman might cumulate a handsome nest-egg by prostitution for a few years, and then return to her own to become a desirable bride and lead a respectable life thereafter.

My subsequent soldiering all the way through Sicily and Italy and into Austria was rife with testing and maturing experiences. And although there is little enough to be said in favor of war, it is worth recording that what used to be called "the comradeship of arms" is no mere romantic illusion. It derives from the fact that war is the only enterprise that gives tens of thousands of men a common and clearly defined target and that puts a premium on cooperation rather than rivalry and personal ambition in attaining this target. And its strongest bond is not only that one's survival depends on the character of the man next in line, but even more the unflattering reality that being afraid together rips off the veil of our fondest self-delusions and stubbornest pretences. Suffice it that I formed friendships then that have lasted half a century. However, so far as my preparation for a career in Arabic studies is concerned, my soldiering belongs to the years that the locusts have eaten.

My frustrations in this respect did not end with demobilization. I was by then determined to work for a doctorate, but I had first to make and save enough money to support myself for several years abroad. I readily got a job at the American University, first as a Library assistant and then as a teacher, but English had a greater rarity value than Arabic there, and it was principally English that I taught. I was also asked to give a course in psychology, but I had only one year's grounding in the subject and I vehemently refused. Reluctantly, I consented to teach modern Middle Eastern history instead. Yet the most unpromising seed can germinate if it happens to fall on fertile soil, and nearly forty years later I was taken aback when, at a meeting of the Middle East Studies Association, a former student approached me and thanked me for having launched him on a career as a historian. The occasion struck me more as a reproach for my half-heartedness than as a compliment.

Of vital concern to me at the time was that my salary was fifteen Egyptian pounds a month for the first year, raised to eighteen the next. Yet I could earn as much as twenty-five pounds a month as a typist with a knowledge of languages. And this I did whenever I could spare the time, during vacations and on a part-time basis during term, at one time carrying a load equivalent to two-and-a-half full-time jobs. When by the summer of 1948 I had accumulated four hundred pounds in the bank, I was ready for the great gamble. Because I had an American B.A., my first thoughts had been to seek a higher degree in the United States, but that was more than my resources could stretch to. Instead, I headed for Britain, where I had an ex-soldier's rights. And for no better reason than that I had fought with a Scottish division and had made friends up North, I chose to go to Edinburgh University.

I had chanced upon a fairly favorable time to start on my career. The war had wakened the Government to the importance of the Arab world. It was soon to forget, but for a while British universities benefited from grants specially earmarked for the development of Middle Eastern studies. I had missed the initial bonanza, but the possibilities of expansion were still such that even before I had completed my degree Edinburgh offered me an Assistant Lectureship—at a salary of four hundred pounds a year!

The Beaten Path

Edinburgh had no mean record in Islamic studies. At the turn of the century, Sir William Muir had been not only a leading authority in the field but also principal of the whole University, and there were those who still remembered him as an imposing figure riding into the Old Quadrangle every morning on a white horse. Incidentally, it was to honor not only him but also his less well-known brother John, a Sanskritist, that the Muir Institute was so named. Retired but still alive was Dr. Richard Bell, as fine a gentleman and as selflessly dedicated a scholar as I have had the privilege to meet. I attended the last of his public lectures, one on the nature of Muhammad's prophetic inspiration, when he was vigorously attacked by Muslim students who assumed that he was denying the genuineness of the Prophet's mission, whereas the point he was making was that—in contradistinction with the Tradition—there was only one Qur'anic passage that could be read as implying that revelation came through a visible agency. He had been succeeded by Dr. William Montgomery Watt, who was to prove as energetic in creating a cluster of departments concerned with Islamic studies as he was productive in his own research. No less of a presence was his wife Jean, whose scholarship was in German but whose experiences in Palestine had also inspired a number of delicate poems. And the departmental library boasted (and still boasts) a long table on which generations of students had carved their names, one of which—next to some misspelt Arabic!—was that of R. B. Serjeant. But in Edinburgh, as indeed in virtually all European universities, the interest was solely in the classical period of Islam.

A great many of the Arabists of the past—not least in Scotland—had been members of the Christian clergy, who studied Islamic thought for comparative purposes. They and the historians had done sterling service for their disciplines, laboring patiently on difficult texts with very few basic aids at hand. For them, acquaintance with Arabic was an indispensable tool, but it was the deciphering of ancient written texts that was necessary to them, not the interaction with a living language.

I was well aware that few would have the good fortune to be as thoroughly immersed in Arabic as I had been. I perceived at the same time that the skimpy attention given to language training was the weak point in the Arabic programs of most Western universities.

The deficiency could to some extent be imputed to an understandable human trait. The adult mind is impatient with the baby food of elementary grammar and is eager to race ahead to a substantial diet. But the result is that

I have on occasion encountered established scholars who labored painfully and wastefully through advanced texts, their attention divided between the subject matter and the basic constructions of the language in which it was formulated.

Yet it was the rigidity of the tradition that was principally at fault. Formal grammar was taught only in the first year, and the anecdote was proudly related that in earlier days aspiring students were handed the two volumes of Wright's *Grammar* and told to return to their august professor when they had learned them! I discovered early in my Edinburgh days that the University had an admirably energetic and enterprising department of Phonetics, two of whose members—Professor David Abercrombie and Mrs. Betsy Uldall—had an interest in Arabic, so I used to take my beginners to them for some instruction in the pronunciation of phonemes that have no counterpart in English, only to be told by old hands that I ought not to waste time on such frills.

The prevalent standard is well illustrated by an incident involving Professor A. S. Tritton—an amiable and lively eccentric who worked assiduously in the British Museum Library long after he had retired and who was invariably kind to me whenever chance took me to the same shelves. Britain still had some toeholds in the Middle East at the time, and a subaltern in Inverness who was being posted to Libya was enterprising enough to buy Tritton's *Teach Yourself Arabic*; but he got as far as the Phonetic Introduction only to be nonplussed by the description of the sound of *'ayn*, so he appealed for help from the author. Airily ignoring the title of his own book, Professor Tritton wrote back that one would have to be a genius to teach oneself Arabic, and he then added: "As for the sound of *'ayn*, don't worry about it—it is no sound at all." The young officer then turned to me and I sent him a tape explaining and illustrating the distinctive Arabic phonemes, but it is surely revealing that a senior Arabist of the day could have completed a long and not undistinguished teaching career without so integral an item in the alphabet having as much as registered in his ear.

The balance of priorities has been much improved since then, but—unavoidably, perhaps—most Arabists in university service are not primarily linguists; they are specialists and researchers in some other discipline, who teach language as a necessary second string to their bow, seldom diverting their energies to the creation of satisfactory teaching textbooks. And it is still to be widely recognized that some of the colloquial forms of the language ought to become integral parts of Arabic programs, not merely to enable casual visitors to the Arab countries to communicate with informants or even to buy onions and carrots in the marketplace, but because the spoken idioms that were once despised are now used by leading writers in their creative works. Furthermore, it is arguable that at all times even the "high" literary language reverberated with echoes of everyday speech, the overtones of which are missed by the unattuned ear.

It is in keeping with their attitude to the language that the Arabists of old gave far less attention to the secular literature, even of the classical period, than to other writings in Arabic. Apart from weighty translations of the *maqamat* which scarcely reveal the richness of verbal ornamentation of the originals and Lyall's rendering of early poetry in antiquated language that Americans (though not the British) find repellent, the only works readily available to give the English-speaking student a taste of Arab literary creativity were those of Nicholson and, among my near contemporaries, Arberry. As for the modern literary output, it had received only the scantiest recognition in the West. There were some translations, the most numerous being of Tawfiq al-Hakim into French. Gibran's original works in English as well as some translations from the Arabic had some devoted admirers. The first volume of Taha Husayn's autobiography had been translated by E. H. Paxton as early as in 1932, but the original edition of Hilary Wayment's translation of the second volume, printed in Egypt, was never sold out. Tawfiq al-Hakim's fictionalized account of his experiences as a provincial law officer had been translated as *The Maze of Justice*, by none other than the man who was later to adopt the name of Abba Eban. But there was not a single book-length study of any aspect of modern Arabic literature in any European language, the most solid critical appraisal being in a series of four articles by Professor (later Sir) Hamilton Gibb in the *Bulletin of the School of Oriental and African Studies*.

The Main Road

So far as my own specialty was concerned, therefore, I had entered a desert, and it was with the express intention of making it blossom that—for my doctoral dissertation, which then became my first book—I chose the most representative Egyptian writer of the time: Taha Husayn. Furthermore, I burdened my study of his work with a lengthy introduction which, together with a concluding chapter, amounted to an early attempt to survey the entire field. Yet no more than five hundred copies were ever printed, and I was told that the book had greater immediate success in southeast Asia than it had in the West, because Muslims in Malaysia and in the Indian sub-continent were looking to the Arab heartland for leadership into modernism yet could read English with greater facility than Arabic.

In my teaching, too, I soon made my peace with the hard fact that in no Western university will there ever be enough Arabists to permit narrow specialization, so I have lectured on language and on literature of all periods, sometimes even on history. I have never regretted these incursions into fields that are at best contiguous to my own, for there are perspectives on the entire culture and even insights into specific issues to be gained even when feeling one's way into the unknown, and there is no better way of learning than to teach!

All the same, I wasted no time in instituting an optional course on modern literature; but hardly anything else in the curriculum tied up with it, and during my first nineteen years in Edinburgh only two students chose to take it.

I was disappointed, of course, but I never doubted that what engaged my interest so persistently and—yes—so passionately was intrinsically valid and must in time prove itself to be so. Nevertheless I felt I owed it to my profession to attach a second string to my bow.

Detours

Casting around for an area of study that might have a bearing on my main interest, I did some preliminary work on classical Arabic rhetoric. I was soon faced with a good deal of confusion in the technical terminology, so I sketched out for myself a long-term project which involved examining the latest manuals first, such as Husayn al-Marsafi's *al-Wasila l-Adabiyya*, produced in the nineteenth century, then working backward in time in order to ascertain when a term first came into use and what changes it underwent.

I had scarcely made a start with this when my colleague Dr. Watt put before me an entirely different proposition, which struck me as very attractive. He wished to write a book on the history of Islamic Spain and asked me if I would contribute several chapters on its literature. I set to with a will and felt well rewarded in pursuing certain features—such as the creation of multi-rhyme poems and the use of the vernacular idiom—which are not without relevance to modern developments. I also realized that very little work had been done on Andalusian prose and was eager to make a start along what seemed to be a profitable new road. Alas, I could not match the speed with which Dr. Watt worked. He soon had the bulk of the book written and was waiting for my much more modest additions. I had little choice but to set down my meager findings and indicate what lacunae needed to be filled.

My greatest reward from this excursus came a few years later, when I was assured that some of my hints had been picked up by other scholars who have ably filled out the lacunae I left behind, for by the late 1960s interest in modern Arabic literature almost suddenly began to germinate and then multiplied as prolifically as a mustard-seed.

How hard it had been to drive the first furrows is measurable not only by the indifference of the many but also by the closed minds of a few who had labored in neighboring vineyards. As late as in 1974 Ilse Lichtenstadter, who had been teaching at Harvard, published her *Introduction to Classical Arabic Literature*, which strayed into its modern sequel, only to dismiss it all in a single paragraph reading, in part:

> The works of the past are accorded high praise by Western critics as well as by Eastern admirers ...The Arabs value their classical heritage highly. However, while praising it, perhaps excessively, they have rested on their ancient laurels and so far have failed to create new masterpieces...This is not to assert that no new writers have arisen in the Arab/Muslim world, only that they have not yet founded a genuine new Arab/Muslim literature rooted in its own soil. Much modern writing deals with topical questions, such as politics, social problems, education, and nationalism, but these works can hardly claim to be art, nor do many of them reach the intellectual refinement of their medieval counterparts. (p. 119)

Whether my own plowing had much to do with breaking such aridly clumped soil into a cultivable loam, it is difficult to say. My first book had had some good reviews, but the only hard evidence I have that it was in demand is that the libraries of both the universities I have served—Edinburgh and Columbia—had their copies of it stolen! In any case, I was glad to return to my first love.

Re-Entry Road

It was then that—mainly at the urging of Dr. Malcolm Lyons—a number of us Arabists functioning in Britain launched the *Journal of Arabic Literature*. Our principal aim was to provide a different outlet from the existing general Orientalist journals, where literature was swamped by theological, historical, and above all philological concerns, and to have it treated strictly as literature. It was also very much our hope that it would serve as a forum for the interchange of ideas, engaging not only Arabists but also Arab writers and academics. How successful we have been in our main purpose I must leave it to others to judge. Unfortunately for our wish to reach out and provoke responses far and wide, we could find no publisher or grant-giving body that would enable us to bring it out cheaply, and its circulation especially in the Arab world has been disappointing.

Petty history is not out of place in this succession of personal reminiscences, so let it be recorded that one of the publishers we approached urged us to give the publication a fancy title, and specifically suggested something taken out of "Arabian flora or fauna." Such associations were the very last we wished to foster, and among the editors they gave rise to ribald coinages, such as *Jath-jath wa Qaysum*, which might have been a challenge even to the experts. For a while I held out for *The Pride of Lyons*, but this too got short shrift. In the end, we came round to the view that catchy titles, like good jokes, are attractive only when first encountered, and—for over twenty years now—the journal has appeared in its stodgy and obvious but easily identifiable name.

Decade after decade, even though safely and comfortably ensconced in an academic chair, I have had the stimulation of sharing in the intellectual travails of a people who had had the making of much history in their hands only to be sorely tested by its recent dislocations. During that time, a succession of literary theories have held sway in academic circles. I have been grateful for the additional insights they have brought, but I have always stopped short of the enthusiasm of some colleagues who saw in one or another of them the sole key to the understanding of all literatures. Necessarily, but also unrepentantly, I have come to each new book with a mind already charged with what chance had accumulated in it, but convinced that what I was about to read was unique and self-authenticating, in some degree reflecting but also in some degree deflecting the movement from which it arose, and therefore demanding of me constant readjustments of all my perceptions, aesthetic or existential.

The ultimate subjectivity of the process seems to me inescapable. What I have been at pains to communicate in all my writings, and ultimately in my *Overview of Modern Arabic Literature,* is no more than a tentative characterization of an ongoing movement, informed (I like to think) by extensive sampling and a broadening horizon, but validated only by whatever measure of coherence it possesses. And what I have passed on to my students and must entrust to my successors is the need to keep it under constant revision.

Side Road

My other venture in scholarship—folk literature—has had a jerky history. Like many an academic who is also a family man, I had claimed the smallest room in my home to house my books and serve as my study. Eventually, like many a family man who is also an academic, my collection of books had grown to such an extent that I had to move it to a much bigger room. In the course of the move, I came across a sheaf of long forgotten papers that brought back a flood of memories.

My father had been very fond of walking and had taught me to enjoy the sport, so that by the time I was nine I used to go on tramps of as much as twenty kilometers with him. Once, when I was about eighteen, we set out for a venture into the countryside around Beni Souef. At one point, I noticed a group of three teenage boys squatting by a small stream, one of them singing to the other two. As we passed by, my ear caught the burden of his song. It told of the treatment peasants got in State hospitals. The refrain, put into the mouths of successive officials from the senior doctor to the junior male nurse, was, "If you don't like it, the door is wide open!"

I was startled. The received wisdom not only in the foreign communities of Egypt but even among many city Egyptians was that the peasantry was a downtrodden mass too apathetic to understand the reality of its condition. A schoolmate whose father was a wealthy landowner used to tell me that when he visited the family estate it amused him to get into their chauffeur-driven car with a cane in his hand, and when he spotted a peasant walking by the roadside he would have the car roll noiselessly by, give the man a whack across the shoulders and shout, "Why don't you look where you're going?" Meekly, the man would reply, "Forgive me, Your Excellency!" What impressed the young tormentor in this was the peasant's stupidity. "Look!" he used to say. "He's an animal! I hit him and he begs my forgiveness!"

The song I now heard was a revelation. But I had yet a great deal to learn. I assumed that such a poverty-stricken lad would do anything for money, so I went up to him and offered him more than he had ever held in his hand if he would come to my house the next day and dictate the text to me. I had reckoned without the diffidence that villagers have towards any outsider (which includes Egyptians in Western clothing), for he promised that he would do anything I wanted, but he never turned up.

I did not get that text, but my curiosity had been aroused. During vacations, I went in search of comparable material. The richest hunting grounds, I found, were the fair-like *moulids* held in honor of Sufi saints. Often, the quest involved long donkey rides, listening to a singer for hours, then cornering him and getting him to dictate one or two items from his repertoire — there were no portable tape recorders then. My difficulties were magnified by the fact that I was particularly fascinated by the narrative ballads, which are extremely long and laden with puns, so that it took a whole day's expedition to pick out and then take down a single one.

When I set off for Edinburgh, I had no thought of leaving Egypt permanently, so I laid my collection aside with every intention of resuming my search, but also with no appreciation of the importance of what I had. With the change in my circumstances and with teaching stretching its tentacles to suck in my time and energies, I lost sight of what I had looked on merely as a hobby. Rediscovering it years later was a new thrill; and I was equally thrilled to find that, amateurish as my work had been, I had been careful in my transcription and had made usable notes.

I picked up the strands with a will and looked for an Ariadne thread to take me further. Progress was bound to be painfully slow. While at home, I read as much as I could round the subject, but the genuine live material could be gathered only in the field. As long as I was based in Britain, my work was neither sufficiently related to my teaching nor sufficiently popular to attract substantial grants, so my visits to Egypt were often years apart, and almost always timed to take advantage of the summer vacations—hardly the most merciful season for the purpose.

In the process, I have had to contend with the indifference not only of Western scholars but also of Arab colleagues who looked upon folk literature as a debased activity unworthy of serious attention, their disapproval sometimes mounting to active antagonism. There are in fact voluminous works, including an M.A. dissertation, denouncing the interest in anything to do with the colloquial idioms as the ploy of imperialists or Zionists intent on dividing the Arabs by weakening their hold on the classical language, which is perceived as a unifying factor. I recall meeting a reputedly sympathetic amateur of folk verse who nevertheless, when I brought up the text of a ballad in which three villains—incidentally described as "Christian Jews"—are sentenced by the Prophet to be burned for an attempted fraud, angrily denounced the ending as "invented by Orientalists" since death by burning is not one of the punishments prescribed by Islamic Law. It did not always help that the slowly growing number of folklorists were often leftists eager to inject an anti-establishment bias into the material.

Furthermore, throughout the period of my greatest activity, the Egyptian authorities were uncommonly stringent in keeping foreigners out of all but the main tourist centers, so I was not allowed to roam about the countryside in search of my material.

Fortunately, I had more alternatives than the Western folklore theorist might assume. There are, in Egypt, pen-and-paper compositions which may be claimed as genuinely folk. Folk singers do perform in the big cities. And I cultivated the acquaintance of Egyptians who possessed material taped in the provinces, which they made available to me. Nevertheless, I was glad of the information and experience I had acquired in my younger days, before the curtain had come down. And after I had moved to New York I received a generous grant from the National Endowment for the Humanities which enabled me to round off my work. The law restricting the movements of foreigners was still on the statute books, but it was no longer rigorously enforced, so I made some recording sallies of my own in Upper Egypt to fill gaps in my knowledge of which I was keenly aware.

Research of this kind—like, reputedly, women's work—is never done. Not even to myself could I pretend that I had plumbed the depths of even the single genre I had concerned myself with. But I was in my sixties then, and not so much daunted by the hardships of field work (which included repeated invasions by fleas) as afraid of being scythed down before I could pass my findings on to a younger generation of researchers. Conscious only that my material could be of use to scholars in more disciplines than any one person could master —to folklorists, social scientists, philologists, and many others— I resolved to write a book of manageable size that would put forward not theory but the facts I had ascertained and a selection of illustrative texts I had garnered.

I next found myself up against a more stubborn obstacle than I had anticipated. One publisher after another—including University presses—turned down the typescript not on grounds of quality but because it had "no known readership." Several would have taken it if I had been willing to suppress the Arabic texts—but these were mostly transcriptions of oral material that would never become available anywhere else. Three years passed before Oxford University Press undertook to print it in the form that I insisted it should have. Even then, they had to market it at an almost forbidding price, and sales in the first three years after its appearance have been paltry.

This neither surprises nor disheartens me. I am as certain of the fertility of this second field I have plowed as I was of the first. It took nearly twenty years for seeds to germinate in this earlier one; it does not distress me that, in this second one, none may sprout in my lifetime, or that it may be someone else's sowing that will grow to maturity. There is an immortality of sorts in such a process.

High Road

Not that I find fulfillment only in such a distant prospect. I have never for a moment regretted my commitment to teaching. I have been offered other jobs—including one with an oil company, that would have paid me three times the salary I then commanded—but I had no hesitation in turning them down. At one time, when war work cast me into tricky situations that called for careful handling of people of different nationalities and in various positions of authority, I did toy with the possibility of a diplomatic career, but only briefly—and this was just as well, for with a Russian mother and without the social and educational background of a Burgess or a MacLean, I would never had been given security clearance!

If the perfect job existed, everybody would be in it. Teaching has its strains and disappointments, not the least of which is that with seniority come increasing administrative duties, calling for skills and proclivities very different from the ones that led me into the profession. And teaching itself has tentacles that suck in one's energies and time. The long vacations are an illusion; but what they and the restricted hours one spends in the classroom mean is that one can choose what to do and when to do it. When my children were small, for example, I could free myself to play with them for an hour before they went to bed. The privilege made time a great deal more precious than is implied when it is equated with money, and the misuse of it a heinous waste.

Teaching is also an occupation in which routine is minimal. Some language courses and even literary surveys are unavoidably repetitive; but I soon learned that a lecture is lively the first time it is delivered, more polished the second time, and stale the third, so for my own sake I made a point of regularly recasting my material. And the ultimate salvation was the sense that one was not teaching a subject but teaching young people, and these were never the same from one year to the next.

Indeed my greatest satisfaction has always come from my relationships with students. From the bright beginner who asked with feigned innocence whether the Arabic word for a human, *insan*, was the root of "insanity" to the graduate preparing not to follow in my footsteps but to refurbish my wares and carry them another mile along the road, they have kept me supplied with the freshness and zest of young minds, the eagerness and idealism of the unbroken, the insights and exploratory keenness of the unstale, and—yes—the sustaining power of intellectual affinity and often the supreme joy of emotional rapport.

Dead End

It has been a good life, but has it been a fully rounded one? I have long admired the great Arabists of yore, such as Lane or Howell, who with very few aids at hand but with infinite patience and constancy of purpose produced immense works of reference that far outlived them. As I consider how much more useful these have been to hundreds of scholars in succeeding generations than many contemporary publications that have sent a ripple through academia, my admiration has grown to a regret that I did not try to emulate them. Arabic studies still need dozens of basic aids that teachers of other languages take for granted—a truly reliable frequency list, a thesaurus, various concordances, dictionaries of idiomatic phrases, lexicons of the various regional colloquials. But the set-up in present-day academia favors not the building of such monuments but the crafting of a clever monograph that offers some startling reinterpretation, some challenge to received opinion, so that like a bale of straw it burns brightly enough to attract attention but is soon reduced to ashes. Edward Lane's *Lexicon* is still the best Arabic-English dictionary of the classical language that we have but would it have earned him tenure in one of today's universities?

The compilation of some of the missing works of reference I have mentioned seemed to call for back-breaking labor, especially before computers became available, and at different times in my career I did try to muster enthusiasm for a collaborative effort to produce some of them. I had no success, but I also realize now that if, instead of preaching, I had set about compiling one of them single-handed thirty or even twenty years ago, the task would be done by now.

In the last class that I taught, I urged my students—an uncommonly gifted set, destined to make a mark in academia—to undertake early in their career one such piece of what I call 'antwork,' to peg away at it at odd moments, perhaps when too tired for the supposedly more creative effort that will earn them immediate kudos, and let it grow slowly into an anthill. If they should follow my advice, I shall glory in the vicarious merit.

Or may there still be time for me to set my hand to yet another plow? I have belatedly realized that—largely because I was eager for my students to drink deep at the sources rather than rely on second-hand material—I have set too little store by literary translations. I did attempt a few myself, but almost always as critical endeavors, aimed not so much at producing a self-subsisting literary text as at bringing to the fore a lesser known Arab writer. But in the aftermath of the award of the Nobel prize to Najib Mahfuz in 1988, I have been forced to think again, to consider whether the spate of good, bad, and indifferent translations that poured onto the market may not have done more harm than good. "Something is better than nothing," I have been told—but is it? I have met several intelligent but non-specialized readers who, having picked up an inferior specimen on the assumption that this was the best that modern Arab writers could offer, are unlikely to venture into that field again. Have I not the experience, and now the leisure, to redress the balance somewhat?

And now that I have bared my soul, I wonder—Was my psychology professor right after all?

CHAPTER 2

Patterns of the Past

Albert Hourani

I had no particular interest in the Middle East or the Arabs throughout my years at school and until my last year at Oxford. I was brought up in a Lebanese emigrant home, in a district of Manchester which had a large Near Eastern population: Greeks and Armenians, oriental Jews, Syrian and Lebanese Christians, and a few Muslim families. Much of the food we ate was Lebanese, we heard the older generation speaking Arabic, there was a constant flow of relations, friends and business clients through our house, but I do not remember that any of this aroused in me the same movement of intellectual curiosity as it did, I think, in my brothers George and Cecil. My mind was turned rather towards English literature and towards history, studied at school in the traditional way: that is to say, it was primarily the study of the development of English political institutions and society. This study of a great, unbroken process of political development, based on sources of an unparalleled richness, is still of absorbing interest to me.

When I went to Magdalen College, Oxford in 1933 as an undergraduate, however, I did not choose to read for the B.A. in modern history, for that would have involved more repetition of what I had done at school than I wanted. I chose rather the B.A. course in philosophy, politics and economics. This was organized by the Faculty of Social Studies, but Oxford at that time had scarcely entered the age of sociology, and the only formal training in what would now be recognized as a "social science" was that in economics. Even here, however, the main emphasis was laid, at least by my tutor, upon the history of economic thought from Adam Smith to Alfred Marshall; J. M. Keynes's *General Theory of Employment, Interest and Money* was published in my last year as an undergraduate, too late for me to assimilate it fully. Politics too was taught in a historical way, by the study of the modern evolution of the British and a few other western systems and of the international relations of the European Powers in the half-century which preceded the First World War. The detailed study of the changing relations between great states, the shifts in alliances, the successive crises and the adjustments in the balance of power in which they ended taught me something which was to help me later; the study of the "Eastern Question," in particular, gave me my first glimpse of the political realities of the Near East, even if they were seen mainly through the prism of the interests and perceptions of politicians and officials in London, Paris, Vienna, Berlin and St. Petersburg.

My main interest in my undergraduate years, however, was philosophy, and this too was studied historically, as a development leading from Descartes to Kant and beyond to modern British empirical philosophy. Behind them lay Plato and Aristotle, but medieval thought was neglected, and Avicenna and Averroes were only names. I spent a term studying Hegel, which was unusual and thought to be rather odd. By the time I finished, Oxford philosophy was going in another direction, away from the historical approach, towards the theory of knowledge and the analysis of the precise meaning of words. I closed my books and I do not think I could now follow a philosophical argument, but something remained from those studies: an interest in the history of ideas and a concern with intellectual method, in particular with the kind of thought which is appropriate when we try to understand history and society. R. G. Collingwood, who became professor of metaphysical philosophy when I was an undergraduate, was the best lecturer I heard during my student days, a man of exceptionally wide reading and broad culture, and a thinker who stood far apart from what was becoming the philosophical orthodoxy of his time; it was largely because of his lectures that I became aware of modern German writing on the nature of historical thought, and in particular that of Wilhelm Dilthey. I also learnt something of Max Weber, although mainly at second hand; his ideas about the way in which we should think about society, and his theory of "ideal types," had a permanent influence on my way of thought.

I learnt something else from my years at Oxford: its tradition of the open door. The basis of the Oxford system of undergraduate teaching was the tutorial, the weekly hour or two spent alone with a tutor, reading and discussing an essay. The personal relationship established in this way made it possible to call upon the tutor at other times, to ask his advice and seek his help, and most tutors, in my experience, were willing to respond; it was a valuable experience to come close to the workings of a mature mind. I shall always be grateful to my tutors, in particular to T. D. Weldon, who initiated me into philosophy; he was invariably kind, and I very much regret that, when we later became colleagues at Magdalen (largely because of his continuing interest in me), we drifted apart, and I never thanked him for all I owed to him.

In my last terms as an undergraduate, my interest in the Middle East awoke quite suddenly. It is difficult to explain these sudden awakenings which occur in early life. Basically, I suppose, what happened was a quickening of natural curiosity about the world from which we came and which was still alive in our life as a family. When my parents settled in Manchester they were not turning away from an old world to a new world of opportunity, in the sense in which so many emigrants to North and South America turned their backs upon their past. They still remained in touch with their native villages and the land from which they came.

My father worked in the cotton export business, first with a cousin already established in Manchester and then on his own. Manchester was then the centre of the world's cotton trade, and he exported cotton goods to Lebanese importers, some of them relations, not only in Beirut and Alexandria but in Sao Paolo and later in West Africa. He and my mother went back to Lebanon many times, built and maintained a home in his native village, and also visited relations in Brazil and the United States. My father had been well educated in the Syrian Protestant College, the American college in Beirut. His English culture was broad and deep; I still have his editions of the English poets, and also a number of essays, in very correct English, which he wrote in his early teens while in the preparatory department of the College. (These were discovered by Marwan Buheiry in the library of Princeton Theological Seminary in a volume called *Essays by Syrian Boys*, deposited there by an American who had taught in the College; it was strange and exciting to come upon my father's handwriting and voice half a century later.) He was also an Arabic scholar, who had been taught, I think, by Khalil al-Yaziji. Sulaiman Bustani's translation of *The Iliad* was his constant companion; I have his copy of it and recently wrote an article upon Bustani.[1] During the First World War he had been the secretary of the Syrian committee in Manchester, had discussed the future of Syria with Mark Sykes, and had been received at 10 Downing Street with a delegation to congratulate Lloyd George upon the occupation of Jerusalem. He had met the Amir Faisal, later king of Iraq, and I remember a stiff lunch when Faisal's younger brother, Zaid, then an undergraduate at Oxford, came to visit us in Manchester. My father talked much about Arabic literature and about "Syria," for which he had an unceasing longing. (He came from Marjayun, then in the province of Beirut but now in the Lebanese republic.) In the tradition he had imbibed from the Syrian Protestant College, he always thought of himself as belonging to an undivided country called Syria that included Palestine and Lebanon; I do not remember he ever used the term "Lebanese" to refer to himself, until Lebanon became independent in 1945 and he was appointed its honorary consul in Manchester.

Impressions received from childhood onwards were given a new depth in the mid-1930s. The general strike of the Arabs of Palestine, of which the newspapers were full, aroused my interest and sympathy, and I also felt the impact of three personalities. One was a friend of my father, Amin Kisbani. A schoolmate of his in the Syrian Protestant College, then a friend in Manchester, he had had a wandering life, and not a very successful one as the world judges success. On visits to England he would come and see us, and his talk opened new doors; I remember the afternoon, eating scrambled eggs in the school café, when he first told me about Ibn Khaldun. A second was Philip Hitti, who came to stay with my parents in Manchester, I think in 1936; he had just delivered his *History of the Arabs* to his publishers in London, and he talked much about it. Someone of more lasting importance in my life was Charles Issawi, who came to Magdalen a year after myself, studied the same subjects, and became a dear and lifelong friend. Among much else he gave me my first glimpse of another Near Eastern world very different from the mountain villages from which my parents came: the polyglot and multi-cultural world of Cairo—a now vanished world depicted in classic form by a later friend, Magdi Wahba, in his "Cairo Memories."[2]

Formal graduate study was scarcely known in Oxford in the 1930s, and even if one wished to pursue it there was little money available. I did well in my final examinations for the B.A., and my college, which was one of the richest in Oxford, was able to find £100 to help me on my next stage. I registered as a candidate for the D. Phil. in Middle Eastern history, but there was no teaching available, as the subject scarcely existed; as my supervisor I was given D. S. Margoliouth, the professor of Arabic, a formidable scholar in fields far from modern history and a kind man beneath a farouche exterior. What I mainly owe to him is that he lent me his set of *Oriente Moderno*, a rich and indispensable source for the political and to a lesser extent the cultural history of the Middle East during the 1920s and 1930s. I never worked seriously on the dissertation and soon abandoned it, but I used the £100 to make my first visit to the Middle East. I went to stay with my aunt in Beirut, and lived for a time also in the house which my father had built for his mother in Marjayun, in the style of the early 20th century: a stone-built house with a red-tiled roof and a verandah shaded by vines from which one could see the light changing on Mount Hermon. I liked what I saw enough to arrange to spend the next two years teaching at the American University of Beirut, the successor of the college where my father had studied.

Those years in Beirut were decisive in more than one way. They gave me my first experience of Mediterranean sunlight, after the half-light of the north of England. It was important to get to know my extended family, or rather my two families, those of my father and mother. I learnt something about myself, and also about the nature of family ties in the Mediterranean world: the way in which ties of blood or connection could give a depth and solidity to all kinds of human relationship, and the values of honour and shame about which social anthropologists were to write so much later. I learnt much too from my colleagues and students at the University. Two colleagues stand out in my memory. One was Charles Malik, the philosopher, newly returned from Harvard and not yet drawn into political life. He brought with him a philosophical approach very different from that which I had learnt in Oxford, and one more congenial to me; we had a small group which met one evening a week to read texts as they should be read, very slowly, lingering over every word, discussing every problem—Plato's *Republic* in the first year, St. Augustine's *Confessions* in the second. The other colleague was Qustantin Zurayq, adviser and friend to the younger Arab nationalists, then in the first flush of his career as a student and teacher of Islamic history; I was acquiring enough Arabic to follow his eloquent and judicious course on medieval Islamic history, the nearest approach I ever had to any formal training in the subject.

The American University was important for another reason. It gave me my first contact with American academic life and with a certain kind of American culture and society. It was still dominated and administered by New England Protestants, some of them with a tradition of several generations of work as missionaries and teachers in the Near East: there lingered in its social life some traces of the Puritan austerity and formal manners of an earlier New England.

The years I spent in Beirut were years of political uncertainty and upheaval. In Lebanon and Syria the treaties of friendship with France, negotiated during the rule of the Popular Front government of Léon Blum, were falling victim to the instability of the political life of the Third Republic. Seeing what was happening, and listening to what colleagues and students said, gave me a harsh view of France and all its works in the Middle East and North Africa. The Mandates for Syria and Lebanon did not, it is true, show French political wisdom at its best, but criticism of French policy could too easily turn into disparagement of all things French; I had never visited France and knew no French men or women, and it took me some years to understand the grandeur of French civilization and appreciate its lasting traces in the countries it had ruled.

These were also the years of the Arab revolt in Palestine, and it made a deep impression on me. The student life of the University was dominated by the issue of Palestine, and by Palestinian students: I remember in particular Burhan Dajani and Isma'il Khalidi, the first whom I met of that remarkable family, and whose son Rashid was to be my student at Oxford a generation later. News, perhaps sometimes exaggerated, of what was happening in Palestine came rapidly to Beirut, and for someone brought up in a more or less unquestioned tradition of English liberalism, it was no doubt salutary to see the British as they were seen by those who lay beneath their power.

At this time I saw the problems of Syria and Palestine in the perspective of Arab nationalism. This was an idea about which I learned in Beirut: that there was an Arab nation of which the emergence to full, independent and united national life was being impeded by British and French rule and by the artificial frontiers imposed upon it after the First World War, and that, if only its energies could be released, it could move into a new and more fruitful period of social and intellectual growth. Apart from the influence of colleagues and students, two books read at that time made a deep impact upon me. The first was *Seven Pillars of Wisdom*, published after the death of T. E. Lawrence in 1935;[3] I now find its style difficult to accept and its view of the Arab movement too simplistically heroic, but it still remains in my view a remarkable book, both for its revelation of an unusual and tragic personality and because of some of its insights into Arab and Syrian society. The other book was George Antonius's *Arab Awakening*,[4] which came out in 1938 and left an impression on me which has never quite been erased; although I would now call into question many of its assertions, and here too I find its view of the subject too simple, I still admire Antonius's narrative power and his understanding of the way in which political decisions are made.

When the Second World War broke out in 1939, I was on holiday in England. There were few Middle Eastern specialists in England at that time, and even my meagre qualifications seemed to be of value. I was offered a position in a research organization set up by the Royal Institute of International Affairs at the request of the Foreign Office; it later became the Foreign Office Research Department. In 1942 I was sent on a mission of inquiry in the Middle East, and on the basis of a report which I wrote I was offered a position in the office of the British Minister of State resident in Cairo; his was a wartime appointment, in order to work closely with GHQ Cairo and with British representatives in the Middle East on the political and economic problems thrown up by the war. I remained there from 1943 to 1945. I do not think any reports or minutes I wrote had any value: from time to time a student working in the Public Record Office will bring me something I wrote at the time, and I usually think it is nonsense. I did, however, acquire some understanding of the politics of some of the Arab countries, and reports which I wrote served as the basis of my first two books, *Syria and Lebanon* and *Minorities in the Arab World*;[5] I do not care for either of them now, and do not wish anyone to read them.

What these years gave me was an opportunity to move about the Middle East and meet some of its leading personalities. I remember several interesting conversations with Glubb Pasha and a long and pleasant one with David Ben Gurion; it was useful to be able to attach a face and a voice to names which came into my reading and writing. I was able to observe at close quarters, from newspapers, conversations and such official papers as I was allowed to see, certain crises which taught me something of the dynamics of Arab political life. The Iraqi movement of 1941, the first of those paroxysms of political feeling which have marked the Arab world in the last half-century, showed me how popular feelings could flare up suddenly and then expire in a kind of frustration and despair; the crises of Lebanon in 1943 and Syria in 1945 helped me to understand the complex relationships between Great Powers and their client movements or states.

I remember also from that period the decisive influence of some of those with whom I worked. Arnold Toynbee was the director of the Foreign Office Research Department and H. A. R. Gibb for a time was head of its Middle Eastern section. I had already read the first volumes of Toynbee's *Study of History*,[6] and at some point I also read what is perhaps the best of his books, *The Western Question in Greece and Turkey*,[7] a classic analysis of the ambiguous and sometimes tragic relationship between Great Powers and their clients. Of Gibb I had then read almost nothing, but I worked with him closely, and his detached, profound analysis of political movements in the light of cultural patterns, persisting over the centuries and slowly changing, left their mark on me. He was at that time bringing to completion the work later published as *Islamic Society and the West*.[8] It had been commissioned by Toynbee in his capacity as Director of Studies at the Royal Institute of International Affairs and was to be one of a series of studies of the impact of modern western civilization on the ancient societies of Asia. The underlying assumption of these studies was that of Toynbee's own book: that the basic units of history are "civilizations," that each has its separate life, moving by its own internal dynamics, and that in the modern period one civilization, that of "the West," is becoming worldwide and threatens either to absorb the others or at least to divert their normal path of development. The Islamic society or civilization was thus to be seen as one of many human societies, but for both Toynbee and Gibb it had a special significance. Toynbee had been an official of the Foreign Office during and after the First World War and had been involved in the settlement of the Near East; he felt strongly that the Arabs had been given undertakings which had not been properly fulfilled, both in Syria and Palestine, and this had distorted the relationship between "the Arabs" and "the West" in ways which would, unless it was remedied, have lasting effects. I held much the same view and, to the extent to which we did so, our writing, I suppose, was "policy-oriented" and therefore perhaps in danger of distorting the historical process.

I should also mention one other personal influence, that of Brigadier I. N. (later Sir Iltyd) Clayton, as whose assistant I worked in the Office of the Minister of State: a man of a kind I had never met before, a military intellectual, with deep wisdom and wide personal knowledge of the Middle East, without the arrogance and over-sensitivity which are the temptations of the academic life. He saw the affairs of the world *sub specie aeternitatis*. When I think of him, I often remember what T. E. Lawrence wrote of Sir Iltyd's older and better known brother, Sir Gilbert Clayton:

> He was calm, detached, clear-sighted, of unconscious courage in assuming responsibility...His own views were general, like his knowledge...he impressed men by his sobriety, and by a certain quiet and stately moderation of hope.[9]

In the two years after the War ended I came closer to being involved in active political life than ever before or after, and did not much like it. I was attached to the Arab Office, an organization created by Musa 'Alami, the most intelligent and interesting of the Palestinian Arab leaders, in order to spread knowledge and understanding of the Arab question, and in particular of the problem of Palestine. I helped to prepare the documents submitted by the Arab Office to the Anglo-American Committee which visited Palestine in 1946, and for another year or so I did similar work in the Office in London. I did not like this kind of work, however, and I do not think I was good at it. I did not enjoy the company of politicians and disliked the way in which they thought; I also found it difficult to accept the endless repetitions of political discourse and the necessity to suppress so many nuances of meaning in order to make a point effectively. I closed this chapter of my life with relief and have never re-opened it. My ultimate sympathies in the matter of Palestine have always been with the Palestinian Arabs, and I am happy to know that they now have many supporters and defenders in the world, but I do not think I need any longer take an active part. I have written nothing which can be called "policy-oriented" since the end of the 1950s, except for one article which I was persuaded to write by David Astor in 1967.[10] I suppose I learnt something which was useful to a historian, however, and Musa 'Alami remains in my memory as a person of great intelligence and integrity, and infinitely complex feelings: I was pleased to be able to help him, and I am grateful to him for kindness over the years.[11]

♦ ♦ ♦

At the beginning of 1948 I was given the opportunity to return to Oxford. I was offered a research fellowship by my old college, Magdalen, in order to prepare to teach the modern history of the Middle East; I took up my post as lecturer in the subject three years later, after another long visit to the Middle East. This began thirty years of immersion in the affairs and society of the University. One could call it a dual society. On the one hand, I belonged to a college, one of the constituent colleges which made up the University. I lived in it until I married in 1955. Living in community was not without its strains, the more so since quite a number of the fellows at that time were bachelors who had little life outside the College, but it was also a source of friendship and enlightenment, as one lived with distinguished scholars and scientists in different fields. I remember in particular many lunches and dinners with C. S. Lewis, a source of stimulation and challenge, for he would not allow loose statements to pass unquestioned. I could not stand up to him in the cut-and-thrust argumentation which he so much liked, but at least he helped me to learn how to make clear and accurate statements.

Life as a teacher and scholar was lived not in the College but in the Faculty of Oriental Studies. That was a time of expansion of "oriental studies" in British universities. A government committee, usually called the "Scarborough committee" after the name of its chairman, had recommended in 1947 that a number of universities should be encouraged to expand the teaching of "oriental" languages and subjects; Oxford was one of them, and it was given the funds to create a number of new posts in Middle Eastern subjects.[12] My wartime colleague, H. A. R. Gibb, was professor of Arabic at Oxford and responsible for this expansion, and my post was one of the new ones to be created.

It may now seem obvious, at least to an American scholar, that a subject such as Middle Eastern history should be taught within departments of history by teachers formed in the historical culture of their time and to students who are themselves mainly concerned with history. In British universities at that time, however, most departments in the humanities and social sciences were reluctant to expand their range beyond the study of British and western subjects. In these circumstances, the policy adopted by Gibb in Oxford was a reasonable one. His aim was to create a nucleus of specialists in various subjects within the Faculty of Oriental Studies; at least they could interact with each other and would have some students to teach, and they could hope to reach out, almost as missionaries, to other faculties in the University. They were to be, as he put it in a later lecture on "Area Studies Reconsidered," amphibians, at home both in "Oriental Studies" and in some other discipline.[13] I was to be the modern historian of this group, and it was hoped that I might in due course arouse some interest in the subject among the main body of teachers and students of history. At the core of this group, Gibb thought, there should be some "orientalists," fully at home in the languages and the central cultural traditions of the world of Islam.

I had taught before the War at the American University of Beirut, but the years after 1948 marked my real initiation into university teaching at a high level. I was never fully at home in undergraduate teaching, but graduate training and supervision were endlessly exciting. I carried on the Oxford tradition of the open door, and it was challenging and rewarding to work with a student at all stages, helping him to define his subject, identify and use the relevant sources, and gradually form his conclusions and embody them in a dissertation. I was fortunate in my first two graduate students. One was Jamal Muhammad Ahmed, a Sudanese scholar of mature mind and literary as well as scholarly gifts, who later became an ambassador and foreign minister of his country.[14] The other was André Raymond, then at the beginning of his career but already fully trained as a historian: he was later to become the most distinguished Middle Eastern historian of his generation.[15] Both of them became my friends, and André helped me to gain some insight into French thought and scholarship. By now I had direct acquaintance with France, and I remember from those years the kindness and courtesy with which I was treated by French scholars who could not have liked the sentiments and opinions which

I had expressed in my first book on Syria and Lebanon. Robert Montagne and Pierre Rondot both reviewed it with care and understanding, and Louis Massignon received me more than once and gave me the privilege of listening to his extraordinary discourse on all things human and divine. I always regret that I never met Jean Sauvaget, who was too ill to receive me when I was in Paris. Later, I was to learn much from the writings and conversation of Jacques Berque.[16]

The 1950s were the period during which I tried to break away from my earlier, purely political and partly "policy-oriented" ways of writing, and to produce something more in conformity with an ideal of detached scholarship directed towards an understanding of the past. This ideal of scholarship I owe largely to Gibb, the most important of all the influences on my mind, but also to other colleagues. I remember with gratitude Richard Walzer, the historian of Greek and Arabic philosophy; he and his wife Sofie had a kind of salon in which, among Bidermeier furniture and with the lovely Monet inherited from her parents looking down at us from the wall, we would meet colleagues and visiting scholars, and where books were discussed and a kind of stock exchange of scholarly reputations was held. Richard taught me the importance of the continuity of scholarly traditions: the way in which scholarship was passed from one generation to another by a kind of apostolic succession, a chain of witnesses (a *silsila*, to give it its Arabic name). He also told me much about the central tradition of Islamic scholarship in Europe, that expressed in German. Another, younger colleague, Samuel Stern, seemed to be the very embodiment of that tradition: of Hungarian-Jewish origin and deeply read in Hebrew as well as Arabic, combining extraordinary learning with flashes of imaginative insight, spreading himself over a wide area, he died young before his books were written, but leaving seminal articles on half a dozen subjects.

Although I learned much from such colleagues, I did not have the training of an "orientalist" or a historian of classical Islam; I was supposed to teach modern history, and that was where the problem lay. It must be difficult for a scholar of the present day to understand how barren the field was at that time. I was, I think, only the second person in Great Britain to be appointed specifically to teach Middle Eastern history; I am not sure whether there were any in the other European countries or in the United States, at that time. I read carefully some of the chronicles and biographical dictionaries—al-Jabarti for

Egypt, al-Muhibbi and al-Muradi for Syria—and they reinforced the idea of the continuity of a cultural tradition; as Gibb pointed out in a famous essay, the biographical dictionaries give us the inner history of Islamic civilization, the preservation, development and transmission of a body of accepted truths.[17] I also read some of the works of European travellers and residents and worked rather desultorily in the Public Record Office, without quite knowing what I was looking for. Middle Eastern archives had not yet been systematically explored. I knew Asad Rustum's collection of Egyptian documents concerning Muhammad 'Ali's period of rule in Syria[18] but could not obtain permission to use the archives when I was in Cairo; the documents in the Lebanese Museum I found accessible and rewarding when I used them during a year as visiting professor at the American University of Beirut; a number of collections of documents from the Ottoman archives had been published, but we were only just becoming aware of the insights into the social and economic as well as the administrative history of the countries ruled by the Ottomans which a systematic use of them could give us. Of modern studies, the first volume of *Islamic Society and the West*, the work written by Gibb in collaboration with Harold Bowen, was published in 1950, and the second in 1957. André Raymond has called it the last great work of European orientalism: a very intelligent attempt to explain the nature of Ottoman society on the basis of literary sources. Two studies by scholars of my generation, both formally trained by Gibb, also provided a solid basis for teaching: Bernard Lewis's *Emergence of Modern Turkey* and A. K. S. Lambton's *Landlord and Peasant in Persia*, works of impeccable scholarship and insight.[19] But there was not much else to recommend to students.

In the 1950s I spent much time trying to write a book about the Arab provinces of the Ottoman Empire in the 19th century. This was to be a continuation of the series on *Islamic Society and the West*, begun by Gibb and Bowen, and to be written within the same broad framework of ideas. It would be a study of the "impact" of an expanding "civilization" upon another which was in "decline." My work on this book faltered, however, partly because I was becoming dissatisfied with this framework of ideas. Was "Islamic society" so stagnant, was it not changing at its own pace and in its own way? Was "western civilization" likely to absorb all others and create a new world unified not only at the level of techniques for the control of nature but at those of the organi-

zation of society and beliefs about the nature of the universe? Were "civilizations" the intelligible units of study which Toynbee had thought them to be?
In 1955 I published a long critique of Toynbee's historical concepts and methods.[20]

There was another range of questions in my mind. How could a society
be studied? By now I was becoming aware of the kind of questions being asked
and work being done by the French historians associated with the periodical
Annales, and they reinforced questions derived from the Marxism which,
along with most of my generation, I had imbibed during my student years. I
thought that history should be a study of the deeper structures of society and
the changing relationships of social groups, but such a study could not be pursued on the basis of the literary sources we were accustomed to use: chronicles,
travellers' accounts, even the records of foreign embassies and consulates,
which saw the societies they studied at one remove and through the distorting
mirrors held up by their native informants.

Although I made some progress with the book, and wrote a first draft of
parts of it, my heart was not in it; I still wished to write it, but not until I knew
more clearly what it should be about, and what questions it should ask, and by
the use of which kinds of source they could be answered. It was with some relief that I turned to a subject not unconnected with it, but which I thought to
lie more within my present scope. Even if "civilizations" were not the authentic
or ultimate units of study, many people in the 19th and early 20th centuries had
believed that they were; the idea that modern civilization was embodied in
Europe, and particularly in western Europe, and that "oriental" peoples needed to enter into communion with it and adopt its values and institutions had
been widespread among influential thinkers and writers and had helped to
form the ethos and policies of nationalist movements, or at least of their leaders and articulate spokesmen. I decided to make a study of the development of
this line of thought among writers in Arabic, particularly in Egypt and in
"Syria" (using that term in its old-fashioned, broad sense). Some work had already been done on particular writers and schools of thought; what I wished
to do was to trace the links between them, to show how one generation of
writers influenced the next, and to show also the process by which certain
seminal ideas, such as those of "civilization," "the nation" and constitutional

government, had been received into the common stock of ideas of writers and readers in Arabic.

I had intended to write a brief study quickly, but it took longer than I had expected. I worked on it from 1956 onwards, and it finally appeared in 1962 as *Arabic Thought in the Liberal Age*.[21] To my surprise, the book has had a long life: thirty years later, it is still in print, it is used for teaching in American and French universities, and it has been translated into Arabic. It seems to have encouraged younger scholars to move over the same ground and make studies of individual thinkers and movements which go beyond my own conclusions or guesses, and often correct them.

I think the book has some merits. It is clearly constructed and easy to read, driving a broad highway through a mass of details, rather as reforming governments have driven wide avenues through the tangle of lanes and alleys in old cities. It shows something about the way in which new ideas were assimilated, not only by means of outright adoption of them but also, and perhaps mainly, by changing the meanings of ideas and words already familiar. I do not make high claims for the book, however. It lays its main emphasis on those writers who accepted ideas from Europe more or less willingly, and sometimes eagerly, but does not give due attention to those who rejected them, or at least accepted them partially and slowly by a cautious adaptation of their own inherited ways of thought, and it does not address the questions why, in what ways and to what extent the ideas of these individual writers were communicated to sections of society, and for what purposes they were used. It ignores the changes in collective "mentalities," habits of thought deeply rooted in established ways of life in common; it was only later that Jacques Berque's *Egypt, Imperialism and Revolution* showed me the importance of trying to discern the two rhythms of social change, that which reforming rulers and elites have tried to impose upon a society and that which it has produced from within itself by its own slow adjustments to a changing world.[22] There was also an implication in the book, or at least in the way it was read, that the active element in social and political change is provided by individual thinkers or lines of them. I do not remember that this was in my mind when I wrote it, but no doubt the way in which it is arranged and written has encouraged readers to come to this conclusion. I may have been too much influenced by a book read years earlier and which had a deep impact on me: Edmund Wilson's *To the Finland Station*, a study of the development of the idea that man could change his social world.[23]

I spent the academic year 1956–57 in Beirut, as a visiting professor of the American University, and once more I was able to observe at close quarters one of those crises—the "Suez crisis"—in which the complex relations of world powers, regional powers and local movements become clear and are subtly changed. When I returned to Oxford I was asked to become director of the Middle East Centre which had just been created at St. Antony's College. St. Antony's was a new college, and one of a new kind: a college for graduate students within a certain broad field, that of modern history and international studies. Oxford University is one of the oldest unbroken institutions in Europe, with a continuous history going back some eight centuries. Like all ancient institutions, it is slow to change as a whole; but the very length of its history has given it a complex structure with many centres of decision, and one such centre can make changes even when the university as a whole is slow to move. When a Frenchman who had made his fortune in the British colony of Aden offered the university an endowment, it seemed good to those who were responsible for it that it should be used to create a college of a new kind: a graduate college, and one where fellows and students would be working in a broad but limited field, within which members of the College would have a shared framework of categories and methods of work and would be rescued from the almost inevitable isolation of graduate study and research. To these ideas the first Warden of the College, Bill Deakin, a man of original mind and capacity for decision, added two more: that Oxford needed to give more attention than in the past to the study of regions outside Europe and North America, and that such study needed to be undertaken—as it was in American universities—by groups of specialists trained in different disciplines but interacting within a "centre." The Middle East Centre was one of those which the College established.

The move from Magdalen to St. Antony's opened what was to be the most creative period of my life as a teacher. I was fortunate enough to find congenial colleagues, among whom I should mention Elizabeth Monroe, the most helpful and unselfish of colleagues, and whose main book, *Britain's Moment in the Middle East*, will continue to be read for its insight into the way in which British policy was formulated and carried out in the later imperial age.[24]

I also remember with affection and gratitude the many dozens of graduate students who came to the College, attended seminars, and in some instances wrote dissertations under my supervision; students came more from the United States, Germany and the Middle East than from Great Britain, and in the earlier years it was even possible to pay for them. It was exciting to create ways of teaching and interacting with them, in a university where graduate studies had been slow to develop. We had a permanent seminar where colleagues as well as students met to exchange ideas; apart from that, I tried as far as I could to keep my door open.

From 1962 this work took on new dimensions. Another government committee, the "Hayter" committee, set up to consider the future of Asian, African, Russian and Slavonic studies, recommended that the government should give funds to expand these studies, but in certain specific directions.[25] In a limited number of universities, there should be created "centres" of regional studies, in the sense in which they were now understood in the United States. In the words of the report, such studies should come out of the departments mainly concerned with the teaching of languages and literature; young scholars fully trained in a discipline such as history or one of the social sciences should be given the opportunity to acquire knowledge of a region and learn the relevant language; once they were fully trained they would return to teach their subject within their own departments, but there should be some framework within which they would be able to interact fruitfully with each other.

Largely, I think, because of what had already been begun at St. Antony's, Oxford was designated as one of the three centres of Middle Eastern studies. Gibb by then had left to become professor and director of the Center for Middle Eastern Studies at Harvard, and it fell to me to take the main responsibility for carrying out the scheme in Oxford. In the course of the 1960s it was possible to create new posts in eight subjects, to choose young scholars to fill them and, in some instances, help them to acquire the training they needed; most of them were to become close colleagues and friends of my later career. Some faculties were more receptive than others. Once more, it was the Faculty of Modern History which proved the most difficult. The great professors—R. W. Southern, Hugh Trevor-Roper, H. J. Habakkuk—were helpful, but college tutors did not on the whole show much interest. The tyranny of the syllabus for the B.A. in modern history was too strong. It was not possible to introduce Middle Eastern options into it, or to attract undergraduates who were studying for it; very few of those who had taken their B.A. in history chose to pursue graduate studies in the Middle Eastern area. On the whole, those of us who taught Middle Eastern history continued to teach undergraduates who were primarily interested in oriental languages and literature and graduates who came from other countries.

This work drew me into university administration and politics, about which I had known nothing. I had to learn how the university worked and to obtain a position in it which would make it possible to carry out the plans made after the Hayter report. In the process I became deeply interested in Oxford University as an institution. For four years I was a member of its central body, the Hebdomadal Council, which met every Monday to debate the affairs of the University and make decisions. This gave me a sense of the continuity and dignity of the ancient University and a knowledge of how decisions were made. I learned how, and within what limits, changes could be made. As A. E. Housman said of poetry, change was either easy or impossible: easy if you knew and were on good terms with those who moved each committee or controlled each fund, impossible once you reached those limits of movement which every institution has. Thus it was impossible to give the Middle East Centre a formal status in the university because of the subtle and complex relationship between the University and the colleges, but for that reason it was possible to do things there which formal status might have made more difficult or impossible. I enjoyed meetings of committees, the interplay of personalities across the table, the process by which decisions were reached; but it is fair to add that I enjoyed those committees of which I was chairman and could arrange the agenda, the order in which items were considered and the point at which votes would be taken and decisions made more than others.

In the 1960s I came to know the New World. My first visit to the United States had been in the 1950s, but I did not go there to work until I was invited to be a visiting professor at the University of Chicago in 1962 and again in 1963. I was later a visiting scholar twice at the University of Pennsylvania, twice at Harvard, and once at Dartmouth College, and I had many shorter visits. These were periods of productive happiness. The great American libraries were a joy to work in. It was good to be really a member of a history department and find that what I wrote was taken seriously by historians of other parts of the world; good too to teach American graduate students, with their eagerness to take from you everything you had to give them. Chicago gave me something of permanent value, my first close contact with the social sciences, and in particular my understanding of the way in which social anthropology can throw light upon history, but it was Harvard which made the deepest impact. After my first year there in 1971–72 I continued to supervise graduate students in Middle Eastern history because Harvard did not make an appointment in that subject for many years after Gibb fell ill and retired; my Harvard students have a special place in my heart, and so does the University. I might have stayed there had I not been involved in the work of carrying out the recommendations of the Hayter report; life is full of doors opening into rooms one has not entered.

After I finished *Arabic Thought in the Liberal Age*, I took up work again on my big book. But I came increasingly to think that I could not finish it. One reason for this was the fragmentation of the mind which is one of the dangers of teaching in a university, particularly one so unstructured as Oxford. We are called upon to do three things, teaching, administration and research, and, unless we are very strong-minded, it is the research which is pushed out at times of pressure, because there is no reason why it should be done on one day rather than another, and also because it is difficult to do it in spare moments; half a day is, for me at least, the minimal unit of serious research or writing.

Apart from that, I gradually came to the conclusion that I did not have the framework of ideas within which I could construct a work on a large scale. The kinds of history which I had practised—political history with its focus on the relations between the European Powers and nationalist movements, and intellectual history seen as a *silsila* of individual thinkers—could no longer hold my attention, and I suspected that neither of them was what a new generation of students wanted. The kind of history which came to concern me more and more was that of social structures, and this would involve other categories of interpretation and other techniques of investigation.

The years from 1965 to 1980 were years of uncertainty, when I was reading new books which might help me to write what I wanted and writing essays in order to explore some of the ideas I learned from them. Among the books which had an influence on my way of thinking, three stand out in my memory. The first was Ira Lapidus's *Muslim Cities in the Later Middle Ages*.[26] This showed me how sources of a "traditional" kind, chronicles and biographical dictionaries, could be used to give new results if new questions, carefully formulated, were asked of them, but it also gave me a key to understanding the nature and development of Middle Eastern cities: the idea of the complex and changing three-cornered relationships between rulers, urban "notables" and—to use Lapidus's expression—the "common people."

Another book of which the influence went deep was Marshall Hodgson's *Venture of Islam.*[27] I had seen a draft of parts of it which Hodgson had given me to read when I was a visiting professor at Chicago, but I had not understood it because the framework of ideas was so new and some of the terms he used were unfamiliar. When it was published in 1974 I was asked to review it, and read it carefully, beginning with the introduction which explains his approach to history and the new terms he had coined. All became clear, and to a great extent I have continued to see Islamic history through Hodgson's eyes. I liked his idea (taken up in conscious opposition to Toynbee's theory) that the only fully intelligible subject of historical study was the Oikoumene, the whole world of cities and settled agriculture stretching from the Atlantic coast of Africa to the Pacific coast of Asia. Within this world, the region stretching "from the Nile to the Oxus" was one of the "core-areas" of high culture and power from early times until the early modern period, and the history of this area in the Islamic period had been Hodgson believed, misunderstood because it had been seen too much from the point of view of the countries of Arabic speech and culture in the eastern basin of the Mediterranean. He thought that we should look further east, to the countries of Persian influence and culture, and that if we did so we should see Islamic history in a different perspective of time: the culmination of power, culture and world-wide influence would then be seen as coming not in the first three centuries of Islam but in the early modern period, the age of the Ottomans, Safavids and Mughals. I learned too from his analysis of the causes of the stability and changes of political systems: the shifting combination of military power, urban interests and legitimizing ideas which turned power into authority. (Behind such ideas in Hodgson's book there may be a reflection of those of Ibn Khaldun, and in some ways it was through Hodgson that I came to understand the originality and importance of Ibn Khaldun.) It was useful too to be reminded that no society is unchanging, and each changes incessantly, at its own pace and within the limits of its own resources. This taught me the danger of trying to use the concepts of "decline" and "stagnation."

A third book which had a deep influence at about the same time was André Raymond's *Artisans et commerçants au Caire au XVIIIe siècle*, published in 1973–74.[28] I was already familiar with some of the ideas in it because of the series of articles on Cairo which he had been publishing since the late 1950s, but the book revealed for the first time the full range of his understanding of urban history. On the basis of a detailed knowledge of the geography of Cairo, Raymond was able to create a picture not only of the economic activities of different sections of the population, but of the ways in which wealth was related to political power: the "political economy" of the city, to use an old expression which has come once more into use, in a sense rather different from that which Adam Smith or John Stuart Mill had given it. Once more, the changing relationship between the holders of power, the urban elite of merchants and the artisans was made clear, and this was done by the first thorough use of a kind of archive of which the importance for the history of Ottoman cities had already been known but was now fully understood for the first time: the documents of the qadi's court, which included not only judicial decisions but registers of property transfers and of the division of the property of deceased persons. Raymond's survey was placed within the context of the changes which were coming in Egyptian society because of the shifting balance of commercial and industrial power. The impact of the commercial and industrial revolution upon the Middle East, from the last quarter of the eighteenth century onwards, was a dominant theme of modern history, and I learned much from the work of two authors in particular: David Landes's *Unbound Prometheus*[29] and E. J. Hobsbawm's wonderful trilogy, *The Age of Revolution*, *The Age of Capital* and *The Age of Empire*.[30]

Some of the essays which I wrote in this period followed a familiar path. They were studies of individual writers: those on Butrus al-Bustani and Sulaiman al-Bustani dealt with a familiar theme, the response of writers to the civilization and culture of Europe,[31] but an essay on Mawlana Khalid, the Naqshbandi shaykh, broke rather new ground for me, since it was an attempt to study a development which could not be seen in the perspective of "westernization," but in that of the continuity of a long and purely Islamic tradition.[32] Other essays, however, were attempts to explore the implications of ideas in the books I was reading. I should mention two in particular. The first was my introduction to *The Islamic City*, a volume of papers given at a conference organized by Samuel Stern, some younger colleagues and myself.[33] The purpose of the conference was to consider certain theories about the specific nature of the "Islamic city" which had been put forward in particular by Massignon and other French scholars, and the conclusion to which we came was that the concept of "Islam," however interpreted, did not suffice by itself to explain the shape or the communal life of mediaeval Baghdad or Cairo: the explanation would have to be found also in social relationships created by methods and patterns of production and exchange, in the relationship between social forces and military power, and in the general constraints of geographical position and limited resources within which all human societies live.

The second essay I should mention was also a conference paper, "Ottoman reform and the politics of notables."[34] In it I tried to use ideas derived partly from our conference on the Islamic city and partly from what I had learnt from Ira Lapidus in order to understand the mass of detailed information which I had acquired from my reading about the nineteenth century. I had been struck by the number of disturbances, mainly but not entirely urban, which occurred in various parts of the Ottoman Empire in the middle years of the nineteenth century. I suggested in this essay that the common factor in them was provided by the changes which a new kind of Ottoman administration, and the expansion of European trade, were bringing about in the relationship between the Ottoman rulers, urban elites and the urban and rural masses; an ancient pattern of social control was being disturbed. This essay seems to have given a number of other scholars a key to understanding which they have found useful: the idea of a specific "politics of notables" appears to have been widely accepted.

At the same time I was writing another series of essays. The search for new categories of explanation had led me to look in a more critical way upon those inherited from a previous generation. Since Edward Said published his book *Orientalism*,[35] it has become almost a fashionable commonplace to point out the connection between "orientalist" scholarship and the expansion of European empires; scholarship and literature are looked upon as having given a justification for imperial expansion and rule. My concern was rather different, with the intellectual genealogy of the principles of explanation to be found in the work of European scholars. With a few exceptions, it seemed to me that scholars working in Islamic studies had not been able to create their own principles from within the field. They had taken over certain ideas from the great systematic thinkers of the nineteenth century and tried to fit the realities of Islamic history and culture into them: in their work it was possible to find the influence of the German philosophers of history, Herder and Hegel, of Schleiermacher's view of the development of religions, of comparative philology and mythology, the evolutionary theories of Darwin and Spencer, and to a lesser extent the ideas of Karl Marx.

I had another concern which to some extent fitted into this: a concern with the relations, as they had been and as they might be, between Islam and Christianity, the two great religious communities which—as I said in one of my essays—had faced each other across the Mediterranean for more than a millenium with a look of uneasy recognition in their eyes.[36] Louis Massignon had suggested, in language of unforgettable beauty and force, what this relationship might be: Islam was Ishmael, the rejected brother, who might be brought back to the fullness of truth by the prayers of Christians and would bring back that sense of the overwhelming greatness of God which Christians were in danger of obscuring. I did not wholly agree with this way of looking at the matter: there was a danger of giving Islam a Christian interpretation which Muslims would not accept, but it posed questions which lay beneath the surface of the essays I wrote on the subject. They included two long studies, "Islam and the philosophers of history"[37] and "Islam in European thought,"[38] some shorter ones, and a series of studies of individual writers: Massignon, Gibb, Hodgson, Berque and, most recently, Raymond. Most of the shorter essays which I wrote during this period were included in two volumes: *Europe and the Middle East* (1980) and *The Emergence of the Modern Middle East* (1981). An earlier volume of essays had been published in 1961: *A Vision of History*,[39] and a later one came out as *Islam in European Thought* in 1991. Between them these four books contain almost all the shorter writings I wish to remember.

I ceased to be director of the Middle East Centre in 1971 and went to Harvard for a year as visiting professor, but when I returned to Oxford I still had some administrative work and a large number of hours of teaching. In 1979 I decided to retire, three years earlier than I need have done. One reason for this was that I no longer believed in myself as a teacher: the gap of the generations between my students and myself had become too great, I was uneasily aware that they were coming to me with questions in their minds which I did not quite understand and was not able to answer. I thought also that I still had a book inside me which I should like to write, and I would not be able to do so unless I could work on it with more of my mind than was available in a busy life as a teacher. I wanted to be able to think about it when my mind was fresh, that is to say, in the mornings. I had a heart attack and a period of ill-health in 1980, but after that I worked for a time as historical consultant to a television series on *The Arabs*; I do not think my advice was taken very often, but the experience somehow helped me to find a structure for the book. Long delayed, it finally appeared in 1991 under the title *A History of the Arab Peoples*.[40]

It might have been, as were Hodgson's *Venture of Islam* and Ira Lapidus's second book, *A History of Islamic Peoples*, a work on the broad canvas of the Muslim world as a whole; and it might have been confined to the history of the last two centuries, in which my special knowledge lay. I thought for a time of making it a study of the end of the great Muslim empires—those of the Ottomans, Safavids and Mughals—and once more I made a first draft of parts of it. In the end, however, I decided to limit the book in space and extend it in time. It became a history of those countries where Arabic was the main language of culture and political discourse, and I extended it backwards to the beginning of the time when what can be called an area of Arab Muslim culture first appeared. Hodgson's book had shown me that the history of the Persian or Iranian region needed to be considered in a different scale of time, and that it should take into account the continuity, or at least the revival in an Islamic form, of an ancient cultural tradition. I do not know Persian, and could not hope to understand this in any depth. If I decided to write about the whole sweep of Arab Islamic history, it was because I had become more conscious than some earlier historians of the importance of the centuries of Ottoman rule in forming what we call the "Arab world," and that we needed to see Ottoman rule and culture not only in the perspective of modern history but also as a continuation, and in many ways as the culmination, of the development of Muslim society.

At times, in making this broad sweep through "Arab" history, it was necessary to look beyond it. I was always aware of Hodgson's principle, that the

Oikoumene of cities and agrarian societies is the only intelligible unity of study. So, in writing about the first centuries when the Muslim caliphate was formed and the religion of Islam was articulated in systems of thought, law and practice, I had to include the whole world of Islam; when writing of the sixteenth, seventeenth and eighteenth centuries, I had to see the history of the Arab countries in the context of Ottoman history as a whole, and look beyond Baghdad, Damascus, Cairo, Tunis and Algiers to Istanbul; the changes of the nineteenth and twentieth century had to be presented within the context of the expansion of European trade and power.

I wrote the book at various times, and without having any clear theoretical framework in my mind. I followed such sources or authorities as I knew wherever they might lead me. Looking back at it now, however, I can see at least four themes running through it. The first is that of the growth and persistence of a cultural tradition, expressed in the Arabic language and carried by an educated elite. Here once more I must acknowledge a debt: Henri Laoust's studies of Ibn Taymiyya helped me greatly to understand the role of this elite in the life of governments as well as that of cities.[41]

Secondly, I tried to do justice both to the unity and to the diversity of that part of the world about which I was writing. I was always conscious of the influence of physical environment and geographical position upon the lives of communities; to live in the Mediterranean basin was very different from living in that of the Indian Ocean. (I suspect, however, that I gave too much attention to the countries lying around the eastern rim of the Mediterranean Sea, and there are problems I may not have fully understood in trying to incorporate the Maghrib or the Gulf or even Iraq into the same framework.) I attempted to give equal weight to local differences and to the links between different peoples; hence the title I gave the book, *A History of the Arab Peoples*, rather than "people" or "nation." The interplay between unity and variety served as a guiding thread in what I wrote about the modern period, when the political unity given by the Ottoman Empire had been lost but Arab national sentiment became explicit.

Thirdly, I took as one of my recurrent themes an idea derived from Ibn Khaldun by way of Hodgson and Lapidus: that of the complex, three-cornered relationship between rulers, urban elites and those whom Lapidus has called the "common people" in town and countryside. I tried to trace the changing alliance of interests between the first two: the rulers defending the fabric of civilized urban life, production and exchange, in return for obedience, financial contributions and the legitimacy which the elite could confer through its control of minds, whether expressed in Islamic terms or, in the modern period, through those of "Arabism." Rulers and urban elite together extended their social control into the countryside, but might at some point come up against another kind of control, exercised by rural lords or leaders in the mountains and steppe and expressed in the language of "tribalism."

Finally, I tried to avoid one of the dangers of writing the history of societies, that of looking at the process in terms of social structure and the relationship between them and political power, while ignoring the consciousness both of collectivities and of individuals, which reflect the social and political process but in some ways are able to control it. The interaction of Power and Wealth creates the "political economy" of a society, but there is also a "moral economy," formed by the interaction of both of them with Truth.

Since finishing the book I have written a few articles, and may write more, but I do not expect to publish any more long books. Of those I have written, the first two books, *Syria and Lebanon* and *Minorities in the Arab World*, were composed in another period of history and of my life, before I had discovered what I really wanted to write. They were perhaps useful at a time when so little had been written about the Middle East, but their life is over; I have never encouraged students to read them or publishers to re-issue them. Some of the shorter essays have more life in them, and so do the two longer books, *Arabic Thought in the Liberal Age* and *A History of the Arab Peoples*. I do not make great claims for them. They are not works of deep or exhaustive research; my threshold of boredom is low, and I lack that quality of obsession with a subject or problem which is necessary to do scholarly work of the highest value. All I can claim is that I have some gift for arrangement, for making clear patterns out of a mass of details, and that I can write in an acceptable way. *Arabic Thought* has already lasted thirty years, and may survive for a few more. *A History of the Arab Peoples* may last as long, as a fresh synthesis of the conclusions of other scholars arranged in a pattern I have devised. That pattern is an old-fashioned one, however; my culture is that of the first half of the present century, not of the present or the future. I am not fully conversant with new movements of historical thought. I think the book will be useful to teachers and students for some time, and it may—like Hitti's *History of the Arabs*—continue to have a certain popular standing after it has become an embarrassment for genuine scholars of a new generation.

I have great hopes in this new generation. I am surprised and pleased to find so many genuine historians now entering our field of study, fully equipped as historians and possessing the technical and linguistic skills needed to use the sources which are now becoming available. There is a "critical mass" of Middle Eastern historians, students and readers, large and solid enough to ensure the continuous development of the subject as a respectable field of historical study.

To this generally optimistic view of the future of Middle Eastern history I should, however, make two reservations. I do not feel confident that British universities will contribute as much to this expansion as those of the United States, France or Germany. The reason for this may lie partly in the mental effects of decolonization: there comes a moment when a nation may turn away from something in its own past. This should be over by now, however: Britain's moment in the Middle East has finished, and active interest may return, as it has done in South Asia (a region, however, where British involvement went deeper and lasted longer). The main reason for my doubt lies in the way in which "oriental studies" are still organized in British universities. The principal energies of teachers of these subjects are given to teaching undergraduates for the B.A. in "oriental studies." In such a course attention is naturally given first of all to the study of one or more languages and their literature rather than to history; moreover, since departments of oriental studies are for the most part small, they tend to lie at a distance from the mainstream of intellectual life in their universities. In that mainstream, the very strength of the British tradition of historical study tends to turn the best students towards the study of British, European or American history, together with those aspects or periods of Asian or African history which can be understood within a familiar framework of the rise and fulfillment of imperial rule. Those who decide to devote themselves to "oriental" history may not find the facilities for intensive and deep study of the languages they need; even if they do, they cannot normally expect more than three years of financial support, and at the end there will be few teaching posts and virtually no research posts available. There is no equivalent of the great French institutes in the Middle East, where a few young scholars in every generation can hope to spend years acquiring a deep and thorough knowledge of a Middle Eastern society and its culture.

Secondly, I believe that the state of our subject will be fragile unless work in Europe and America is solidly rooted in, or linked to, work by indigenous scholars. The flowering of Turkish historiography which we associate with such names as that of Halil Inalcik has had, I think, a salutary effect upon European and American students of Ottoman history, but the situation appears to be less satisfactory in Arabic and Persian history. There are some excellent Arab historians, and to some extent the ways in which they look at the past have had an influence upon their colleagues in other parts of the world: I am thinking of such writers as 'Abd al-'Aziz al-Duri on early Islamic history[42] and Abdullah Laroui on the Maghrib[43] and Kamal Salibi on Lebanon.[44] They work under great difficulties, however: secondary and university education in Arab countries is weak; there are a large number of universities, not a few preeminent ones where scholars can form a "critical mass;" in most countries their freedom to think and write as they please is limited; some of the best remain in Europe and America after they finish their studies, or when they give up their hopes of continuing their work in their own countries. This is a source of weakness for all of us who work in this field. Before everything else, the writing of history is an act of self-reflection of a collective consciousness, a community taking stock of its own past and what has made it what it is, creating its own principles of emphasis and categories of explanation.

Notes

1. A. Hourani, "Sulaiman al-Bustani and the Iliad" in *Islam in European Thought* (Cambridge, 1991), 174–87.
2. M. Wahba, "Cairo memories," in D. Hopwood, ed., *Studies in Arab History* (London, 1990), 103–15.
3. T. E. Lawrence, *Seven Pillars of Wisdom* (London, 1935).
4. G. Antonius, *The Arab Awakening* (London, 1938).
5. *Syria and Lebanon* (London, 1946); *Minorities in the Arab World* (London, 1947).
6. A. J. Toynbee, *A Study of History*, vols. 1–3 (London, 1934).

7. Toynbee, *The Western Question in Greece and Turkey* (London, 1922).

8. H. A. R. Gibb and H. Bowen, *Islamic Society and the West*, vol. 1 (part 1, London, 1950; part 2, London, 1957).

9. Lawrence, *Seven Pillars*, chap. 6, 57.

10. "Palestine and Israel," *The Observer*, 3 September 1967.

11. Hourani, "Musa 'Alami and the problem of Palestine, 1933–1949" in H. Nashabé, ed., *Studia Palaestina* (Beirut, 1988), 23–41.

12. Foreign Office, *Report of the Inter-Departmental Committee of Enquiry on Oriental, Slavonic, East European and African Studies* (London, 1947).

13. Gibb, *Area Studies Reconsidered* (London, 1963).

14. Hourani, "Wednesday afternoons remembered" in *Islam in European Thought*, 61–73; J. M. Ahmed, *The Intellectual Origins of Egyptian Nationalism* (London, 1960).

15. Hourani, "L'oeuvre d'André Raymond" in *Villes au Levant: Revue du Monde Musulman et de la Méditerranée*, vol. 55/56 (1990), 18–27; "The achievement of André Raymond," *British Journal of Middle Eastern Studies*, vol. 18, no. 1, 5–15.

16. Hourani, "In search of a new Andalusia: Jacques Berque and the Arabs" in *Islam in European Thought*, 129–35.

17. Gibb, "Islamic biographical literature" in B. Lewis and P. M. Holt, ed., *Historians of the Middle East* (Oxford, 1962), 54–58.

18. A. Rustum, *al-Mahfuzat al-malikiya al-misriya*, 4 vols. (Beirut, 1940–43).

19. B. Lewis, *The Emergence of Modern Turkey* (London, 1961); A. K. S. Lambton, *Landlord and Peasant in Persia* (London, 1953).

20. Hourani, "Toynbee's vision of history" in *Europe and the Middle East* (London, 1980), 135–60.

21. *Arabic Thought in the Liberal Age* (London, 1962).

22. J. Berque, *L'Égypte, impérialisme et révolution* (Paris, 1967); English translation, *Egypt, Imperialism and Revolution* (London, 1972).

23. E. Wilson, *To the Finland Station* (London, 1941).

24. E. Monroe, *Britain's Moment in the Middle East, 1914–1956* (London, 1964).

25. University Grants Committee, *Report of the Sub-Committee on Oriental, Slavonic, East European and African Studies* (London, 1961).

26. I. M. Lapidus, *Muslim Cities in the Later Middle Ages* (Cambridge, Mass., 1967).

27. M. G. S. Hodgson, *The Venture of Islam*, 3 vols. (Chicago, 1974); Hourani, "Marshall Hodgson and the venture of Islam" in *Islam in European Thought*, 74–89.

28. A. Raymond, *Artisans et commerçants au Caire au XVIIIe siècle*, 2 vols. (Damascus, 1973–74).

29. D. Landes, *The Unbound Prometheus* (Cambridge, 1969).

30. E. J. Hobsbawm, *The Age of Revolution: Europe 1789–1848* (London, 1962); *The Age of Capital, 1848–1875* (London, 1975); *The Age of Empire, 1875–1914* (London, 1987).

31. "Bustani's encyclopedia" in *Islam in European Thought*, 164–73; "Sulaiman Bustani and the Iliad," see note 1.

32. Hourani, "Sufism and modern Islam: Mawlana Khalid and the Naqshbandi order" in *The Emergence of the Modern Middle East* (London, 1981), 75–89.

33. Hourani and S. M. Stern, ed., *The Islamic City* (Oxford, 1970).

34. "Ottoman reform and the politics of notables" in *The Emergence of the Modern Middle East*, 36–66.

35. E. Said, *Orientalism* (London, 1978).

36. "Western attitudes towards Islam" in *Europe and the Middle East* (London, 1980), 4.

37. "Islam and the philosophers of history" in *Europe and the Middle East*, 19–73.

38. *Islam in European Thought*, 7–60.

39. *Vision of History* (Beirut, 1961).

40. A *History of the Arab Peoples* (London, 1991).

41. H. Laoust, *Essai sur les doctrines sociales et politiques de Taki-d-Din Ahmad b. Taimiya* (Cairo, 1939).

42. 'Abd al-'Aziz al-Duri, *Bahtih fi nash'at 'ilm al-tarikh 'ind al-'arab* (Beirut, 1960); English trans. L. I. Conrad, *The Rise of Historical Writing Among the Arabs* (Princeton, 1981).

43. A. Laroui, *L'histoire du Maghreb* (Paris, 1970); English trans., *The History of the Maghrib* (Princeton, 1977).

44. K. Salibi, *The Modern History of Lebanon* (London, 1965); *A House of Many Mansions* (London, 1988).

CHAPTER 3

The Education of
J. C. Hurewitz

J. C. Hurewitz

On enrolling as a Ph.D. candidate in history at Columbia University in 1936, I elected the modern Middle East as an area of academic specialization, even though I knew that it was at the time essentially a nonexistent subdiscipline not alone on Morningside Heights but in American higher education.

A respected school of historiography in the United States still viewed Thucydides as the Father of History. But many American practitioners, trained in the 19th-century German tradition, favored Herodotus for that title, naming his rival a journalist whose fame rested on a contemporary account of the Peloponnesian War. When I finally reached the dissertation stage of Ph.D. candidacy, I chose Thucydides as my model, determined as I was to demonstrate that the analysis of an unfolding international crisis may be seen as part of an historical process and can be carried out with the exacting standards of dispassion. That is what I sought in my first book, *The Struggle for Palestine*.

The study established my credentials as an historian of the contemporary Middle East. It had originally been framed as a doctoral dissertation in history at Columbia University. Before Pearl Harbor I had spent three years in the region on a graduate fellowship, originally granted on the eve of the award of my M.A. degree and renewed in the field. I thus left for the Middle East with little more than vague plans to undertake research for a doctoral dissertation even before meeting the residence requirements for the Ph.D. I was not aware nor did I think of looking into the history department's formalities on advance approval of dissertation designs. I did not even seek its endorsement from the field for a study of "Americans in Ottoman Palestine" in the 19th and early 20th centuries. I simply framed and pursued the project. If twenty years later one of my students had proposed such a topic, I would have refused to sponsor it unless the candidate demonstrated research skills in Arabic and Osmanlı (Ottoman Turkish) as well as Hebrew. By such criteria, I could not possibly have found departmental support in the 1930s.

At that time Columbia offered no courses on Middle East history other than the ancient period and segmental coverage in Jewish history. The only other offerings on the region consisted of Semitic languages—Arabic, Hebrew, Amharic and such ancient languages as Aramaic and Ugaritic (almost as speedily as it was being deciphered)—and related classical literature. Into this class fell Columbia's anemic oriental studies. Even instruction in Persian history and Farsi had stopped on the retirement of A. V. W. Jackson the year before I reached Morningside Heights. Courses in theology, admittedly, were offered at adjacent theological seminaries. But they were not my dish.

It is clear that I had brought to Columbia a developed interest in Palestine. In my sophomore year at Trinity College in Hartford, Conn., where I was born, I recall appealing to its president, Dr. Remsen B. Ogilby, an Episcopal cleric by training, for permission to take my junior year at the Hebrew University in Jerusalem for full or part credit toward the B.A. He politely but unequivocally dismissed the appeal. The attempt to revive an ancient language could only fail, since there was no successful precedent. Ponder the efforts to revive Gaelic in Ireland, he advised, and be thankful for escaping a fruitless experiment.

Not long thereafter, Dean Thurmon L. Hood, a professor of English literature with a chosen interest in the 19th century and a focus on Robert Browning, sought my aid. Browning, he informed me, had studied Hebrew, and the Dean was driven by an urge to follow in the Victorian bard's steps. And so I devoted a marginal part of my junior year in the vicarious Middle East experience of teaching our Dean at his gracious home the Hebrew alphabet and biblical grammar, using as text selective chapters of Genesis.

How I wished that the top administration could get their act together.

My interest in Palestine, it is also clear, reached back even earlier, indeed, as far as I can remember. Palestine was a brand new country, not yet independent, but with a fixed if also controversial profile, and in it a Jewish National Home was rising with the international sanction of the League of Nations and with Great Britain as trustee. The national home and its patron were challenged, sometimes violently, by an articulate but poorly organized Palestine Arab nationalist movement. An orthodox rabbi, my father was born in Russian Poland but ordained in Lithuania, where he met and married my mother in 1888. At that time my parents were among the multiplying residents of the world's largest Jewish community of the day who were fleeing from the Pale of Settlement and the brutality of tsarist Russia. Mostly, they headed for the United States, as did my parents, who reshaped their lives and raised their family in freedom. I was the youngest of twelve children. On my birth all but one were still alive.

At about the time of my father's emigration to the US, his father upon becoming a widower settled in Jerusalem to live out his declining years. Indeed, he was buried there in 1899. Ties to Palestine were reinforced by a strong family interest in Zionism. An authority on the religious philosophy of Maimonides, my father wrote two books in Hebrew on the subject and in person delivered the manuscripts to the printer in Jerusalem. One appeared in 1927 and the other six years later, each in an edition of perhaps fewer than 1,000 copies. My father became his own distributor. Even with some attrition by marriage, we remained an ample family and were lucky to be living in a three-story home, with a spare room in the attic where the unsold stock was kept.

Despite my major in philosophy at Trinity, I gave equal time to history. My interest centered on modern Europe, I suspect, because Britain, France and Italy had brought into their empires most of the Middle East and North Africa. Responsible for leading me to Columbia was the history department chairman, who had earned his Ph.D. there. He explained that, while Columbia offered no direct instruction on modern Middle East history, neither did any other American university. (He was wrong on that point, as I learned much later. Albert Howe Lybyer in the interwar decades had been teaching in alternate years a survey course on Ottoman history at the University of Illinois without collateral instruction by colleagues and without duplication elsewhere in the country.) I would nonetheless receive excellent training in historiography by some of the ablest and most incisive practitioners.

In the fall of 1936 I enrolled in the graduate history department, for a start studying with among others Salo W. Baron (the world's preeminent Jewish historian), William L. Westermann (with the ancient Mediterranean and Near East as his circuit, but also, as he told me, drawn in 1919 into President Woodrow Wilson's advisory team at the Paris Peace Conference, when he became a lifelong advocate of the Kurds), Carlton J. H. Hayes (his kick, the rise of modern nationalism in Europe) and Allan Nevins (a prolific historian and biographer in the American field and, after retirement, the father of oral history). In 1936 Nevins coordinated the colloquium on historiography, which all doctoral candidates in the discipline had to take. Each week one of the professors led the discussion on his subfield based on advance reading of selections from related classics. In the absence of manuals that became plentiful after 1945, Nevins devoted the opening meetings to the stuff of the professional historian. We learned about the nature of historical inquiry and the varieties of oral and written evidence and their assemblage and assessment as well as putting a research design together. I also worked with Dr. Abraham Halkin in modern literary Hebrew to help me build on an earlier base in the liturgical language.

As the first recipient of a fellowship for the Hebrew University from the Berwitz-Gollin Foundation of St. Louis, I reached Palestine in mid-July 1937. Fresh out of Columbia with a one-year M.A., only introductory training in the discipline and no more than peripheral exposure to my elected specialization, I had to find my own way. It was thus clear that, as an aspiring scholar of the contemporary Middle East, I would cut my academic teeth by putting to the test, in the still largely barren field of modern Middle East history, the styles and techniques of those history classics into which I had dipped and those that I might later consult.

In the field what I learned I learned without structured guidance. There was at the Hebrew University, it is true, a School of Oriental Studies. But like oriental studies in Europe, it centered attention on theology, the humanities and languages with almost no attention to the social sciences. Comprehensive courses on the history of the concluding Ottoman century were simply nonexistent. The curriculum at the American University of Bayrut—medicine, nursing and engineering excepted—was still essentially that of an undergraduate liberal arts college. However, individuals were still around in the late

1930s who had lived through the major part of the period of my research concern. In Jerusalem for about a year I boarded at the home of David Yellin, a third-generation native of the city, widely respected across communal lines for his concerns about public welfare, and professor of medieval Hebrew poetry, fluent also in Arabic, English and Turkish. In Bayrut I befriended Dr. William T. Van Dyck, the son of the co-translator into Arabic of the Bible and the founder in 1866 of the medical school at the Syrian Protestant College (renamed in 1920 the American University of Bayrut). Even as octogenarians, they commanded remarkable memories of life under Ottoman rule and after. They shared with me their libraries and at times personal papers. But I am getting ahead of myself.

With three months to find my bearings before the start of a new academic year, I decided to put the unexpected free time to double duty. On application, I was accepted as a volunteer worker at Qibbutz Mishmar ha-'Emeq, south of Haifa, to begin converting biblical Hebrew to the modern spoken language and to sharpen my skill in reading contemporary literature, so as to prepare for university lectures in the fall. Exposure to the members of a leftist collective, which advocated cooperation with the Palestine Arabs even in the midst of their three-year revolt, would also enable me to identify at first hand the issues in dispute. Equally important, a week before I stepped ashore, the comprehensive Royal Commission report was released along with a White Paper ratifying the Palestine partition proposal as British policy and announcing that a second commission would refine the specifics. Whitehall's action sparked weeks of obsessive argument by, between and among Britons, Arabs and Jews in the three languages and then some. What a juncture to enter the scene. And what regrets that I had not yet begun studying Arabic.

Mishmar ha-'Emeq's library featured local newspapers and journals with a small selection of books in Hebrew, Arabic and major European languages. Saturday nights were given over to public meetings on issues of the day for guest workers as well as qibbutz members. In my two-month residence, partition was the unvarying theme: Would it open the doors of Palestine to rescue the Jews of central and eastern Europe, already threatened by the spread of Nazism and Fascism? Would the Arabs, so deeply aroused, acquiesce? If not, would Whitehall be likely to proceed in the face of emphatic Arab opposition? In either case, how would the announcement of splitting the country affect intercommunal relations? Since two members of Mishmar ha-'Emeq sat on the executive of its federation of collectives, the forum drew participants from nearby villages belonging to the same wing of socialist Zionism. The brief encounter opened my eyes to the complex dynamics of Zionism, a vibrant purposive unity amid an articulate disunity.

In mid-September, a few weeks before the start of the academic year, I moved to Jerusalem to settle in. The Hebrew University had a magnificent campus on Mount Scopus, with a panorama of Old and New Jerusalem on the west and the red sands of the Judaean Desert on the east, an excellent library, ample classrooms, a student commons of sorts, choice gardens full of biblical flowers cultivated by the university botanist—but no dormitories. A student identity card, I soon learned, opened many doors, even that of the American-born university president, Dr. Judah L. Magnes, who had lived in the country since 1907. After listening to my still inchoate dissertation plans, Magnes introduced me to Edwin Samuel, the son of Palestine's first High Commissioner and a member of the incumbent HC's inner advisory circle. Edwin, I quickly learned, had also studied at Columbia, and out of that common experience grew a lasting friendship. He seemed to know everyone of consequence in the country and shared my interest in the history of modern Palestine. On many questions raised by my developing research project, he knew residents in Jerusalem and beyond to guide me to the sources. In the research-friendly setting his introductions proved that interviews across the rigid communal lines of the Mandate's cosmopolitan capital were feasible.

The first and, for my project, the most productive introduction led me to George Wadsworth. The US Consul General applauded my unfolding dissertation plan to trace the origins and rise of US interests in Ottoman Arab Asia, with Palestine as the centerpiece. My subject seems to have been inspired by Tyler Dennett's *Americans in Eastern Asia: A Critical Study of the Policy of the United States with Reference to China, Japan and Korea in the 19th Century.* The ponderous title suggested its probable derivation from a dissertation. I had a hunch that the types of evidence the author had uncovered in investigating the underpinning of US policies toward China, Japan and Korea might also be relevant for West Asia—missionaries pursuing proselytes and good works, exporters and importers chasing a fast buck, scholars seeking to explore little-known but richly cultured lands and record the findings, a much larger tribe of travelers bent on immortalizing "unique" adventures, and US consuls and their unpaid agents keeping an official inventory of such goings-on. Although the specifics at the two ends of the massive continent bore little resemblance, Dennett had identified for my exploratory use classes of evidence that proved pertinent.

Wadsworth shared my desire to chart and analyze the development of an American presence in this part of the *Mashriq* (Arab East). He himself had entered the region via Lebanon on the eve of World War I, either to teach at the Syrian Protestant College or to serve on the staff of the US Consulate General. I recall, not the direction of his move, but its date—1915. Such a career qualified him as an old Middle East—or, in his usage, Near East—hand. The State Department, Wadsworth explained, had recently instructed the chiefs of the diplomatic and consular missions everywhere to pack for shipment to the US all official records dated 1910 and earlier. Pending their transfer, Wadsworth offered me free access to the packaged files lying in dead storage in a one-story stone guardhouse of the walled-in attractive consular compound, an Ottoman relic of the turn of the century. With little persuasion, I launched the research almost immediately. I was given a desk, a typewriter, the requisite stationery, a key to the otherwise unused building and free access five days a week from 8 to 5.

The consulate lay halfway up Mamillah Road. On its continuation over the crest of a hill into Rehavyah, a new section of Jerusalem favored by settlers from Germany and Central Europe, was my new home, a rented room in the apartment of a newly arrived Hungarian couple to whom the university's foreign student advisor had led me. An alley that separated the consulate from its adjacent building led to a five-minute shortcut to the YMCA, with the only swimming pool in the city. As a water nut even then, I interrupted with refreshing muscle-stretching exercise the grinding daily rounds of building a database.

The unexpected treasure trove at the US Consulate could easily entrap me, if I were not careful. I was in danger of learning more and more about less and less by squirreling facts away without enlivening reference to the relevant evidence in the public domain (books, articles, brochures, reports) or available in interviews of individuals who might have taken part in the societies, institutions, public affairs and episodes noted in the consular record books. More important, my fellowship committed me to enroll in the Hebrew University, then the only one in the *Yishuv* (settlement), as the Jewish Community was known. I had neglected none of these. I began meeting students who had registered in earlier years and were familiar with the rules, the routine and the opportunities. Mostly, they were refugees from Europe who found the Hebrew University routine familiar. Attendance records were not kept. Students might come or go at pleasure, so long as they met the written requirements (papers and exams).

The course offerings on the whole seemed to have little bearing on the research goal that I was trying to define. Understandably, instruction on the growth of the Yishuv in the 19th and 20th centuries received primary attention, as did traditional orientalism with its focus on Islam as theology and religion. The offering in Islamic art was distinguished. Courses in Arabic, Turkish and Persian were also available, but fluency in Hebrew was indispensable, since that was the language of instruction. What I instinctually did was identify the most eloquent lecturers in courses not too remote from my focused interest so that I might rationalize the decision as a mode of acquiring the skill to take notes from acknowledged masters of a rapidly developing language.

Within the Yishuv I found my own way. On individuals and groups in the society beyond, mentioned in the consular documents, I conferred from time to time with Edwin Samuel as also with new friends that I was cultivating in Jerusalem and elsewhere. The new friends among resident Jews and Arabs (Muslims and Christians) led me step by step to the well informed on communal affairs. But it was Samuel who guided me at the outset to European and American residents—archaeologists, missionaries and millenarians as well as British officials. I put to the test the value of oral evidence with Mrs. Bertha Spofford Vester, the acknowledged head of the American Colony of Jerusalem.

As predicted, she invited me for tea in her magnificent salon, still kept in the opulent Ottoman imperial style with colorful rugs and brilliantly polished brass trays, copper vases with floral displays, and a large mangal or brazier. The chairs and sofas were tastefully upholstered in the style of the French monarchy. I was her only guest that early evening, bursting with questions on the origins of the Colony in the 1880s and its survival into the mandate in a mode that differed so radically from its original conception. I did not reveal that the consular papers were, on balance, less than flattering. I simply plumbed her memories on why her parents had left Chicago with a small retinue to build a new life in the Holy Land. She did not dodge any question, and the flow of response came, not in sentences, but paragraphs. She happily permitted me to take notes, which I later typed on 5 x 8 cards for my databank.

Skip to the fall of 1938, when I returned for another interview at high tea to find answers to new questions that had cropped up in the interval, again taking full notes. As I later began the transcription, I abruptly stopped. The new message echoed the old. From the dual exercise, I learned two lessons: reread the notes of a first interview before going on to the next; and global repetition signals the need to wrap one's attention around likely reasons for the deliberate concealment.

To return to the actual sequence, in a few weeks of close review of the Jerusalem consular records, I recognized their true value: a convenient inventory of relevant data, (relatively) authoritative on official policy, of variable reliability on the rest. Besides, the US was only a marginal player in Ottoman external politics and until 1906 US consuls and diplomats in Ottoman Asia were political appointees, not professional foreign service officers. Under the "spoils system," on each change of administration in Washington, they were rotated out of office. As capital of the mandate, Jerusalem became center stage for the domestic and external politics of the new country. In the final half-century of Ottoman rule the political geography of the region had presented a wholly different aspect. Under the reorganized and, after a lapse of 250 years, recentralized provincial system put together in stages under the Tanzimat by the Sublime Porte between 1841 and 1864, the Jerusalem sancak or provincial district was attached to the Damascus vilayet. In 1887 it became an independent sancak or quasi vilayet (as had Lebanon from its creation in 1861), so that the kaymakam reported not through a vali but directly to the Ministry of the Interior in Istanbul.

To learn about the northern half of the country under late Ottoman rule, it was clear, I had to go to Bayrut. A note from Wadsworth to Ely E. Palmer, the Consul General there, served as entree to the larger and more formal post with its more plentiful files. Palmer installed me and the boxed records in a large vacant room equipped with two desks and two typewriters in a part of the building with marginal traffic. Almost immediately the personnel manager, on her own initiative, recommended my hiring an English-speaking typist, once in consular employ, to transcribe documentary extracts of my selection. With the local pound pegged to the French franc, a favorable exchange rate made it practicable to employ the typist nearly full-time even on my modest stipend. The sancaklar (provincial districts) of Acre and Nablus embraced what became mandated Palestine's north. The Bayrut records helped me reconstruct the range and depth—or perhaps more aptly the marginality—of US official interest in the entire area of the later Palestine mandate and confirmed that Americans were drawn chiefly to Jerusalem, Jaffa and Ramallah in the south.

The Bayrut consular archives reached back to 1833, although the post was run by an unsalaried British national, officially titled an honorary US consular agent. He was succeeded starting in 1850 by salaried American consuls, and the post was raised in 1906 to a consulate general. The Jerusalem consular archives dated to 1857, when the first American incumbent was installed. It did not become a consulate general until after the ratification of the mandate in 1923.

On the American yardstick Bayrut was a small town of perhaps 150,000 people. But it was the country's largest city, the capital and, more important at the time, the seat of French authority in its mandate which embraced Syria. As the home of AUB, Bayrut had become in the interwar years the center of American cultural presence in the Mashriq. In the humanities and the social sciences, the university offered essentially undergraduate instruction, not very useful to my purposes of graduate research, although its library of some 65,000 volumes, in which I enjoyed guest privileges, proved helpful for occasional reference. Even before arrival I knew that my interests would best be served by centering research on the consular files and pursuing leads to interview those who had experienced Ottoman rule.

The problem of housing proved much easier to resolve than I originally had feared. An American visiting professor of education at the Hebrew University told me that his daughter, who had accompanied her parents to the Middle East, was enrolled in AUB's medical school. She led me to some fifteen or so American male students of medicine and dentistry, all roughly my age, who had formed an off-campus cooperative dormitory by renting a large house on Rue Bliss within view of the stunning campus, overlooking the Mediterranean from Ras Bayrut, the city's promontory that descended to the sea. They employed two maids, one doubling as a cook to prepare all three meals each day, and a handyman who kept the premises clean and doubled as a waiter and gardener. Welcomed to the cooperative, I was assigned to share a room with a dental student. My roommate did not object to my typing at the day's end, when I culled entries for the databank from the daily rounds at the consulate (within easy walking distance) and occasional interviews. Away from the cloistered residence, I had ample scope practicing French and developing a facility in the Syro-Palestinian dialect of spoken Arabic. I returned to Bayrut a year later for a second research stint at the Consulate, and on both occasions took side trips to Damascus in order to familiarize myself with the terrain.

Early in 1938, on my return from the first trip to Bayrut, I applied for permission to consult the files of the former British Consulate in Jerusalem, which I learned had been stored in the Palestine Government's Office of Migration and Statistics. When I discussed the matter with the then Commissioner for Migration and Statistics, Eric Mills informed me that on the outbreak of war in 1914, the archives had been burned to prevent their falling into Ottoman hands. I therefore wrote to the Librarian and Keeper of the Papers at the Foreign Office in London to find out whether, if I went to England, I might be allowed to consult the records there. No need for that, Stephen Gaselee, the Keeper, replied. The requested "archives ... are now in the custody of the High Commission for Palestine," and suggested that I seek the necessary permission there. When I returned with Gaselee's letter in hand, an embarrassed Mills apologized, declaring that he had already received a copy of the letter. He went on to explain his orders to deny applicants access to the materials on the ground that the likely traffic of such requests would exceed his office's capacity to handle the flow.

Needless to say, I was treated to the same courtesies given by the American consulates. The British collection, in greater and more illuminating detail than the American, chronicled social, economic and political developments in the sancak. Understandably, references to Americans were incidental, though often pertinent and at times insightful. Decades later I was astonished to learn from Ann Lesch, then one of my Ph.D. candidates, that, in rummaging through the Colonial Office papers for her dissertation, she had come upon my application. After conferring with Foreign Secretary Lord Halifax, Gaselee was directed to recommend that, if Colonial Secretary Malcolm MacDonald "sees no objection, the High Commissioner might be asked to grant, at his discretion, the facilities desired by Mr. Hurewitz." In a Colonial Office minute, attached to these papers, it was noted, "From the [return] address—c/o Professor David Yellin, of the Hebrew University—this is evidently a reputable request."

The outbreak of war in September 1939 put an end to my circuits of the mandated beat. By then I had begun studying Arabic at the Hebrew University with Professor S. D. Goitein, a founder of its School of Oriental Studies and later a world renowned historian of Arab-Jewish relations and a long-term fellow of the Institute for Advanced Study in Princeton. I also registered for a seminar with Professor Richard Köbner, an eminent refugee historian from Germany whose theme that year was varieties of European imperialism in the Middle East. When I heard Köbner speak, I could not always tell whether it was in Hebrew or German or, at times, a combination of both. But whatever he was saying was decidedly worth pondering. History, as you might have gathered, has many fathers. Leopold von Ranke, the founder of 19th-century "objective historicism," was Köbner's. He in turn trained a number of scholars whose later eminence in social sciences reached far beyond Israel's unmarked land borders. For his seminar, I drafted sample dissertation chapters.

In view of "the already limited facilities for travel from Eastern Mediterranean ports to the United States…and the existing uncertainty as to how long even such restricted facilities will be available," ran a notice to US citizens in Palestine from the American Consulate General in Jerusalem at the time of Dunkirk and Italy's entry into the war in May 1940. It urged "the advisability of returning to the United States with the least possible delay." It took two months longer to arrange direct passage from Port Sa'id, Egypt, to New York via the Cape of Good Hope on the *Al-Nil*, a Khedival liner that had never before left the Mediterranean. The date of departure was finally fixed for 15 August, with an expected travel time of thirty-five days.

That decision focused my mind on packing a three-year accumulation of consular transcripts (I am thankful, in retrospect, that instant copiers were still two decades into the future), sample dissertation chapters, my first book reviews in local periodicals, interview notes, maps and especially books (mostly memoirs and travelogues as well as dictionaries and other reference works), articles, brochures, broadsheets and bulletins from American, British and German missionary, millenarian and archaeological societies, Arab nationalist and Zionist groups, clippings from the press and just plain memorabilia. The burden was somewhat eased by Wadsworth's offer to send to Washington via diplomatic pouch seven hefty parcels of the top copy of notes and transcripts of the Jerusalem and Bayrut US consular papers. That at least virtually assured safe delivery to the US of most of the official documentary evidence for the dissertation. That was much on our minds in the summer of 1940 as the media chronicled in banner headlines the two-pronged battle for Britain by the Luftwaffe over the Isles and by the Nazi submarines in the Atlantic.

All the rest was crated, with all documentary and written contents accessible for examination by the wartime government censor. My luck had lingered on. Edwin Samuel, by then Commissioner of Migration, doubled as censor and personally reviewed the miscellany. He of course knew all about my research. After asking the standard questions, cutting off parts of maps and admiring selected items in my budding library on the Middle East, Samuel had the two crates nailed shut, wired and sealed. Sixty-six days after weighing anchor at Port Saʻid the *Al-Nil* debarked in Manhattan—time enough for me to change from hunt-and-peck to touch-typing. In this light, the $800 fare did not seem excessive.

On returning to Columbia in the fall of 1940, I still had to satisfy two more years of residence requirements for the Ph.D. American history had become my disguised major in the department. I enrolled in or audited pertinent general courses, notably with Henry Steele Commager, later my dissertation sponsor. In a Commager seminar on "The Reform Movements in the U.S. 1830–50" I was allowed to stretch the time span for a paper on "American Millenarians in Palestine, 1866–1900." I also resumed studying with Baron for my orals minor, and branched into sociology and international law and relations. After Pearl Harbor, acceleration became the rule. The oral examination in history in the spring of 1942 was the first hurdle, formal acceptance of "Americans in Ottoman Palestine 1820–1918" the second. A special language project for the study of Egyptian colloquial Arabic, financed by the US Government and sponsored by the American Council of Learned Societies, filled much of the summer and fall.

My study of Arabic landed me, after conscription into the army, in a Signal Corps camp in Warrenton, Va. Yet even before basic training as a soldier and in cryptology had ended, the Signal Corps lost interest in Arabists, for the American and British campaigns had made a clean sweep of Axis troops from North Africa. It was then that, in uniform, I was reassigned to the Near East Section of the Research and Analysis Branch of the Office of Strategic Services in Washington. The section director, Professor E. A. Speiser, a brilliant archaeologist and philologist on loan from the University of Pennsylvania, had read my "Arab Politics in Palestine" in the bimonthly *Contemporary Jewish Record* (December 1942).

Speiser was seeking a scholar with expertise on the Palestine problem and research experience in Arabic and Hebrew and, after an interview, requested my transfer. The commander of the Warrenton camp notified the OSS personnel office that the request had been turned down on the ground that Hurewitz was indispensable to the Signal Corps. Speiser phoned me to ascertain the duties that accounted for the rejection. Every morning, I explained, our unit moved logs from one side of the road to the other; in the afternoon we returned them to the original site. Speiser enlisted the aid of the top-ranking uniformed officer in the hierarchy of the mixed civilian-military intelligence agency. Within twenty-four hours I received orders to proceed to Washington.

After a month-long security check in comfortable seclusion in a Maryland OSS camp, I was finally delivered to my new office and notified that, while promoted from private first class to corporal, I was nonetheless given the same title as that of my civilian colleagues—senior political analyst. Significantly, the Near East Section of R&A, along with the Africa (including the Maghrib) and South Asia sections, was a unit within the European Division. R&A as a whole had been deposited in Foggy Bottom in a former skating rink preempted by the federal government. The converted rink housed in a single room all sections of R&A. Shortly thereafter we moved for the war's duration and beyond to a nearby adapted apartment building where each geographic unit was given its own separate quarter.

As research analyst on the Palestine Mandate (including Transjordan), I was told, I would be responsible for a weekly report on domestic politics in the

Mandate and repercussions of the unresolved Arab-Zionist dispute in the Arab East and among Zionists and pro-Zionists in Europe, Britain and the Commonwealth and the Americas. Since Fridays and Saturday mornings were given over to the weekly country roundup, I would be expected to devote the other days to longer analyses of timely issues, mostly of my own choice. I was told to request newspapers and other publications from Palestine as a primary source of information, to be enriched by data from the classified traffic of the departments of State, Army (along with its air force until it was elevated in 1944 to the status of an independent department) and Navy as well as from other branches of the OSS and occasional classified papers that the British shared with us. Other duties called for evaluating signed reports from the Pentagon's intelligence units.

On asking for the existing files on Palestine, I was handed the entire collection—two folders, one with an article on Arab nationalism and the other, with one on Zionism, both in public print. I promptly ordered all Palestine dailies, weeklies and monthlies in Arabic, Hebrew and English. Three copies of each along with a parallel flow from every country of our ambit, embracing Turkey and Iran as well as the Arab East, reached our office twice each week from OSS Cairo within forty-eight to seventy-two hours of the date on the latest issue. Two sets might be clipped, we were advised, and the third had to be deposited in the Library of Congress.

It did not take long to appreciate that I had been invited to join a unique, uninterrupted scholarly seminar on the Near East at war, for which at government expense I was ordered to update my familiarity with the contemporary history of Palestine and keep abreast of unfolding developments with the support of the best evidence available to Washington. More than that, I had to bear in mind that my own research and analysis would be critically reviewed by colleagues, each assigned a particular geographic or functional duty. Each of us saw the total daily classified traffic on the Near East, which encouraged our cultivating a regional perspective. From time to time we also cooperated in areawide evaluations, such as a study of evolving interests of the USSR in the Near East after its entry into the war in June 1941, as the context for forecasting its likely postwar regional strategy.

As section director, Speiser infused into our work a 5,000-year perspective on the overall region. Originally trained as a biblical scholar, he developed a deep interest in the civilization of ancient Mesopotamia (present-day Iraq), where he had directed a series of archaeological digs. His writings reflected an inclusive interest in the ancient civilization of the region. Along the way he deciphered and published a grammar on Hurrian, an ancient Mesopotamian language. The first year's sales were seven. By the war's end, the first printing of 100 copies was exhausted. The weekly reports often contained one of Speiser's pieces on contemporary Iraq, many of whose political leaders he had met.

The Near East section brought together a thoughtful, lively and congenial group. Harold W. Glidden, with a Princeton Ph.D. in Arabic, at first covered Egypt, Sudan and the Arabian Peninsula. Early in 1944 Franz Rosenthal joined our section in a corporal's uniform to share Glidden's load. After the war, on the appearance of *A History of Muslim Historiography* (1952) and his translation of Ibn Khaldun's *The Muqaddimah* (3 vols., 1958), Rosenthal earned worldwide esteem as a universalist in Arab and Islamic studies. His impressive output continued into his retirement from Yale University with a translation of *The History of al-Tabari*, vol. 1, that included a biography of the 9th-century prolific world historian. In most of 1944, Rosenthal replaced Glidden in the latter's absence on loan to OSS Cairo. On Glidden's return to Washington, the two once again redivided the chores. As a longtime educational missionary in Iran, T. Cuyler Young kept track of the wartime reshaping of the shahdom's public affairs under Anglo-Soviet occupation and the presence of a US Persian Gulf Command of some 28,000 engineering and transportation troops, to forward through this corridor a quarter of American Lend-Lease aid to the USSR. An interwar instructor at Robert College in Istanbul, Harvey P. Hall with the cooperation of Kerim K. Key, an American citizen of Turkish birth, kept a close eye on Turkey, the region's sole country to cling to its neutrality until early in 1945. Turkey thus served as a center for international intrigue, engaging all the major belligerents in their rival diplomacy, propaganda and undercover operations. Also in 1944, Dr. Herbert J. Liebesny, a Viennese-trained lawyer who had worked with Westermann at Columbia on legal practice in the ancient Near East, developed expertise on the interplay of Western and Islamic law among the Arabian states in the Gulf.

Early in 1945 I was one of twenty-five uniformed men in R&A to receive a direct commission and, on demobilization in October, was promoted to the rank of first lieutenant. At the same time R&A, retitled the Office of Intelligence Research, was assimilated into the Department of State. Speiser had already returned to the University of Pennsylvania; Rosenthal followed at the turn of the year, to his post as professor of Semitic languages at Hebrew Union College in Cincinnati. By the time I entered the Department, my bailiwick had been expanded to encompass Iraq. We performed our accustomed tasks—the preparation of weekly and special reports. And we remained in the same offices, since the swelling Department at the time was still crammed into what later became the Executive Office Building of the White House, with no room to spare for divisional accretions. By then my desk had, in effect, been transformed into the Department's repository of active "historical" files on the Palestine problem.

On the initiative of Foreign Secretary Ernest Bevin, the US joined its ally in an Anglo-American Committee of Inquiry on Palestine and Related Problems. At the time of its formation, Evan Wilson, the diplomat in charge of the AACI's American secretariat and a close friend and squash partner, apologetically explained that, because of the Foreign Office recommendation, no "Americans of Arab or Jewish extraction" would accompany the inquirers to Europe and the Middle East. However, in the Washington hearings that kicked off the investigation, I briefed the researchers in the US secretariat and, while they remained in Washington, directed to them a steady flow of classified background papers.

A few weeks after the appearance of the AACI report in the spring of 1946, Loy Henderson, the director of the Office of Near Eastern and African Affairs, invited me to serve as political adviser to President Truman's Cabinet Committee on Palestine, in actuality a committee of alternates appointed by the secretaries of State, War and the Treasury and none with prior experience on Palestine. The Secretary of State named as his representative Henry F. Grady, who, after receipt of a doctorate in economics at Columbia, rose to become CEO of the President Lines and had just returned from a mission to observe the first postwar election in Greece. He was joined by the Secretary of War's alternate, Goldthwaite H. Dorr, a prominent New York attorney with a Columbia law degree. Their styles clashed. Grady refused even to skim the classified reports on the issues of his curiosity, insisting instead on oral briefings. Still, he seemed to command total recall for the later rehearsal of scenarios on America's role as Britain's peaceseeking partner. Dorr, on his side, wanted me simply to identify the major issues on which he sought the relevant reports. His appetite for the written word was voracious, and his visual memory easily matched Grady's aural absorption. By the time Herbert E. Gaston came on board as the Treasury Secretary's appointee, I had undergone emergency surgery and did not take part, as intended, in the Anglo-American exchanges in London.

Nearing the end of sick leave, I was traced on Sunday, 21 July, to my sister's summer cottage in Connecticut by an urgent call from the Department of State to return to Washington as soon as possible. On arrival at the Department the next morning, I was instructed to find a copy of the provincial autonomy plan, presented to, but rejected by, the AACI because of American opposition. The British team, headed by Sir Norman Brook, the Cabinet secretary, had pulled the plan out of the Foreign Office wastebasket, arguing that, if it were not accepted, the Palestine dispute would go to the United Nations for settlement. Grady reported that the American team agreed in principle to take another look at the scheme in the light of the Cabinet Committee's terms of reference and cabled the Department that "Copies of the plan without maps are in the Anglo-American Committee files," placed in the care of Hurewitz.

President Truman, I was told, needed a dozen copies as soon as possible, for he planned to reassemble the AACI's US members in the White House on Wednesday to ascertain why they had originally turned down the proposal of Sir Douglas Harris, its author and the Colonial Office expert on Palestine. There was, for me, I pointed out, an impediment. The so-called AACI files were in the original twenty-five or so trunks of papers of that committee and its staff. The trunks had simply been deposited, with their contents unsorted, on the unused top floor of a government building a block away from the Department. I did not have the trunk keys. Besides, my doctor forbade my lifting heavy objects or remaining for long in a bent posture. If the trunks were placed unlocked on tables, I was confident that I could produce the first copy in less than an hour. Never had I received such prompt treatment in Washington. The desired report, immediately classified top secret and photostatted in the requested number, was delivered to the White House under guard before noon. This time, it was the President who, in effect, tossed into the White

House shredder the proposal, renamed in London after marginal editing the Morrison-Grady and in Washington the Grady-Morrison plan.

Meanwhile, a month or so after the Japanese surrender in September 1945 and before our collective transfer to the State Department, I had informed the chairman of Columbia's history department of my desire to return to the campus to complete the suspended dissertation requirement and sought his guidance on the procedure for changing the theme. I explained that, on the advice of Professor Speiser, my R&A supervisor, I wished to propose as a new working title one that derived from my Washington experience—"The Impact of the War on Arab and Jewish Politics in Palestine." The new study, I went on, would analyze the forces that, in the context of World War II, had reshaped the social and economic as well as political structures and aspirations of the two communities in Palestine.

The spring of 1946 proved crowded. I married and was no longer free to make plans without taking my wife's wishes into account. The history department formally approved the revision and assigned Commager and Baron to joint sponsorship. Both accepted the shared role with reservation, since neither viewed himself as a Middle East specialist. The Social Science Research Council approved my application for a Demobilization Award, as my dissertation fellowship was called. That, along with the veterans' education stipend and Miriam's salary as a staff researcher for *Fortune* magazine, would enable us to tide over my preoccupation with the slippery analysis of an ongoing breakdown of a contested mandate that had in the aftermath of the war exploded into a regional dispute and was in the first postwar year dividing the US and Britain and seemed about to entice Soviet meddling. I was already intrigued by the prospect of carrying the analysis through the mandate's end, which seemed imminent as I began to collect my massive data. Clearly, Thucydides' model returned to my mind. His dispassion was unexceptional. But the geographic scope of his coverage did not reach beyond a small peninsula.

My section chief in OIR persuaded me to seek unpaid leave from the Department of State. Given the uncertainty of academic employment, I saw that as a pragmatic step. At about the time of my leaving Washington, my R&A colleague, Harvey Hall, chosen editor of the new *The Middle East Journal*, the first American quarterly devoted wholly to the region, invited me along with

Glidden, Liebesny and Young to serve as advisory editors. The journal's patron, the Middle East Institute, founded in May 1946, was closely linked to the School of Advanced International Studies, which the Johns Hopkins University of Baltimore later absorbed as an extension in Washington. I continued as an advisory editor until 1981, when I also resigned from the Institute's board of governors on which I had sat since 1964.

Completing the dissertation took, not one year as I had originally estimated, but two and one-half. For one thing, I pushed back the starting point to the outbreak of the Palestine Arab revolt in 1936 and then carried the analysis forward to the mandate's lapse in May 1948. By the time the first draft was ready in July, it exceeded 1,500 pages with "The Road to Partition" as a working title. The outlandish length arose from my aim to produce a carefully documented, calm analysis of the emotional contest between Arabs and Jews in Palestine and its interplay in regional and world politics. I treated the several positions at whatever length the available evidence and clarity dictated. I knew then, and even more now, that a dissertation in such detail on any subject, even one so bedeviling as that of Palestine, was unconscionable. Before the defense, I therefore cut the draft down to 932 pages of which 190 were single-spaced notes. The annotation, I might add, comprised almost wholly references to sources, for I felt then, as I do now: if the discussion is important, it belongs in the text; if it is not, it should be left out of the notes.

The dissertation was defended in May 1949, but the degree was not conferred until September 1950, when I finally complied with Columbia's requirement for prior publication. The examining committee encouraged me in the belief that my work had commercial potential. But their efforts failed to find an interested publisher. I enlisted the help of a literary agent, and W. W. Norton accepted the manuscript on condition that it be cut a further third after adding a post-mandate epilogue. Before returning the manuscript, I also changed the title to *The Struggle for Palestine*—but not until the book's production had reached the galley stage.

By the turn of 1949 I began to crawl out of a shell of self-imposed seclusion to assess the job market. In a gesture to entice me back to Washington, former associates commissioned an evaluation of the first election in Israel, set for the end of January. While the analysis was still under way, the ubiquitous Edwin Samuel turned up, this time surprisingly from Philadelphia. He was teaching at the Dropsie College, a graduate institution for Hebrew and Cognate Learning. He had come to the US, on a year's leave as head of Israel's program for training civil servants, to help launch Dropsie's new Institute on Israel and the Middle East. It was an early US experiment in infusing contemporary social science courses on the Middle East into existing instruction on related humanities and languages. Samuel was delegated to invite me to replace him as instructor on regional politics in 1949–50. I had just begun working as a political affairs officer in the UN Secretariat at Lake Success. Once the director of the Division of Security Council Affairs approved the application to reduce my work week during the academic year to four days, I agreed to teach a year-long course on regional politics.

The Dropsie College attracted graduate students seeking a nontheological academic career in Jewish history, with emphasis on the biblical (including Assyriology and Egyptology) and medieval periods (including Islam) and selective coverage of the later rise of Jewish mysticism along with associated Semitic languages (ancient and modern), with primary attention to Hebrew and Arabic. The college also included a department of education for training teachers for Jewish parochial schools, which included a comprehensive introduction to the history of education from ancient Greece to the 20th century. To this base, the Institute on Israel and the Middle East was attached. The College faculty, the Institute included, did not exceed fifteen; the student body (not all degree candidates), 125. Roughly ten percent of the students were graduates of Christian theological seminaries, some not degree-seeking candidates who took the classical offerings. So, too, was an Arab student, an alumnus of Fuad al-Awwal (renamed in 1953 Cairo) University, who commuted from Princeton.

Mine were two-semester regionwide lecture courses, one each year, with an enrollment ranging between six and twelve. In my coverage, the Middle East embraced Egypt, Sudan and non-Soviet southwest Asia to the eastern frontier of Iran. All the books still in print that I ordered for student use were on the open shelves at the start of the year. The students worked hard. I found it especially helpful as a setting to structure comprehensive introductory lecture courses on the Middle East. But despite the depth of Dropsie's intellectual reach, the college was too small and its focus too narrow to grow into a dynamic, innovative center for the study of the modern Middle East.

President Abraham A. Neuman, however, always cooperated when I suggested ways of sharing with the community Dropsie's Middle East concerns. Early in 1952, for example, the College sponsored a public discussion on the Anglo-Egyptian crisis brought on by the inability of the two governments to agree on terms for revising the 1936 Anglo-Egyptian treaty on which Britain's access to the giant Suez Canal Base rested. I invited Dr. Muhammad Hasan al-Zayyat, the cultural affairs officer of the Egyptian Embassy in Washington, to join me in a public debate on the issue. The program drew a lively audience in the full auditorium. Zayyat gave the Egyptian case and I outlined Whitehall's, after first reinforcing his argument. When the meeting adjourned, some two dozen Egyptian students assembled at the foot of the stage to congratulate Zayyat. "We came here to heckle you," admitted one, approaching me, "but you deprived us of the opportunity."

By then I was also teaching on Morningside Heights. Indeed, two years earlier, Professor Schuyler C. Wallace, chairman of the Department of Public Law and Government and director of Columbia's School of International Affairs, had invited me to join their expanding foreign area program. My candidacy had won the strong endorsement of the dissertation examining committee, in particular Commager, Baron and Speiser (who sat as visiting examiner). Also supporting me was Franz Neumann, who, before coming to Columbia as a professor of political theory, had seen my reports at OSS, where he was R&A' s chief expert on Nazi Germany.

Wallace explained that Columbia had just received a grant from the Jewish Agency for Palestine to establish a graduate Center for Israel and Jewish Studies. He wondered whether I would accept a two-year contract to offer single-semester courses on the political and social institutions of Israel and on the Palestine problem in international politics and year-long courses on political institutions in the Middle East, the diplomatic history of the region (later retitled international and regional politics in the Middle East and North Africa) and an annual two-semester seminar for M.A. and Ph.D. candidates. The courses would be spread over two years. My semester load would not exceed three listings. Wallace advised scheduling Israel and Palestine in the evening to attract extension as well as full-time students. If the experiment prospered, we might then explore prolonging the contract. I would receive the rank of lecturer with a salary of $4,000 before taxes, or half that of the UN after taxes.

Miriam had stopped working before the birth of our older daughter eighteen months earlier. Since I would have to resign from the UN Secretariat, we both agreed that I ought to keep the Dropsie post with its $2,000 stipend so as to fill part of the gap.

For the evening lecture course on Israel in the fall of 1950 the turnout surpassed Wallace's expectations and mine—more than forty students, including a few from the UN. Similarly, the size of the year-long introduction to Middle East politics exceeded thirty students, even though it was given mornings. In the second semester, attendance at the evening lectures on Palestine matched those on Israel.

My office was in one of the small turn-of-the-century buildings on 117th Street between Amsterdam Avenue and Morningside Drive, known as Deans' Row, that Wallace had appropriated as SIA director. I shared the third floor of our building with Leland Goodrich, who also in 1950 switched from Brown University to become our man on international organization. William T. R. Fox also in the same year left Yale to head the Institute on War and Peace Studies, just founded by Dwight D. Eisenhower, Columbia's new president. Going and coming we had to pass the open door of Schuyler's office on the second floor where he offered easy access. He had been the Ruggles Professor of American Public Administration. By the time of our arrival he was devoting full time to administration. Most commonly, Schuyler's campus negotiations were pursued curbside, anywhere between the Men's Faculty Club at the southwest corner of 117th Street and Morningside Drive and halfway up to the frontage of No. 429, on the north side, where our offices were located. To conclude a deal often no more was needed than a nod. A brief note of confirmation promptly followed.

Wallace's shift of professional interest from American government to international affairs grew out of the Naval School of Military Government and Administration that he ran for Columbia in 1942–44 under contract with the US Navy. On his initiative, with liberal seeding from the Rockefeller Foundation, the university trustees approved the opening in 1945 of the School of International Affairs with a two-year curriculum culminating in a Master of International Affairs degree. Associated eventually with SIA (later SIPA— School of International and Public Affairs) were eight foreign area institutes, founded one by one in the first two postwar decades. The Russian (later Harriman) Institute, also with Rockefeller support, opened in 1946, followed three years later by the East Asian and the European (later renamed Western European) institutes, both largely underwritten by the Carnegie Foundation. The remaining five—the Middle East, East Central Europe, Latin America (and Iberia added later), Africa and Southern Asia—came into being between 1954 and 1967.

In the winter of 1950–51, No. 429 and the well-worn path to the Men's Faculty Club were abuzz with plans for ten-year financing by the concerned Islamic governments of three new centers—on Iran, Pakistan and Turkey. Actually, the talks with the first two governments had received high visibility in 1949. Indeed, it was then that the University conferred an honorary degree on the Shah, which assured the plans wide publicity, to say nothing of his good-will, long before he had aroused the implacable enmity of the 'ulama. That publicity also hastened the formation of the Center for Israel and Jewish Studies, which, as we have seen, came to life well ahead of the others. The prime mover was Ernst Jackh, an old Turcophile whose career reached back to the Kaiser's Germany. He had received a doctorate at Heidelberg in 1899 and in 1915 was appointed professor at Berlin, where in the interwar decades he later presided over the Politische Hochschule. An outspoken opponent of the Third Reich, Jackh had received political asylum in the US before I first met him on my return to the campus in 1940.

From the time of the UN General Assembly's adoption of the partition plan for Palestine in the fall of 1947 and the rise of Israel several months later, Jackh pursued Wallace, as the University architect of the foreign area institute program, with an enviable—or annoying—persistence, depending on where you stood, to create a Middle East Institute. Wallace resisted the pressure on two grounds: its high cost and, no less important, the fear of introducing into the campus the stubborn disputes that were already growing the postimperial Middle East into the world's most fractious region, pitting successor states, ethnic communities in plural societies and superpower "clients" against one another, not to mention the rivalry of American and European oil companies in search of concessions. When Jackh finally received a green light to raise funds, even of government origin, to experiment with individual centers on segments of the Middle East that might in due course be welded into a region-al institute, Wallace may well have concluded that he would at least find momentary relief from ceaseless badgering. If nonetheless the funds did turn up, the University would at least benefit from the feasibility test.

With Wallace's clearance Jackh faced no resistance in enlisting the cooperation of Salo Baron. Together they raised the money in 1950 for a Center for Israel and Jewish Studies, which had brought me to the campus. That very act, in turn, speeded up Jackh's concluding arrangements with the three governments. The Iranian and Pakistani centers opened in the fall of 1951, and the Turkish Center a year later. Unlike Israel, which could not release academic specialists so soon after independence, the sponsors of the three other centers sent to New York, usually for a year at a time, their ablest English-speaking professors chosen by the pertinent Columbia departments from the supplied short lists.

The initial breakthrough was attributable to Jackh and Baron's persuading the Jewish Agency to give Columbia a five-year grant. The Agency was the international coordinating, administrative and fund-raising body that brought Zionist and non-Zionist Jews together in the common cause of assuring the transition from a national home in mandated Palestine to a sovereign Israel and from the sponsorship of the League of Nations to that of the UN.

The centers accomplished two purposes: they helped to fund the training of students in the respective national languages, and the visiting scholars offered lecture courses in their fields and took part in an interdisciplinary seminar that I chaired from the outset. This proved as much a learning experience for the participating faculty as for the students. All of us in different degrees and in our several styles were gleaning insights into one another's cultures, enhanced by abiding friendships. The enriched mutual understanding then found its enduring way into books, articles and dissertations. Of equal immediate importance was the availability of professional guidance for Columbia students and faculty in field research by scholars from major Middle East countries, long before American research centers were established in Istanbul, Tehran and Karachi.

Just glance at a sampling of our visitors: From Turkey, Ömer Celal Sarç, an economist and a world-renowned statistician with a Berlin Ph.D., highly respected former rector of the University of Istanbul and courtly gentleman with an astounding judgment of the abuse of demographic and fiscal data by Middle East governments, who lectured and conducted a seminar on economic development in Turkey. Halil Inalcik, the century's most creative historian of the Ottoman Empire and the Turkish Republic, who inspired a generation of post-1928 historians to learn Osmanlı and put it to research use in the region's richest national archives that in our time were being restored to researchable order from the jumble inherited by the Republic. Şerif Mardin, dean for many years at Boğaziçi University (successor of Robert College), a Stanford-trained political scientist who, in the path-breaking *Religion and Social Change in Modern Turkey*, gained an international reputation as the leading sociologist of religion in secular Turkey. A permanent addition to our staff in 1952 and later chairman of the Department of Middle East Languages and Cultures, Tibor Halasi-Kun had earned a Ph.D. in Turkic philology at the University of Budapest in 1936 and lived for nearly a decade and a half in Turkey. He negotiated Turkey's generous gift to Columbia's library of major works in Osmanlı and modern Turkish and was the founder of the American Research Center in Turkey.

From Iran: Sadeq Rezazadeh Shafaq, with a B.A. from Robert College (1918) and a Ph.D. from the University of Berlin (1929), was trained in literature, philosophy and law. Known also as a poet, he wrote a history of Persian literature and in his two-year visit to Columbia (1952–54) did not surrender his seat in the Iranian Senate. Lotfali Suratgar, a professor of English and comparative literature at the University of Tehran, with unshakable fidelity to his native Shiraz. Sayyid Dr. Hasan Taqizadeh from Tabriz, an independent-minded political leader with solid academic credentials, active in his country's public affairs for half a century, stretching from the constitutional revolution of 1905–06 and membership in the first and second Majlis through service in the mid-1950s as the speaker of the Senate; in between he headed Iran's diplomatic missions to Paris (in the mid 1930s) and to London (in World War II). The two diplomatic appointments sandwiched his professorship of Iranian history at London's School of Oriental and African Studies. Ehsan Yarshater, with a D. Litt. from the University of Tehran and a Ph.D. from London, came to Columbia in 1958 and joined us permanently, later becoming the Hagop Kevorkian Professor of Iranian Studies. He taught courses on ancient, medieval and modern history and launched the *Encyclopaedia Iranica* and the al-Tabari translation project, thus reviving the strong interest in Iran at Columbia that had prevailed earlier. Dr. Fouad Rouhani, OPEC's most cultured Secretary General, filled in one semester of Yarshater's two-year leave (1964–66). Equally gifted in music (an excellent piano player) and botany as well as law in which he received a doctorate at Oxford, Rouhani translated Plato's *Republic* into Farsi.

From Pakistan: Sir Muhammad Zafrullah Khan, an early foreign minister of the Islamic state. Ishtiaq Husain Qureshi, an early minister of education with a Cambridge Ph.D. in history. An authority on the Mughal Empire, he offered courses on the history of Islam in the subcontinent and on Pakistan. In the five years that he remained at Columbia, he also took regular part in our interdisciplinary seminar. Recalled to Pakistan in 1961 by President Muhammad Ayub Khan, Qureshi founded and ran an Islamic Institute at Lahore and later became Vice-Chancellor of the University of Karachi.

From the Arab states: My earliest recruit was Charles Issawi, whom I first encountered at Lake Success, as he relates. At the same time we invited Majid Khadduri, professor of Middle East politics at SAIS, to teach Islamic law and to take part in our interdisciplinary seminar. Khadduri remained with us until my return from a year of field research in 1959. He and I had an informal exchange arrangement in the 1950s and '60s, each to fill in when the other was absent on sabbatical or research leave. In 1954–55, Muhammad Hasan al-Zayyat, with an Oxford Ph.D., lectured on political and social movements in Islam in the 19th century and their influence on contemporary affairs. 'Aziz S. 'Atiyah, an Egyptian-born student of Arab history, with a B.A. and D.Litt. from Liverpool and a Ph.D. from London, taught Arab history in 1956–57. 'Abd al-'Aziz al-Sayyid, with an Oxonian doctorate in English literature, a former minister of education in Egypt and on leave from his directorate of the Arab League's Educational, Cultural and Scientific Office, lectured on Arab education and joined our integrated seminar. In addition, Joseph Schacht, a world renowned authority on Islamic law and an editor of the second edition of the *Encyclopaedia of Islam*, succeeded Arthur Jeffery as professor of Arabic in 1959, after a year as visiting professor.

The integrated—and integrating—seminar for end-to-end area studies proved invaluable in arousing expanding student awareness of the realities of the polycultural Middle East. It proved equally valuable for the American and the guest instructors. The guests' early education as a rule was national, not regional. They inclined toward positing a larger degree of uniformity than was warranted, on the ground that almost all regional states are Islamic. For one thing, their populations speak languages that are structurally different, even when they use a common alphabet and partake of a limited vocabulary overlap. There too Turkey deviated after October 1928 when Arabic gave way to a Latin alphabet, while in Central Asia and the Transcaucasus Cyrillic had displaced Arabic by Soviet fiat. Besides, in syntax and etymology Arabic shares much more in common with Hebrew (since both are Semitic languages) than with either Turkish (a Ural-Altaic language) or Farsi and Urdu (members of the Indo-Iranian family).

In developing regionwide courses, year-long collective teaching alerted the professors to the common and divergent structures and practices among and within the Middle East states and thus the need for comparison and contrast, lessons that we passed on to the students. Students from the Middle East in our program—growing in numbers over the years—were prone to feel that they could breeze through the instruction and the training exercises effortlessly. Such students were rudely awakened. Those who persevered put to great advantage their language fluency. Even then, some had to overcome yet another common disability—the need to master the rigorous canons of research in the social sciences. For only rarely did their received education equip them for the demands of such original inquiry.

It did not take long to realize that we were all apprentices. The growing need to blend the purposes and techniques of two or more social sciences in our own on-the-job education and research—and thus to devise modes of training our students—became manifest to Issawi and me in the 1950s. Truman's Point Four, with its focus on exporting American technology to the agrarian and pastoral Middle East, was launched with an unmistakable focus on modernizing agriculture. This dictated our training degree candidates in political science as well as economics or, more accurately, in the amalgam of the two—political economy. How else would it be possible to explain such an inherent contradiction in the US proclaimed goal of using Point Four to promote stability when by simply weaning the peasants away from traditional practices, the American strategy was itself contributing to instability? In the second half of the decade, as Issawi points out, we put the hybrid discipline to work on Middle East oil.

Meanwhile, quite independently we were both also drawing heavily upon sociology, anthropology and law to deepen our interpretations of the region's societal trends as they bore upon our "separate" disciplines. And, undeniably, both of us are addictive historians. On my side, I resisted viscerally the pressures of the political scientists to impose irrelevant Western models and the accompanying jargon on the analysis of Middle East political institutions and behavior.

In the fall of 1954 I returned from nine months of research leave to the Middle East (broadly defined to include Pakistan and Afghanistan) and Western Europe. Reacquaintance with the new face of my prewar haunts and updating sources of information in that zone were one intent of the excursion. This time I benefited from the enlargement of my entourage to a family of four. The experiment yielded three-dimensional insights into the local societies and into Turkey, where Miriam and our two daughters rented an apartment in Ankara, while I ventured into Iran and its adjacent states. Visits to Sudan, Turkey and Iran as well as to Pakistan and Afghanistan expanded the area of my personal exposure in the field. All along the way, as also in Rome, Paris and London, I collected books and documents.

I had hardly resettled in my Columbia office, when Wallace invited me—in his accustomed informal style—to become the first director of the Near and Middle East Institute, whose formation he had announced in the spring. The offer was tempting. But I did not succumb. On reflection, I did not want administration to distract me from teaching and research at the developing stage of my academic career. On Wallace's retirement in 1962, Charles Issawi succeeded to the Institute directorship for a two-year term. Then John Badeau came on board directly from the ambassadorial post in Cairo, and on his retirement in 1971 I assumed the duties until 1984.

The Council on Foreign Relations in 1953 published *Middle East Dilemmas: The Background of United States Policy,* which I had originally roughed out in 1951–52 in background papers for a study group of Council members. Four decades later, the thrust of the analysis remains valid: the major conflicts in the region at the time—over the Palestine mandate's succession, the nationalization of the AIOC concession in Iran and Cairo's abrogation of the 1936 Anglo-Egyptian treaty—entangled Britain, not the USSR, and thus inhibited the immediate application of America's containment strategy.

In writing the Council book, I drew heavily on the materials that I had assembled in the field before Pearl Harbor, as also on a hectographed collection of documents that I had assembled in the summer of 1951 for classroom use in the next academic year. It was an introductory course on the diplomatic history of the Middle East as our program then defined it, from Egypt and Sudan to Iran's eastern frontier. The enthusiastic response of colleagues at Princeton and SAIS as well as of students encouraged me to publish a larger collection. To fill in major gaps I gathered official records and related papers unavailable for the 1951 experiment, while crisscrossing the Middle East and Western Europe. Most rewarding was the search at the Services des Archives of the Quai d'Orsay in Paris and at the Public Record Office and the India Office Library in London. On my return home I enriched the American collection with the help of the historical division of the State Department. My model was one of Commager's books on American history, prefacing each entry with a brief essay and a list of readings. Foreign language materials were reduced to English. By the summer's end of 1955 the manuscript went to press. *Diplomacy in the Near and Middle East*, released on the eve of the 1956 Suez crisis, received free publicity from Secretary of State John Foster Dulles, photographed at the airport clutching the two volumes on his way to an international conference in London called by the Eden government to deal with the crisis.

Framing that work removed all doubt that the prevailing literature on international politics in the Middle East from the 16th century to the early 20th was almost uniformly Eurocentric. Largely the product of British, French and Russian scholarship, the judgments still dominated the study of the interplay of European and Middle East relations well into the opening decades after World War II. Nor could I fully escape their bias—in essence, that the power relations from the outset had always favored Europe—in my choice of documents, since those were virtually the only ones available in public print. Efforts to correct the balance were only partly successful. And this, in turn, could hardly fail to affect my analysis.

In my pre-career self-training on the Middle East I recognized that Turkish would be indispensable for balanced insights into the 19th-century background of those Arab provinces of Ottoman Asia that unfolded into British and French mandates after World War I. However, I had just begun the formal study of Arabic and, given my commitment to open-ended research for a dissertation, concluded that one language at a time was all the traffic would bear. Not until a decade and a half later, in the summer preceding my first postwar revisit to a much expanded field, did I at last start teaching myself Turkish. By then, my interest in the Ottoman Empire had widened and deepened as I developed introductory courses on the region's comparative and international politics and came to appreciate the Ottoman legacy not to the Turkish Republic alone but virtually to the entire Arab world, with the notable exception of Morocco.

Miriam and our two daughters once again accompanied me in 1958–59 when a Guggenheim fellowship and sabbatical leave enabled me to engage in extended archival research in Istanbul, Cairo, Tehran, Paris and London. Primary attention was given to the Başvekalet Arşivi (Prime Ministry Archives) in Istanbul to plumb the official records for reconstructing the evolution of Ottoman diplomatic practice. I was seeking answers to a variety of questions. Why did it take so long for the Ottoman regime to institute reciprocal resident diplomacy, which had been the norm on the Continent since the 16th century? After all, the Ottoman Empire had become a Continental power as early as the mid-15th century, on the conquest of Constantinople (Istanbul), and solidly entrenched itself in southeastern Europe in the century that followed. Why then did it not become a founding member of the European State System at the Peace of Westphalia (1648)? The common explanation—that, as an Islamic regime, it had automatically cut itself off—seemed much too facile. When precisely did the Sublime Porte become a dependency of Europe—at Küçük Kaynarca (1774), during the Napoleonic wars (1798–1815) or the Greek War of Independence (1821–29), at Hünkâr Iskelesi (1833) or even later?

In brief, I was set on demonstrating the gross inadequacy of the one-dimensional analysis that so typified the Western treatment of the Ottoman conduct of foreign policy. The Ottoman archives, one of the oldest and richest in the world, presented overwhelming difficulties even for fluent users of the language, one of which I was not. The multiple styles of calligraphy and handwriting apart, vocabulary and usage, as in all dynamic languages, changed over the half-millennial collection. The index to the deposits comprised catalogues that were not consistent, prepared as they were by successive advisers. And they were far from complete. Happily, Fahir İz, joint compiler of a set of Turkish-English and English-Turkish dictionaries, found a young instructor to ease my transition from modern Turkish to Osmanlı, and Halil İnalcik recommended as a part-time assistant one of his own students, then engaged in dissertation research at the archives.

In the Hariciye Odası or Foreign Ministry division, housed in its own building in the archival compound, the core of the collection, though much smaller, was research-ready because the collection had been organized for active policymaking. The deposits, largely in French, dated only from 1857, with a smattering of items reaching back to the 18th century and deposited there by the Republic's foreign ministry, under whose custody that segment of the declassified records had been placed. But I also discovered major gaps. For example, absent from the collection on Cyprus were the files for 1878, at the time of the Berlin Congress and the transfer to Great Britain of the island's de facto sovereignty. The archivists expected to find missing files in Abdülhamit II's Yıldız papers, which at the time were impounded because the sorting was still underway.

The evolving diplomatic usage of the Ottoman regime had not been probed systematically, not even by Turkish scholars. I was able, very early, to determine that the primary reason for its failure to conform to European procedures had less to do with religion, as generally held by the concerned European diplomats and their historians including those in Turkey, than with commerce and also, until the 17th century, with the sultan's military superiority. I first shared my findings with scholars attending the 25th International Congress of Orientalists in Moscow in 1960 (see *Middle East Journal*, Spring 1961).

In that report, I outlined the evolution of Ottoman diplomatic practice from its Islamic origins in the 14th century to its becoming in the 19th century the first non-Christian regime to accept fully the European style of reciprocal continuous or resident diplomacy, ahead of Iran and even of China and Japan. Turkish scholars were just starting to nibble at Ottoman experiments in reciprocity (1793–1821), but neglected the antecedents altogether. So too did the European scholars, even though the diplomatic style went far to explain the empire's political, economic and military relations with the Western powers. "Instructively," as I pointed out, "there is no entry on 'diplomacy' in the first edition of the *Encyclopaedia of Islam* (see the entry on 'Elçi' in the 2nd ed., 1965) while the article on 'Tanzimat' dismisses foreign relations in two sentences. It makes no reference whatsoever to the Europeanization of Ottoman diplomacy, which undeniably was as much a product of the innovating zeal at Istanbul in that period as were the changes in military organization, education and law" (*MEJ*, op. cit., 142).

The generally accepted interpretation of many major disputes between the Ottoman Empire and European powers did not resolve inconsistencies in the evidence. A glaring example was the USSR's insistence at the Potsdam Conference in 1945 that its claim to share with Turkey the defense of the Straits rested on the Sublime Porte's pledges in secret treaties of 1805 and 1833 to close the waterway to the naval vessels of all but the riparian powers of the Black Sea. The claim in that form traces back to *Bosfor i Dardanelly* (St. Petersburg, 1907) by Sergei Goriainov, the director of the tsarist central imperial archives. It was never challenged by Western European or Turkish diplomatic historians. On the basis of documents that I discovered in the Ottoman archives I exposed the Russian claim "to treaty precedents for what it is—a long-perpetuated diplomatic and literary fraud" (see my "Russia and the Turkish Straits," *World Politics*, July 1962). I sent copies of the article to Soviet scholars whom I had met at the Orientalist Congress. Three years later I was introduced to an international lawyer from the University of Moscow at a reception in New York. I asked her if she could explain the silence with which my paper had been received in her country. After all, I went on, in 1953 Soviet reviewers of *Middle East Dilemmas* had dismissed me as a tool of Wall Street and the oil monopolists. To which she replied, "What could we say?"

Early in 1959 a week-long conference, sponsored by the SSRC Near and Middle East Committee, took me to Tehran. Gathered in the shahdom were social scientists from eleven US universities, all pursuing field research that year. The twenty-one conferees intermixed postdoctoral scholars and Ford-financed Ph.D. candidates working in Turkey, Egypt, Lebanon, Iran, Israel and Kuwayt. The papers, circulated in advance, summarized the projects and research experience in each place with an assessment of available data. It was a novel venture, proposed by Dankwart A. Rustow, that deepened the comparative insights of the authors and helped enrich the SSRC Committee file on research conditions for American scholars in accessible regional countries.

On my return to New York in the fall, I encountered for the first time the newly formed American Association for Middle East Studies, a nonpolitical and nonprofit educational body that was fostering interest in the Middle East at the undergraduate level in colleges and universities across the country. The AAMES directed its attention to institutional rather than individual needs through academic conferences and summer faculty institutes. It began the program without benefit of systematic information, after discovering that no office, governmental or nongovernmental, was keeping track of numbers, distribution or quality, to say nothing of course titles, the identity of disciplines and instructors, the state of library resources and the procedures followed in a near-perfect textbook vacuum. To find its bearings, the Association set about seeking the missing data.

By the spring of 1961, when the AAMES employed me to evaluate the national condition and the needs, the list ran to 330 faculty members and 180 institutions. John Badeau, Roderic Davison, Charles Ferguson, Charles Issawi, William R. Polk and William D. Schorger served as my area advisory committee at the planning stage. For technical guidance on procedure, I consulted colleagues at Columbia (Herbert Hyman, David B. Truman and Schuyler Wallace) and Donald N. Bigelow of the US Office of Education in Washington. With their guidance, I framed two questionnaires, one for instructors and the other for college presidents or concerned top university administrators. Analysis of the two levels, it was felt, would make it possible to uncover problems of administration and teaching and offer a basis for in-depth analysis. The respondents added new names, so that ultimately questionnaires reached 201 institutions and 393 faculty members, which probably represented at least 90 percent of the universe.

Highlights of the findings were that national interest in the Middle East at the student and institutional undergraduate level seems to have taken off after the 1956 Suez crisis—and to have moved up to ever higher levels in the succession of Middle East crises after that which have recurrently captured prime time on the electronic media and banner headlines in print. If viewed as a nationwide effort, the forward thrust of the late 1950s was mostly spontaneous, uncoordinated and lacking in direction. Colleges about to adopt courses on the Middle East, as also on other foreign areas, thus had nowhere to turn for counseling services. "At present far too many schools," I warned, "have undertaken Middle East instruction with untrained teachers, poor libraries, and nonexistent teaching aids. Instead of instructing the students, they are simply turning the uninformed into the misinformed."

Like the undertrained or untrained area instructors, the overtrained—that is, the alumni of the Middle East centers employed by the colleges—discovered that their departments commonly limited them to a single one-term regional course each year or even every other year. Nor were they offered incentives to do further research in their specialties. In this climate, expectations of developing into recognized foreign area experts seemed doomed from the outset. In the circumstances, I pointed out, "The means of putting the skills of the Middle East specialists everywhere to proper use have never been systematically explored. The underemployment of area specialists, it is safe to assume, is a general condition in American undergraduate non-Western studies, and not one limited to Middle East studies." To pick up the slack, there was limited scope for the AAMES. But the primary obligation rested with the US Office of Education under the National Defense Education Act of 1958 and with the national and regional associations of the many varieties of American colleges and universities.

By then, the time had come to enlarge my definition of the Middle East for teaching and research by adding the Maghrib in the west and Afghanistan in the east. In retrospect, my decision flowed in part from the emerging reality of the steadily enlarging Arab League. Besides, the Ottoman Empire at its height had embraced virtually all the Arab world, and Atatürk's realism in Turkey's dealings with Europe had deeply impressed the new interwar leaders in Iran and Afghanistan. What I needed for the next transition was another year of research leave, which Schuyler Wallace approved on my receipt of a fellowship for 1962–63 from the Center for Advanced Study in the Behavioral Sciences at Stanford, California. The Center provided an idyllic setting for scholars to test and evaluate the premises of their disciplines and to teach one another new skills. That was what Charles Issawi and I seemed to be encouraging at Columbia in our continuing quest, respectively, for a definition of the economic and political culture of the region, with steady enrichment by our visiting scholars from the Middle East.

Ralph Tyler, the director of the Center, assembled the thirty-nine fellows then in residence, soon after our arrival in September, to explain the ground rules. Tyler had met very few of us in person before. We scrambled in our seating. Yet he knew each fellow by name, as he introduced us to one another. In his opening remarks, he had it just right: "Many of you have come here to write or finish a book; the others, to cultivate new intellectual friendships and attend one another's seminars. At the end of the year, the authors will regret their failure to take regular part in the seminars, and the seminarians, to do more writing. In either case, most of you will leave with a sense of accomplishment. That's what the Center is all about."

The ambiance suited my purposes exactly, enabling me to steer a middle course. Even before arriving at Stanford, I had decided to compare differing styles of British, French and Russian imperial conquest and governance of adjacent, predominantly Islamic territories. I was thoroughly familiar with the British experience and decided to use that as the frame of reference. For such specialized reading and research, the Center's library was hardly equipped. But the fellows enjoyed generous borrowing privileges at Stanford and Berkeley. By the year's end, I put the new skills to work in an analysis of regional and international politics in the newly defined Middle East (in Georgiana G. Stevens, ed., *The United States and the Middle East*, 1964).

Soon following, and far more important, was *Middle East Politics: The Military Dimension*, to which I was lured against my initial wishes. I was still at the Center, in the spring of 1963, when John Campbell, the director of the studies program at the Council on Foreign Relations, called from New York to invite me to serve as research secretary for a discussion group on the military in the Middle East. As I had done a decade earlier, I would be expected to convert my papers, enriched by the discussion, into a publishable book. I respectfully declined, on the ground that I was not the best candidate. A few days later, Campbell phoned again, informing me that it was not an invitation but a command by Grayson Kirk, then president of Columbia and of the Council and chairman of the Council's committee on studies. As a dutiful servant but a firm believer in academic freedom, I agreed conditionally to serve as the research secretary of the study group but delayed my decision on the book until I could test the wisdom of the project in the opening meetings.

After the very first background paper, I told Campbell that the theme struck me as valuable not to national policymakers alone but to academics and concerned citizens. If we agreed to embrace the area from Afghanistan to Morocco, I would commit myself to a book on one further condition: I would have to find a way of gaining access in Washington to the unclassified basic data available to the government. Campbell approved my terms and offered the Council's help in gaining entry into the engaged federal agencies. I preferred to keep his offer as an available option but take the first steps on my own.

I immediately phoned Sherman Kent for an appointment. A former history professor at Yale, Kent had headed OSS R&A Europe and thus bossed my wartime boss. In 1947 he joined the CIA on its creation and by 1963 had reached his pinnacle as chief of the Office of National Estimates, just two notches below that of the DCI. As a quondam professor, he advised me not to seek such materials from the CIA, for he remained sensitive to the sensitivities of academia. That was farthest from my mind, for I too was sensitized to the prevailing feelings on the campus. I simply sought his advice on two matters: Was my hunch correct about the steady flow into the nation's capital of such unclassified data from and on the Middle East? If so, where could I find it? Yes, to the first question. On the second, he phoned his wartime deputy in R&A Europe, Dr. Rudolph Winnacker, first recruited from the University of Nebraska history department and remaining in Washington to rise by the 1960s to the post of Historian at the Pentagon.

At a Pentagon lunch that very day, Winnacker informed me that I was in luck. In May 1963, he reported, President Kennedy had issued an executive order whose thrust was essentially this: the US is flooded daily with unclassified reports on the armed forces and associated politics from all sovereign states across the globe. Most of the material, while germane, was never put to analytical use. It was simply filed, cluttering the storage facilities. The executive order proposed that a dozen scholars or so, covering different regions of the world, be assigned to evaluate the information for its immediate and longer value. So far, only a half-dozen of the intended assignments had been made, but the one on the Middle East was still open. Would I be interested in a Defense contract carrying a generous honorarium (including expenses) running into six digits? I promptly turned it down, on the ground that I had a prior commitment to the Council on Foreign Relations. He then trimmed the offer to fit my needs.

Under the executive order, whose number I forget, I was designated .007 (which amused my family), given the right—after security clearance—to consult not only the unclassified traffic but all records through top secret, and assigned Fred Haynes, a marine colonel fluent in Turkish, as my liaison with the federal agencies. Since I was assured access to classified papers, I proposed a clearance review of a sample chapter, so as to fix in my own mind the Defense Department's conditions for releasing the manuscript of the completed book and thus avoid time wastage at the verge of publication. The sample chapter raised only one type of violation—the failure to round out all official statistics of the US and foreign governments on monetary outlays, weapons inventories, size of the ranks and the like. Also on the prohibited list, I learned through prodding for more caveats, were references to the personal affairs of political leaders here and abroad.

Neither prohibition created difficulties in the Pentagon or the State Department. The nineteen tables of data that I ultimately structured (in the pre-computer age) on force levels, official outlays and GNP for each of the eighteen Middle East governments under analysis, or for Western and Soviet Bloc economic and military aid to the region, raised no eyebrows. The Pentagon cleared the 850-page manuscript in two days. State took two weeks because the foreign service officer on the Jordan desk, I later learned, was absent on annual leave at the start of the clearance process. Before submitting the manuscript for review by Washington, I had tested the analysis in the manuscript with a sample of responsible officers of the armed forces. The book was translated in 1977 into Turkish for officer training in Turkey's General Staff College. Three years later the College published the book in paperback for public sale.

◆ ◆ ◆

When I was first approached to contribute to this book, I was casually asked how I happened to be drawn into Middle East studies. Among the random memories that rolled off my tongue came mention of my founding membership in the SSRC Committee on the Near and Middle East. That seemed to strike us as a central point in the invited autobiographical note. Undeniably, an eight-year seat on the SSRC Committee left me with insights into the indebtedness of the widening Middle East segment of American higher education to the national professional consortium that had spawned the Committee and nurtured it until the ACLS became a joint sponsor in 1959. That experience formed an essential aspect of my training as a regionalist. Membership on such a committee is a collective learning process for joint action in the common good. Yet in the brief recounting of my relevant education, I found it difficult to extract those elements carrying my fingerprints and impossible to fit them into the chronological tale. I therefore set the exercise aside for the wrap-up.

A comprehensive analysis of the SSRC agenda to set standards and goals for training and research on the Middle East, discover talent and funds for underwriting such research, and frame guidelines for graduate training centers on the region goes on awaiting its author. To the input of the committee's sponsor would have to be added that of the engaged universities, the private foundations and ultimately the US Government. Despite liberties one cannot escape taking in a précis of this complexity, searching for my own component while keeping the detail to a bare minimum proved impossible.

Consider the occasion. President Truman had formally proclaimed the outbreak of the Cold War in his 1947 doctrine on the global containment of Soviet and world communist expansionism. The discard of the peacetime remnants of isolationism in American foreign policy immediately produced a sustained sense of crisis in Washington, and, to act on it, an early restructure of the federal government's Executive branch with abiding effect. The departments of the Army, Navy and Air Force (without loss of separate identities) were merged into a Department of Defense (which swallowed whole the once Department of War). The State Department's requisite reorganization and enlargement took much longer, delayed in large part until the agency's move to its giant newly built quarters. The Central Intelligence Agency's view of its mission to help wage the Cold War proved far more ambitious than that of its OSS model in World War II. The CIA on birth became a permanent executive body with a generous—if hidden—budget. All its personnel had to be recruited afresh. Its very existence stirred the armed forces' intelligence units to corresponding and, within the Pentagon, also competitive growth. Piled on these demands, with the coming in 1950 of US country programs for technical aid to nonindustrial regions, was a rising quest for experts by those divisions in the departments of Agriculture and Commerce dealing with the Middle East. Washington's appetite for trained analysts, in brief, was growing insatiable.

To help fill the State Department's openings for missing expertise, it had established a Foreign Service Institute, offering to its personnel and new recruits innovative courses in the major dialects and modern literary Arabic as well as the region's other primary languages. For the coverage of economic, political and social problems in their historical context, the Department enlisted as instructors experienced foreign service officers on home duty. FSI could hardly carry the Department's load, let alone satisfy the appeals for rescue, notably from CIA and the Pentagon. State also placed promising young officers in academia for a year of language and area study. Thus Hermann Eilts, later ambassador to Saudi Arabia and then to Egypt, was sent in 1950–51 to the University of Pennsylvania to study Arabic with Franz Rosenthal; he and Helen Eilts also registered for my course at Dropsie. But farming young diplomats of promise out among the few training centers was still only experimental at this stage.

Sustained pressure for speeding up the formation and expansion of the Middle East center network in the universities thus came from the nation's capital, untypically without even a gesture of fiscal generosity. The federal government's paralysis arose from diehard isolationists who early in 1950 rallied to the reckless campaign of Senator Joseph R. McCarthy to ferret "red agents" out of federal agencies, State foremost among them, and also from the top universities. Even after McCarthy's formal censure in 1954, the lethargy lingered on until the near coincidence of his death in 1957 and the Soviet launching of *Sputnik*. Only then was the Eisenhower Administration excited to action. In response to the President's lead, the Congress in 1958 at last adopted the National Defense Education Act that explicitly underwrote important segments of selected major training centers on all foreign areas, with liberal student grants and loans. On the NDEA list the Middle East ranked high, commonly just after the USSR and China.

It is in this context that we can best understand the birth and early unfolding of the SSRC Committee on the Near and Middle East.

The SSRC in the fall of 1946 had named a Committee on World Area Research to identify foreign regions of growing American national concern, to evaluate the state of the art in American universities and to administer a program of area fellowships and travel grants funded by the Carnegie Corporation of New York that would in each instance illumine the contemporary culture of a major foreign area. The CWAR built upon the experience of the joint committee on Latin America, which the SSRC, the ACLS and the National Research Council had founded in 1941. On the CWAR's advice the SSRC formed the first postwar committees: on Slavic Studies (1948) and Asia (1949) jointly with the ACLS, but as the sole sponsor of the one on the Near and Middle East (1951). On why it went its own way with the Near and Middle East Committee, I can only speculate.

As the national professional association of the humanities, the ACLS had actually had the first crack at framing a plan for guiding American higher education to meet the Cold War challenge in the Middle East. But it missed the chance. The Rockefeller-funded ACLS survey Committee on Near Eastern Studies, after a two-year study, issued in November 1949 a report that clung too slavishly to prevailing practice. The ACLS appears to have named its own committee on the Near East in 1950 with these guidelines. Presumably because the university response was less than tepid, it dissolved the committee in 1953.

As in the past, the curricula of most American colleges and universities still derived from a view of American culture as the product of Western civilization, a blend of the Judaeo-Christian(-Islamic) and Greco-Roman legacies, with little more than a bow to human achievement elsewhere in the world. The Middle East, it is true, won an extra nod in those larger universities—and theological seminaries—that listed oriental studies. Customarily, the courses were grouped in a language-based Semitics department. But the regional fragments of oriental studies were collected in essence from ancient (at times also medieval) history, religion (now and then with law thrown in), archaeology and related classical languages (dead and living).

What was new about the emerging foreign area studies in the US after 1945 was their focus on the social sciences with greater heed to the modern age and the spoken and literary languages of the contemporary Middle East. This was the thrust of the SSRC mandate to its Near and Middle East Committee.

For our present purposes, the American system of higher education comprised universities and four-year colleges only. Even under that narrow definition, it was a divergent and loosely structured one, made up of only public (state and municipal, but no federal ones for there were none except those for training officers of the armed services) and private (which subdivided into nonsectarian, church-related and land-grant) institutions. The system served American society and the US Government in its own special way. A small but slowly growing voluntary network of foreign area centers began building a community of academic specialists who might help round out the staffs for training experts to meet the demands of the federal agencies in conducting the Cold War or to be hired as professors in the undergraduate schools. The latter were expected to enlarge the circle of informed citizens, as they indeed did in the long haul.

Since we were starting afresh, we gave highest priority to staffing the Middle East centers. There were five by 1951—Columbia, Dropsie, Michigan, Princeton and SAIS—plus two others—Harvard (1955) and UCLA (1958)—while I still sat on the SSRC Committee. In the embarking years of the first five, all except SAIS were competing with federal agencies for the tested talent on the Middle East. Most of the latter had originally been recruited by OSS R&A and given invaluable experience in wartime analysis of contemporary regional issues in historical context. Because of its location in Washington, SAIS shared desired experts with OIR/State. For the early economy SAIS later paid the price of stunted growth of its regular staff.

SSRC's inaugural Near and Middle East Committee, dating to February 1951, was supposed to be one of the social scientists centering on the modern period. It comprised archaeologists (George C. Cameron, Michigan, chairman, and E. A. Speiser, Pennsylvania), a physical anthropologist (Carleton S. Coon, Pennsylvania), a geographer (Douglas D. Crary, Michigan), an economist (Peter G. Franck, American University), a philologist (Richard N. Frye, Harvard), an Ottoman and Turkish historian (Lewis V. Thomas, Princeton) who joined us in 1952, and two political scientists (Majid Khadduri and myself). The chairman of the CWAR (Robert B. Hall), an East Asian geographer, sat as an ex officio acting chairman throughout the spring of 1951 for his Michigan colleague, then absent on overseas research.

Hall excepted, none of us—certainly not I—had had any earlier firsthand experience with the inner workings of the SSRC or its service to academia. As a consortium of seven members—the American associations for anthropology, economics, history, political science, psychology, sociology and statistics—the SSRC played the role of their interest group. The ACLS was the mirror image for the humanities. Between them, the two national organizations represented in effect the interests of American higher education.

While I may not speak for my colleagues, I suspect that they were reacting much as I to the gentle but persistent guidance of the SSRC officers and staff in the committee meetings. From the first meeting, Pendleton Herring, the SSRC president, and Bryce Wood and Joseph B. Casagrande, the committee's successive staff associates, pressed us to think about research projects that would contribute to the solid anchorage of each social science discipline to the region. For doing that the Committee mounted a conference at Princeton in October 1952 on "The Near East: Social Dynamics and the Cultural Setting." The activity revealed that social science research on the region was still swaddled. The exception was Speiser's essay on "Cultural Factors in Social Dynamics in the Near East," an original analysis in the author's usual multimillennial perspective. Sydney N. Fisher edited the papers for a book titled *Social Forces in the Middle East* (1955).

With the naming in the fall of 1955 of Cuyler Young, head of the Princeton center, as chairman, the face and pace of the committee changed emphatically. Gone were the archaeologists. To fill their slots came humanists (one from Canada) with modern scholarly concerns and dedicated commitment to language teaching and religion. Khadduri and I, the only holdovers, were joined by: Hamilton A. R. Gibb (moving from the Laudian Professorship of Arabic at Oxford to the directorship of the new Center for Middle Eastern Studies at Harvard), William D. Schorger (cultural anthropologist, Michigan) and Wilfred C. Smith (Islamic theology, McGill) and, without a formal seat, Harvey Hall (editor, *The Middle East Journal*, and starting in 1956 a staff member of the Ford Foundation's International Training and Research Program).

After the sluggish opening years, the reshaped Committee moved into high gear. It centered its attention on shoring up the national base for training of social scientists for research on the contemporary Middle East. In the spring of 1956, the Ford Foundation approved a grant of $50,000 in support of the Committee's work. With assured financing, the Committee commissioned blueprints for intensive instruction in the region's primary languages and for the regular procurement from the field of the pertinent vernacular literature (serials and official publications as well as books) of central interest to social scientists. For the Committee's guidance in the next academic year, it appointed subcommittees in the major social sciences to draft reports on the basic needs and priorities of each discipline for deepening our knowledge of the region.

On a selective evaluation of the subcommittees' accomplishments, the Committee invited some twenty-five additional scholars to a conference in the spring of 1957 on "Fields of Research in Middle East Cultures: Anthropology, Politics and History." The Committee also introduced that year at Princeton a Ford-financed five-year consortial rotational summer program for intensive instruction in Arabic, Persian and Turkish; the other participating centers included Columbia, Harvard, Michigan and SAIS. Jointly with the Library of Congress and the American Library Association, a subcommittee fashioned standard transliteration systems from Arabic, Osmanlı and Persian. In that year, too, aided by the Ford Foundation, the Committee instituted and administered an annual program of grants-in-aid to postdoctoral researchers, designed largely to encourage young area specialists to continue field research.

It should be observed that the incentives for aspiring foreign area scholars to do research in the field, the accelerated language instruction and the collective arrangements for regional library services were all under way by the time that the federal government stepped in as an inclusive guarantor of foreign area centers and their recruitment of talented students. More than that, the NDEA program leaned heavily on the half-dozen-year head start of the Ford Foundation. Indeed, had the Foundation not gone to the rescue as pump-primer as early as 1952, the national effort would have been substantially retarded at the time the US Government belatedly came aboard.

Incidentally, Herring's sensitive antennae caught the first signals of the immanence of the Ford Foundation as generous patron of foreign area studies. As early as June 1951 he consulted each of the relevant regional SSRC committees, ours among them, on their most urgent wants. With the proposals he went to California to confer with Carl Spaeth, the Foundation's president.

That meeting and the ensuing dialogue helped yield as early as 1952 the International Training and Research Program that, in retrospect, acted as the interim underwriter for all foreign area centers, with the Rockefeller Foundation and the Carnegie Corporation of New York still picking up many pieces.

But the job of the private foundations did not abruptly stop on the Congressional passage in 1958 of the NDEA and of the Dingell amendment to Public Law 480, which carried the cumbersome title of the Agricultural Trade Development and Assistance Act of 1954. The NDEA, as we already know, offered generous annual subventions in support of foreign area training center projects as well as large numbers of fellowships to graduate students majoring in foreign language and area studies. The Dingell amendment authorized under PL 480 the use of blocked local currencies, accruing to the account of the US Government from the sale to the Third World of American agricultural surplus, for a comprehensive library procurement plan managed by the Library of Congress in close cooperation with the participating university libraries. The Library of Congress opened regional offices in 1962 in Cairo (to cover all Arab countries, Turkey and Cyprus) and Karachi (Iran as well as Pakistan) and in 1963 in Tel-Aviv (Israel).

With the surplus local currencies the regional offices purchased books, serials and official publications sought by the American center libraries. The surplus currencies ran out in Tel-Aviv in 1973, Cairo in 1979 and Karachi in 1985. Although the regional office in Israel was closed at the time that the local funds were exhausted, the other two were still active in 1993 in the LC's successor Cooperative Acquisitions Program offering binding services for monographs and serials and two preliminary printed catalog cards with every title sent from the region. Moreover, the Cairo office employed country representatives throughout the Arab world, and office staff paid frequent acquisitions visits to the individual states in its ambit. From the start, the services from the field assured prompt and standard catalog entries, thanks once again to the Committee's initiative in winning the cooperation of the LC and the ALA for a uniform style of transliteration.

One of the most productive features of the close cooperation with the LC was the preparation of two sets of negative microfilms of available complete runs of the major Arabic newspapers, one for the LC itself and the other for the University of Chicago, as the university depository for the center network.

In our first Committee discussion of the possibility of such a deal, as early as 1955, I described my own experience at the dissertation stage. I had conferred in 1947 with the section head at the Library of Congress for permission to check the accuracy of some of my summary references to Palestinian Arabic newspapers that OSS had sent there regularly for acquisition, only to be told that none had ever been removed from the original boxes packaged by our wartime office. I was also informed that, because of the poor quality, the folded newsprint had begun to disintegrate. Fortunately, in my own case, I was able—at much greater cost and loss of time—to procure photostats of many items from the Hebrew University library in Jerusalem. The section head bemoaned the fact that the Congress paid liberal attention to acquisition but often seemed reluctant to cover the expenses of upkeep.

At the inaugural meeting of the Committee in 1951, the SSRC staff gave each of us a copy of *A Program for Near Eastern Studies in the United States* (Washington, 1949), sponsored by the ACLS. I have already asserted that the SSRC Committee rejected its assumptions as well as its proposed guidelines because it looked backward rather than forward in recommending practical steps for coping with the unprecedented challenge of the Cold War.

Also circulated for our guidance was the *Report of the Interdepartmental Commission of Enquiry on Oriental, Slavonic, East European and African Studies*, chaired by the Earl of Scarborough and commissioned by the British Foreign Office for the guidance of the Quniquennial Review Committee when it factored the next series of government grants into what the Americans were labeling foreign area studies. Like the SSRC committees on Slavic and Asian Studies before us, we praised the abiding British dedication to sound language instruction. But also like our fellow committees, we dismissed the rest of the Scarborough report for its persisting belief in theology, philosophy, philology and literature as seemingly the sole building blocks of regional history and culture.

All the greater was the SSRC Committee's pleasure in 1961, when Great Britain's University Grants Committee issued the *Report of the Sub-Committee on Oriental, Slavonic, European and African Studies*, to read the high praise for American (and Canadian) accomplishments in foreign area studies in the interval. Sir William Hayter and his subcommitteemen, as guests of the Rockefeller Foundation which also had modestly subsidized Britain's parallel program in the 1950s, made the rounds of the major American foreign area centers, including those at Columbia. The compendious analysis of the origin and growth of the US system and its comparison with the British one endorsed with enthusiasm the American achievement.

CHAPTER 4

The Shaykh's Story
Told by Himself

Halil Inalcik

Part I: The Story of How I Became an Historian

At the time of my graduation from the Teachers' College of Balıkesir in 1935 I had only two options open to me. I could either have immediately started to work as an instructor at a village primary school or sat for an entrance exam to qualify for advanced training at the main Teachers' Training College in Ankara to become a secondary school teacher. During the summer of 1935 an unexpected new possibility presented itself. Atatürk had recently founded a new institution in Ankara called the Faculty of Languages, History, and Geography in the hope of providing a scholarly foundation for the theories of Turkish history with which he was then experimenting. To serve as the faculty of this newly founded institution he had invited a number of German professors, most of them refugees from Nazi Germany. It was planned that forty students, selected by means of examinations administered in Ankara and Istanbul, would initially be admitted with scholarship. In principle, graduates of the lower teachers' colleges were ineligible to sit for this exam and university-level education was only an option for graduates of the regular high schools' College. But because the Faculty of Literature, History, and Geography had only just been created, that summer an exception to this general rule was made and the competition was opened up to graduates of all the teachers' colleges throughout Turkey. We learned only later that it was through the intercession of Afet Inan that this exception had been approved.

Afet Inan was herself a graduate of a teachers' college for women, and it was during one of Atatürk's inspection tours at her school that he had first met her. Later on he adopted her, took her into his own household, and sent her abroad to Switzerland for advanced training. In so doing Atatürk was in effect grooming her for the role she later fulfilled as the representative of his ideas and pedagogical views concerning the Turkish theory of history. It was in recognition of her own background as a graduate of one of Turkey's teachers' colleges that Afet Inan in the summer of 1935 used her influence to secure this unprecedented opportunity for that year's graduating class. Years later when I became a member of the Turkish Historical Society I met her face to face.

Afet was the lifelong collaborator of Atatürk and she worked closely with him concerning all aspects of the Turkish theory of history. After Atatürk's death in 1938 she married Doctor Inan and acquired his surname. My recollection of her is of a kind-hearted, gentle woman who, while leaving no important scholarly legacy in her own right, nonetheless had a profound impact on the development of the historical profession in Turkey.

In 1935 I sat for the entrance exam to enter the Faculty of Languages, History, and Geography and was admitted. I was given the opportunity to study with scholars of international standing. The faculty had been created and organized with a view to promoting the development and study of a particular approach to history known as the Turkish historical thesis. Among the German professors who were founding members of the faculty were Anne Marie von Gabain in the fields of Chinese Studies and Turcology, E. Landsberger in the field of Sumerology, Hans Güterbock in the field of Hittitology, W. Rubens in Indic Studies, W. Eberhard in Chinese Studies, and a professor of Geography Herbert Louis. During the mid 1930s fields such as Hittitology, Sumerology, and archeology were particularly popular because of their presumed relevance to the Turkish theory of history then being promulgated. My first inclination was to study Chinese language, culture, and history, but I ultimately chose Ottoman history. As I now recollect the main factor which influenced my choice was the consideration that this period of history was better documented and possessed richer source materials than any other period of Turkish history. In addition, because my main interest in history was its social and economic aspects, I had no desire to devote a lifetime of study to the mastery of extinct languages and their long since abandoned scripts. It is also possible that my growing up in Istanbul, the capital of the former empire, had a sentimental influence on my choice of fields.

Had it not been for the opportunity offered by Afet Inan's opening the entrance exam to recent graduates of the teachers' colleges it is very likely that I would never have become an historian at all. One of my first teachers at the faculty was Professor Muzaffer Göker, who pursued a dual career in academics and politics, although his abiding interest was in politics. By Göker we were given instruction in political history. The other historian on the staff was Bekir Sıdkı Baykal, who had just returned to Turkey from Germany after receiving his doctorate. Above all others it was from Professor Fuad Köprülü, who had taken responsibility for teaching the history of the Middle Ages, that I learned the most. Köprülü was the Turkish scholar whose works most influenced my own genesis as an historian. As a student in his seminars at the faculty I also greatly profited from his personal guidance. In those days we students revered Köprülü as a master scholar with command over the two broad fields of history and literary history. Köprülü on his part felt an intellectual debt to the Russian orientalist V. V. Barthold, and the influence of this Russian scholar on Köprülü's research agenda and methodology is clearly detectable.

It was thanks to Köprülü's support that I was able to stay on at the faculty as a research assistant following my graduation. As one of the original graduates of the new faculty I felt a kind of missionary duty to contribute to the task which our patron Atatürk had set for us—namely, to provide a scholarly framework for teaching the Turkish historical thesis at all educational levels. Atatürk's aim was to liberate the Turkish nation from its status as a religiously-based society of the Middle Ages and to create conditions for modern Turkish statehood. Atatürk sought to give a new meaning to the study of Turkish history, making it the means of revealing the truth about the nation's past origins to the people and imbuing them with pride in their Turkic roots as well as a collective sense of their national identity. In essence Atatürk's task was to create a national identity *ex nihilo,* and he firmly believed that the development of a national historical consciousness would play a crucial role in that process. Atatürk was particularly sensitive to the negative image of the Turk in the West, which he attributed to the effect of six centuries of crusading conflict with Europe under the Ottomans and their predecessors. He saw this casting of Turkey in the role of adversary by the West as one of the principal causes for the national tragedy suffered by the Turks in the nineteenth century and the downfall of their once powerful world empire in the twentieth. Because Westerners, in their minds and in their literature, equated the Turk with Ottoman imperial ambitions, he felt that Turkic history as a whole tended to be viewed negatively. Atatürk felt that interpretations were still confused and mostly dominated by distortions, inaccuracies, and deliberate falsification of the facts. This situation troubled Atatürk, not only as leader of his country but also as a common Turk. He continued to cherish the idea that the new nation state of the Turks which he had helped to found in Anatolia would soon take its rightful place among the modern Western nations and gain acceptance as their equal. In any case, the Ottoman state had already in the final century of its existence (1822–1922) begun an intensive process of westernization which lent some credibility and feasibility to Atatürk's dream.

During the 1930s Atatürk devoted a good deal of his attention and energies to developing the Turkish historical thesis. In 1930 he summoned a group of the Republic's top historians, which included Fuad Köprülü, Sadri Maksudi Arsal, Yusuf Akçura, Halil Edhem Eldem, Şemseddin Günaltay, and Işmail Hakkı Uzunçarşılı to help found the Turkish Historical Society. He also commissioned them to write a new general history of the Turks from earliest times to the beginning of the twentieth century. The title given to the book was *The Main Outlines of Turkish History* (Türk Tarihinin Ana Hatları). The formative ideas around which the book was framed may be summarized as follows:

- Turkish history begins not with the arrival of the Seljuks to Anatolia in the late eleventh century, but rather dates from the era of the Hittites and Sumerians.

- The first discovery of agricultural techniques and systems of writing by man are attributable not to the peoples of the ancient Near East, but rather to the Turks of Central Asia. Central Asia was the point of dissemination of advanced civilization to other parts of the globe.

The part of the *Main Outlines* book that was devoted to the Ottoman Turks was written by Işmail Hakkı Uzunçarşılı. Uzunçarşılı's approach emphasized the institutional structure of the state. While still a student at the teachers' college in Balıkesir; I had already been exposed to the Turkish historical thesis, mostly through official publications distributed by the Turkish Historical Society. The texts based on the *Main Outlines* book was required reading in all of Turkey's schools during the early 1930s, and it was from this book that I gained my first inkling of what it means to study history. But even in those early student days I had already begun to realize that nationalist-inspired writing of history, although understandable as a reaction to western cultural bias and chauvinism, itself led to many excesses and an unscientific romanticizing of the past. In spite of this realization, however, after a lifetime of work as a professional historian I remain convinced that the need to correct distorted views of the Turks prevalent in western historiography still exists. Indeed it is my consciousness of this continuing need that has given inspiration to much of my scholarship. Unaware of the wisdom of Atatürk's vision at the time, I realized only later that it was pursuit of this politically crucial goal which motivated Atatürk to expend so much of his time and energy in the intellectual and pedagogical spheres. Today the early prototype versions of the Turkish historical thesis have been universally abandoned both by the scholarly community and by the public at large. Consequently, books in a genre similar to the *Main Outlines* book are no longer required reading in Turkey's schools. But Atatürk's foresight in establishing the Faculty of Language, History, and Geography as a center for the scholarly study of Turkish culture provided the essential framework for later discoveries in many fields of research, and these discoveries have contributed greatly to a better understanding of both Turkish and ancient Near Eastern history and civilizations. For example, the strides made in Turkish archaeology were only possible thanks to the institutional framework provided by Atatürk.

On the subject of the negative effect of superficial and fallacious interpretations of Turkish history by western historians let me mention a single example. Franz Babinger in his book on Mehmed the Conqueror describes this Ottoman ruler, the true founder of the Ottomans' *imperium*, as a sadist who derived pleasure from the torture and killing of human beings. Babinger emphasized throughout his book that the sultan's sole objective in undertaking his campaigns was the amassing of booty and slaves. Babinger saw no need as an historian to examine the conditions which led the Conqueror to embark upon his uninterrupted campaigns. As his main source of information on the Conqueror Babinger made use of documents found in the libraries and archives of the Ottomans' foes in the West and made little effort to restore balance to his account by referring to the historical documentation found in the Ottoman archives. It is astonishing to note that despite such glaring deficiencies in the work, Babinger's book on Mehmed the Conqueror still enjoys considerable popularity. Historians who confront and contradict entrenched popular views and write histories aimed at challenging these views are unfortunately all too rare a breed.

Part II: Intellectual Influences

I count among the historians who have had a profound effect on my own scholarship two principal figures. The first of these, Fuad Köprülü, who guided my historical interests during my early years of training, I have already mentioned. The other great historian with whom I was lucky enough to be associated was Paul Wittek. My first meeting with Professor Wittek was in 1949, when he had already been appointed as Professor of Turkish Studies in London at the School of Oriental and African Studies. During my one and a half year's stay in London I regularly attended his afternoon seminars at the school, which sometimes lasted from three to four hours. Among the other regular seminar participants at that time were Bernard Lewis, Victor Ménage, Vernon Parry, and Elizabeth Zachariadou. In these seminars Professor Wittek sometimes addressed set themes and other times engaged in discussion and offered his opinion about recently published works in the field of Ottoman studies. Occasionally one of the seminar group would present his or her research to the assembled company and discussion and criticism would ensue. Wittek had a sharp, critical mind, and his criticisms were unforgiving and sometimes devastating to those on the receiving end. He had absolutely no toleration for those who made use of old Ottoman historical texts in an uncritical manner. Wittek's greatest contribution to Ottoman studies was his application of western scholarly methods for text analysis to the earliest sources for Ottoman history. It is indeed unfortunate that the task of critical text edition and analysis which he commenced in the 1940s has not yet found any worthy or willing successors or devotees.

Two main approaches on the origins of the Ottoman state and its first rulers still dominate the recent literature. According to one approach, the stories relating to the origin of the Ottoman dynasty as told by the early chronicles are pure fabrication with no basis in historical fact and must be dismissed altogether as historical evidence. The second approach accepts these stories at face value without subjecting them to critical analysis. The truth of the matter is more complex than either approach would allow. In fact, the stories relating to Osman Gazi derive from two separate sources. On the one hand there is the factual chronicle tradition which derives from epic historical writing and reflects fourteenth-century conditions. But woven into this genuine narrative tradition are later additions by historians belonging to an era when the Ottoman empire had grown in size and stature who tended to idealize the state's origins in order to lend legitimacy and greatness to the dynasty. The task which now remains for serious modern historians to undertake is to separate those parts of the narrative which originate in the fourteenth-century epic story from the later accretions. The methods which might be followed to accomplish this task are as follows:

- testing the accuracy of the facts mentioned in the narrative against documentary evidence, such as *wakf* deeds, now coming to light concerning the earliest periods of Ottoman history

- carrying out extensive field research in the regions of northwest Anatolia which figure most prominently in the narrative accounts

Through application of the above-mentioned methods in some research that I have lately been conducting I have made some significant progress in untangling the confused record of the reigns of the first two Ottoman sultans, Osman and Orhan. Naturally, the easiest solution to the problem is just to declare the stories wholly unreliable. But, when these narrative stories are subjected to a careful and critical examination, they reveal a great deal that is historically relevant. It is certainly the case that the historical compilations of the late fifteenth century, as exemplified by the histories of Aşik Paşa-zade, Neşri, Ruhi, Idris Bidlisi, and Ibn Kemal, contain a number of ideologically motivated additions whose purpose was to exalt and lend legitimacy to the dynasty. These additions reflect the challenges which the Ottoman state faced at various stages in its later history and the reactions of its leaders to those challenges in the form of political assertions. Such assertions and claims embedded in Ottoman historical writing become particularly prominent in the aftermath of Timur's defeat of Beyazid I (1389–1402) and the ensuing collapse of Ottoman imperial unity and territorial integrity.

It is, in my opinion, particularly unfortunate that in a spirit of revisionism gone awry a new generation of Turcologists in England have begun to attack the legacy of Wittek's scholarship, completely forgetting the fact that it was his pioneering research that first opened up the early Ottoman period to serious investigation. They accuse Wittek of being governed by sentiment rather than scientific method in his historical approach. Such accusations against Wittek are both unfounded and unfair. Wittek in his assertion that the *ğaza*, or holy war, on behalf of Islam constituted one of the dynamic elements in the constitution of the early Ottoman polity, fully recognized that the Ottomans used this appeal to Islamic loyalty for their own reasons of state. To deny that beliefs and belief systems exerted a primary influence over human behavior and social norms and to relegate them to a position of secondary importance in the interpretation of history reduces processes of historical change to simple mechanistic determinism. It is rightly argued that history is the study of man in his *meaningful acts* in society.

The interpretation of Ottoman history in Turkey has passed through several distinct phases in recent times. Following the abolition of the sultanate and the emergence of modern Turkey, historians and social scientists under the new political regime tended to focus their scholarly interest on the pre-Ottoman epochs of Turkic history and the origins and spread of Turkic culture. The main agenda for research at this stage of national development was the search for the cultural and political origins of the Turkish people. The nationalist urge was already strongly felt in the period following the empire's defeats in the Balkan wars of 1912–13. During the teens and twenties of the current century a strong nationalistic trend dominated indigenous schools of historical writing on the Ottoman empire. During this period the main intellectual figure was the first Turkish sociologist, Ziya Gökalp. Following the path first blazed in the works of Emile Durkheim and Gaston Richard, Gökalp's writings assured the predominance of the positivist and collectivist schools of sociology in Turkey. As a result of Gökalp's overpowering influence historical work that emphasized nation and national culture gained preeminence in the period. Fuad Köprülü's innovative research into the origins of Turkish culture meshed closely with the intellectual fashions of the period. Köprülü identified the origins of Turkish literature in Central Asia, traced its spread via the dispersed Turkic tribes of Iran and Asia Minor, and founded a school of integrated studies based on his discovery of the common roots of Turkic culture. By examining the development of Turkish folk culture on a trans-Asiatic basis Köprülü attempted to identify and describe the uniform characteristics of this geographically widespread literature. Köprülü sought to identify the main features both of the general Islamic milieu of Central Asia and the Near East in the second millenium A.D. while at the same time revealing the peculiar character of the Turks' religious and cultural expression within that broader tradition and context. His work on the popular sufi orders of Anatolia (especially the *babai*, *kalenderi*, and *bektaşi* orders) was a milestone in the scholarly examination of Turkish cultural life during the Middle Ages. In this work he was courageous enough, given the fact that the book was first published in 1918, to draw attention to the fact that the nomadic Turkic peoples who had formally adopted Islam still retained the strong imprint of their pre-Islamic, shamanistic tribal beliefs. There can be no doubt that despite its excesses this positivist and nationalistic approach to the study of Turkish history and culture represented an important advance in Turkish historiography since it removed the study of Turkish and Ottoman history from the limited and confining context of Middle Eastern and Islamic history and placed it within its more appropriate global geopolitical as well as interdisciplinary contexts.

The directions taken by Turkish historical research in the 1930s had a close connection with the developing international economic crisis of the period, which had a strong disruptive effect on Turkey as well. During the 1930s Atatürk focused his attention on Turkey's economic policies and sought formulas and social policies to relieve the plight of the masses. During this period interest in socialism and socialistic writing were on the upswing. A new attitude towards the social sciences in general began to reveal itself and in this intellectual climate we again find Köprülü as one of the leading figures. By founding a new periodical called *The Journal of Turkish Legal and Economic History*, whose first issue appeared in 1931, Köprülü gave direction to the new trends in historical research. Immediately after he had founded this new journal Köprülü was invited to the Sorbonne to give a series of lectures, and during his stay in Paris he was greatly influenced by the work of two of his French colleagues, Lucien Febvre and Marc Bloch, both of whom were active in the new areas of historical research. While one group of Turkish researchers progressed in research on the history of institutions and remained in the tradition of Durkheim and his followers, the new history focusing on social and economic issues began in this period to attract an ever growing interest.

Around this time (the early 1930s) Ömer Lûtfi Barkan, who had recently completed his studies at the University of Strasbourg, where Marc Bloch was active, also returned to Turkey. As one of the pioneers of Turkish social and economic history Barkan began to devote himself to archival research and became a specialist in the field of Turkish agrarian and legal history through his detailed investigation of the Ottoman tax and population registers of the sixteenth century.

As I began my studies at the Faculty of Languages, History, and Geography in Ankara in 1935 it was these trends in historical research that focused on the social and economic dimensions of Ottoman history which predominated in the historical profession. In other words historical training in Turkey during the 1930s gave precedence to the history of institutions and to social and economic history. In these fields it was the scholarship of Köprülü and Barkan that gave direction and inspiration to the new generation of historians in the thirties. My own persona as historian bears the indelible mark of these two Turkish scholars. Their influence can be clearly seen in my doctoral thesis, in which I concentrated on the social effects of the Tanzimat reforms and investigated the role played by unresolved social and economic problems in the relationship between landowners and peasants as a factor in the 1841 and 1850 Nish and Vidin uprisings respectively.

The French influence on Turkish historical writing continued to be felt and after the work of Fernand Braudel took a fundamentally different tack. When Braudel's *La Méditerranée* was first published I happened to be in Paris. In 1950 I had set out from London to take part in the *International Congress of Historical Sciences* then being convened in Paris. During the course of the Congress Braudel's recent book, written in a new style and representing a fundamentally different historical perspective, had engendered lively discussion and debate. After reading the book I came to the, for me, exciting conclusion that for the first time in European scholarship the Ottoman empire had been presented and approached from an entirely new objective angle.

In his work Braudel presented his view that the Ottoman empire, far from representing an alien world on the eastern fringes of the Mediterranean, was in its social, demographic, and economic structures an integrating part that closely paralleled the lands of the western Mediterranean. Instead of seeing the eastern and western Mediterranean lands as separate and mutually incompatible worlds, as had most of his predecessors, Braudel saw the two halves of the sea as existing in a close commensality and mutuality of contact and influence. Braudel believed that the only way to understand Mediterranean history was not to separate it into its European and "oriental" (i.e., Ottoman) components, but rather to view it as an integrated whole. Braudel's interpretation of Mediterranean history came closer to reflecting historical realities than the portrayal by any of his predecessors. Braudel, as a student of the human geographer Vidal de Lablache, introduced revolutionary new methods to the study of history with his concepts of geographical determinism and, I believe, a Bergsonian understanding of historical evolution over the *longue-durée*. As a matter of fact, it is well known that Braudel in many ways continued in the path opened by Lucien Febvre and Marc Bloch, who had developed the concept of total history. This approach to history insisted on the need to study society based on the assumption that it was not made up of isolated events and structures, but rather existed and changed as a whole within the context of its given institutional and environmental framework.

Braudel attempted to apply these concepts of total history with its emphasis on material conditions to his study of Mediterranean societies, including Ottoman society. But he acknowledged the limits of his information concerning the Ottomans and described the empire as "a zone of formidable uncertainty." In the late 1940s, as he was writing his book on the Mediterranean world, there were very few detailed studies on either Ottoman institutions or economic conditions that he could rely upon, and he was frequently led into serious errors of interpretation by his dependence on the deficient secondary literature. Nevertheless, despite all his faults, Braudel was a gifted historian who wrote elegantly on many of the fundamental questions of Ottoman history, and his work raised important questions for future research. Each of the questions raised by Braudel opened up new areas of research for Ottoman historians, and his book *La Méditerranée* undoubtedly left a profound impact on Turkish historiography. Barkan was the first Turkish historian to write a review of Braudel's work introducing it to the reading public in Turkey, and at the same time Barkan conducted research of his own into questions raised by Braudel's book. Shortly afterwards I too, in a review of Mustafa Akdag's article on economic conditions in Ottoman Turkey, touched on the importance of Braudel's historical conceptualization for the study of Ottoman realities. In this paper I placed particular emphasis on Braudel's ideas concerning the universal effect throughout the Mediterranean economy of global phenomena such as the invasion of American silver and the European demographic boom of the sixteenth century. On the occasion of Braudel's visit to Turkey at Barkan's invitation, I was able to make his personal acquaintance. The influence of Braudel's approach on world historiography is today generally accepted, and his influence on Turkish historiography has been equally profound. When Braudel was preparing the second edition of *La Méditerranée* Barkan supplied him with the results of his own research in the realm of Ottoman price history.

Distortion of Ottoman history can arise from a number of different sources, both scholarly and nonscholarly. There are those distortions which arise from uncritical use of the sources, but the larger problem comes from either nationalist or other doctrinaire (e.g., Marxist) bias. The effect of these may be observed in Balkan and Arab historiography. Beyond the regional nationalist biases there exists also distortion which arises from anti-Ottoman prejudice of broader scope. Such prejudice originates from trends such as Eurocentrism and political forces such as colonialism. In the beginning stages of the development of modern Turkish historiography, which coincided with the creation of the Republic of Turkey as an independent political entity and the dominance of westernizing ideologies, Ottoman history was interpreted from an unsympathetic secularist point of view. Understood in the context of political developments in the Near East and Balkans during the early twentieth century these nationalist tendencies in historical writing are perfectly understandable. It was an unavoidable precondition of national awakening and self-realization throughout the region that the Ottoman regime which preceded national liberation should be reviled as oppressive and backwards. According to this theory the developmental potential of the Balkan nations had been suppressed as a result of their subjugation by a retrogressive, rapacious, and exploitative class of Turkish overlords during the centuries of Ottoman rule. None of the Balkan historians wish to acknowledge the historical fact that side by side with the indigenous peasants lived large numbers of Muslim settlers who as pastoralists and cultivators of the land were also tax-paying *reaya*. Muslim and non-Muslim *reaya* living as neighbors in the same land shared the same material conditions and standard of life. For the Arab historians too the concept of an oppressive Ottoman exploitation served as a convenient scapegoat and explanation for their own countries' backwardness vis-à-vis Western Europe. But it was also during the period following World War Two that the Ottoman documentary and archival record began to be exploited. This development gave rise to revisionist trends in historical writing that challenged the credibility of some latent anti-Ottoman prejudices found in the literature. It was the Hungarian historians that took the lead in the field of archival research. Lajos Fekete and his successors made a particularly valuable contribution to Ottoman documentary studies. Following the trend started by the Hungarian historians, Yugoslav, Bulgarian, Roumanian, Albanian, and Greek historians all began to rely on the Ottoman documentary record as the most trustworthy source for the history of their countries during the early modern era. The document-based studies conducted by these historians have concentrated mostly on topics such as institutional history, demography, social and economic conditions, and the phenomenon of urbanization. Beginning in the 1970s the Arab historians, like their Balkan colleagues, began to conduct research in the Ottoman archives.

Among the other intellectual trends which have influenced scholarly study of Ottoman history, sociological theory has also played a noteworthy role. Social historians and sociologists belonging to both Marxian and Weberian schools have attempted to apply their models to Ottoman history. These various efforts have resulted in the development of new, sometimes very interesting, directions for research. Because there are broad areas of Ottoman social and economic history that still remain inadequately studied and understood, premature generalization by the social scientists remains speculative and cannot be confirmed on a factual basis. Yet sociological concepts and generalizations both help to formulate questions for historical research. Inspired by class conflict or patrimonialism, a new generation of Ottoman historians has emerged whose interpretations of history are equally influenced by the works of historical sociologists such as K. Wittfogel and E. Eisenstadt.

In recent years a fashion has developed for tackling major problems in Ottoman history from the theoretical perspective offered by historical sociology. Underlying this approach is the assumption that these methodologies are so powerful an interpretive tool that they will be capable of resolving complex problems in historical research even though their practitioners may lack the appropriate skill or knowledge to make proper use of the first-hand narrative and the documentary evidence. If there is a proper task for history it is not to formulate generalizations divorced from both time and place but to investigate concrete events and developments in time and space. The recent rekindling of interest in hermeneutics and textual study among historians should therefore be welcomed as a needed reaction, and a positive development.

Those who would seek to define my place in contemporary historiography on the Ottoman empire by citing my earliest studies fail to see the evolution which my ideas have undergone since I first started writing history in the 1940s. As I see it, my historical writing falls into several clearly distinct periods. I was exposed to the Marxist interpretation of history through the lecture notes of Yusuf Akçura at the Ankara University's Faculty of Law, which I read while a student. The Marxist approach to Ottoman history achieved its strong influence in the 1970s during the time of the revolutionary leftist movement in Turkey. In those years, because of economic stagnation, Turkish students who could not find jobs were in constant agitation and began to seek the causes of Turkey's social and economic underdevelopment in the Ottoman legacy. The majority of the young writers focused their research on the topic of Ottoman social structure, reaching the conclusion that Turkish underdevelopment had its explication in Marx's Asiatic Mode of Production theory. When seeking empirical evidence to support their theories these writers turned primarily to the historical researches carried out by Barkan, Mustafa Akdag, and myself. The questions raised by the Marxist writers bore a close resemblance to the kinds of questions raised in Braudel's work. One of the forerunners of the Marxist historical school in Turkey was Sencer Divitçioğlu.

Divitçioğlu took as his theoretical base Marx's Asiatic Mode of Production. Divitçioğlu's work had a sustained influence on Turkish historians and social scientists in those days. Huri Islamoğlu-Inan, one of the new generation of social historians who studied with me, and Çaglar Keyder, a sociologist, are among the best representatives of this new school of research. In their research they adopt Marx's concept of social formation as their basic working model. This concept runs parallel in many ways to Braudel's concept of total history. As an historian, Islamoğlu-Inan somewhat modifies the classical theory of the Asiatic Mode of Production and her work attempts to clarify the peculiarities of the Ottoman social system that differentiated it from other Asian societies. I myself made a concerted effort during the 1980s to deepen my own understanding of some of the questions raised by the Asiatic Mode of Production debate. In particular, I began to undertake archival research and collect data that could shed light on questions such as the alienation and concentration of land in the hands of the members of the elite and their exploitation of peasant labor, the basic characteristics of the Ottoman agrarian regime, price movements, and rural-urban relations. It rapidly became clear to me that the AMP theory gave inadequate explanation for certain features of the Ottoman case. My work in the archives established, without any room for doubt, that the basis of the Ottoman land tenure system in the classical period (1450–1600) was the *chift-hane* system, a system that evolved within the framework of a highly centralized bureaucratic state structure for the purpose of regulating the productive capacity of the large masses of peasant households. It appears that Marx's theory, which he had developed by examining social relations in the context of the Indian subcontinent, represents not a universal phenomenon but a peculiar historical case. The theory put forth by Marx was that peasant society was subjugated to a class of military overlords who extracted the surplus agricultural production of the agrarian underclass by sheer force. Such a theory contradicts Marx's general theory of social formation based on relations of production. Such practices were not general throughout Asia as the AMP label would imply. In this limited context social structure evolved, AMP argues, not through economic articulation, but rather as the result of political suppression. The Ottoman *chift-hane* system on the other hand was based on *a particular economic articulation* through processes that can be documented from the archival record.

In 1977 Immanuel Wallerstein convened an international conference at Binghamton to celebrate the inauguration of the Fernand Braudel Research Center. At this conference I presented a paper on the influence of the Braude-

lian school on research in the field of Ottoman social and economic history
and attempted to summarize research progress on a number of questions
raised by Braudel's approach. Wallerstein's interest revolved mostly around the
question of the place occupied by this large imperial land mass within the
western capitalist world economy. Wallerstein's peripheralization theory was
discussed in search of consensus on the important questions of when, how, and
how far the Ottoman economy was incorporated into (that is peripheralized
by) the European world economy. Wallerstein's views were of keen interest to
Turkish historians and when, later that year, the First International Congress
on the Social and Economic History of Turkey was convened in Ankara,
Wallerstein was invited to take part. At that conference Çaglar Keyder and
Huri Islamoglu-Inan, together with other young sociologists and historians,
had the opportunity of meeting Wallerstein in person, and they later sent their
students for study at the new center in Binghamton. At the State University
of New York in Binghamton a research group emerged and Çaglar Keyder
himself later joined the Center as a member of the University's Sociology Department. This research group began to take an active role by sponsoring conferences and preparing publications relating to the question of the place of the
Ottoman empire in the context of Wallerstein's peripheralization theory. This
research trend started at Binghamton soon found followers in other circles,
and McGowan's book on Ottoman social and economic history is an example
of the new school of research. Islamoglu and Keyder also published some
thought-provoking studies relating to the AMP theory and peripheralization.

In Wallerstein's view the Ottoman empire, like China, possessed a nearly
self-sufficient "imperial" economy. Economies of this type represented challenge to European economic penetration. According to Wallerstein such imperial economies represent a separate category which remained essentially
independent from the European capitalist world economy. But the Ottoman
empire was different from China in that its geographical location on the eastern shores of the Mediterranean traditionally drew it into very close trading
relations with Europe. The Ottoman empire was an important source of raw
materials such as cotton, leather, wool, and dyes for European industries. But
at the same time it acted as an important market for European export of man-
ufactured goods, woolen cloth in particular. Over time the close trading relations between Europe and the Ottoman empire grew to such proportions that

they began to transform the social and economic structure of the Ottoman society. Under these latter circumstances, the Wallerstein school argues, the long-delayed peripheralization of the Ottoman economy did in fact occur. To investigate this process of peripheralization in the Ottoman empire, the Binghamton research group began to carry out empirical studies. The present state of research seems to indicate that the true peripheralization of the Ottoman economy did not take place before the second half of the eighteenth century. Professor Reşat Kasaba at the University of Washington in Seattle is one of the leading figures among the young researchers currently working in this field. Debate on the process of marginalization of Turkey's economy is not a new phenomenon; the *kadro* movement of the 1930s had also discussed Turkey's reduction to a semi-colonial status by the European capitalist economies. Wallerstein's group has, however, developed a more penetrating methodology for studying this phenomenon, and they exert a growing influence over studies on the late Ottoman empire.

Part Three: Major Studies

I completed my doctoral studies between the years 1940 and 1942. The subject of my doctoral thesis was the effect of the Tanzimat reforms in Bulgaria. During the course of my research I was fortunate enough to discover at the Dolmabahçe Palace in Istanbul a special collection of documents on the Bulgarian question compiled for Abdulhamid II. The papers, amounting to ten volumes, were originally preserved in the Başbakanlık Archives. I made a special study of those documents relating to the Vidin uprisings of 1841 and 1850. The reports sent by the governor of the province and confirmed in details of the reports by special investigators sent from Istanbul indicated that land disputes between the landowners and the Bulgarian peasants and corvees lay at the root of these rebellions. We know that when similar reforms had been attempted in Bosnia-Herzogovina, land disputes and corvees had given rise to discontent and uprisings there too. Thus, already at the time of my doctoral research I had begun to focus my attention on questions such as land tenure and peasant problems. Around the same time Ömer Lûtfi Barkan was also carrying out his research on the land question in the sixteenth century. As for myself, the land and related questions have remained a constant focus of my research throughout my academic career. In the years following 1942, when I completed my doctoral thesis, I continued to conduct research on the Tanzimat era of Ottoman history in both its internal and international aspects.

In 1953, as the five hundredth anniversary of the conquest of Istanbul approached, historians in Turkey began to focus their attention on the historical significance of this event and on the reign of Mehmed II in general. I too took part in these activities and began to collect information in the archives relating to this period of Ottoman history. In the forty years since 1953 on the basis of this research I have published quite a number of studies on the subject of fifteenth-century Ottoman history. In addition to the information on Mehmed II's reign gathered from the Başbakanlık archives, I discovered that the Bursa *sicillât* (law court records) also contained important information. The series of kadi registers from Bursa begins in the 1460s, and the last three years of Mehmed's reign (1479-81) are covered in detail in a bulky register. Because the material in the Bursa *sicillât* is mostly concerned with city life in Bursa, the direction of my research turned to areas such as Ottoman urbanism, trade, crafts, silk trade, industry, and the position and administrative activities of the kadis of Ottoman cities. Soon after beginning my research I realized that the *sicillât* constituted a source of capital importance for Ottoman social and economic history. Later on I also made use of the Istanbul *sicillât* for my research and, in fact, a large part of the documentation that I have used throughout my years of research in Ottoman history came from local court registers.

In the period between 1935 and 1950, before I began carrying out my own research in these records, a number of studies had been carried out under the auspices of the *Halk Evleri*. Most of these studies had been published in obscure journals, and the work was mostly done by high school teachers as opposed to professional historians. Because of their location in the provinces, these records had remained mostly inaccessible to professors from the Istanbul and Ankara faculties. The publication efforts of the period 1935–50 suffered somewhat from disorganization and lack of consistent standards. But whatever its publishing flaws the corpus of original documents selected from the *sicillât* that took shape in these years served to provide reliable first-hand information on important subjects, such as local developments and economic practices, popular movements in rural areas, brigandage, and a great deal else.

In later years local studies grounded in information extracted from the court records of Ottoman cities also became popular in other parts of what had once made up the empire. Historians in Syria, Egypt, and the Balkan countries all came to realize the importance of the Ottoman *sicillât* records as a source for their own history. In Syria Abdulkerim Rafeq; in Egypt André Raymond and A. A. Abdurrahim; in Bulgaria G. Galabov, Berov, and S. Dimitrov, and in Bosnia Hamid Krashevliavić, A. Sučeska, H. Shabanović, Hamid Hadzibegić, and others all published studies based on these local records. So far as Turkey is concerned, a decision has now been taken to collect the local records presently housed in museums and other municipal buildings in the provinces and house them under one roof at the National Library in Ankara.

Towards the end of 1953 the subjects of research around which my interest was beginning to concentrate had already become clear. The major axes around which my research was to revolve were the land question and the Ottoman timar system, Ottoman social and economic history, and urbanization in the Ottoman empire from the beginning of the fifteenth century. While I was conducting my research in the Başbakanlık archives on the *tahrir* registers of Mehmed II's era I came across an extremely interesting and valuable document belonging to the period of Mehmed's father, Murad II. This register, dating from 1432, was the timar register for the sancak of Arvanid, or Albania, which I published in book form in the year 1954. This publication was the first full edition of an Ottoman land register in Turkey. The only earlier effort in this field was Lajos Fekete's publication of the Estergom register in Hungarian translation. The timar register of Albania contained documents relating to the period 1432 to 1455 and provided important information shedding light on the Ottoman timar regime. It also provided insight into problems connected with Ottoman settlement in Albania and the identity of local Christian families that were incorporated into the Ottoman timar system. The other registers relating to the period of Mehmed II which I was studying at the same time revealed the existence of Christian timariots in other parts of the Balkans controlled by the Ottomans. These research findings demonstrated to my satisfaction that the feudal-military aristocracy representing the pre-Ottoman regime preserved their status in Ottoman society as timariots. This discovery completely invalidated the widespread claims that the Ottoman conquest had led automatically to the expropriation of Christian landowners by the Muslim conquerors. The Balkan historians took a keen interest in my research find-ings. The article on the continuity from Czar Stephan Dushan's empire to that of the Ottomans, published in Turkish in 1953, was translated into Serbo-Croatian by Nedim Filipović and published in Sarajevo. In a history of Greece written around that time by A. Vakalapoulos mention was also made of these new discoveries. Today it has become generally accepted by all Balkan histo-rians as a fact of history that most of the military aristocracy remained in place after the Ottoman conquests and did not yield its place to a new landholding class from Anatolia.

My researches on the period of Mehmed II contradicted the findings of the German scholar Franz Babinger, who was conducting intensive research of his own, and my critical review of his book on the Conqueror and his time appeared in 1953. This review brought an end to the cordial relations that had existed between us up until that time and to this day I regret my loss of his friendship under such circumstances. In his research Babinger hardly used the contemporary Ottoman archival evidence and ignored the principal Ottoman narrative source for the Conqueror's reign written by the contemporary states-man and intimate of the court Tursun Beg. As for myself, I have been able to exploit only a small fraction of the material I have collected during a lifetime of study in the Ottoman archives. The material which I have collected would more than suffice for a comprehensive study of the Conqueror's reign super-seding all previous work on the subject. A proper understanding of the reign of Mehmed II, which coincided with the time when the Ottoman empire and the traditions of Ottoman rule and sovereignty attained their classical form, is critically important for understanding subsequent periods of Ottoman history. There is no doubt that his reign constitutes one of the most important turning points in Ottoman history. It was at this time that the Ottoman empire finally emerged onto the stage of world history as one of the major players after more than half a century of uncertainty that lasted from the beginning of the four-teenth century to 1453.

In the 1950s I became interested in the history of the Crimean khanate. My father had immigrated to the Ottoman empire from Crimea in either 1905 or 1906, and my family background gave me a personal as well as pro-fessional reason for pursuing this interest. My first research into this topic had been completed in 1944 when I studied the establishment of Ottoman suzerainty over the khanate in 1475. In addition to this early study I have published a number of articles relating to the structure of the Crimean khanate, its position within the Ottoman imperial system, and its relations with Russia.

In 1949 one of my students brought me the manuscript of an old history that he had found in his village. Study of the manuscript revealed that it was a previously unknown Ottoman chronicle covering the events of the Varna Crusade of 1444. Recognizing that this work was an original Ottoman example of the *menakibname* type that gave authentic and detailed information about John Hunyadi's campaigns against the Ottomans, I decided to publish the source together with Mevlut Oğuz, the student who had first brought it to me for study. After its publication scholars in Hungary, Poland, and Roumania expressed a keen interest and saw immediately that the text revealed many important and previously misunderstood aspects of the Varna Crusade. This publication, together with my edition of the 1432 timar register of Arvanid, helped to provide a clearer picture of conditions in the Ottoman empire during the reign of Murad II (1421–1451). I also made a separate investigation of the registers of *wakf* endowments from Murad II's reign preserved in Ankara at the General Directorate of Pious Foundations. It can now be said that the combination of these three sources enables us to gain better insight into Ottoman realities in the first half of the fifteenth century.

Sultan Mehmed II was the first Ottoman sultan to codify the existing Ottoman law, and during his reign two separate law codes were promulgated. I have made a detailed study of these two law codes in particular and have also published a number of studies on Ottoman law in general. One reason for my interest in law is that starting from my high school years I was in close touch with Sadri Maksudi Arsal, who was a friend of the family. During my high school years I helped him to transcribe drafts of his work on Turkish legal history from Arabic script into Latin letters for the printers. When we used to meet in his study he would also occasionally describe his research projects to me. I have a vivid memory of fighting off drowsiness during these sessions when he would explain, sometimes for hours at a time, about subjects which as a teenager must have been mostly over my head. But though I had little appreciation of these private lectures at the time, I later realized that I had derived quite a lot of benefit from listening to Sadri Bey. During my first year as a student of the Faculty of Letters I simultaneously attended lectures at the

Faculty of Law, and throughout my life I have maintained a strong interest in law.

In 1956 I edited, together with Dr. Robert Anhegger, a collection of legal rescripts belonging to the reigns of Mehmed II and Beyazid II. Simultaneously a French translation of these laws was prepared by Nicoara Beldiceanu, while Franz Babinger published a facsimile edition of the text. This translation, which was prepared after our edition had been published, contained many serious mistakes. The review which I published concerning the translation unfortunately resulted in my losing another friendship.

As a result of my researches into the Ottoman law codes and *tahrir* registers I had come to an important conclusion concerning the Ottoman agrarian regime. Based on my research I now felt ready to describe the origin and general character of the Ottoman system of taxation. In my article in Turkish entitled "Raiyyet Rüsûmu" I established for the first time that land taxes such as the *chift resmi* had to be understood within the context of a more general system which determined and defined the legal and social status of peasants. According to the dictates of this system it became clear to me that the cultivator of a plot of land sufficient to provide for the needs of a peasant family paid the full *chift resmi*, the cultivator of half that amount of land paid the half *chift resmi* and represented the second tier of the landed peasant class, while cultivators with less than a half *chiftlik* of land constituted the lower tier of the landed peasant class. That these categories were the significant ones determining social and economic status became clear from the *tahrir* registers themselves, where taxpayers were listed as belonging to one or the other of these three categories. It also became clear that the land as well as the family cultivating the land were registered together as one unit. Peasant families representing a certain potential labor capacity were entered into the registers not as individuals but as production units, i.e., the *chift hane*. As becomes clear from Ottoman archival records, it was the *chift hane* which gave definition to the village social categories within the context of the Ottoman imperial land regime.

By means of centrally maintained registers the Ottoman administration was thus able to organize and categorize the land and the labor of the entire rural economy and keep it under its own control. My research had revealed this system which lay at the very heart of the Ottoman imperial administrative system. It was this system, the Ottoman *chift hane* system, that determined the other basic Ottoman administrative practices and forms such as the *tahrir* system itself, and it was also the means by which the amount and character of land and personal taxes were determined. In my later research I discovered that prior to the Ottomans in regions where the agricultural production was characterized by dry farming, similar systems for regulating the peasant labor and land had existed. From the time of the late Roman empire onwards imperial rulers throughout the Mediterranean lands had developed such systems for maintaining control over their primary source of revenue, i.e., the land and peasant. The Ottomans, introducing very few changes of their own, merely perpetuated existing norms and practices. For their part they had as their principal concern preserving the peasant land-family units in the conquered territories as productive tax-yielding entities. The Ottomans had little interest in or incentive to carry out radical changes affecting peasant society. The Ottomans carried neither social nor religious revolution to the rural society they conquered.

It is possible, thanks to the preservation of the extremely rich Ottoman archival record—from *tahrir* registers, to law codes, and law court registers—to establish in detail the actual material conditions which prevailed in the rural parts of the empire. Through the Ottoman records and knowledge of the social and institutional conservatism of the Ottoman regime we are also able to reconstruct a fairly clear picture of what peasant life and agrarian conditions must have been like in the Balkans and Anatolia under the pre-Ottoman Seljukid, Byzantine, and even Roman imperial regimes. Because very few documents from the pre-Ottoman period have been preserved, our knowledge of these periods remains imprecise. But under the light of a detailed knowledge of the Ottoman *chift hane* system some aspects of these earlier regimes can be clarified. Thus our original study on the Ottomans' "Raiyyet Rüsûmu" opened the way to a broad new area of research in both Ottoman and comparative contexts.

I consider as one of the most critically important aspects of my work as an empirical historian my efforts in the realm of document and text publication. In the early years I turned my energies in this sphere to documents pertaining to the Tanzimat reforms. As mentioned above, in 1954 I published the full edition of a timar register of Arvanid. At the same time I published a collection of documents on the reign of the Conqueror and on the city of Bursa. The series of documents on Bursa (over five hundred) has continued with a sequence of articles in the journal *Belgeler*. Most recently I have prepared for publication the customs register of the port of Caffa covering the years 1487 to 1490. I also collected for publication Ottoman rescripts of justice from the sixteenth and seventeenth centuries. I have published the texts of Ottoman law codes and coedited with R. Anhegger a collection of regulations dating from the reigns of Mehmed II and Beyazid II. At present I am preparing an edition and translation of three principal Sultanic Ottoman law codes. The first of these is the law code of Süleyman I, the second is the so-called *kanun-name-i cedid* compiled in the early seventeenth century, and the third is the law code of the sancak of Aydın. For this project the text is being prepared according to the principles of critical text editions, and the text is accompanied by annotations and a full English translation of each of the three codes. The work is being supported by a grant from the National Endowment for the Humanities and publication is anticipated during 1993.

Another text publication which I am currently preparing in collaboration with Gilles Veinstein and M. Berindei is the customs registers of Kilia and Akkerman from the late fifteenth and early sixteenth centuries. With the publication of the Caffa register, this material will provide the basic source for Black Sea trade in the fifteenth century.

Part Four: Major Projects

Over the course of my professional career I have undertaken a number of long-term projects which I hoped would provide a foundation for further study in the field of Ottoman historical research. Some of these projects have already been completed; others are still in progress.

One of these projects concerns the *sicillât* of Bursa. When I first began to work on these records in the early 1950s they lay in heaps in one of the cells of Mehmed I's medrese in Bursa, covered with dust and dirt. After I had already worked for several years in Bursa I had the idea of proposing a new home be found for these important records and approached the General Directorate of Museums in Ankara with a plan for preserving and cataloguing these records. The idea was enthusiastically received, but since the first stage in the plan was to send the registers to Topkapı Sarayı in Istanbul for rebinding, I soon became the victim of my own suggestion's success. When the registers were sent to Istanbul for cleaning, repair, and rebinding, they became inaccessible for research for quite a long time. Eventually the registers returned to Bursa and were housed in a special archive at the city's Archeological Museum. Once they returned to Bursa these registers attracted the attention of both the Turkish and the international scholarly community, and publications based on these records began to proliferate.

Many years later, in the 1980s, I turned to the *sicillât* of Istanbul as a potential source for the history of the empire's capital city. The Istanbul *sicill* archives are now housed in the Müftülük of Istanbul and contain close to 10,000 volumes. This archive was created during the reign of Abdulhamid II (1876-1909) when a resurgence of interest in the Islamic sciences and particularly Islamic law manifested itself. The archive was placed under the jurisdiction of the Sheyh-ül-Islam. During Abdulhamid II's time the archive was carefully organized and classified and a catalog of the holdings was also prepared. This archive is of first-rate importance not just for the history of the city of Istanbul but more generally as a source on Ottoman urban life, crafts and trade, and legal history. I had thought for a long time that there was a need to develop some kind of organizational framework by which this important source for Ottoman history could be fully exploited and research results published and disseminated. While so much important scholarly research had been carried out on Byzantine Istanbul, it seemed to me shameful that such a major source for the history of the Ottoman city should lie unexploited and indeed almost completely ignored. I became determined that this important source should gain equal recognition with the Başbakanlık and Topkapı Sarayı archives as a major center for research on Ottoman history. With this in mind I established contact with the Müfti of Istanbul, his honorable Selâhattin Kaya, and with his assistant at the Müftülük's archive, Abdülaziz Bayındır, and I began immediately to encourage some of my doctoral students at Chicago to carry out their research there. I also had the idea of setting up a small team of qualified researchers who could take charge of publication efforts based on the Istanbul *sicillât*. Through consultation with professors Abdullah Kuran and Zafer Toprak of Bosphorus University I sought advice on establishing a foundation devoted to the promotion of this project. The mayor of Istanbul, at that time Bedreddin Dalan, was also approached for his ideas on the subject. Later on the planning committee was widened to include professors Nurhan Atasoy, Cemal Kafadar, and Gulru Kafadar, but because our sources of funding were still inadequate the project's realization had to be delayed. In the end a solution was reached whereby the project would be directed under the auspices of the Center for Art History of Istanbul's Faculty of Letters with funding from the Koç Company. At the present time work continues on transposing the contents and information contained in these registers into data banks by use of computers and other technical aides. During the early stages of this project a part-time research staff of three assistants is working to process the information in a systematic fashion. The publication of the first register of the kadi of Istanbul is anticipated shortly. It is the hope of the project organizers that once this first in a series of studies and monographs on the Istanbul *sicillât* is published it will serve to publicize the project and further stimulate interest.

There are very few peoples in the world who are as well endowed with such rich historical sources for their own national history as the Turks. The variety of archival evidence found in Turkey is something unique. For the past fifty years, ever since I began my first work in the field of Turkish history, I have been a strong advocate of the necessity for setting priorities that will ensure the preservation, scholarly classification, and openness of access of the Turkish archives.

In 1985, in collaboration with his excellency former ambassador Ismail Soysal, we organized a colloquium in Istanbul on the archive question. The prime minister, his excellency Turgut Özal, and a number of archive technicians and specialists took part in this colloquium and, following the meeting, it was decided by the government to allocate generous funds for the purpose of archive development and modernization. At the present time the Ottoman archives in Istanbul are on the way to becoming an international center for scholarly research on a par with the London and Paris archives. Hundreds of cataloguing personnel are now working to classify the millions of documents preserved at the archives, and for the first time a trained cadre of archivists is now in place in Turkey. If we recollect that from the ruins of the Ottoman empire there emerged more than twenty independent nations, the need for historians from these countries to turn to the Ottoman archives for the illumination of their own historical pasts is obvious. In addition, the Ottoman empire is one of the great empires of world history on a par with the Chinese and Roman empires. In addition to Ottomanists, historians, and other specialists, the Ottoman empire holds a particular interest for sociologists and other social scientists. For example, K. Wittfogel and E. Eisenstadt both devoted a significant portion of their works to the case of the Ottoman empire.

The journal *Belgeler* (Documents), which is published under the auspices of the Turkish Historical Society and on whose editorial board I currently serve, has been published continuously since 1964. This journal serves as one of the principal mediums for the publication of documents relating to Ottoman history.

One of the most significant archival sources for the study of Ottoman history is the series of registers, numbering more than 260 volumes, called the *Mühimme*. The *Mühimme* registers were those registers in which matters discussed by the Imperial Council were summarized in the form of imperial rescripts, or *fermans*. More than thirty years ago I presented to the Turkish Historical Society my idea of publishing each of the *Mühimme* registers in a series of volumes. The essential elements of my proposal were as follows:

- each of the Mühimme registers should be published first as a facsimile

- each volume would be accompanied by a detailed alphabetical index of proper names and technical terms

- each volume would be accompanied by an introduction serving to indicate the peculiarities pertaining to that specific volume

I was convinced that this plan would meet best the needs of the scholarly community. I was aware at the same time that previous efforts at summarizing the contents of the registers and publishing simplified versions of the texts in modernized Turkish had failed to provide material which was of any use to serious scholars and historians. Regretably, the executive committee of the society voted against adopting my suggestion on the grounds that it would prove too expensive. I still remember with disappointment that among those who rejected this proposal were my historian colleagues. Had the project been undertaken thirty years ago as I had hoped, by now the major universities of the world would each have on their library shelves the full 260-volume set ready to serve as the foundation for all serious studies in Ottoman history.

Another of the most important series of registers for historical research contained in the Başbakanlık archives are the *tapu tahrir* registers. These registers, numbering more than 2,000, are today preserved mostly at the Ottoman archives in Istanbul but also in part at the General Directorate of Deed Registration in Ankara. The importance of this fund was first demonstrated in studies carried out by the late Ömer Lûtfi Barkan. Since the 1940s they have formed the subject of active publication both within Turkey and internationally. In our opinion however, despite the flurry of interest in publication, no ideal method of publication has yet developed that fulfills the requirements for scholarly use. For instance, let us take the Hungarian publications based on these registers which, because they are published only in Hungarian translation, become essentially inaccessible to scholarship outside Hungary. Had these registers been transcribed in the original language they would have remained much more accessible to the international scholarly community. As for the publications in Turkey, there has been an unfortunate trend, referred to above, toward simplification and modernization of the Ottoman texts. In my opinion, a system similar to that which I had earlier proposed for the publication of the *Mühimme* registers, which envisaged providing facsimiles of the texts with notes and indices, would be the most suitable method for scholarly use. It should be recognized that these publications are not intended for the general public's use and should be designed only for use by specialists.

Six years ago in 1986 I proposed to the Turkish Historical Society a project for organizing the publication of these imperial land registers in a scholarly and systematic fashion. In this project I proposed as the initial task the job of publishing all the registers of the reign of Süleyman I that pertain to the areas contained within the present day borders of Turkey as a series of volumes. The method for preparing these volumes would conform to the above indicated publication specifications. The *tahrir* registers contain information on the population and economic conditions of villages, towns, and cities indicating also the value and amount of agricultural production. These censuses were carried out by the state for the purpose of estimating tax revenues and establishing social groups. Consequently, when, according to the project's plan, all the *tahrir* registers pertaining to Turkey from the reign of Süleyman I have been published, it will be possible to map out in full detail the demographic and economic resources of Anatolia as they existed 400 years ago. The executive committee of the Turkish Historical Society agreed to accept this project into their general plan, and a committee composed of specialists on the *tahrir* registers was established. At present we are pursuing contacts with the General Directorate of State Archives in Turkey to identify those individuals who will be able to take charge of the task of publication.

A project that I was fortunate to bring to fruition was the creation of a permanent organization for research on Ottoman social and economic history. To launch this project I conceived the idea of convening an international congress and, with the agreement of the Dean of the Faculty of Arts and Letters, Emel Dogramacı, and the Chairman of the Department of Economics, Osman Okyar, Haccetepe University was chosen as the site for the first international meeting. The meeting took place in Ankara in 1977.

Throughout the world since the Second World War the fields of social and economic history had emerged as areas of growing interest and concern for historians. Following the opening of the Turkish Archives after 1930 both in Turkey and in the Balkan countries a number of important studies relating to those fields were produced, and the social and economic aspects of Ottoman history began to be studied in greater depth. By bringing together researchers working in these fields a number of new areas for research were identified and the meeting served as a positive impetus for the further development of Ottoman studies. Subsequent meetings were held in Strasbourg (1980), Princeton (1983), Munich (1986), Istanbul (1989), and Aix-en-Provence (1992). To give permanence to these efforts and to encourage future research, we created an International Commission for the Social and Economic History of Turkey. The founding members of this commission were, apart from myself, Osman Okyar, Emel Dogramacı, Kemel Karpat, Bernard Lewis, Irene Mélikoff, William H. McNeil, Nikolai Todorov, and Immanuel Wallerstein.

My most recent project in the realm of Ottoman social and economic history has been to organize and edit a textbook designed to synthesize current research advances. As partners for this project, which, according to the original contract with the publishers (Cambridge University Press), was to cover the whole period from the beginning of the empire to its final collapse within

750 pages of text, I approached five well-known specialists working on specific periods of Ottoman History—Suraiya Faroqhi, Bruce McGowan, Donald Quataert, Mehmed Genc, and Halil Sahillioğlu. In the end, the last two members of the group withdrew from the project. I undertook to prepare the portion of the work covering the period 1300–1600, and Faroqhi, McGowan, and Quataert took on the responsibility for each of the successive centuries to the close of the nineteenth century. As a replacement for Sahillioğlu, Şevket Pamuk agreed to write the segment on Ottoman monetary history. After years in preparation the book has finally been completed and sent to the publishers. We hope that it will be ready for distribution in 1993. The book is on the one hand designed to answer some of the questions raised by Braudel in his now classic book on the Mediterranean world and on the other hand to correct, while at the same time complementing, the work of Wilhelm Heyd on the Levant trade. It is our belief that in this book we have convincingly demonstrated the important economic role played by the Ottoman empire in world history, a role which was until now either imperfectly understood or mostly overlooked.

Another project with which I am now involved as one of the chief responsibles is the *History of the Scientific and Cultural Development of Mankind* being sponsored by UNESCO. The fifth volume of this work, currently planned as a seven-volume set, covers the period 1500–1800. Professor Peter Burke from Cambridge University and myself are sharing duties as editors of the fifth volume, and we have already agreed upon the general plan for the volume. At present, approximately sixty percent of the chapters have been written and final publication is scheduled for 1996.

In addition to serving on the editorial boards of a number of journals, I have taken a personal role in founding and perpetuating two specialized journals devoted to Ottoman studies. The first of these is *Archivum Ottomanicum*, which I founded in 1969 together with Tibor Halasi-Kun (+1992), and the second is the *Journal of Ottoman Studies*, founded in 1980 together with Nejat Göyünç and Heath Lowry. These two journals are the only journals that are exclusively devoted to Ottoman studies as opposed to the more general context of Turcology or Turkish history. In the category of general journals covering all these fields the leading journals are *The Journal of Turkish Studies* (Cambridge, MA) under the joint editorship of Şinasi Tekin and Gönül

Tekin; *International Journal of Turkish Studies* (Madison, WI); *Turcica* (Paris); and *Türk Dünyası Araştırmaları* (Istanbul, 1980–). In addition, *Türkologischer Anzeiger*, published annually in Vienna since 1975 under the directorship of Andreas Tietze, gives a comprehensive listing of worldwide publication on both Turcological and, more specifically, Ottoman-related subjects.

We are currently working on a project for the preparation of another kind of practical work designed for researchers wishing to conduct research in Ottoman history. Our plan is to prepare a work organized as a dictionary of Ottoman technical terms. The preparation of such a work has now become a necessity as the numbers of students and specialists concentrating their research on the Ottoman archives continues to grow. To start with I proposed to two distinguished Turkish colleagues, Cemal Kafadar of Harvard University and Nejat Göyünç of Konya University, that the three of us work together on this project. Later on Şinasi Tekin joined us. While taking note of the efforts of our predecessors in the field, such as Mehmed Zeki Pakalın, Midhat Sertoglu, and Reşat Ekrem Koçu, for our own work we plan also to incorporate into the volume the results of our own research over the years preserved on index cards.

Part Five: America

In the years between 1943 and 1972 I taught Ottoman history at the Faculty of Languages, History, and Geography at the University of Ankara. I became an assistant in 1942, was promoted to *doçent* in 1943, and became full professor in 1952. In 1956, in addition to my teaching at the Faculty of Languages, History and Geography, I also taught Ottoman administrative history and the history of the Turkish Revolution at the Faculty of Political Science, Ankara. On several occasions during this period I was invited to be a visiting professor at various American universities. I came to the School of International Affairs at Columbia University in 1953–54. In 1956 I was awarded a Rockefeller Fellowship to spend one year as a research fellow at Harvard University; and in 1967 I spent one semester at the Department of Near Eastern Studies at Princeton University.

Prior to 1971 I had never considered the possibility of moving permanently to the United States, but in 1971 the History Department at Harvard

University invited me to deliver two lectures, and the idea of my joining the department on a permanent basis was discussed. Around the same time, Professor Thomas Naff of the Department of Oriental Studies at the University of Pennsylvania invited me to join his department on a five-year contract, but because I had not yet made up my mind about leaving Turkey permanently I felt that I should not accept such a long-term offer. The next year, 1972, brought a very handsome offer from the University of Chicago as University Professor with responsibility in the Department of History for teaching and supervising research in Ottoman history. During the 1970s Turkey was in the throes of student riots sparked by the revolutionary left movement, and it was becoming increasingly difficult to maintain order in the university classrooms. Guns were being shot off in the corridors, confrontations between the students and the police became a daily occurrence, and there were many student fatalities as well. During the time of the funeral processions for these students the Faculty was routinely closed and all academic work ground to a halt. In such an atmosphere, it became virtually impossible to carry out either teaching or research, and so I decided to broach the matter of leaving Turkey for America with my wife Şevkiye. Şevkiye and I had been married since 1945 and by that time she had become chair of the Arabic department at the Faculty and an established scholar in her own right. I knew that accepting the offer at Chicago would entail considerable sacrifice for her. When, however, she agreed to accompany me, I accepted the offer from Chicago and we moved to Hyde Park, taking with us our grandson Gökhan, who had been born two years earlier. From 1972 to present I have lived in Chicago, and having grown up in the densely urbanized environment of Istanbul, I quickly adjusted to life in one of America's big cities. My home near the shore of Lake Michigan is only 20 minutes walking distance from the University.

When we arrived the spirit of the history department at the University of Chicago was William McNeil, author of the *Rise of the West*. I had met this paragon of global historians twice previously at meetings in Venice and Madison, Wisconsin. It was McNeil's ambition to make the history department at the University of Chicago into a center where specialists representing all areas of the globe could gather, and with this view in mind it would have been unthinkable that Ottoman history should fail to be represented in the department's program of study. Among the other members of the department at that time were Europeanists, such as the department chair, Karl Morrison, a specialist on Medieval European history; Erich Cochrane, a specialist on the Italian Renaissance; and Leonard Krieger, an expert on European intellectual history. The Asianists included Donald Lach, author of *Asia in the Making of Europe*, and the historian of China Ping-ti-Ho. This distinguished group of scholars gained Chicago's Department of History a reputation as one of the world's foremost centers for historical research. At Chicago it was possible to attend an interesting guest lecture delivered by an expert in the field nearly every day, and interdisciplinary work in social sciences was particularly encouraged through the medium of specialized seminars and the work of the Committee on Social Thought. Chicago's library, which contains over four million volumes, also acted as a stimulus to serious historical research. In my opinion developing nations should follow America's example in devoting resources to their libraries as a critically important stimulus to both education and modernization. The University of Chicago, as an institution which places primary emphasis on original research and publication, allows its professors the maximum degree of freedom in determining their teaching preferences and priorities. As a result, I was able to adjust my teaching schedule with a view to achieving harmony with my own current research interests, thereby widening the scope of my research to include new topics, while at the same time making optimal use of my spare time for publication activity. In my opinion the University of Chicago provides the ideal working environment for scholars. Following my retirement in 1986 I remained active at the university and continued to oversee the progress of my doctoral students' work. At the same time I have maintained close ties with my colleagues.

Turning now to the situation of Turkish Studies at the University of Chicago, it may be said that the beginnings of the program date from the academic year 1962–63, when Richard Chambers was first appointed to the Department of Near Eastern Languages and Cultures. Shortly before my arrival at the University of Chicago, Fahir Iz had been invited to join the NELC as Professor of Turkish Language and Literature. After Professor Iz's retirement and departure from Chicago, he was replaced by Robert Dankoff, a productive expert in the field of Turcology. At the University of Chicago it has been possible for graduate students, after completing their elementary language training, to conduct original historical research using Ottoman sources.

During my years at Chicago I trained twelve such advanced graduate students and all of them conducted primary research in the Ottoman archives of Istanbul, wrote original doctoral theses, and now hold positions at a variety of universities. As they have progressed in their careers they continue to publish original scholarly contributions relating to the history of the Middle East during the Ottoman centuries. My primary goal in training these graduate students was always to prepare them as experts in Ottoman archival research, and my courses were always organized with that goal in mind. I made it a matter of principle to work very closely with my advanced doctoral students to ensure that they avoided the sad fate of some other so-called experts whose teachers and advisers allowed them to defend theses and even publish books knowing that their students command of Ottoman Turkish was only barely adequate.

In recent years the efforts at modernizing archive administration and the decision to liberalize access to the Ottoman archives has broadened the possibilities for conducting serious research into Ottoman history. Because these archives serve as the repository for the national histories of more than twenty countries that have emerged from the former empire, it seems inevitable that the most important universities will want to create or maintain positions for Ottomanists within the general framework of historical studies.

We have noted with regret a recent trend at some universities where Ottoman studies and Turcology have been eliminated for financial reasons. Unfortunately, at my own institution, the University of Chicago, the position I had occupied was allocated to other fields and at present Ottoman studies is not being maintained at its former level. This is a particularly unfortunate development since a solid infrastructure for Ottoman studies had been created during my tenure at the University of Chicago. Particularly noteworthy in these developments was the creation of an important collection of Ottoman documents for researchers. The core of the collection was contributed by the late Professor Alexandre Bennigsen, who brought with him to Chicago an impressive number of microfilms from the Başbakanlık and Topkapı Sarayı archives. To this fund I added microfilms of a number of documents and manuscripts that I had collected over the years in the libraries and archives of Turkey. After photo-duplication, binding, and classification of this material, the university's library was enriched by a collection of Ottoman documents and historical manuscripts. It may be said without exaggeration that the collection of Ottoman documents now housed at Chicago's Regenstein Library constitutes one of the richest sources for research on Ottoman history outside Turkey. Using this material it would be possible to write any number of doctoral theses. At present the archive is being used by students and professors who make research visits to Chicago from all parts of the United States.

Apart from this archival material, Regenstein Library also houses one of America's richest collection of printed books in Ottoman and modern Turkish. In view of all this effort at building up a program of Turkish studies at the University of Chicago, it would have been unthinkable to abandon it or allow it to languish. Some of my colleagues at the university who shared this sentiment began serious efforts to raise endowment funds to found a chair in Ottoman Studies. Through a matching funds agreement, whereby half the money will be supplied by the Turkish government and the other half by the University of Chicago, a decision to create such a chair has recently been reached. Both the university's president, Hanna Gray, and the former Prime Minister of Turkey, Turgut Özal, gave their personal approval to these undertakings, and some significant progress towards the goal of funding this chair has already been made.

One of the intellectual traditions of the University of Chicago is the emphasis it places on interdisciplinary research and contacts. My own appointment at the university was principally in history, but I was also a member of the Department of Near Eastern Languages and Cultures and took an active interest in their activities. Within this department the languages and cultures of all the Middle Eastern countries from ancient Egypt and the civilizations of Mesopotamia to those of the present day are all taught. Collaboration with both students and faculty from this department has been of great benefit to me, and occasionally we have conducted joint seminars on closely related areas of research. For me one of the most interesting of these joint seminars was the comparative study of palace organization in the premodern societies of the Middle East. From the work of this seminar it emerged that some of the main features of palace organization, such as the division into male and female residential quarters, can be traced as a continuous tradition as far back as ancient Mesopotamia. In my opinion, neither the Ottoman empire, nor for that matter the Umayyad or Abbasid caliphates, can be properly understood and explained without reference to ancient Mesopotamian and Iranian civilizations.

These ancient civilizations bear a close affinity to their historical successors in many areas, such as concepts of state and kingship, taxation and landholding, traditions of urbanism and trading practices and, more generally, economic philosophy and social structure.

One of the most unforgettable memories of my two decades at the University of Chicago relates to the visit from Turkey of a group of sufis belonging to the Halvetî order. Led by their *sheykh*, Muzaffer, a group of more than twenty dervishes gathered in the university's chapel to witness a performance of the *sema* ritual of dancing and worship. For the occasion the chapel was filled with students and other observers. When the rituals were completed, *sheykh* Muzaffer joined some of the audience at a different location to respond to their questions. Some of the *sheykh's* disciples, both American and German, were also present. As the questioning began, the limits of Muzaffer's understanding of Islamic mysticism and sufi philosophy were soon revealed. Muzaffer's actual profession was bookseller at Istanbul's central book market, and his grasp of some theological concepts was not that profound. During the question and answer session he faltered a bit in some of his responses and finally lost his temper. Despite this momentary embarrassment, however, the evening as a whole was a great success and remains as one of my most truly memorable experiences at the university. The dervishes' cries in their repeated invocation of God's name reverberated off the chapel's ceiling filling the air with spiritual intensity, and I was genuinely moved. It struck me that such an event taking place in America's heartland could only have transpired through the miraculous intercession of the Prophet Muhammad himself.

Two of the most memorable and significant scholarly meetings that I participated in during my years at Chicago were the colloquium on slaves and slavery jointly organized by myself, Ralph Austen, and J. Coatsworth, and the conference on the age of Süleyman the Magnificent organized by myself and Richard Chambers. The latter conference was organized as an international symposium and the conference papers are currently in the process of being published.

I met my future wife Şevkiye when we were both studying Arabic at the Faculty of Languages, History, and Geography in Ankara. We were married in 1945, and in 1948 our daughter Günhan was born. A little more than twenty years later she gave birth to our grandson Gökhan. In 1989 my wife Şevkiye passed away. She had been not only a life's companion to me but also a colleague in scholarship and work partner. After completing her studies in Arabic language and literature, she became a faculty member and later department chair of the program in Arabic language and literature at the Faculty of Languages, History, and Geography at the University of Ankara. She prepared a scholarly edition of the *Layla wa Majnun* stories of Kays ibn Mulawwah and prepared an unpublished doctoral thesis on passages from the Arab chronicles relating to the Ottomans.

♦ ♦ ♦

In the foregoing I have described in my own words my life and accomplishments and failures in accordance with the Turkish proverb: "Şeyhin kerâmeti kendinden menkûl." (All the great deeds of the shaykh are related by the shaykh himself.)

CHAPTER 5

A Set of Accidents?

Charles Issawi

Sunt bona, sunt quaedam mediocria, sunt mala plura quae legis hic.
Aliter non fit, Avite, liber.*
—Martial, ep. I:16

I entered my chosen field of study, the Economics of the Middle East, in a roundabout way and reached the one on which I have been working for the last thirty years, the Economic History of the Middle East, relatively late. I went up to Magdalen College, Oxford, in 1934, with a scholarship in Modern History, but read PPE (Philosophy, Politics and Economics), concentrating on Economics. There I formed a lifelong friendship with Albert Hourani, who was also taking PPE and who helped me in innumerable ways.

At school my favorite subjects had been history and chemistry, but I never considered getting a degree in either. In the absence of any research facilities in chemistry at that time in Egypt, chemistry would have meant fixing dyes in a textile plant, or something equally exciting. And there were no jobs in history. Besides, I wanted to improve the world and thought economics was a

---

* "There are good things, there are some mediocre things, there are many bad things in what you read here. No book, Avitus, was written otherwise."

powerful tool for that purpose. I still think it is useful, though nowhere near so powerful.

At Oxford I had a brief encounter with Orientalism. A classical, as well as a modern, language was required of all undergraduates and (perhaps mistakenly) I had no wish to study Greek or Latin. However, a clause in the University statutes stipulated that students of "Asiatic or African descent" could take instead Arabic, Hebrew, Persian, or Sanskrit. I proclaimed loudly that I was an African of Asiatic descent and got the waiver. For two terms, along with half a dozen men, I sat at the feet of D. S. Margoliouth, with whom we read *Al-Fakhri* and *Sharh al-Baidawi*. His erudition was fantastic, but I had never heard anything resembling the sounds that issued from his throat when he spoke Arabic—which means that I had never met an Orientalist. I cannot say I was wildly excited by the course (especially since he omitted all the juicy bits saying, "That is not a nice passage") but managed to pass my examinations, which is more than the two other Arab students did. Their amazement and indignation were boundless: *"He* failed *me!"*

I also had my first live encounter with British socialism in the person of the able and prolific economic historian G. D. H. Cole. At school I had read his *Intelligent Man's Guide to Socialism and Capitalism*, which, together with Bernard Shaw's books, converted me to socialism. I happened to learn that his brother-in-law (the one Christian in a family of heathen Postgates) was headmaster of a British school in Cairo and managed to meet him and drop a broad hint about my admiration for Cole. "Would you like a letter of introduction to him?" Would I like a letter to God! I cherished the letter and, after one of Cole's lectures, gave it to him. "You are from Egypt, are you?" "Yes, Sir." "I met lots of Egyptians, dozens of them—didn't like them, didn't like them at all." "Oh!" "At the Peace Conference—Labour Party—asked me to meet representatives of many oppressed nationalities—didn't like any of them—didn't like them at all." I fully sympathized; I could see the poor man, badgered by Indians, Armenians, Irishmen, Poles, Jews, Arabs, and others, each convinced that theirs was the only cause in the world. And I had my first glimmering of the fact that there is no one as insular and xenophobic as a British socialist. But this encounter in no way dampened my respect for Cole or weakened my enthusiasm for socialism; an enthusiasm that lasted for another ten to fifteen years and has left traces to this day.

The tutoring we got at Oxford was unmatched. Twice a week we sat with our tutors, singly or in pairs, and read out our essays. A stony silence was followed by a devastating demolition of our essay and suggestions as to how it might be improved. I remember very vividly one such experience, on Kant's *Analytic.* I never worked so hard in my life—reading, thinking, walking to get my ideas straight. I then wrote what I thought was a masterpiece. The only comment was "Fine, now put this into English."

My philosophy tutor, T. D. Weldon, a bachelor, was truly exceptional in his devotion to the College and students. We had a standing invitation to drop in every evening, drink his beer, and discuss philosophy, until 11 PM when he shooed us off. He affected great cynicism: If the Germans want Czechland,[1] let them have Czechland. If they want Jugland,[2] let them have Jugland. And so on. But during the vacations, I am told, he wrestled with the souls of prison inmates. My economics tutor, Redvers Opie, was also able but, being married (to F. W. Taussig's daughter), he had less time for us but invited us to musical afternoons. He had studied at Harvard and kept on telling us how excellent things were in America, which we received with great skepticism. He knew his Marshall backwards (all eight editions) and drilled us in it. On the other hand he didn't really understand what Keynes was trying to say and we were equally confused; it took us some years to absorb Keynes.

I should add that, to please my father, who thought I would make a good lawyer (he was surely mistaken), I entered my name in the books of the Inner Temple in London and conscientiously ate my dinners there, three times a term, for three years. I even passed an examination, intending to take the rest after my graduation from Oxford. However, by the time I did graduate, it had become clear to me (and to my father) that I was not going to become a lawyer, and the matter was dropped.

By a strange coincidence, while I was eating my dinners at the Inner Temple my future colleague, Bernard Lewis, was doing the same at the adjacent Middle Temple. He too had no intention of becoming a lawyer but was also trying to please *his* father. He too took a couple of exams and then went on to greener pastures.

As an undergraduate I was a member of the Labour Party and the Oxford Union and occasionally participated in debates. Oxford was a very lively place politically, and my contemporaries included Harold Wilson, Edward Heath,

Denis Healey, Roy Jenkins, Reginald Maudling, Keith Joseph, Christopher Mayhew, and other future ministers.

I did well in my final examinations but neither I nor my tutors suggested I continue with graduate work. I was anxious to start "doing things" and had no desire to pursue an academic career. And their attitude was, "If you want to write a book, go and do it, but why waste our time and yours in writing it here?" As a result, none of us stayed on for graduate studies, and none regretted it. I now realize, of course, that I should have gone to Harvard or Columbia and got a Ph.D. in economics, which would have given me a technical training that would have been very useful. But since perception usually lags a generation behind reality, my picture of American universities corresponded to what they had been in 1910, and it never occurred to me to go to one. I had dreamed of studying at Heidelberg or Tübingen, but in 1937 German universities were hardly attractive.

On my return to Cairo in 1937 I was appointed as secretary to the Under Secretary at the Ministry of Finance. Since I did not have an Egyptian degree, a special dispensation had to be obtained, and the Official Gazette solemnly announced that, at its last session, the Cabinet had taken several decisions, including a credit of several million pounds for public works and the appointment of Charles effendi Issawi to a Grade Six post in the Ministry of Finance at a salary of £E 15. My work, at the center of what was by far the most important and powerful Ministry, gave me a panoramic view of the Egyptian economy, of which I of course knew nothing. It also gave me a good insight into the workings of the Egyptian bureaucracy, which, unsatisfactory as it was, was probably far more efficient than those of the other Arab states. The centralization was horrendous. The transfer of the most minor of officials from one town in Upper Egypt to another required the signature of the Under Secretary, and so did the promotion of a Lecturer in the Faculty of Arts. My boss, Amin 'Uthman pasha, usually came in at 6 PM—we used to say he came for Dawn Prayers—to find a heap of files two feet high on his desk. Of these he managed to dispose of perhaps six inches before being caught up in the day's work.

After a year I moved to the National Bank of Egypt, a private British-run organization that performed some of the functions of a Central Bank. After a training in banking, I was put at the head of a small research unit. One of our duties was to prepare a monthly bulletin, which ceased publication during the Second World War but resumed later to become perhaps the most useful and reliable source of information on the Egyptian economy.

While at the bank I also served for two years as secretary to the Governor and attended board meetings, thus becoming acquainted with Egypt's financial elite. They were not inspiring, except for the President, Ali Shamsi pasha, a cultivated and enlightened man, to whom I privately referred as *le roi soleil*. Our research unit kept a good set of files on the Egyptian economy, and I read all the available literature, which was meagre although far more abundant than on any other Middle Eastern country. The main books were by P. Arminjon (1912), M. A. Rifaat (1935), A. E. Crouchley (1936), and Wendell Cleland (1936). There were also a few, mostly mediocre, doctoral theses presented at French or Swiss universities and a few even more mediocre volumes in Arabic. However, some excellent articles were published in the 1930s, mainly in *Egypte Contemporaine*, the journal of The Royal Society, by such authorities as C. Bresciani-Turroni, J. I. Craig, E. Minost, E. Hallett, Hamed 'Azmy, R. El-Shanawany, and M. A. Zahra. The fact is that it was only in the late 1930s and 1940s that well-trained Egyptian economists came back from England, men of the calibre of Muhammad 'Ali Rif'at, 'Ali al-Gritly, and Nazmi 'Abd al-Hamid, to be followed in the 1950s and 1960s by even better graduates of American universities. I got to know these men through my work at the Bank or at meetings of The Royal Society, where I gave occasional lectures or papers and wrote articles for *Egypte Contemporaine*. I also contributed to *al-Majalla al-Jadida*, a review edited by the well-known writer Salama Musa.

I felt the lack of a comprehensive study and when, in the summer of 1942, my good friend and former classmate Albert Hourani suddenly popped up in Cairo and showed me the manuscript of his book on Syria and Lebanon. I was fired with what would be called "Socialist emulation" in the Soviet Union and elsewhere vulgar jealousy. By March 1943 I had the typescript of *Egypt: An Economic and Social Analysis*, which Albert smuggled out of the country. It was a comprehensive and analytic study that contained lots of purple prose, but it was an angry and intemperate work—even though I still believe it was right on fundamentals. War conditions delayed publication until November 1947, and it immediately ran out of print. Belatedly the government banned it in 1950. This afforded me a rare pleasure. In 1958, having returned to Cairo and the monarchy being gone, I bought some books in a bookshop and gave my name and address. "Oh, you are Mr. Issawi," said the owner. "We have your book in the basement. It is banned by the police." For a brief moment I felt like Lenin. For some years my book—and its much fuller, more analytic and more judicious successors—*Egypt at Mid-Century*, published in 1954 and translated into Russian, and *Egypt in Revolution*, published in 1963 and translated into Hebrew—was the only one of its kind. In the 1960s, however, a spate of excellent studies came out by Bent Hansen, Donald Mead, Robert Mabro, Mahmud Abd al-Fadil, Samir Radwan, and, more recently, by John Waterbury and Alan Richards. In addition there are numerous very good books on more specialized topics, such as population and agriculture. Altogether, by now Egypt is far better covered than any other Middle Eastern country, and perhaps than any in the Third World.

At this point I should perhaps say something about my two bosses. Amin 'Uthman pasha, the Under Secretary—and later Minister—of Finance, was a very well educated man with law degrees from both Oxford and Paris. He had an excellent command of English and a good one of French. He was an outstanding football player, very active in Old Victorian affairs, and a very loyal alumnus of Victoria College, where he taught Arabic translation. He was energetic, straightforward, scrupulously honest in financial matters, and enlightened in his views. His fatal flaw was his attachment to Britain. I once heard him make a speech in which he said that the Anglo-Egyptian union was an indissoluble marriage. The British, who on the whole enjoyed the marriage, knighted him, but the vast majority of Egyptians wanted a swift divorce and therefore regarded him as a British stooge. I do not think he was. He really believed that a close alliance with Britain (as provided for by the 1936 Treaty, in the conclusion of which he had played an important part) was in Egypt's best interests. But Egyptians were not concerned with such subtle distinctions, and he was assassinated in 1946 by a Muslim Brother.

Sir Edward Cook was a Cambridge mathematician who had risen in the Indian Civil Service to become Acting Financial Member of the Viceroy's Council. We got on very well and he often asked me to spend an evening with him since his eyesight was poor and he liked being read to. Once he requested me to read Pericles' speech, and when I had finished asked me if I knew anything about the translator. "Oh, yes," I replied eagerly. "He was one of my professors at Oxford, Sir Alfred Zimmern." I was then going to tell him, with much glee, how Zimmern had gone off with another don's wife and, a few weeks later, called on the ex-husband to apologize and explain. "Don't give it a thought, old chap," said the latter, "I have been waiting for it to happen for many years." Luckily I remembered, just in time, that Sir Edward had left his wife for another woman!

He told me a story I have always wanted to record. In 1920 or so, when Gandhi's resistance movement was at its peak and the Provincial Governors were urging strong action, Cook walked into the office of Lord Reading, the Viceroy, and noticed that he was very preoccupied. "Would you like me to return later?" he asked. "No, do stay. It is very refreshing to discuss the budget for a change." After a long silence Reading said: "I know I am right. I feel it in my bones. Cook, I belong to a race which has been persecuted for two thousand years because it took premature action against an agitator." Reading held out until the popular movement had scared enough prosperous Indians to make it possible to arrest Gandhi.

Early in 1943, my life nearly took a turn which would have put it well off course. I received, through a common friend, an offer from the Regent of Iraq, 'Abdul Ilah, to go to Baghdad and serve as his political advisor. He and I had been good friends at Victoria College in the early 1930s. My answer was brief, "Do you want both of us to be shot within six months?" He countered with another offer, would I serve as his economic advisor? This was much more sensible and tempting, but luckily I had just received another offer, from the American University of Beirut ((AUB). I often wonder how things would have turned out if I had gone to Baghdad. I probably would not have stayed there very long.

The job I was offered at the AUB was in the Political Science Department, to replace Cecil Hourani, who had joined the British army. Soon after my arrival we had a major crisis when the French authorities arrested the Lebanese President, Prime Minister, and several deputies. A group of us hurriedly wrote a pamphlet in English and Arabic, "The Problem of Lebanese Independence," which was clandestinely printed, conveyed to us in a cart hidden under a heap of tomatoes, and distributed to the U.S., British, and Soviet embassies and other institutions. We felt just like the Carbonari!

Those were the first of the Golden Years of Lebanon, which lasted until the end of the 1960s—a period of hope, intercommunal harmony, economic expansion, and intellectual florescence. For me, they were very happy and educative years. I taught Comparative Government and Political Theory, as well as a course in economics. I learned a lot from my excellent colleagues Charles Malik, Constantine Zurayk, Sa'id Himadeh, Roger Soltau, George Hakim, Husny Sawwaf, Anis Frayha, Zeine Zeine, and others. I should also mention Bayard Dodge, the last of the great AUB presidents. He was one of the few saintly people I have been privileged to know. At the same time he was a shrewd businessman. I was also, eventually, to discover that he was a very good scholar. When I was at Columbia, in the 1960s, he asked me to help him get his excellent *Fihrist* published by Columbia University Press, typically adding that he would see to it that the press did not lose money on the deal. There are few requests with which I complied with greater joy.

At my initiative, and that of George Hakim, we founded the journal *Silsilat al-Abhath al-ijtima'iya*, which later became *Al-Abhath*. I served as Editorial Secretary, translator, compiler of the Chronology, and general bottle washer and learned much about the Arab countries, of which I had been utterly ignorant. In particular I benefited from the company of that splendid man, Sa'id Himadeh, whose pioneering books on Syria, and Lebanon, Palestine, and Iraq were literally the only available economic studies on those countries.

Unlike my AUB colleagues, I kept in touch with the other, French, end of Beirut. [As the wife of my chairman, Mrs. Roger Soltau, put it, "For most AUB people the world ends at Hembekidis' Pharmacy," situated just outside the campus. Or, in the words of one of my francophone Jesuit friends, "Do occasionally get out of your gilded ghetto."] My main contacts were my Cairene friends Louis and Andrée Chédid (he later a distinguished scientist and she one of France's outstanding writers). I wrote several articles for a good review that appeared for a few years, *Les Cahiers de l'Est*, and gave some lectures at the Cénacle du Liban, a political and cultural forum.

In 1945–46 I received an offer from Swarthmore or Haverford (I cannot recall which) to teach International Relations, a subject that did not appeal to me. If I had accepted, my subsequent work would have been very different and, from my present vantage point, less interesting since so many people have been working in that field.

In my Political Theory course I touched briefly on Ibn Khaldun and, since there was no translation other than De Slane's of 1868, I decided to put into English the sections dealing with the social sciences. My translation was published in 1950 under the rather silly title of *An Arab Philosophy of History*. It proved successful, selling some 20,000 copies and being re-translated into Spanish, Bengali, Malayan, and Indonesian! Perhaps the greatest compliment it has received was when the newly founded review, *Past and Present*, quoted a passage from it as reflecting the journal's point of view on what historiography is all about. Recently it has been reprinted. Of course it has been superseded by Franz Rosenthal's complete and monumental translation, but only the other day I received a request to reproduce a sizeable chunk of it.[3]

While at the AUB I was asked to prepare a study on the economy of Palestine for presentation to the Anglo-American Commission of Inquiry in 1946. Part of it was included in *The Future of Palestine* (Arab Office, London, 1947). The exercise taught me a good deal about both the Arab and the Jewish sectors of Palestine.

Subsequently, the Arab Office asked me to serve at its Washington bureau, and I welcomed the opportunity both to strike a blow for the good cause and to see the United States. I edited *The Arab News Bulletin* and lectured and debated extensively, pointing out that the creation of a sovereign Jewish state would not only be unjust to the Arabs but would also cause great upheavals in the region—a notion entertained by few at that time. Moreover, the creation of a Jewish state in Palestine would not improve the situation of Jews elsewhere, who would continue to form the majority of the Jewish people. The horrors inflicted on Jews by Hitler demanded a worldwide solution, in which all countries, including the Arab ones, should bear part of the burden. I still think I was right on all three counts, though of course the situation has greatly changed since then. But there was no resisting the arm-twisting of the U.S. government on the foreign delegates at the UN; some of them, like the Cuban, held out, but most succumbed to the pressure because of the possible repercussions on their country, for example, the Liberians. As it was, the U.S. got just enough votes to pass the Resolution in the General Assembly. I vented my feelings in *The Arab News Bulletin* with a quotation from *Measure for Measure*:

> O it is excellent
> To have a giant's strength; but it is tyrannous
> To use it like a giant.

With the Arab Office running out of funds, owing to inadequate support by the Arab governments, and my former Dean showing reluctance to take me back, I applied to the World Bank and received a tentative offer with the understanding that I would be put to work on a region other than the Middle East since the Bank did not want its staff to negotiate with their own or neighboring countries. I wonder what things would have been like if I had accepted. Probably I would have become a development economist with a specialization in Latin America. However, in the meantime I was urged by a good friend, Zaki Hashem, who worked at the UN Secretariat, to apply for a post at that organization. I approached another good friend, Charles Malik, for advice. In his humorous way he said, "My friend, if you work for the Bank you know for whom you are working—American capitalism. If you work for the UN, you don't know for whom you are working." As it happened, I received a firm offer from the UN and joined the Economic Affairs Department of the Secretariat in February, 1948. The intention was that I should work for the projected Economic Commission for the Middle East, patterned on the ones for Europe, the Far East, and Latin America, with headquarters in Beirut. The prospect of living in Beirut on a UN salary and being able to travel all over the region was very appealing. Unfortunately for my daydreams, Israel soon became a member of the UN and therefore entitled to membership on the Commission. The Arab governments said, "No thanks, not now," and the matter was postponed from one session to another. Finally, it became clear that the Commission was not going to be formed. By then I was enjoying my work at the UN and also life in New York. We decided to stay and, eventually, become American citizens. I may add that I received offers from the AUB to return but turned them down. If I had gone back to Beirut, I am certain I could not have achieved half of what I did in the United States. The stimulus and opportunities were just not there, and the experience of equally able colleagues who remained at the AUB shows how great were the difficulties of doing serious work there.

When I joined it, the Department of Economic Affairs at the UN had some excellent economists, such as Michal Kalecki, Jacob Mozak, Folke Hilgerdt, and Hans Singer, as well as some very able younger men, and it produced some very good reports.[4] In the 1960s, however, the UN's work expanded enormously, the quality of its personnel seems to have deteriorated, and the reports suffered correspondingly.

My years at the UN were happy and productive. I learned a great deal from my contacts there and elsewhere. As at the National Bank, I learned to work to a deadline and to deliver my manuscript on time even if keeping it for a few more weeks would improve it somewhat My economic analysis improved. My knowledge of other regions greatly increased. I began to put the Middle East in its world perspective and to understand that some of its problems were peculiar to itself but that most were shared with other less developed countries. I also realized that people of different nationalities and cultural backgrounds could work together quite satisfactorily. My favorite example, just across the hall, was a unit consisting of a French Jesuit, a politically conservative Israeli, and a Soviet Russian who worked together very happily on Natural Resources. On the other hand, there were sharp divisions between members of the staff on ideological lines.

I was assigned to a small Middle East Unit, of which I eventually became the head. Our main task was the preparation of the *Annual Review of Economic Conditions in the Middle East*, patterned on the reports issued by the various Regional Commissions. In addition we read and commented on papers written in other parts of the Department and briefed the experts sent to Middle Eastern countries and evaluated their reports. Many of the latter were very interesting, giving a picture taken at the factory or field level. One theme kept recurring, both in the Middle East and in other less developed countries: the workers learn quickly and efficiently to *operate* machinery, but they do not *maintain* it. It is worth noting that, in his *Memoirs*, Nubar pasha says exactly the same thing about the Egyptian railwaymen in the 1850s. As an unkind critic once said, "In the less developed countries Churchill's famous appeal should read, 'Give us the job and we will finish the tools.'"

Another task to which I was assigned was land reform. I helped prepare a preliminary report, *Land Reform: Defects in Agrarian Structure as Obstacles to Economic Development* (1951), and was active in issuing and analyzing the questionnaires we sent to all countries and in writing the first report on *Progress in Land Reform* (1954). For both documents, the main work was done by that excellent woman, Doreen Warriner. I learned a great deal about agrarian problems, past and present.

On being hired, and somewhat to my surprise, I was informed that I was an expert on the Middle East and set out to become one. I learned Persian and enough Turkish to read such exciting literature as the *Bulletin of the Chamber of Commerce of Izmir*. I also read all there was to read on the Middle East, which was very little. I asked an Iranian colleague, Taghi Nasr, what were the best sources on the Iranian economy. As solemnly as he could, he said, "The best source is still Herodotus." In fact, the whole literature consisted of R. N. Gupta's flimsy account, *Iran: An Economic Study* (1947); three doctoral theses, in French, by Iranians; and such gleanings as could be found in the general books by Wilber, Haas, and Elwell Sutton.[5] For Turkey there was Donald Webster, *The Turkey of Ataturk* (1939); Barbara Ward, *Turkey* (1942); Akif Erginay, *Le budget turc* (1948); Şefik Bilkur, *National Income of Turkey* (1949); and Max Thornburg et al., *Turkey: An Economic Appraisal* (1949). For Iraq, Syria, and Lebanon there were the prewar books by Sa'id Himadeh, mentioned earlier; Gabriel Menassa, *Plan de reconstruction de l'économie libanaise* (1948); and photocopies of reports by the British consulting firm, Alexander Gibb.

For Palestine there was, in addition to Himadeh, *The Economic Organization of Palestine* (1938); P. J. Loftus, *The National Income of Palestine* (1944); and Robert Nathan et al., *Palestine: Problem and Promise* (1946), as well as a set of good government reports on population, landholdings, etc., and another set on various aspects of the Jewish trade unions and cooperatives. Egypt has been discussed earlier and there was nothing on the Arabian peninsula.

As for books covering the whole region, there were the monographs issued by the Middle East Supply Centre; A. Bonné, *The Economic Development of the Middle East* (1945); Doreen Warriner's excellent, *Land and Poverty in the Middle East* (1948); and some very good chapters in A. R. Prest, *War Economics of Primary Producing Countries* (1948).

As regards statistical sources, Egypt, Iraq, and Turkey issued annual year-books covering many aspects of society and the economy; Palestine (and sub-sequently Israel) had a monthly bulletin; and these countries, as well as Iran and Syria-Lebanon, had foreign trade bulletins and budget estimates. The UN *Statistical Yearbook* and *Monthly Bulletin* had just begun to be published and the International Monetary Fund and Food and Agriculture Organiza-tion were preparing the first issues of their bulletins. In these circumstances, the annual *Review* which we brought out was, for some years, by far the most comprehensive available survey of the Middle East.

The state of the art may be illustrated by an incident that happened in late 1948. Two highly respected statisticians from our National Income Unit came to see me and asked whether I had any *per capita* income figures for the Middle East. "Only for Israel," I answered. "But we need them," they said. "The Fifth (Budget) Committee of the General Assembly assesses all member states ac-cording to a formula which has, as one of its variables, the *per capita* income. Can't you provide us with some estimates? They are purely for internal con-sumption and will not be published." Eager to oblige, I started thinking. I had done enough work on Egypt to feel that I could supply an approximate figure. "Put $100 for Egypt," I said, which they did. "Turkey?" "Rather better off than Egypt. Put $125, and also for Lebanon." "Thank you so much. Syria?" "A little worse off than Egypt." This was true then, not now. "Put $85." "Iraq?" "The farmers are worse off than in Syria, but there is some income from oil, put $85." "Iran?" "I haven't the foggiest idea, but Iran and Iraq sound so much alike, and both have oil, put $85." "What about Yemen? "What," I asked, "is your lowest figure for a member state?" "Paraguay, $50," they said. "Put $40." "Thank you so much. You have been very helpful." "Not at all. Always ready to oblige."

I thought that was the end of the matter, but it was not. In the spring of 1949, the FAO (Food and Agriculture Organization) had a chapter on the Middle East in its *Annual Survey*. It began, "The Middle East is a poor re-gion—here are some illustrative figures," and proceeded to give my guesses! I was dismayed but consoled myself with the thought that since the *Survey* was mimeographed it would soon decompose and be forgotten. That fall, I went to Beirut with the Economic Survey Mission headed by Gordon Clapp, Gen-eral Manager of the Tennessee Valley Authority. When the time came to write our report, someone asked, "Are there any *per capita* income figures on the Middle East?" I tried to hide under the table, but some fool said, "There are the FAO figures." So my guesses came out *in print*, and for the next few years found their way into all sorts of regressions and correlations. "The evil that men do lives after them." Fortunately, by the mid-1950s more reliable estimates began to come out and mine faded into well-deserved oblivion.

In 1950 I received an invitation to give a course on the economy of the Middle East at the Harvard Summer School. I was thrilled, promptly accepted, and spent six very pleasant weeks at Cambridge. Another participant in the Summer Session was Sir Hamilton Gibb. We had never met but he had been extremely kind to me and helped me publish my first two books. Of course he was very reserved and tried to confine the conversation to small talk, such as the shoes sold at Filene's,[*] but he could not help being interesting all the same. I think my course at Harvard was the first course on the economics of the Middle East anywhere, though it is possible that Alfred Bonné had given a similar one in Jerusalem. It formed the basis for the courses I was to teach over the next forty years at Columbia, Princeton, and New York University.

At the UN I got to know J. C. Hurewitz, who worked in the Department of Political Affairs but then left to teach at Columbia. In the spring of 1951 he called and asked me if I would like to lunch with some of the Columbia economists, and I eagerly accepted what I thought was to be a purely social occasion. At that time, the Economics Department at Columbia was at the height of its glory. It had what was probably the best set of economists in the world—J. M. Clark, Ragnar Nurkse, George Stigler, Arthur F. Burns, and Arthur R. Burns (known to the students as "Fluctuations" and "Reform" Burns, respectively), Cecil Mills, Carl Shoup, James Angell, Abram Bergson, Joseph Dorfman, Albert Hart, William Vickrey, Carter Goodrich, Harold Barger, David Landes, and others. To my great surprise Arthur R. Burns, the Chairman, asked me if I could teach a course on Middle East economics, once a week, in the evening. I gladly accepted and received the required permission from the UN, which was very helpful in such matters. And so, as my wife said, I returned to academia like a drunk to a tavern, but by the back door.

---

[*] A local department store

My only previous contact with Columbia had been in 1949, when I thought of enrolling as a graduate student. The Chairman, James Angell, looked at my record and book and said, "We would very much like to have you, but have you thought of the mechanics? Two hours commuting each way from Lake Success [Headquarters of the UN] on top of an eight-hour day and you'll be in hospital in six months." That was the end of my velleity to get a doctorate—instead I was to dispense dozens of them over the next forty years.

To all intents and purposes the Middle East Institute at Columbia consisted, at that time, of J. C. Hurewitz, who taught history and politics, and Tibor Halasi-Kun, who taught Turkish language and culture. That of course does not include the Department of Middle East Languages and Cultures, which had such fine scholars as Arthur Jeffery and Isaac Mendelsohn, nor the eminent Jewish historian Salo Baron. Later we were to gather a highly distinguished group—Joseph Schacht, John Badeau, Ehsan Yarshater, Gerson Cohen, Nina Garsoian, Karl Menges, Edward Allworth, Dankwart Rustow, Kathleen Burrill, and others. I think I can claim we were second to none.

Our Dean of the School of International Affairs and father-figure was Schuyler Wallace, to whom I owe so much and who was one of the finest of the many fine people with whom I was privileged to work. I have seldom met so generous a man, and never one on whom power sat so lightly. He and his beautiful and gentle wife, Esther, did everything they could to make us feel at home; Columbia was a marvelous place to be in.

After I had taught for three years, Schuyler asked me whether I would like to join Columbia full-time. It took me and my wife ten minutes to decide, although the offered salary was lower than what I got at the UN—and, unlike the latter, was of course taxable. With much difficulty, I obtained a year's leave of absence from the UN, not wanting to burn my bridges. After a few months, I told Schuyler I would very much like to stay, provided I got tenure. The Economics Department, to which I had been appointed as Associate Professor, said they would look into the matter and began the usual procedures. In the meantime Schuyler took the question up with the Provost, who looked into my file and said, "But he *has* tenure." That was Columbia for you! When I see the agony through which young people pass nowadays to get tenure I cannot help feeling I had it easy. On the other hand, when I consider all the grants, leaves, and other sweeteners they enjoy, I am not so sure. My first sabbatical was in 1961, when I was 45; all my books and articles till then were written while carrying a full-time job, except for a few weeks of unpaid leave I took from the UN in 1953 to finish up my *Egypt at Mid-Century*. After that, the only leaves I had were one sabbatical from Columbia and two from Princeton. Still, on balance, I do not envy the younger generation and wonder whether, if I were starting today, I would have chosen an academic career.

My teaching at Columbia consisted of a course on the economy of the Middle East—at first for a whole year and later for a semester—and another on land-tenure. Later I gave a course on the modern economic history of the Middle East, discussed below. I also gave an introductory economics course at the School of International Affairs, which I called—informally— "Economics for Illiterates." It was the most demanding course I have ever undertaken, but also the most exciting and rewarding. At the beginning of the year I interviewed all entrants into the school. To those who had taken three or more semesters of economics as undergraduates I said, "Enroll in Gary Becker's course, and may the Lord have mercy on your soul." To the others—ranging between 60 and 100—I gave a course which was very different from Econ 101. I tried to make them understand what were the basic problems that *any* economy faced and how they were dealt with in the Western, Eastern, and Southern economies; I used a minimum amount of mathematics and jargon. The student response was very good, and many told me later that it had started them on a serious study of economics, some eventually getting Ph.D.'s in that subject.

I also participated, along with one or two visiting professors, in J. Hurewitz's seminar, which we optimistically referred to as "The Integrated Seminar." It was taken by all graduate students working on the region, who explored in it the topic on which they proposed to write their dissertation. Jay conducted the seminar in a masterly way, and I learned a great deal by watching him. First he would ask the students to "define their problem"—most did not even suspect they had one. He would make them come up to the blackboard, which they did with as much enthusiasm as soldiers leaving the safety of their trenches to advance into no-man's land. He would badger them and push them around, and many must have felt like strangling him. But they finally came out of it all with much clearer ideas. Many excellent dissertations were born in that seminar, but quite a few were sunk.

Also with Jay I gave a seminar on Middle East oil, he covering the political and I the economic aspect. In our first year we had students from Vene-
zuela, Iran, and Iraq, and it was perhaps no coincidence that, the following
year, OPEC was founded!

I had some very good students, drawn from a variety of disciplines and
backgrounds. My impression—which may be colored by my strong reaction
to the 1968 agitation—is that the quality improved steadily until the late
1960s, and then fell off sharply. My main difficulty was persuading good
economists to work on a Middle Eastern topic, unless they had some Middle
Eastern connection and already knew one language. Although we kept on receiving job offers for well-trained economists who knew Arabic (or, less frequently, Turkish or Persian) it was impossible to persuade a student who was
putting so much effort into learning economics to take on the additional burden of a difficult Middle Eastern language—or, for that matter, of Japanese,
Chinese, or even Russian. Besides, economists regard "area studies" as "below
dignity"; they honestly believe that economics is, like physics, independent of
time and space and that their theories apply to all cultures and periods; they
are, of course, right, but only in a very narrow sense, and the institutional and
cultural factors can make all the difference in any given situation. As a result,
I sponsored only about ten doctoral dissertations in my twenty years at Columbia, and somewhat more master's theses. However, I earned my keep by
being the second reader of a very large number of dissertations on Middle
Eastern history, politics, and geography. Among those students, Eliyahu
Kanovsky, Samir Makdisi, Alfred Musrey, Carol Greenwald, Fatemeh
Moghaddam, and Manuchehr Parvin have made valuable contributions to
Middle East economics and Hrair Dekmejian, Irene Gendzier, Ann Moseley
Lesch, and John Waterbury to politics. Other students have done well in government and business. I also served as Director of our Institute in 1962–64,
but my tenure was not memorable; I followed Eisenhower's (and Ibn Khal-
dun's) precept—that the best ruler is the one who does least.

In 1958 I collected a set of articles I had written in Arabic, and others that
I translated from English, in a book published in Beirut under the title *Mush-
kilat Qaumiyya*. A couple of years later I had the satisfaction of seeing a copy
in a bookshop in the old quarter of Tunis. More to the point, I co-authored,
with Mohammed Yeganeh, *The Economics of Middle Eastern Oil*, published in

1962. I had recruited Yeganeh in 1948, from among a group of Iranian graduate students, to work in our unit at the UN. We soon took to each other, and our friendship survived the acid test of co-authorship. As far as I am concerned, he has all the virtues, and when Dr. Mossadegh visited the UN I told his colleague, Dr. Baghai, that Yeganeh was the best young man in Iran. He later rose to high office, including Governor of the Central Bank and Minister of Finance, and was almost the only one of the Shah's ministers whom the Revolutionary government did not accuse of malfeasance.

Yeganeh was deeply, indeed passionately, interested in petroleum—I once told him that, just as Spinoza was "intoxicated with God," he was "intoxicated with oil." We shared an office and I remember his whoop of joy when he came across the first firm figures on the cost per barrel in Saudi Arabia and Bahrain on pages 25,008 and 25,022 of a U.S. Senate report; they were the first for the whole region. He knew an immense amount about oil and I learned a great deal from him about that fascinating industry. I suggested writing the book but he did at least two-thirds of the really important work; the book could well have been written without me—though it probably would not have been—but certainly not without him. It was a useful work since, before anyone else, we asked the important and awkward questions regarding cost, price, investment, and returns. Some of our conclusions were startling, e.g., that net annual returns on company investments in the Middle East averaged, in 1948–60, some 67 percent per annum!

When we started our work I told that wise old man Terry Duce, the Vice-President of ARAMCO, that we were writing a book on oil. "Can't be done," he said. "Those who know about oil can't write and those who can write don't know anything about oil." When we had completed our manuscript we showed it to the man in charge of public relations at ARAMCO, who promptly photocopied it and sent it to half a dozen companies. We received some thirty single-spaced pages of comments. Fortunately, none questioned our findings and we were easily able to meet the main suggestions, some of which struck me as odd—for example, they strongly objected to the word "control" in, say, "the seven major oil companies control 80 percent of reserves, 56 percent of refineries," etc., but were perfectly happy when we substituted "own." The book was translated into Arabic and published in Baghdad—and was used as a textbook in Saudi Arabia. Unfortunately, a Japanese translation was never completed because of the translator's death. The book received good, though few, reviews and was probably the best study available until the 1970s; the events of that decade naturally changed the situation beyond recognition. I returned to oil in 1972, when I wrote a pamphlet on *Oil, the Middle East and the World* for the Center for Strategic and International Studies in Washington. In it I concluded that since demand was increasing rapidly, supplies were getting tight and control was passing from the hands of the companies to those of the governments; dependence on Middle East and North African oil was growing fast and the price of this oil "will rise, steadily and appreciably, over the next decade or two" (p. 74). This forecast, like others I have made, correctly identified the trend, but missed out on the timing and magnitude! Later in the 1970s I wrote a couple of articles on oil and then dropped the subject.

An interesting consequence of my pamphlet was my involvement in a law suit. I received a call from a very distinguished law firm asking whether I could prepare a brief and serve as an expert witness in a suit between two largish oil companies. I was asked to argue that a rise in oil prices could have been foreseen at the time the contract was made and did so with a clear conscience. Fortunately, the suit was settled out of court.

In the late 1950s I began to feel unhappy with my work on Middle Eastern economics. For one thing, I realized that one could no longer keep up with the area *as a whole*, though one could and should continue to teach it. Too many things were happening in the Middle East and too many changes were taking place. Material was becoming much more reliable and abundant. I became convinced—and still am—that economic research on the region should be carried out by institutions, preferably those on the spot, like Central Banks. Where this is not possible, bodies like the World Bank and International Monetary Fund, which have both access to unpublished information and a large qualified staff, could do a very good job. The establishment of the UN Economic Commission for West Asia, with headquarters first in Beirut and then in Baghdad, was a further step in the right direction. A list of articles published in its *Studies on Development* (1988) includes "A Macro-Econometric Planning Model of the Syrian Arab Republic," "Manpower and Employment Planning in Iraq and the Syrian Arab Republic," "Economic Structure, Foreign Trade and Capital Needs of Yemen in the Second United Nations

Development Decade," etc., as well as a Bulletin giving ample details on the National Accounts of Bahrain, Egypt, Iraq, Jordan, Kuwait, Lebanon, Oman, Qatar, Saudi Arabia, Syria, the United Arab Emirates, and North and South Yemen. Of course these studies should still be taken with a large pinch of salt. The rigor of the analysis should *not* blind the reader to the fact that the underlying data are often shaky. Nevertheless, they indicate the progress made.

Individuals have also made many valuable studies. I have mentioned some on Egypt; for Turkey there are the books by Z. Y. Hershlag and William Hale; for Iran the ones by J. Bharier and J. Amouzegar and M. Fikrat, and more recent ones by H. Amirahmadi and M. Parvin and by K. McLachlan; for Israel by N. Halevi and R. Klinot-Malul and by Y. Ben-Porath; and for Iraq by E. Penrose. Useful books have been written on Kuwait and Saudi Arabia by R. El-Mallakh and F. Al-Farsy, respectively. Syria and Lebanon still remain to be done. Many years ago a Lebanese student—an excellent econometrician—was urging me to write a book on Lebanon. "Me?" I replied, "*You* should write one." "No," he answered, "I can only work with much data, but you can with little." The prospect does not seem to have attracted others, but I should mention the book edited by André Raymond on Syria (in French).

In addition to these country studies, there are very good books on the region as a whole, for example, Yusif Sayigh's *The Economics of the Arab World*; Charles Cooper and Sidney Alexander (eds.), *Economic Development and Population Growth in the Middle East*; Marion Clawson, *The Agricultural Potential of the Middle East*; Galal Amin, *The Modernization of Poverty*; and, just out, Alan Richards and John Waterbury, *Political Economy of the Middle East*, an outstanding piece of work.

There have also been many good articles, published in the *International Journal of Middle Eastern Studies* (IJMES), the *Middle East Journal* (MEJ), and in more technical journals. I have not mentioned works in other European languages because there have been very few, but there is a growing literature in Arabic, Hebrew, Persian, and Turkish. The fact is that, in striking contrast to the situation in the 1930s and 1940s, there are now hundreds, or even thousands, of highly qualified economists in the Middle East. Most are engaged in government or business, but many are doing very valuable research as well. The future is safe in their hands, and also in that of American economists working on the region, whose numbers have grown immensely. When the

Middle East Studies Association was founded in 1967, I may have been the only member who had any interest in economics—I was certainly the only one among the 'Founding Fathers' of the Association. By 1989, however, of the approximately 1,600 members, 52 members, or 3.25 percent, gave their discipline as Economics; moreover many of these members, as well as some persons outside the Association, have founded the Middle East Economic Studies Association, which has been quite active and now has a membership of about 100. The 1990 meeting lists 75 active participants in 13 panels. And the *International Journal of Middle Eastern Studies* regularly carries economic articles, some of them highly mathematical; I am not sure it should, since they are unintelligible to 95 percent of the readers, but perhaps this makes sense until such time as a journal specifically devoted to Middle Eastern economic matters is founded.

To go back in time, around 1960 I began to feel that I ought to change my field, or rather to acquire a new interest. Schuyler Wallace, to whom I mentioned this, said, "What about Economic History?" I realized he had hit the bull's eye. My approach to economics had always been historical, and not mathematical. I had certain comparative advantages, such as a fair knowledge of general Middle Eastern history and a set of Middle Eastern and European languages. I had grown up with French and Arabic as well as English, picked up Italian from my schoolmates and in the streets of Alexandria, taught myself German shortly before the war and Spanish in the 1940s, and I learned Russian in return for the compliment the Soviets paid me by translating my *Egypt at Mid-Century* in 1958; the latter was helped by the fact that I had picked up some Polish by osmosis from my wife. As mentioned earlier, I also taught myself Persian and some Turkish at the UN. Above all, modern economic history was a field in which almost no work had been done and which, as far as I knew, no one was studying.

I was certainly lucky in my timing, but I also, perhaps, showed some prescience. In 1960, the field was empty; at present, there are several excellent scholars working in it. I was lucky to get in when I did, but it is also possible that I helped to stimulate interest in the subject.

I have given elsewhere a fairly extensive review of the available literature, which I will summarize very briefly.[6] For the medieval period a good amount of research had been done and a few first class scholars were active—Eliyahu

Ashtor, Aziz Atiya, David Ayalon, Claude Cahen, Ahmad Darraj, Aziz Duri, Andrew Ehrenkreutz, Subhi Labib, Maxime Rodinson, Avram Udovitch, and, above all, S. D. Goitein. For the early modern period, there were the writings of some fine Ottomanists—Omer Lutfi Barkan, Halil Inalcik, Bernard Lewis, Robert Mantran, and Stanford Shaw. But for the nineteenth century, I said that the state of knowledge was like the schoolboy's definition of a net: "a bunch of holes tied together with string...The trouble is that, here, the holes are so wide that rather large fish can easily slip through, while the string is so weak that one cannot be sure of keeping what one thinks one holds."[7] Only two good general surveys had been made—on Egypt A. E. Crouchley, *The Economic Development of Modern Egypt* (1938), and on the Ottoman Empire A. D. Novichev, *Ocherki Ekonomiki Turtsii* (1937). Several useful books had appeared in Egypt on Muhammad Ali, at his centenary, by such scholars as Moustapha Fahmy, Ali al-Gritly, Ahmad al-Hitta, and others; there was also David Landes, *Bankers and Pashas* (1958), and Abdel Maqsud Hamza, *The Public Debt of Egypt* (1954). On the Ottoman Empire there was *Tanzimat* (1940), a collective work, and a recent study by E. R. J. Brünner, *De Bagdadspoorweg* (1957), as well as older works on the Public Debt and the Baghdad railway. There was also a good unpublished thesis by Saleh Haider, "Land Problems of Iraq" (1942).

Meanwhile, unbeknown to me, several excellent scholars were beginning to till various corners of the field. At Oxford, Roger Owen was writing *Cotton and the Egyptian Economy* (1969), to be followed by *The Middle East in the World Economy* (1981) and various articles. In Paris André Raymond was at work on his monumental *Artisans et commerçants au Caire* (1973), Dominique Chevallier on *La Société du Mont Liban* (1971), Lucette Valensi on *Fellahs tunisiens* (1977), and other scholars such as Miège, Nouschi, and Despois. In Jerusalem Gabriel Baer was writing *A History of Landownership in Modern Egypt* (1962), to be followed by *Egyptian Guilds in Modern Times* (1964) and other books and articles before his untimely death. At Harvard Helen Rivlin's *Agricultural Policy of Muhammad Ali* (1961) was just about to appear. And in Moscow a group of young scholars were doing valuable research, notably A. L. Fridman on Egypt and I. M. Smilyanskaya on Lebanon.

In 1960 I started a course on the Economic History of the Arab World and put together a reader, *The Economic History of the Middle East* (1966), and thereby hangs a tale. I had just begun working on my project when I got a call from an eminent economic historian inviting me to a conference on the Economic History of Asia. He told us he would like to commission six books (one each on the Middle East, India, Southeast Asia, and Japan and two on China) to consist of translations of sources, critical notes, bibliographies, etc. An application would be made to the National Science Foundation for $125,000 for *each* book. We all drooled and gladly accepted to do our bit. Very sensibly, the NSF turned the project down, so I went to Schuyler Wallace and told him I would like $900 to cover costs of translation and photocopying. He said, "Make it $1,200," which I readily did. As it turned out, my total expenses were $1,060, and I offered to return the balance to his Administrative Assistant. "Don't ever do such a thing again," she said. "It confuses the accounts. Just spend the money." I learned another lesson in economic history.

The book consisted of articles and extracts from reports in various European and Middle Eastern languages, with introductory essays and notes, a glossary of terms, a note on weights and measures, and a fairly extensive bibliography. It obviously met a need, since it sold quite well, went into paperback, and was widely used and quoted. This encouraged me to write more scholarly documentary histories—*The Economic History of Iran* (1971, translated into Persian), *The Economic History of Turkey* (1980), and *The Fertile Crescent* (1988, translated into Arabic). All these volumes followed a uniform pattern: a large number of unpublished documents from the British, French, U.S., Austrian, and Ottoman archives; and translations from books, articles, and reports in Arabic, Armenian, Hebrew, Persian, Turkish, French, German, Russian, Italian and Dutch (of course I got help with some of these languages!) grouped by topic (Agriculture, Industry, etc.), preceded by essays and notes, and followed by a note on weights and measures, plus a full bibliography. These books do not make for exciting reading and their sales have been low, but they are the only ones of their kind and serve a useful function.

However, I never thought I was writing bestsellers. The fact is that very few people are interested in economic history, and fewer still in the economic history of a backwater like the nineteenth-century Middle East. I suspect that many people would agree with Carlyle's description of economics as "the dismal science" and a few with Henry Ford's "History is bunk," from which it presumably follows that economic history is dismal bunk. This is a pity for as

J. H. Clapham put it, "Of all varieties of history, the economic is the most fundamental. Not the most important; foundations exist to carry better things ... But economic activity, with its tools, fields, trade, inventions, and investments, is the basement of man's house."

Indeed one can say that social relations stand out most sharply in the economic field; it is there that power relations and clashes and cooperation between various social groups can be most clearly discerned. And economic activities tend to leave records that are more abundant than most, that are less ambiguous, and that lend themselves most readily to measurement and quantitative analysis; all of which does not, however, mean that all reality can be reduced, directly or ultimately, to economic factors.

In 1979, although *The Fertile Crescent* was still in its early stages, I decided that the time was ripe for a synthesis and began work on *An Economic History of the Middle East and North Africa* (1982, translated into Arabic). I had a great piece of luck: I sent back the copy-edited manuscript the day before I had a heart attack. Although I recovered well and have led a normal and active life, I doubt whether I could have borne the tense and sustained effort needed to hold together a book covering such a wide subject, as distinct from the more mechanical and compartmentalized work needed for the documentary histories. In this book I let myself go, and it is more interesting than its predecessors; it is at once a textbook and one designed for the general historian or economist; it has sold well in hardcover and paperback and has been extensively used.

In all my writings on economic history, I have avoided controversy and methodological debate and have refused to follow prevailing fashions or jargon. My objective has been to provide solid material in a field where it was sorely lacking. Not that I am a blind empiricist who believes that the accumulation of facts makes history. I fully subscribe to Werner Sombart's dictum: "No theory, no history."[8] Economic history, like other branches of history, is not just an assemblage of facts but a study of problems, an analysis of data and theories, in which the two are as inseparable as form is from matter. However, one must immediately ask, Which theory? Whose theory? My answer is the classical theory taught in the West for the last two hundred years, the theory of Adam Smith, Ricardo, Malthus, John Stuart Mill, Jevons, Pareto, Marshall, and Samuelson and the mainstream development theory of some of those thinkers and Schumpeter, Colin Clark, Simon Kuznets, J. R. Hicks, Roy Harrod, Ragnar Nurkse, W. A. Lewis, Albert Hirschman, and others. This theory is based on the centrality of the market and market mechanisms. I know that some highly learned and intelligent historians, like Karl Polanyi and M. I. Finley, have assured us that the concept of market, and its associated mechanisms and phenomena, is very misleading when applied to ancient times, including Rome. But the more I read Roman and Middle Eastern history—and even ancient Mesopotamian—the more I am impressed with the market phenomena displayed, such as rise and fall of prices, inflation, specialization of production, flow of bullion. And I am in deep sympathy with John Hicks, who made the Rise of the Market the central theme of his very stimulating incursion into history, *A Theory of Economic History*, tracing its origins to remote antiquity.

This theory supplies us with many sturdy tools that can help us work on the historical material: Opportunity Cost; Diminishing Returns of Factors of Production; Maximization—most of the time most producers and consumers act rationally, i.e., they seek to obtain the desired output with the smallest possible input of resources or, alternatively, to get the greatest possible output from the factors of production and materials at their disposal; Equilibrium—the market provides an equilibrating mechanism which, by raising or lowering prices, sets in motion forces that increase or decrease supply and demand; Marginal Productivity of Factors of Production; and lastly, for monetary phenomena, some version (more or less refined) of the Quantity Theory, at least to the extent that a large increase in money supply will, unless offset by other factors, tend to raise prices and a decrease to lower them, and a theory of foreign exchange that relates changes in the balance of payments to fluctuations in exchange rates and an equilibrating flow of bullion or other means of payment.

Needless to say these economic forces work within a social context that differs from place to place and are affected by a variety of geographical, religious, political, social, legal, customary, and other factors. Take Maximization, for instance. What—if anything—do people seek to maximize? income? capital? satisfaction? prestige? leisure? security (i.e., minimize risk)? Anthropologists working in different parts of the world have come up with very different answers. Some, like Clifford Geertz in his study of Moroccan bazaars,

maintain that the responses are economically very rational, though the underlying constraints may be different; others see much less rationality and more
custom and tradition. Clearly, the economic historian must be fully aware of
the non-economic factors at play and not force a factitious economic clarity on
a murky picture.

My findings have not been sensational. I have tried to describe the inte-
gration of the Middle East in the world economy and its effect on various aspects—population, trade, transport, agriculture, industry, finance, etc.
Whenever possible, I have quantified. I also tried to measure the impact of
these changes on the living conditions of various classes and groups. I tried to
show why, around the turn of the century, they aroused a nationalist reaction
which accelerated after the First World War and resulted in taking over the
economy from the hands of the foreigners and minorities who had previously
controlled it.

I have done little work on pre-nineteenth-century economic history but
feel rather strongly about one of my conclusions: Europe overtook the Middle
East in the late Middle Ages and not, as is so often maintained nowadays, in
the sixteenth, seventeenth, or even eighteenth century. And this was due primarily to two facts: European technology, particularly in the field of energy,
began to develop much earlier and European birth rates (and probably death
rates) were much lower, owing mainly to later marriage, enabling Europe both
to produce a larger surplus available for productive investment and not to
waste that surplus on mere "vegetative growth." In other words, the causes of
Europe's subsequent economic domination are intrinsic (the accumulation of
physical and human capital) rather than external, i.e., the profits of trade and
the loot of empire. Of course the latter helped greatly, and so did the accretion
of strength due to the colonization of the New World. By the same token, the
primary causes of the poor performance of the Middle East were internal, and
not the retardation inflicted on it by the impact of Europe, or of the World
Economy as in recent formulations. In, say, 1500 the Middle East was just less
efficient; that is, less technologically advanced, less literate, and less economically dynamic than Europe. This of course does *not* mean that later on, say in
the eighteenth century, European competition, and in the nineteenth century
European imperialism, did not have adverse effects on the Middle East.[9]

Of all the currently fashionable schools of economic history the one centered around the French journal *Annales* seems to me to take the non-economic factors most fully into account. But before discussing this theory a few words may be said about the Cliometric school, which enjoys great prestige in the United States. Its hallmark is the attempt to fit historical data into econometric models and it has come out with some significant, though strongly contested, conclusions, such as the profitability (or non-profitability) of slavery in the *antebellum* south. It is evident that such models can be applied only where abundant, reliable, and consistent data are available, and this is definitely not the case in the Middle East until after the Second World War. For example, to take the most obvious and fundamental series, population, the first census in Lebanon and Syria was taken in 1921–22 (and none has been taken since in Lebanon), in Turkey the first was in 1927, in Iraq in 1947, in Iran and Sudan in 1956, and in the Arabian peninsula in the 1960s; the one exception is Egypt, where an incomplete census was taken in 1882 and a complete one in 1897. Similarly, except for Egypt—and more doubtfully Turkey—no reliable foreign trade statistics are available before the 1920s, or even later. In these circumstances, econometric models are out of the question. But the papers on Egypt by Bent Hansen—an excellent economist turned economic historian—show how rigorous analysis can be used to produce impressive and highly significant results. If, as I hope, these papers are collected in a book, they will constitute a milestone far beyond any reached so far by other travellers in our discipline. And the benefit of applying rigorous economic analysis to available data has been clearly demonstrated by Şevket Pamuk (a student of Hansen's) in his book on foreign trade and the balance of payments, *The Ottoman Empire and European Capitalism, 1820–1913* (1987).

The *Annales* school is very much aware of the role of the non-economic factors and of the importance of taking them into account. First of all, it stresses the effects of physical and human geography, which tend to be ignored or treated as constants by economists. I should perhaps point out that in a region like the Middle East, which lies at the edge of the main rainfall systems of the old world (the Monsoon and Atlantic), fluctuations in precipitation are frequent and violent and have a decisive influence on agriculture and other economic activities. Hence any rainfall cycles that may be discerned could go a long way toward explaining the course of economic and social change. As far as I know, the only systematic study on this subject was by Karl Butzer in *Erdkunde* (XI) 1957.

Secondly, the Annalists are very interested in a set of disciplines closely related to economic history, such as sociology, anthropology, psychology, archaeology, and art history. This is particularly important in the Middle East which, in the last seven or eight centuries, has undergone less transformation than, say, Europe, which means that its old "structures"—to use a favorite Annalist term—have survived in a better state and are still very relevant. Microstudies at the level of the village, urban quarter, or tribe carried out by geographers, sociologists, and anthropologists with a historical vision can be of incalculable help to the economic historian—one thinks of Xavier de Planhol's studies on Turkey and Jacques Weulersse's on Syria. Another field in which they have done excellent work is demography, e.g., Daniel Panzac, *La peste dans l'empire ottoman* (1985). Here it may be pointed out that the absence of parish registers in the Middle East means that the work done on medieval and modern Europe cannot be duplicated, but the Ottoman archives offer an alternative source which is just beginning to be explored, as the writings of O. L. Barkan and Michael Cook on the sixteenth century and of Enver Ziya Karal and Justin McCarthy on the nineteenth-century show. For the Arab countries, the court archives (*sijills*) represent a rich mine which is only just beginning to be exploited.

For a person trained in economics, the analysis done by this school falls far short of its descriptive power. The construction of models and their testing is almost completely absent and the laboriously compiled statistics used are not subjected to the revealing torture to which Cliometricians put them. The Annalists seem to have taken biology, rather than mechanics and hydrostatics (so beloved by economists), as their model and in this they could claim the support of the high priest of modern economic analysis, Alfred Marshall. But whatever one's views, one cannot but acknowledge the great contribution made by them to the study of the Middle East and, even more, North Africa.[10]

As for Marxism, I believe that its central thesis holds very well for European history. This can be summarized in two statements: first, history is a progression from Antiquity through Feudalism to Capitalism and thence to Socialism (the last seems somewhat dubious); and, secondly, the transition from one stage to another is due to changes in the Mode of Production (because of changes in technology and other factors) and the struggle between the classes formed by each mode—landlords, bourgeoisie, and proletariat. This scheme does not fit the Middle East at all well because both the modes of production and the social classes of the latter differ significantly from those of Europe.

Take Feudalism, for instance. The Islamic *iqta'*, as Claude Cahen, Bernard Lewis, and others have pointed out, is different from the European fief; the Ottoman timar is somewhat closer, but still dissimilar. *Iqta's* were granted by the monarch for a lifetime and were revocable, whereas fiefs were hereditary; *iqta's* were scattered, fiefs mostly consolidated; European lords built castles in their fiefs and lived in them and therefore had a basis of local power, whereas most *iqta'* holders dwelt in cities; in principle, there was no serfdom in Islam, unlike Europe, but in practice there was little difference between the two; lastly, in the Middle East, unlike Europe, judicial power was exercised by the government-appointed *qadi*, not the *iqta'* holder. More generally, state control was much greater in the Middle East than in Europe, which had a strong, independent, hereditary aristocracy.

Similarly, the Middle Eastern bourgeoisie was very weak compared to the European. Guilds were the breeding ground of the bourgeoisie in Europe, but whether they even existed in the Middle East in the pre-Ottoman period is still a matter of controversy and it is generally agreed that in Ottoman times they were weak and served mainly as an instrument of government control rather than as an expression of the class interests of merchants and craftsmen. More generally, in the Middle East property was always precarious and the bourgeoisie was very feeble. The contrast in the fates of the Karimi merchants and the Hansa is highly indicative; the Karimis covered a far wider and richer area and were probably much better off, but they vanished without trace.

In the Middle East authority was in the hands of the military and bureaucracy. The military were Mamluks and Janissaries, i.e., foreign slaves, who certainly did not represent an *economic* class and whose power was not hereditary. The bureaucracy was indigenous and more hereditary, but it too was not a class engaged in the process of production.

Marx seems to have been aware of the inapplicability of his model to Asia and left two very suggestive manuscripts, "Pre-Capitalist Formations" and "Grundrisse," which were not published until 1939. He also has some keen observations on what he called the Asiatic Mode of Production, which consists essentially of small self-sustaining peasants and a strong bureaucratic state based on the need to control irrigation. I have always found this model applicable to Egypt and said so in my first book, written in 1942, long before Wittfogel popularized the notion of the Hydraulic Society. It may also be applicable to medieval Iraq, but surely not to other parts of the Middle East—Turkey, Iran, Syria, and still less Arabia, where there is so little hydro!

I shall discuss the next school of thought, the Dependencia Theory, very briefly. It is concerned mainly with explaining why the economic center of the world (Europe and then the United States) is so rich and the periphery (Latin America, Africa, and Asia) so poor. The brief answer is that the former sucked in the resources of the latter and at the same time distorted its economic and social structure by imposing Dependency upon it. This model, which was developed by students of Latin America and Africa (including an Egyptian, Samir Amin), may fit those two continents but not the Middle East. First of all, relations between Europe and the Middle East go back for more than 2,000 years, in only the last 200–300 of which was Europe the stronger partner, militarily and economically. Secondly, unlike the other continents, its population was neither enslaved nor ravaged by disease but, on the contrary, grew prodigiously under the European impact. Thirdly, it did not have any mineral wealth to plunder and its soil was not devastated. The one exception is oil where, from the 1920s to the early 1950s, the share of the Middle Eastern governments in the net income generated by the industry was only some 20 percent, but this soon rose to 50 and over and since 1973 has been above 90 or even 95 percent. Lastly, available information shows that, until 1914, the trend in the region's terms of trade was upward and that since then the international purchasing power of the government's net take per barrel of oil has risen sharply.[11] Of course many of the harmful effects that European political and economic domination is alleged to have imposed on the periphery did in fact occur in the Middle East—the devastation of the handicrafts and the inhibition of factory industry, the waste of borrowed capital and the consequent debt burden, the distortion of the social structure, and so forth. But where Dependencia has been most remiss is in ignoring the defects in the basic economic, political, and social structure of the Middle East, which long antedate the

European impact and which, in my opinion, are largely responsible for its poor subsequent performance.[12]

A variant of the Dependencia Theory is elaborated by Immanuel Wallerstein in his impressive *The Modern World-System* (3 vols., one to follow). This has had a marked impact on an able group of Turkish scholars, e.g., Çaglar Keyder, Reşat Kasaba and others who have examined nineteenth-century Ottoman history mainly from the angle of its incorporation into the world economy.[13] Their work, and that of such American scholars as Bruce McGowan and Donald Quataert, has greatly expanded our knowledge. In this context I may also mention Haim Gerber, Nahum Gross, and Gad Gilbar in Israel; Abd al-Rahim Abd al-Rahim and Ali Barakat in Egypt; Boutros Labaki in Lebanon; and Muhammad Salman Hasan in Iraq, without in any way implying that they belong to this school of economic history.

♦ ♦ ♦

Economic history has absorbed most of my energy during the last thirty years, but I have made incursions into other fields and written many articles on historical, cultural, and—occasionally—political topics. Many of these articles were republished in *The Arab World's Legacy* (1980); others are scattered in various journals. In 1973, *Issawi's Laws of Social Motion* was published. I think it was the only serious work I have written, containing such profound truths as Issawi's Law of Petroleum (formulated circa 1951)—"Where there are Muslims there is oil; the converse is not true"; the Path of Progress—"A shortcut is the longest distance between two points"; On Revolutions—"Revolutions revolve 360 degrees"; On Roosting Chickens—"At any given time a certain number of chickens are coming home to roost. The politician's main efforts are directed toward keeping them off his perch during his tenure of office;" and other such gems of wisdom. I was very fortunate to find a very able cartoonist, David Pascal, to illustrate the book. Unfortunately it fell flat and received exactly one review—although it has been widely quoted and in the most unexpected publications. An expanded edition, with additional cartoons by Pascal, has been brought out by Darwin Press (Princeton, 1991) and I hope this one will be more successful. I also revised and edited a translation of a book by Raif Khuri under the title *Modern Arabic Thought: Channels of the French Revolution to the Near East* (1983).

I have also dabbled in literature, publishing verse translations of German and Arabic poetry, and have contributed a short article to *Persuasions*, the journal of the Jane Austen Society of North America. Of all my writings these are the ones of which I am most vain. Since my retirement I have indulged my natural tendency to dissipate my efforts and have written on topics unrelated to my discipline or field. For example, in 1989 I published an article on Shelley in *Encounter* and one on "The Costs of the French Revolution" in *The American Scholar*, as well as one with the rather pretentious title of "Empire Builders, Culture Makers and Culture Imprinters" in the *Journal of Interdisciplinary History*. I also tried to help my alma mater's fund raising campaign with "In Praise of Oxford," in *The American Oxonian*.

I have run ahead of myself and must now turn back to 1974, when I received an offer to move to Princeton. The first time, I declined since we were perfectly happy at Columbia, and we both felt we were too old to move. However, when the offer was renewed, after much hesitation we accepted it and went to Princeton in 1975, to the Department of Near Eastern Studies. There were many "pull" factors: an excellent Near East faculty, including Bernard Lewis, Avram Udovitch, Carl Brown, Rudolf Mach, Roy Mottahedeh, and others; the best Near Eastern library collection in the country; splendid students; a beautiful campus; and, not least important in a time of inflation, a distinctly higher salary. The main "push" factor was the deteriorating state of New York City.

Leaving Columbia was a wrench but I have never regretted my decision. Although city-bred, I have always preferred a more rural environment, and the trees at Princeton are wonderful. Working conditions are more favorable and I believe I was able to do more research than I would have at Columbia, where committees and administrative work were taking much of my time.

I supervised about the same number of doctoral and master's dissertations as at Columbia, but here there were also numerous Senior Theses. I have had some excellent students, notably Timothy Mitchell, Christopher Taylor, Ami Ayalon, Arnon Groiss, and Timur Kuran. I profited greatly from conversations with my colleagues—but then I had done so at Columbia. In many ways Princeton is more provincial than Columbia, and the lack of professional schools and of a very large faculty makes a difference. Curiously enough, there is less contact between faculty in different departments than there was at Columbia, at least when I was there. But I have been involved in several interesting projects—Income Inequality in Egypt and in Turkey, the Modernization of the Near East, the Modernization of Inner Asia, Christians and Jews in the Ottoman Empire, the Economic History of the Islamic Middle East, the Age of Suleyman, and, most recently, the Greek Millet in the Ottoman Empire. For most of those I wrote papers, for others I read and commented on the other contributions. I have always said that Princeton is for the very young and the old and Columbia for the years in between. I was very lucky to get them (and Oxford) in the right order.

I formally retired in 1986, at the age of 70, but have kept very active, reading, writing—and teaching. In fact my secretary says I am not retired but recycled. My department kindly let me keep my office and secretarial help, which made all the difference. At Princeton I gave some Freshman Seminars and precepted. I have also been giving a graduate course at New York University. The latter has brought me full circle to the one I started with at Columbia in 1951; it is an evening course, and attracts mainly older people who work during the day, a very interesting group. I should perhaps point out one more fact, that in all my work I have made very little use of research assistants. This was a mistake, since they could not only have saved me much effort but also, by checking my statements and figures, have helped me avoid certain errors. I think my failure to seek such assistants arose from two feelings. First, I always thought it would be more trouble to explain what was needed and to direct an assistant than to do the work myself. And, secondly, there was the reluctance to apply for research funds and grants. At Princeton I did not really have the second excuse since I could have obtained the necessary funds quite easily, but before that it would have needed quite an effort, which I was not prepared to make.

Before concluding, I think I should return to the topic with which I started and briefly survey the state of the Middle East, which I have been studying for so long. Casting my mind back to the UN days, in the late 1940s, neither I nor any responsible person I know would have believed that the Middle East would have achieved as much as it did, still less that the developing countries would do so well. We all greatly underestimated two factors: the effects of contemporary technology and the upward pull on the whole world of the un-precedentedly long and powerful economic boom in the advanced countries since 1948. In addition the Middle East profited uniquely from its enormous oil resources and the sharp rise in the government's take per barrel since 1950—total government revenues were $58 million in 1947, $5.8 billion in 1970, and $200 billion in 1980. This, and the huge amount of foreign aid re-ceived—over $100 billion in economic aid from the United States and more than $12 billion from the Soviet bloc, not to mention other donors—has en-abled the region to achieve much. Infrastructure has been greatly extended and improved. Land reforms—successful in Egypt and Iran, less so in Syria and Iraq—have been carried out. Irrigation works have been built, agriculture has been intensified, and its output has risen at 2–3 percent per annum, not a bad figure though too low to meet the needs of the growing population and the increased demand for food. Vast new industries have been set up, but most of them are uneconomic. Most impressive have been the improvements in health and education. Life expectancy at birth has about doubled—from 30 years to 60 or over—and the school population of the three large countries, Egypt, Iran, and Turkey, rose from 4 million in 1950 (it was 3 million in 1938) to 29 million in 1986; in the other countries, which started from a much lower base or from scratch, the rates of growth were far higher. There are some 50,000 Arab students in the U.S. alone, and before the Revolution another 50,000 from Iran. There are thousands of scientists, agronomists, economists, and other technicians and tens of thousands of engineers, some of them of very high quality. And women play a much more prominent role in economic and social life, though their position is now threatened by Muslim revivalism.

All these achievements, which have far exceeded my expectations and, I think, those of any reasonable observer, have, however, been largely offset by unforeseen adverse developments. First, population growth—one would have assumed it would continue at 1 percent per annum, or a little over; instead it shot up to 3 percent. Secondly, the nationalization of large sectors of the econ-omy and the proliferation of bureaucratic controls has greatly reduced efficien-cy. Lastly, and most important, the huge defence expenditures—which in some countries have absorbed 20 percent of Gross National Product and more—represent a crushing burden.

On balance, the peoples of the Middle East are better off today than they were forty or fifty years ago and they live in a more modernized and interesting society. They have also achieved a far greater degree of independence. But their frustrations are perhaps even greater than they were, and one cannot envisage the future of the region without foreboding.

◆ ◆ ◆

This, then, is the story of my uneventful and not too exciting—though to me very interesting—professional life. On the face of it, it looks like a series of unrelated accidents. If Cecil Hourani had not left the AUB, I probably would never have entered academic life. If the Arab Office had not offered me a job, would I have come to the United States, and if so when? If I had returned to the AUB after finishing my stint at the Arab office—which was my original intention—I would probably not have stayed in this country and would surely have followed very different academic pursuits and produced much less. If I had joined the World Bank, instead of the UN, my interests would have diverged far from the Middle East. If I had not recruited Mohammed Yeganeh, and if we had not become such good friends, I would not have studied petroleum at all seriously. If I had not met J. Hurewitz, I would probably never have joined Columbia. If I had not followed Schuyler Wallace's suggestion and taken up economic history, the best part of my work would have remained undone. And so on, and so forth.

Eppur si muove[*]—and yet it has a certain logic. I started with a knowledge of English, Arabic, and French and a familiarity with Egyptian society. I was always fascinated by the social and cultural impact of the West on the Arab world. I had, from my childhood, a love of history—every kind of history, including all periods and cultures. I majored in economics and was very interested in economic and social problems. I had a facility for learning languages. Surely it makes sense that these elements would have come together to make of me an economic historian working on the Middle East and a dabbler in the cultural history of the region.

---

[*] "And yet it moves!" (Galileo)

As I write these lines, I have entered my 75th year, i.e., I am now "old old" rather than "young old." Throughout my life I have been like that eighteenth-century man who "often tried to be philosophical, but cheerfulness kept on breaking in." I always thought that the proper epitaph for me would be:

> He never wrote his treatise on Ephesus
> But he was thanked in all the prefaces.

Indeed I have been mentioned in scores of books, dissertations, and articles, and for that I am truly grateful. But now I think more *gravitas* is in order, and I often recall Goethe's fine poem, of which this is an accurate but inadequate translation:

> On the mountain tops
> All is at rest;
> Hardly a breath
> Stirs in the crest
> Of the trees;
> The birds in the woods are still.
> Only wait, you too will
> Soon be at peace.

Notes

1. Czechoslovakia
2. Yugoslavia
3. Incidentally, I was offered generous financing by both UNESCO and the Bollingen Foundation for a complete translation but refused saying that first I was not equipped to deal with many subjects covered by Ibn Khaldun, such as *fiqh* and astrology, and secondly that I was not a German who could sit for ten years on such a project. Fortunately, a German was available—Rosenthal.

4. For a fuller account, see Charles Issawi, "As It Was Then: Studying the Middle Eastern Economies in the 1940s," forthcoming.
5. For a fuller discussion on the various countries, see Charles Issawi, "Recent Books on the Middle East Economics," *Pakistan Horizon*, vol. 2, no. 3 (Sept 1949), 156–65.
6. "Economic History of the Middle East to 1914," Middle East Studies Association Bulletin vol. 2, no. 2 (May 15, 1968) 1–14.
7. *Ibid.*
8. The following pages draw heavily on two of my articles, "Economic History and the Middle East," Middle *East Studies Association Bulletin*, vol. 8, no. 1 (Feb 15, 1974) and "Schools of Economic History and the Middle East," in Charles Issawi, *The Arab World's Legacy* (Princeton, 1981), in which these questions are discussed more fully.
9. I have discussed these matters in three articles: "Europe, the Middle East and the Shift in Power: Reflections on a Theme by Marshall Hodgson," *Comparative Studies in History and Society*, vol. 22, no. 4 (1980); "The Middle East in the World Context: A Historical View," in Georges Sabbagh (ed.) *The Modern Economic and Social History of the Middle East in Its World Context* (Cambridge, 1989), 1–28; and "Technology, Energy and Civilization: Some Historical Observations," in the *International Journal of Middle Eastern Studies*, vol. 23 (1991), 1–9.
10. *Principles of Economics*, 8th ed. (1920), 50, 315–16, 323, 461, 777.
11. Charles Issawi, *An Economic History of the Middle East and North Africa* (New York, 1981), 38–41.
12. I have discussed this question at some length in "The Middle East in the World Context: A Historical View," in Georges Sabbagh (ed.) *The Modern Economic and Social History of the Middle East in Its World Context* (Cambridge, 1989), 1–28.
13. See, for example, an issue of Review (Spring, 1988), brought out by the Fernand Braudel Center, "Ottoman Empire: Nineteenth Century Transformation" and Huri Islamoglu, *The Ottoman Empire and the World Economy* (Cambridge, 1987).

CHAPTER 6

A Lust for Language

Ernest N. McCarus

"He doesn't listen to *what* you say so much as *how* you say it."
—Adele McCarus, referring to her husband

The one consistent thread throughout my life has been my love for language. In the first grade of elementary school in my native Charleston, West Virginia, I loved "English Class," where we learned to spell words with little paper squares with letters printed on them. Winston's *Simplified Dictionary* for students soon became my personal bible, and I could not wait to take Latin in ninth grade, much to the amazement of my older brothers who were then struggling through it. In high school I took four years of Latin, two of French, and two of Spanish, all that was offered. I tackled Perry's *Sanskrit Primer* and took extracurricular classes in German and modern Greek from immigrants, and from our own Syrian Orthodox priest I took introductory lessons in Arabic, which consisted of penmanship and reading words in a beginner's primer from Lebanon. Although my parents, who had emigrated from Kfeir, Lebanon, in 1910 and 1914, spoke Arabic to each other, they spoke English with us children and we did not learn more than a few words and phrases of "kitchen Arabic"; this aural exposure did, however, give me a feel for the language that I could not have gotten in school. In high school I ordered a copy of Thatcher's *Arabic Grammar* by mail from a University of

Chicago bookstore and read through it twice; this was my formal introduction to Arabic.

Later, as a sophomore at the University of Michigan majoring in French and Spanish, I decided to take a course in Arabic; the only course offered was a third-semester reading course. Professor William O. Worrell, who I later learned was an authority not only on Arabic but on Coptic as well, accepted me on the basis of a brief reading test. There were two other students in that class, a specialist in Fine Arts and a missionary, both women. We read the adventures of Sinbad the Sailor; I found the going a bit adventurous at first, but by the end of the term I was assisting the other two students in navigating those waters.

I had gone to the University of Michigan in September 1940 to major in Romance Languages. After Pearl Harbor I signed up for Russian and Japanese and audited intensive Military French, not knowing how I was going to use any of them in the prosecution of the war effort. Army Intelligence recruiters came along and invited the Japanese class to sign up, which I did without finishing the term. I was a member of the first class of Company A, Army Intelligence Japanese Language School at the University of Michigan set up by Professor Joseph K. Yamagiwa and taught by Nisei and Issei from the West Coast who had been rescued from the "relocation centers" set up for Japanese-Americans in the war hysteria. After six months thirty-five of us were selected early to go for advanced training at Camp Savage;, Minnesota, near Minneapolis, where, after seven more months of intensive language and military training, we were commissioned as second lieutenants. Before my studies were over I had studied so much Japanese that the University of Michigan saw fit to award me a Bachelor of Arts degree in Japanese *in absentia*!

From Camp Savage a small number of us were assigned to Signal Intelligence in Arlington, Virginia, where I was involved in translating intercepted coded Japanese messages. After a year in strategic intelligence there I volunteered to join a newly formed tactical unit whose mission was to intercept Japanese voice transmissions in combat and translate them on the spot.

The war ended two weeks after we arrived on Okinawa, and my unit was sent on to Seoul, Korea, for the occupation. I thoroughly enjoyed those ten months in Korea and, although I had hoped to learn a lot of Korean while there, I spoke Japanese almost continuously, perfecting my oral and aural skills. On becoming eligible for separation from the service I elected to take a civil service position in Tokyo for a year, serving as a team captain in the Japanese-English translation section of the Allied Translation and Interpreting Service of MacArthur's General Headquarters in Tokyo. It was a truly remarkable experience to see the rapid rebuilding of the bombed out regions of Tokyo and other cities—except for the building in Hiroshima, preserved in its devastated state as a monument for peace—during the twelve months I spent in Japan.

(I was to have a remarkable experience with the Japanese language seventeen years later, when I returned to Japan as a senior consultant for the Ford Foundation to tour fourteen universities across Japan for consultations with Japanese professors of English who had previously spent a year at the University of Michigan English Language Institute specializing in English as a Foreign Language. The preceding summer I had tried to review my Japanese but found I could not compose a proper sentence. Immediately on my arrival in Tokyo, however, I responded to the environment and began speaking as if I had never left Japan. On the first night there a Japanese asked me how many years I had lived in Japan, and later I was told that I had no foreign accent in my Japanese. To me this was a dramatic illustration of the value of sustained intensive training—two years of full-time study in my case—and of the necessity of associating linguistic forms with their native environment, again two years of residence in Korea and Japan. I have since tried to speak Japanese on any occasion that presents itself, and even today I find that Japanese words and expressions suddenly come to mind, of their own volition as it were, in response to particular situations or stimuli.)

In 1948 I returned to Michigan to get an M.A. in Spanish, thinking that America's future was tied to Latin America. In the course of this study two things happened that were to affect the course of my life. First, I took courses in Linguistics—then called "Linguistic Science"—from Kenneth L. Pike and Charles C. Fries, and immediately knew that linguistics was central to my life. Knowing a language is a pleasure in itself; but learning to see patterns and structures in what at first might seem a chaotic jumble of facts is thrilling. For that is the essence of linguistics: to analyze and codify the regularities in language in such a way as to explain irregularities, or to create new, grammatically correct text. From Pike I learned the importance of methodology, of knowing what one's underlying assumptions are and of testing them out with data. His procedures for phonemic analysis—collect the data, formulate a hypothesis based on commonalities in the corpus, prove or refute that hypothesis on the basis of more data, and then modify the hypothesis as appropriate—are of course the classical Scientific Method and have never been supplanted by other subsequent theories or methodologies of linguistic analysis, generative or other. The second major event was Dr. Fries' hiring me as a Teaching Assistant, teaching English as a foreign language, for four years in the University of Michigan's English Language Institute. During these four years I was intimately exposed to the theory and practice of the "oral approach" to foreign language teaching, of which Fries was one of the leading theoreticians and practitioners; his English Language Institute was a pathfinder organization which served as a model for subsequent ones. The principles followed there I later applied to the teaching of Modern Standard Arabic; I believe my unpublished *Elements of Modern Standard Arabic* (1955) and my *Elements of Contemporary Arabic, Part I* (1962) were the first applications of contemporary foreign language pedagogy to Modern Standard Arabic (MSA), wherein MSA is treated like a living spoken language. The weekly staff meetings of the English Language Institute were in effect seminars, where Dr. Fries would discuss the principles and procedures involved in each phase of the program of instruction.

It was at one of these meetings that he described how best to introduce new material: Give the overall picture first and then deal with the constituent parts. In explaining how a baseball game works, to use Fries' favorite example, first explain what it takes to win the game and then define strikes and outs, innings, and so forth. I have always found this to be an important guiding principle. My affiliation with the English Language Institute was to provide the link to my eventual occupation.

In 1948 George C. Cameron was brought to Ann Arbor from the Oriental Institute at the University of Chicago to establish the Department of Near Eastern Studies, with the goal of providing coverage of Biblical Studies and ancient, medieval, and modern languages and civilizations of the present-day Arabic, Hebrew, Persian, and Turkish-speaking lands. He right away recruited scholars such as George Hourani, George Mendenhall, George Makdisi,

George Grassmuck (dubbed "George the Fifth"!), William Schorger, Andrew Ehrenkreutz, Oleg Grabar, and other leaders in their fields.

In 1951 George Cameron took an expedition to Iran and Iraq to study that area from a multi-disciplinary point of view. He had arranged for William Schorger and graduate students John Anderson and William Masters to participate representing anthropology (but Bill Schorger spent the period in the American University of Beirut Hospital with hepatitis), Douglas Crary for geography, Ralph Solecki of the Smithsonian Institution for prehistoric archeology, and was in need of a linguist to round out the disciplinary coverage. When he consulted with Dr. Fries, the latter recommended me, given my Lebanese background. By then I had received an M.A. in Spanish and had just completed my preliminary exams in linguistics. Dr. Cameron was able to arrange for Carter Zelznik, a history student, and me to apply for Rockefeller fellowships, which we did successfully. The expedition spent the spring and summer of 1951 in Iraq, with a three-week motor trip to Iran; we drove to Tehran and up to the Caspian shores, and Carter and I also flew down to Esfahan—a city of truly magnificent architecture!—and Shiraz, the home of Hafez and Sa'adi.

My mission was to do a study of Kurdish. We engaged as my interpreter-informant Mr. Abdul-Qadir Qazzaz, a native of Sulaimania who was an official in the Ministry of Post and Telegraph in Baghdad and whose Kurdish and English were both excellent.

The expedition first camped on the outskirts of Rowanduz, in northeastern Iraq, and I began my field research there. It soon became apparent that there were major differences between the Rowanduz and Sulaimania dialects of Kurdish and, since my goal was to capture the Sulaimania dialect, which was considered by most Kurds as the most prestigious dialect of Kurdish and indeed was the dialect used in textbooks, print media, and other publications, I decided to move on to Sulaimania itself. After a short time there Mr. Abdul-Qadir was obliged to return to Baghdad for personal reasons, but I had in the meantime established connections with two teachers of English, Mr. Fuad Rashid and Mr. Majid Sa'id, both of whom had an excellent command of English.

I spent most of the next two months or more working primarily with Majid; my procedure was to go around town talking to shopkeepers and others, taking notes in my notebook, and then, while everyone else was having their afternoon siesta, I would sit in my hotel room analyzing my data to see what gaps still needed to be filled in, and so forth. Although I had already picked up a lot of Iraqi Arabic dialect, I pretended with strangers not to know Arabic so that they would speak to me in Kurdish. Indeed, I was sometimes asked why I was studying Kurdish and not Arabic, the national language. Majid and Fuad often took me in the evenings to the Officials Club, where we sat and drank and would talk with other professionals, and where I could also discuss matters of Kurdish structure. On some occasions we would drive out to a picnic area called Sarchinar, where we would take refreshments and where I was also able to record Kurdish texts and live music.

On one occasion I was called to the office of the *mutasarrif*, where I was told that I was no longer permitted to stay in Sulaimania. When I drove back to Baghdad we determined that the authorities were concerned over my talking to so many people. George Cameron was able to renew my permission to work there through the good offices of the High Commissioner of Education, I believe, but first I had to list the names of all the individuals that I knew in Sulaimania; the names of two students were crossed out and I was told I could talk to the remaining names on the list but to no one else. It seems that the Central Government was afraid of communist activities on the part of anyone there!

I was able to complete my field research, which became my dissertation and was eventually published by the American Council of Learned Societies in 1958, *A Kurdish Grammar: Descriptive Analysis of the Kurdish of Sulaimania, Iraq*, a study of the phonology, morphology and syntax of that dialect. I later prepared in Ann Arbor, with Jamal Jalal Abdulla of Sulaimania, *Kurdish Basic Course* as well as three readers (newspaper, essay, and short story) and a dictionary, under an NDEA (National Defense Education Act) grant that George Cameron obtained for the Department in 1960.

On our return to Ann Arbor George asked me to teach Lebanese Arabic and to relieve George Hourani of some of the literary Arabic instruction. I was happy to do so but said that I would need a native speaker of Lebanese Arabic to help prepare materials and assist in classroom instruction. That was authorized and, by chance, I met a Lebanese student from Beirut named Adèle Haddad at a Near Eastern Studies Department picnic who was majoring in

Political Science and who wanted employment. We hired her and I began preparing furiously for an intensive course in Lebanese Arabic for that summer of 1952, preparing dialogs with Miss Haddad, working out grammatical notes from informants and whatever published materials I could find on Arabic dialects of the Levant. It was a highly successful course, and I believe that the participants absorbed a great deal of Arabic in those eight weeks. One participant, the historian John A. Williams, told me later that even after many years in Cairo someone would still ask him "*Inta shaami?*" (Are you Syrian?), still finding traces of Lebanese Arabic in his speech. William Brinner, Norman Itzkowitz, and Robert Crawford were also in that first class.

Miss Haddad remained my teaching assistant for three years. Although she was an outstanding instructor, after three years I sacrificed that advantage, in those pre-Affirmative Action days, when I married her. When later on she became a public school teacher of French she applied many of the principles of foreign language pedagogy that she had learned in her teaching of Arabic, so further extending Charles Fries' oral approach.

That fall I decided to teach colloquial and literary Arabic the "natural" way, the way Arabs learn it. I taught Lebanese colloquial the first semester and then added literary Arabic using Jochanan Kapliwatzky's *Arabic Language and Grammar* the second semester. It was another instance of the operation's being a success but with the patient dying; at the end of the year the students did not command either the colloquial or the literary. While it is true that this experiment was hardly carried out under controlled scientific conditions, I was sufficiently sobered by it to realize that the Arab has no option in the order in which he learns the dialect and the literary forms and that what is "natural" might not necessarily be the soundest from a pedagogical point of view. I believe that it is more difficult to master a complex system like Modern Standard Arabic, where, for example, the selection of vowels both internal and word-final affect so much the meaning of the word, after one has mastered a largely overlapping colloquial system which is far more streamlined, one with much less significant detail and where a large degree of flexibility in its vocalism is permitted. This matter of how to teach the proper mixture of Modern Standard Arabic and a dialect is still a live issue today, forty years later; my impression is that younger teachers of Arabic today favor teaching the colloquial first or else a mixture of colloquial and literary, the "natural" approach, while my generation generally favors learning Modern Standard Arabic first and then learning a dialect later in the game, after a reasonable control of MSA has been acquired. Today many different experiments are being carried out, involving varying ratios of MSA and colloquial, and time will tell what the most effective approach is for any particular body of learners. The naturalness of the mix between MSA and the dialect will in any case depend on the amount of the student's exposure to Arab society in its native habitat.

I was employed first as an instructor; I taught Arabic language full time until I completed my dissertation in 1956, when I was promoted to assistant professor. In 1958 I accepted a two-year appointment as a Foreign Service Reserve Officer in the U.S. Department of State, serving as director of the Foreign Service Institute (FSI) School of Arabic Language and Area Studies in Beirut. Three conditions had to be waived in order for me to be approved for the position: my wife was not yet an American citizen, so that process was speeded up; Foreign Service officers are not permitted to be assigned to their spouses' native countries, and that was waived; and there was a hiring freeze on at that time, which had also to be overridden.

That was the summer of the *hawaadith* in Lebanon—the civil insurrection which prompted Eisenhower's sending in the marines. When I arrived in September the FSI school had been without a director since the previous February, and the number of students had dwindled to eight. The number was built up to thirty-one by the time I left; they included Richard Murphy, Morris Draper, and Michael Sterner of the Foreign Service and George Thompson of the U.S. Information Service, to mention a few of the more prominent. I basically followed the established curriculum, introducing such changes as Arabic Only on the school precincts, memorizing proverbs, and weekly randomized vocabulary tests; I also gave weekly lectures in English on Arabic structure from a linguistic point of view. We established—or maintained— cordial relations with the Honorable Donald Maitland, the director of our British counterpart school in Shemlan, the Middle East Centre for Arab Studies.

I had visited the FSI school in 1957 during a visit to Lebanon; at that time there were two directors who ran the school in the morning, as it were, and were free in the evenings for their own research. I thus had the idea that I would be able to conduct a great deal of research of my own during those two years in Lebanon. As it turned out I spent a full day at the office, took work home with me evenings, and was involved in Embassy activities many weekends as well.

When my term ended I was replaced by a senior Foreign Service Officer and, since he did not know Arabic, two junior FSO's. It was nevertheless a valuable experience for me professionally in terms of Arabic linguistics, and I benefitted greatly from the trips I took to Turkey, Iran, Iraq, Israel, Egypt, and the Gulf, either to inspect their post language programs or for briefings on study trips with other FSO's. As a section chief I attended the Tuesday morning staff sessions with the ambassador, the Honorable Robert McClintock. The U.S. Embassy in Beirut was large enough to be interesting but small enough for me to get a good view of how a diplomatic mission functions in its various capacities.

In September 1959 I participated in a week-long Colloquium on the Teaching of Arabic to Non-Arabs, together with Fernando de la Granja (Madrid), Charles Ferguson (Center for Applied Linguistics), Ahmad Lakhdar (Rabat), Hussain Monés and Ali Makki (Institute de Estudios Islámicos, Madrid, the host institution), Charles Pellat (Paris), G. F. Pyper (Amsterdam), Paul Rivinc (Saint Cloud, Paris), Elias Terés Sábada (Madrid), R. B. Serjeant (School of Oriental and African Studies, University of London), Berthold Spuler (Hamburg), Laura Veccia Vagliere (Naples), Felix Walter (UNESCO), and Hans Wehr (Münster). We discussed current and preferred teaching methodologies, current instructional materials, problems with Arabic orthography and printing, a recommended order for teaching the structures of Arabic, and the desirability of creating a Basic Arabic lexicon for instructional purposes. The name "Contemporary Arabic" was adopted as a term for modern literary Arabic; Charles Ferguson and I used it for our early textbooks, but the name never gained currency and was eventually replaced by "Modern Standard Arabic."

When I returned to the Ann Arbor campus in 1960 I found two major changes: James Bellamy had replaced George Makdisi (who had gone to Harvard) in medieval Arabic studies, and George Cameron had obtained a major grant from the Office of Education for the preparation of instructional materials in Arabic, Kurdish, Persian, and Pashto. I had agreed to work on the first two, with the assistance of Adil Yacoub from the FSI school in Beirut and Jamal Jalal Abdulla from the Institute of Kurdish Studies at the University of Baghdad; Herbert Paper and Ali Jazayery worked on Persian; and Herbert Penzl and Oscar Echeverria-Aguilar worked on Pashto. (Ripley's *Believe It Or Not* deemed it noteworthy that "Paper and Penzl" were involved in writing textbooks at the University of Michigan!) We rented offices for the project, which, although officially only part-time, in practice dominated all phases of my life. In the next five years I produced five readers in Modern Standard Arabic (the *Contemporary Arabic Reader* series, which is still in print) and the *Kurdish Basic Course*, three Kurdish readers, and a Kurdish-English dictionary, which are also still in use, especially after the Gulf War. A special feature of the Arabic readers is that, except for the newspaper volume, they come in two parts, one containing the original texts and the other with the vocabulary and notes arranged in order of appearance in the text, in effect "visible vocabulary," to facilitate learning through extensive and rapid reading.

In 1963 AATA—the American Association of Teachers of Arabic—was formed at the initiative of Charles Ferguson. Its goal was the professionalization of the teaching of Arabic; more specifically, "the enhancement of study, criticism, and research in the field of Arabic language, literature, and linguistics" to quote the AATA's own description of its activities. In 1967 Fergie asked me to put out a newsletter for the association, which I did—*An-Nashra*—for seven volumes; it was then taken over by Frederic Cadora of The Ohio State University, who renamed it *Al-ʿArabiyya* and raised it to the status of a respected professional journal. Its current editor is Mushira Eid of the University of Utah.

The AATA has been very successful in reaching its goals, not only publishing the journal but also presenting its own very useful panels at its annual meetings as well as those co-sponsored with MESA (Middle East Studies Association of North America), sponsoring workshops on various aspects of teaching Arabic language and literature and on proficiency teaching and testing, and so forth. The AATA has created an *esprit de corps* in the profession and has become the collective voice of teachers of Arabic. It has served as a model for the creation of its sister associations, the AATP for Persian language and the AATT for Turkish. The AATA sponsors for students an annual contest for the translation of Arabic literature into English. I served as president of AATA in 1973 and on the Executive Board on different occasions.

In the early 1960's Charles Ferguson headed a number of teachers' workshops on the teaching of Arabic. They were followed in 1966 by a workshop at Columbia University, headed by Peter F. Abboud, devoted to Arabic instructional and testing materials; this workshop recommended the preparation of an intermediate level textbook for MSA following up-to-date methodologies and a proficiency test. Since the intermediate level of Arabic would depend on how the elementary level was constructed, it was decided that an elementary MSA textbook should be prepared first. At a follow-up workshop at Princeton in 1967 subcommittees prepared papers on the structures to be covered on the elementary level and a recommended order, a survey of extant instructional texts, an ideal methodology, and so forth. In addition, a separate committee consisting of Raji Rammuny (chair), Salman Al-Ani, and Sami Hanna prepared a draft proficiency test for Modern Standard Arabic which included a taped section for aural comprehension. The proficiency test was revised in 1974 by Raji Rammuny (chair) and Salman Al-Ani, Najm Bezirgan, Sami Hanna, and Darlene May. This test was remarkable in that it included not only the taped aural comprehension component but also a written component—both translation and free composition in Arabic. When the CASA (Center for Arabic Study Abroad) program adopted this *AATA Arabic Proficiency Test* as its selection test, many Arabic programs across the nation felt the need for the first time to include oral drill as well as composition in Arabic in their Arabic language curricula. While one should not teach to a test, this does show the power of a test in helping determine the direction that language instruction takes. It has remained in active use until recently, when it was replaced by a more extensive proficiency test, Rammuny's *New Arabic Proficiency Test*.

In the summer of 1968 a committee of Peter Abboud (chair), Najm Bezirgan, Wallace Erwin, Mounah Khouri, Raji Rammuny, and me met for ten weeks in Ann Arbor, Michigan, and prepared *Elementary Modern Standard Arabic*, a textbook which found immediate acceptance in the Arabic teaching field. People were surprised that this book could have been prepared in only ten weeks, but the secret was in the planning—Peter and I had during the previous year consulted with experts in foreign language pedagogy and in Arabic language instruction and the entire committee had met on two weekends in the previous spring to plan, under Peter's inspired leadership, the objectives and approach, the tasks of each person, and sample lessons including a draft first lesson. Thus when we assembled we were ready to start producing on the first day. Four of our group were native speakers of Arabic and two were native speakers of English; four had had linguistic training while one was a specialist in Arabic belles-lettres and one brought a social-science background. The native speakers composed or selected the texts and prepared some drills, while the English speakers prepared the grammar notes and other drills. We all read and edited every thing that the others had prepared, and Peter was responsible for the overall editing of the lessons. *Elementary Modern Standard Arabic* was innovative in teaching all four language skills of Modern Standard Arabic, just as modern European languages are taught. It was an intensive and exhausting summer, but we all worked well together, enjoyed the daily feelings of achievement, and ended up all friends with each other in spite of all the pressures we had undergone.

George Cameron was one of the last department chairs appointed for life at the University of Michigan. In 1969, after twenty-one years, he retired from that position, having established one of the strongest programs in the nation on our area. I was appointed his successor and served two terms, for a total of eight years. During this period we maintained the programs and even grew in certain areas, but I consider one of my prime achievements was, like George's before me, the maintaining of harmonious and collegial relations among the department faculty in spite of personal differences on the matter of the Arab-Israeli conflict. One professor of Arabic is a naturalized Palestinian and one Hebrew professor is a naturalized Israeli; they have over all these years cooperated in teacher training workshops, in exchanging ideas and teaching concepts, and so forth. I am happy to be able to say that that conflict has never been waged in our department.

In early 1967 I represented the University of Michigan at a meeting at the Social Science Research Council office in New York to set up a program to send advanced students of Arabic for a year's study in the Arab world; Muhsin Mahdi of Chicago and William Brinner of Berkeley were other Arabists in attendance. We decided to name it the Center for Arabic Study Abroad, and Muhsin was the first to pronounce the acronym, CASA. CASA incorporated the summer program that Fred Cox at Portland State College had set up at the American University in Cairo and added the academic year program, providing a twelve-month commitment for the student. Bill Brinner obtained an Office of Education grant for Berkeley, and the program started that summer.

It is a matter of record that the CASA program has been one of the most successful programs of its kind for any language. One of the key reasons for that success, in addition to a devoted administrative and teaching staff over the years and the serious commitment of the student fellows, lies in the advanced level of study involved. In my opinion elementary language courses should be taught in the States, where the teachers are presumably familiar with the problems particular to American speakers of English. Further, no matter how intensive, the beginning student can only proceed at a slow pace, so that I would even advocate an elementary course taught during the academic year rather than in a summer session, given a real choice. On the upper intermediate or advanced level the students have mastered the new, "alien" concepts and structures and their absorptive capacity for new vocabulary and expressions is far greater, well suited to intensive language study. The stateside directors have been William Brinner and Mounah Khouri at Berkeley, me at Michigan from 1974 to 1983, followed by Farhat Ziadeh at Washington for five years, and now Gerald Lampe at the School for Advanced International Studies, Johns Hopkins. The executive directors resident in Cairo include Lorne Kenney, Roger Monroe, ElSaid Badawi, John Hunwick, William Granara, Sherman Jackson, Mahmoud Al-Batal, and now Alaa Al-Gibali.

CASA's history has been characterized throughout by creativity and innovation. The core of the fall term is a rapid reading course where literally thousands of pages of Arabic fiction are read and where the use of the dictionary is proscribed; by the end of the term the students have not only mastered that body of vocabulary for the most part but in the process have learned to scan any kind of new material; they have been weaned from the use of the dictionary (although it is never dispensable to any one!). During my tenure we tried a super-advanced level for alumni of the year program but, in our final evaluation, determined that we lacked the faculty necessary to present such a program in proper fashion. The four "CASA II" students, however, John Eisele, Michael Fishbein, David Hirsch, and Margaret Larkin, were excellent students and profited greatly from the work. CASA III, on the other hand, was a success: a summer brush-up program designed for area faculty who had studied Arabic but now needed to reinforce it. CASA III is now dedicated to a particular theme each summer, such as social science or teaching Arabic as a foreign language (TAFL). Also during John Hunwick's tenure we instituted the FSI oral interview type of test, which has now been adapted by the American Council of Teachers of Foreign Languages as the Oral Proficiency Interview (OPI). Dr. Margaret Omar Nydell, then director of the FSI Arabic school, which had moved from Beirut to Tunis, came to Cairo a number of times to train CASA faculty in administering the oral interview test. It is not only a reliable instrument for measuring the individual's linguistic and cultural progress but also a powerful diagnostic tool which can guide the students and their teachers in identifying areas of strength and weakness in the mastering of the language.

In 1983 I was appointed director of the Center for Near (now "Middle") Eastern and North African Studies at the University of Michigan, which I held for three terms, until 1992. William Schorger had established the Center in 1961 with an NDEA Title VI grant and major Ford Foundation support. He added strong coverage of North Africa to that already existing for the Near East; his work as director was continued by Allin Luther (Iranian Civilization) and then Ernest Abdel-Massih (Arabic, Moroccan, and Berber linguistics), whom I succeeded.

Directing the Middle East Center became the major thrust of my life due to several causes. First, I considered the Center's role in promoting Middle Eastern and North African studies at Michigan as of top importance and undertook whatever I deemed necessary to that end. Secondly, the Center administrative staff consisted of an administrative assistant, Mary Ringia, and an outreach coordinator, Elizabeth "Betsy" Barlow, each of whom was incredibly competent, creative, pro-active, industrious, dedicated, and effective; with such support there was no stopping us. It was also at a time when cross-disciplinary and cross-areal interests were developing, and we responded fully to our faculty's and students' interests there. We developed joint M.A. degree programs with the University of Michigan Law School, the School of Business Administration, and the School of Public Health and joint annual lecture series with the Law-School (on Islamic Law), the Program on Women's Studies, the Business School, and with the other area centers on campus. We successfully vied for a five-year Rockefeller Foundation humanities grant to bring two distinguished scholars or writers each year to interpret Middle Eastern peoples through their literatures and for a five-year Andrew W. Mellon grant to support Middle Eastern and North African Studies at the University of Michigan through student fellowships, a visiting Near Eastern language instruction professor, and inter-areal activities, which needless to say have enriched our program immensely.

The Center has made an important contribution to area studies at Michigan. In recent years the ten or so directors of area studies and related centers and programs have come together to form a committee to deal with matters of common interest; as chair of that committee I became the informal voice of area studies on campus in university-wide committees.

An early instance of cooperation among the five Title VI area centers at Michigan, along with the Great Lakes College Association and the Associated Colleges of the Midwest, was the creation of the Program for Inter-Institutional Collaboration in Area Studies (PICAS). Thanks to major grants from the Ford and Andrew W. Mellon Foundations and from the Pew Memorial Trusts, PICAS has brought hundreds of talented students from PICAS colleges to Beloit College or to the University of Michigan for intensive summer study of languages not available at their home campuses and has brought a large number of faculty members for long-term or short-term projects on the University of Michigan campus, either for personal research or for curriculum development. There have been other minor programs, such as conference and lecture support. I have served as project director since 1989, although the burden of making PICAS successful has fallen on the capable shoulders of William Kincaid, the Executive Director since its inception.

The Center for Middle Eastern and North African Studies at the University of Michigan is primarily a service and administrative rather than an academic unit—our main purpose, as I saw it, was to get funds from whatever source possible for student scholarship support and to support full faculty teaching and research on the area. The Center at one point added multidisciplinary B.A. and M.A. degree programs for those in need of a general overview of the area. When I became director there were under ten candidates at each level; by the time I left the Center the numbers had risen to ten-to-fifteen B.A. and over thirty M.A. and joint-M.A. degree candidates. When the Center first initiated the M.A. degree I had thought it unnecessary, that it would duplicate the terminal M.A. degree program of the Near Eastern Studies Department. It is now clear that the Center degree is multidisciplinary in a way that no department would permit, since the bulk of the courses would be outside of that department, and that it provides a most important service for those graduate students who are entering Middle Eastern Studies at the graduate level and for graduate students in the various disciplinary departments who want to add a Middle Eastern-North African perspective to their studies.

Through all of this administrative service I have at the same time been teaching full time; originally I taught elementary and intermediate Modern Standard Arabic language and literature and colloquial Levantine dialect, with an occasional offering in Comparative Semitic linguistics or Kurdish language. In the mid-sixties I was joined by Raji M. Rammuny, then a Ph.D. candidate in Education, who team-taught with me the semi-intensive elementary MSA courses. Soon after that Ernest T. Abdel-Massih, a Ph.D. candidate in Linguistics, joined us, with the two of us team-teaching intermediate-advanced MSA. Eventually Raji and Ernest took over the elementary and intermediate intensive courses, with Raji developing courses in advanced composition, business Arabic, and Teaching Arabic as a Foreign Language and Ernest's offering courses as well in Moroccan and Egyptian dialects and Berber language. I was then teaching Arabic (and Kurdish) linguistics exclusively; Trevor LeGassick was covering modern Arabic literature; and James Bellamy, medieval Arabic literature including the Koran. At the time of Ernest's untimely death in 1983 we certainly had a remarkably strong program in Modern Standard and dialectal Arabic, as well as extensive sets of publications for teaching these various forms of Arabic as well as Berber and Kurdish.

In 1987 Mushira Eid, professor of linguistics at the University of Utah and mentioned earlier as editor of the AATA journal *Al-'Arabiyya*, initiated, with great foresight, energy, and skill, the Annual Symposiums on Arabic Linguistics and in 1988 founded the Arabic Linguistic Society (ALS). The object of the ALS, according to its constitution, is "the advancement of the study of the Arabic language within current approaches to linguistics." Along with others I actively participated in both endeavors, and in 1992 had the honor of being elected president of the Society. Although still small in membership, the Society has an arrangement with John Benjamins Publishers to publish the papers given at the annual symposium, and an important series of publications on Arabic linguistics has resulted from these meetings.

In 1992 my term as Center director came to an end and I was looking forward to only teaching full time, without additional administrative responsibilities. Feeling that I would have much more time at my disposal I offered Kurdish language this fall in addition to my usual two courses on Arabic linguistics; I have five students in the course, including two auditors. I find that my involvements in many activities, both my own and others', continue, however, and I am as short of time now as I was before. One of my current involvements is a project I began in 1969 along with Peter Abboud, Wallace Erwin, and Raji Rammuny to establish a computer database of one hundred thousand words of post-World War II Arabic prose to serve as a basis for a comprehensive study of the syntax of Modern Standard Arabic. We made considerable progress until our funding eventually ended in the seventies, and the project then lay dormant all these years. This year I received a grant from the University of Michigan's Office of Vice President for Research to resume the project; this grant enabled me to engage K. Dallas Kenny as a Graduate Student Research Assistant to develop a data management program and then complete the storing of the data. Once completed it will be possible to retrieve instances of any syntactic construction, morphological form, or lexical item with its contextual meaning and usage for analysis, for constructing instructional materials using "live" material, for statistical studies, and so forth. We have just about completed the data management program and look very much forward to entering the data. I feel that, when completed, it will be a major research facility at the disposal of researchers and teachers of Arabic.

I am very excited about a project that Dr. Jonathan Rodgers, the University of Michigan Near East Librarian, and I have submitted to the National Endowment for the Humanities to fund two graduate student interns to work on Middle Eastern book backlogs at the University of Michigan and at the Library of Congress over the next five summers. This follows up on a grant that I received in the spring of 1992 from the Michigan Office of the Vice President for Research for two graduate students to work on the backlogs at those two institutions in the summer of 1992. They did outstanding work., achieving far more than their supervisors had expected: Roberta Dougherty catalogued the entire University of Michigan MacGregor collection of Arabic astronomical and scientific manuscripts and Shiva Balaghi catalogued a significant number of Arabic, Persian, and Turkish manuscripts and lithographs at the Library of Congress. If awarded, this grant will permit graduate students to make accessible to faculty and student researchers important collections that otherwise are lost to scholarship, in the process developing their own library research skills and, as in the case of our two interns above, further their own personal research.

The few analytical articles that I have prepared have been in festschrifts and have not received much general notice. Although I am probably associated primarily with textbooks I am proudest of the article "A Semantic Analysis of Arabic Verbs," which appeared in 1976 in *Michigan Oriental Series in Honor to George G. Cameron*, edited by Louis Orlin. In it I first analyze the two tenses of Arabic in terms of function, aspect, and timing and then classify verbs into statives, activities, acts, and inchoatives on the basis of the meanings of the imperfect indicative and the active participle forms. Since the analyses have withstood the test of time I believe the study provides important insights into the meanings of the indicative and active participle forms.

At this point in my life I have the option of retiring from the University or continuing to teach indefinitely. I have always loved to teach, and would give it up with reluctance. But I am also very much looking forward to the time when I can complete the various projects I have begun, both analytical and pedagogical, and perhaps even to master all the software programs that I have acquired. In any case I am sure that whatever I do will involve language and languages.

And perhaps some day I will be able to listen to what people say and how they say it both at the same time.

CHAPTER 7

The Unconventional Education of a Syro-Lebanese American

George Makdisi

I was born on Learned Street, on the East Side of Detroit, two miles or so away from downtown. My first memories are of home in a second floor flat on Congress Street, across from the playground of Barstow Public School. We were a family of seven children, two born in Lexington, Kentucky, the others in Detroit; I was the middle child. The first decade of my life was that of the "Roaring Twenties." I remember the whispered mention of the "Black Hand" and stories about the smuggling of whiskey from Canada between Windsor and Detroit, across the Detroit River. One such story was about the shooting of a smuggler who, it was said, took twenty-four bullets in his stomach and lived to tell the tale. I went to grade school at St. Maron's, a couple of blocks away, and played on the public school playground across the street from our home. It was the period of the "Charleston," of the ten-cent movie and five-cent popcorn, of Harold Lloyd, Tom Mix, and Laurel and Hardy, of Al Jolson and the first "talkies." It was the period of Prohibition, the Crash, and the Great Depression.

Two early dates have always stood out clearly in my mind. The first is 1930, the date of the train trip which took the family from Detroit to New York for embarkation to Lebanon; I can still see the train moving out of the station, separating me from my friends as it sped on its way away from my hometown. I remember standing at the window watching the cows pasturing and farmers working in the fields. The second date is 1937, the year of my return to the States, when I was seventeen, and of the long trip from New York back home to Detroit on the Greyhound bus.

The family arrived in the Lebanon of 1930 in the last days of summer, at harvest time. A few weeks later I was enrolled in the public school in my father's town of Halba, capital of the district of 'Akkar, a town of some five thousand inhabitants, lying at the foot of a hill, overlooking the plains of 'Akkar, about twenty-seven kilometers to the north of Tripoli. The ancestral home, nestling among fruit trees and vineyards at the top of a hill, was only a few miles away from the Mediterranean with its unforgettable sunsets. On rainy days we could see the sheets of rain approaching from the direction of the sea, over the plains and towards us, with no tall buildings to hide the sight.

Lebanon had been, for a decade or so, a French mandate. Halba, like the city of Tripoli, had been a part of Syria added to Lebanon by the League of Nations. My parents had gone to the States in 1913, just before the First World War. They went first to Lexington, then to Detroit when Ford inaugurated the five-dollar day for his workers, revolutionary wages at the time. It was as Syrians that my parents had gone to the States; close to a quarter of a century later they came back as Lebanese.

There was a great family reunion in Halba, hugging and kissing and cries of joy, interspersed with fervent invocations and the giving of thanks to God for a safe journey from a distant land—and this in Arabic, a language not unfamiliar to my ears but which I could not speak. (When my parents had spoken to me in Arabic, my answers were in English; I understood mostly by the tone of voice, rather than by the words.) But now this kind of communication was no longer possible, especially with my cousins, some of whom were of my age. It was they who introduced me to the wonders of my father's property, and other cousins on my mother's side introduced me to hers in another town, both of which properties a city boy could only view as veritable Gardens of Eden. One had only to reach up and pull down a luscious piece of fruit, ripe fruit: figs, grapes, and pomegranates. At my father's home was a huge carob tree, below and to the left of the old homestead, the branches generously laden with its sweet, broad bean, chocolate-brown fruit. Nothing anything like this in Detroit! Trees there I had seen; they had leaves, but no fruit. It was a long time before I could again get used to "barren" trees.

But my paradise of delights was not without its drawbacks. English had not prepared me for the local public school. Cousins and neighborhood children of my age, and younger, could speak this Arabic with frightful fluency. Back in Detroit only Big People spoke that way. These little tots were already reading books in Arabic and in French, the two official languages of the mandate, and I had yet to learn the alphabet. There was little consolation in discovering that French had the same alphabet as English; the words did not always make American sense. On my first day at school I was assigned to a classroom where the students were younger, much younger, and shorter. Being the oldest and tallest of the bunch served only to exacerbate my feelings of shame.

My mother provided me with a tutor, a favorite cousin, who was a teacher in my mother's town, Karm 'Asfour ("Bird's Vineyard"). He tutored me on weekends and holidays and throughout the summer that followed that first traumatic school-year. Strongly moved by the desire to join students closer to my age, I worked long and hard, and finally succeeded in closing the gap that separated me from them. The second school year found me sporting a medal for being first in French and, later that year, another for being first in Arabic. In 1935, four of us in the highest class accompanied our teacher to Tripoli to take the Arabic and French exams for a diploma. I remember the French *dictée* was a section out of a novel by George Sand. We all passed successfully, to the delight and great pride of our teacher. The diploma was the first to be acquired in the history of the town's public school, all to his credit. It was a magnificent document divided into two solemnly written sections, one in French, the other in Arabic, in beautiful calligraphy and entitled "Certificat d'Etudes Primaires Elémentaires." I still have it, larger than any of my other diplomas, more than three times the size of the French doctorate.

The "Certificat d'Etudes" is, of course, the first and lowest diploma in the French system of education, but it represented the highest level of instruction the local public school could then offer. I had now just turned fifteen, of an age to be sent to a larger city for instruction. But the necessary funds were not available; the depression, severe, had caught up with the family. I had to stay home. Besides working on the property, planting grapevines and trees (olives, almonds, figs, pomegranates), I took to reading French classics of the seventeenth century and the poetry of al-Mutanabbi, and I memorized and recited the verses of several favorite poems of that author. Throughout that year, I exchanged books with friends and read everything I could get my hands on.

I had a consuming love for the literature of seventeenth-century France. In the last year of public school in Lebanon, I had played the leading role of a shortened version of Molière's *Le Bourgeois Gentilhomme*, that of Monsieur Jourdain, the nouveau riche who was surprised to learn that one could write a love note only in prose or poetry and that, whenever he spoke, he was speaking prose and had been for forty years, even when asking his maid to fetch his *pantoufles*! Later, at the University of Michigan, I was to play the role of Chrysale in Molière's *Les Femmes Savantes*.

Besides Molière, I read Corneille, Racine, and La Fontaine. I read the same plays and fables in poetry over and over again in the little French paperback editions of the *Classiques Larousse*. I knew many parts by heart, especially from Corneille's *Le Cid*. Later in Paris, I was taken aback by the irreverence shown by my landlady's daughters who made fun of the play for which I had long ago had such a special feeling. Antoinette would recite the words of Don Diègue, the old insulted father of Don Rodrigue, who asked his son to defend his honor: "Rodrigue, as-tu du coeur?" Instead of the son's courageous answer, Marie-Claire would answer Antoinette, "Non, j'ai du pic!" One could not help joining in the laughter, but not without some sense of committing blasphemy.

Though I could not understand all that I read—there was much that went over my head—I found that the repeated reading of a book, a play, or poem enhanced my understanding of it beyond the help afforded by a dictionary. One needed only time, patience, and persistence. Time was a commodity I had in ample supply; the other two came easily to one who feared being left behind once again. All through that fallow school-year I had the encouragement of my mother who assured me that "Knowledge, my son, knowledge!" was a very precious thing ("al-'Ilm, *ya ibni, al-'ilm!*"). As I worked on our land, I recited poetry out loud, at the top of my lungs, with the birds as my audience, and a surprise visit now and then by the *natur*, the vineyards warden of my father's town.

I also did some reading that year in modern literature, especially of my favorite writer, Jibran Khalil Jibran. I remember reading his essays in *Dam'a wa 'btisama*, which I later came across in translation as *Tears and Laughter*, *al-Arwah al-mutamarrida* (Spirits Rebellious), and especially his poem *al-Mawakib*

(Processions), translated as *The Procession Poems*, with the refrain, "*a 'tini 'n-naya wa-ghanni...*" (Pass on the reed to me and sing...) as well as other writings by Jibran. In Modern French literature I remember reading *Les lettres de mon moulin* of Alphonse Daudet and *Mon oncle et mon cure*, known more by its title than by its author, Alice Cherdonnel. I remember them for they were lent to me by a lovely girl of my age, from a nearby town, named Suzanne, whose grandmother always sat as chaperone when I paid the family a visit; the grandparents had been our neighbors in Detroit. The grandmother was a grand old lady who showed me every kindness during these visits but never ceased to remind me that Suzanne was destined for my godfather's son back in the States. For light literature in Arabic, I remember reading detective stories in which the hero was a certain "Jeems Reedangh" (James Reading?), whose name I have not been able to find in English language detective stories.

The following year, the financial state of the family having improved, I was sent off to study at a seminary school belonging to the diocese of Tripoli, which was situated some twenty kilometers to the east of that city. The student body was made up of interns and externs, some of whom prepared for the priesthood. My studies at this school were heavily weighted toward the literary and the philological, and though we studied *physique* and *chimie*, this was done without the benefit of laboratories. Here I had the good fortune of being taught by a Frenchman, Jean Grosjean. He was the first Frenchman I had for a teacher, and he spoke some English. Hardly six or seven years older than we students, he was teaching in Lebanon in lieu of his military service. He was later to become a poet and writer. (During the war, on military leave of absence to Paris, I went to pay him a visit in a suburb of the city. We subsequently collaborated on the translation of a couple of poems of al-Mutanabbi, eventually published in the *Nouvelle Revue Française*, an experiment to see what could be accomplished by an Arabist and a non-Arabist poet, translating Mutanabbi into French poetry. We did this, on and off, for a period of some ten years, a week or so each year, at his summer home, not far from the *Paraclet* that Abélard had long ago offered to Héloise and which was being run as a farm as recently as twenty years ago.)

Shortly before the end of that school year I learned of the long awaited return to Detroit. In anticipation of the trip, which I had often been told would one day become a reality, I began to make an effort to improve my fourth-grade English which had lain dormant for seven years. But my current studies left little room for a sustained effort. Moreover, I was painfully aware of the limited nature of my English vocabulary. (I have a sample of my composition in a letter written home from the school, a photocopy of which one of my sisters gave me some years ago). When I read aloud, in an effort at self-teaching, I was not sure which syllable should get the accent; and as the time spent on English was beginning to impinge upon my school work, I finally lost confidence and gave up. I had wanted so much to improve my knowledge of English, at least to bring it back to what it had been. The fourth grade had not provided me with much American literature, nor even with English grammar as such. American schools did not give the sort of grammar instruction one learned in Arabic and French.

The trip back from Lebanon took me from Beirut (a city I had seen once before, on arrival in Lebanon), to Villefranche and Marseille, thence by train to Paris and Le Havre, and finally onto the *Ile de Grasse*, bound for New York. On the *Ile de Grasse* I made the acquaintance of a French-American family from Rumford, Maine, which made for a pleasant nine-day trip. The family consisted of the mother and two children, Madeleine, of my age, and her brother, Pierre, some four years younger. There were other Americans on board ship with whom I conversed in English, asking them questions about their hometowns and listening to their speech. These conversations helped me get the accent on the right syllable of many a word over which I had puzzled back in the mountains of Lebanon. I gained some confidence when it appeared to me that my English was not as bad as I had thought. However, I remember trying to pronounce the two words that kept appearing on the billboards all along that interminable trip back. "Coca Cola" was written in great big letters, in a faintly familiar calligraphy. I sounded them out quietly as they slipped past the bus: "Co*ca* Co*la*," with the accent on the last syllable of each of the two words. These and other mispronunciations were eventually cleared up in the days that followed my return.

Once back in Detroit, French and Arabic receded into the background. They belonged to another world, one that I felt had nothing to do with America. Unforgotten, they nevertheless lay tucked away in the memory's folds. I had other things to learn and a lot of catching-up to do. Detroit had not yet changed; it was not to lose the beauty of its boulevards and its better quarters until the post-war period. I was elated to recognize the streets and buildings where I had lived, played, and gone to school.

I registered at St. Joseph's High School near Gratiot Avenue, a school run by the Christian Brothers. (The school shut down sometime after the Second World War.) After exams and credit for certain subjects, I was placed in the tenth grade, mainly for English composition and to learn typing and short-hand. It was essentially a year of remedial learning, which would place me the following year in the eleventh grade. I attended classes the first half of the day; the second half was spent working in my godfather's grocery store. There was just enough time for me to go to the movies on my way from school to work, a break which I found helpful as a change of pace between the two activities and a chance to improve my vocabulary and to purge my American accent of its foreign influence. My part-time formal education was thus supplemented by the movies, which gave me an abiding taste for American "Westerns," and by the job of serving customers in my godfather's store.

I delighted in the radio shows of the '30s, such as *Amos and Andy* and *Jack Benny*; in the Andy Hardy series of movies, in which Andy had man-to-man talks with his father, the judge; and in the "Road" movies of Bob Hope and Bing Crosby. I saw Bob Hope on stage in those days when feature movies were followed by variety shows. I fervently wanted to catch up with all that I had missed during those seven years in Lebanon.

Life back in the little town in Lebanon was without electric power and, therefore, no radio and no movies. Still the small town was not without its particular charms. Singing could be heard on many an evening, a strong clear voice flowing across town in the starlit night or coming from the hills behind, from the grapevine trellised summer shanties. The quiet moonlit nights were so bright that one could easily read the pages of a book and observe the moon's silver beams reflected in the waters of the Mediterranean beyond. No one could remain indifferent to that vast celestial vault on those clear summer nights, contemplating the beauty and majesty of God's creation, marveling at the sight of the myriad luminous stars, all the more resplendent for the lack of city lights. The simple life of that little town, tucked away in the backwaters of Syro-Lebanon, free of the many distractions of modern civilization, had its redeeming features. Back in Detroit I soon forgot about the starlit nights and had little time for the kind of reading I used to do. The atmosphere and the orientation had changed.

At high school in Detroit in the late 1930s what was most surprising, in comparison with the Franco-Lebanese system left behind, was the relaxed way in which education was approached. It was not unusual to spend the greater part of a literature hour in class discussing student government, planning strategy for the sale of tickets for a football game, or hiring an orchestra for the junior or senior prom. Many an hour meant to be spent on Shakespeare's *Hamlet* or Oliver Goldsmith's *She Stoops to Conquer* fell victim to the exigencies of extracurricular activities during their various seasons. There seemed to be as much time spent on sports and social activities as on the development of the intellect—an experience which, for me at the time, was a relaxing change from the regular rigidity of my previous schooling. In Lebanon the sports we enjoyed at school were racing, football (really soccer), and volleyball, which I particularly liked; but no sport commanded the kind of enthusiasm lavished on it in Detroit. In Lebanon, during recess, we often pursued another sport, quizzing each other on poetry or on Arabic grammar to see who could win the match; we sometimes conspired to find some arcane principle of grammar with which to trip our omniscient prof, who knew the textbook by heart, including the footnotes, much like the "Grammarian" of Browning's poem. I began to relax at St. Joseph's High School, attending full-time as a junior and senior and joining as many activities as I could, no longer in need of the movies as a break between school and work or as an extracurricular course in the American English of the "Westerns."

It was during these high school years, while walking the distance of some twelve blocks between home and school and becoming acquainted with other parts of the city, that I was reminded now and then of French. I began to take notice of the names of long familiar streets and places and to become conscious of their French origins: St. Antoine, Orleans, Riopelle, Joseph Campau, Bellevue, Grand Boulevard, Belle Isle (Detroit's "beautiful island"), and many other street names—some pronounced close to their original French and with the accent on the right syllable, others not so close. And, of course, the name of the city itself, the French *détroit*. This first conscious experience of French in the town of my earliest years meant for me that French was not foreign to Detroit.

I graduated from high school at age twenty, two years later than the norm. For the next two years, again for lack of funds for college, I wanted to try my hand at different jobs, including an attempt to sell magazines and encyclopedias; but as I could not earn enough commissions to pay the price of lunch, I gave up the attempt at door-to-door sales and went back to working at what I knew best—groceries. In 1937, with the money I had saved I began to learn to play the violin. This began after a visit to the Detroit Institute of Art, where on a Sunday afternoon I had heard classical music for the first time—an orchestra of numerous violins played the fugues of Johann Sebastian Bach. After a few months of weekly lessons, I was mercifully cured of the attempt when I heard Heifetz play Tchaikowski's Violin Concerto in D Major. From then on I gladly deferred to the great virtuoso, some of whose concertos I still have on 78s. I then took up dancing, Ballroom and Ballet (the latter mainly to improve performance in ballroom) and did so with great enthusiasm and enjoyment. But to succeed at Ballroom one had to have funds for dance routines and costumes; as for Ballet, one had to have begun at a tender age. Nevertheless I was good enough to win travel expenses and a scholarship to study ballroom dancing in New York City.

Once in New York, on learning that a New York resident could attend college tuition-free at the College of the City of New York, I contemplated a return to studies. Apprehensive as to whether I could qualify, I was encouraged to apply for admission by a friend's brother, who had himself successfully attended the college while gainfully employed. But since the academic year had already begun, I had to wait to register for classes the following year and so took a part-time job working for the Atlantic and Pacific Tea Company (A&P). Then one day in December of 1941, while I was having Sunday dinner with the family of a friend, the announcement came over the radio around one o'clock in the afternoon that the Japanese had bombed Pearl Harbor. Less than two months later I was drafted for service in the Army.

The War had not taken me by surprise. Back in September, 1939 I had read the headlines in the *Detroit Free Press* about Germany's invasion of Poland. There was talk about our getting into the war sooner or later. That meant young men around my age would be recruited. My godfather had been in the First World War, and when there was a lull in our work at the store he told me many stories about the War in France. I knew a friend of my father's who had lost his voice from being gassed during that war and could speak only in whispers. In 1939, war was still some distance away from us, and it was not altogether certain that we would get into it.

When the time did come, I served for a total period of almost four years, first in the States, then, from December, 1943 in the European Theatre of Operations. Having had combat duty from the invasion of Normandy on June 6th, 1944, through the crossing of the Elbe and the end of the War in Europe on May 8, 1945, I had earned eighty-seven points, two more than necessary to be discharged from the Army. But the war was still going on in the Pacific, so I was flown back to the States from Wiesbaden on a high priority in order to be part of an instructing cadre in the Pacific Theatre of Operations. Several weeks went by with nothing to do but wait and while away the time on leaves of absence from Fort Meade, Maryland, to nearby Washington. After having been ushered into the Army by the bombing of Pearl Harbor, I was to be ushered out by the bomb that brought the holocaust to Hiroshima. A few weeks later I was mustered out of the Army of the United States.

The date was September 17, 1945, and I was once again a civilian. Mustering out pay was three hundred dollars and a ticket for travel home. The State of Michigan gave its veteran sons bonuses of up to five hundred dollars, depending on their length of service, and I was eligible for the full sum. I was eager to begin university studies. My first impulse was to make a beeline for Ann Arbor and the University of Michigan, and I did so after spending a few days home in Detroit to see the family and get my bearings. I lost no time in signing up for the GI Bill, which offered me the maximum period for a university education, forty-four calendar months (which translated into something more than five academic years), plus tuition, books and supplies, and a monthly stipend for food and lodging.

Because of the influx of veterans of the Second World War, the University had delayed the opening of the Fall term to accommodate them. I remember the beauty of the campus of the University of Michigan on that autumn day of my first visit, with the leaves beginning to put on their displays of color, some of them beginning to fall gracefully to the grass below. The first person I met there, between the Library and Angell Hall, was Professor Bement, professor of Old French, who answered my queries about the University and gave me advice on registration for courses.

I began University studies at age twenty-five, seven years older than the non-veteran student. I was painfully conscious of the time I had lost, not only the war years, but also the year catching up in Lebanon, the year catching up at high school in Detroit, and the years between High School and Pearl Harbor. I had a faint feeling of the emotions I had experienced in Lebanon: the feeling of having to run hard in order to match the level of my studies with the level of my age, while younger classmates went past at an effortless pace. I wondered whether I was not too old to benefit by the experience. When I confided these feelings of futility to a sympathetic professor of French literature at Michigan—Professor Denkinger, who was a native of Switzerland—he assured me that my maturity, motivation, and enthusiasm for learning would serve me well.

Michigan admitted me as a "special" student during the first semester, pending final determination of my status at the end of that period. Because of advanced credit for courses taken in the Army and for proficiency exams in Arabic and French taken at the University, I found myself a senior at the end of the summer term following the first academic year. I graduated from Michigan at age twenty-seven, considering myself fortunate that I had at least shortened the educational gap from eight years to six. It also helped to know that a good many of my classmates, also war veterans, were graduated with me at an age not so far from my own.

My time at the University of Michigan slipped by in high gear. Throughout that period, my day would start at five in the morning. At the Student Union in Ann Arbor I was ready to begin work on the textbooks by the time the building's caretaker opened the main door. Among the courses I was taking were American history and political science. My fellow students had had rudimentary versions of these subjects at the elementary and secondary levels; I was experiencing them for the first time. I had long been familiar with Congress as the street on which I had lived as a boy and had later come to learn that it was a branch of government in Washington, but my mind was fuzzy about its exact functions. I had to do advanced study of both history and political science without the benefit of prior elementary knowledge. Once again I had that old and awful feeling of being the tortoise, laboring past the proverbial hare who could overtake me at his leisure, hence the necessity of studying at the crack of dawn. But I soon learned that to compete with myself, from one level of achievement to the next, was more encouraging and more satisfying than comparing myself to others.

The study habits I developed at Michigan have since become ingrained. My work day begins at a quarter to six in the morning; it ends in the evening at five. At a younger age, I often worked longer hours. Early to bed, and early to rise, cut down considerably on social life. I kept the Lord's day as a day of rest, and still do so. When on vacation, I take books and notes and other materials with me, even if they rest untouched in the trunk of the car for the whole period; just having them there, in case of need, is reassuring; and there is always a library in which to work on rainy days.

Finishing studies for the Bachelor's degree at Michigan in two years and a summer had deprived me of two undergraduate years. Since I had by this time decided on government work, I applied to the School of Foreign Service, Georgetown University. This gave me the opportunity of continuing my studies at an undergraduate level in history, political science, international law, and economics while working toward my preparation for government work. I received a second Bachelor's degree after the first year, during which I carried a "course load" of twenty-two hours. The following year I completed courses for a Master's degree in Modern European History and taught classical Arabic for two years, 1947–49, at the School of Advanced International Studies (SAIS), which was later to become part of the Graduate School of Johns Hopkins University. I also assisted at the Foreign Service Institute of the State Department, acting as a drill-master—a "native informant"—in Levantine colloquial Arabic. It was here that Charles Ferguson, Director of the Foreign Service Institute (later a colleague at Harvard then Professor of Linguistics at Stanford) advised me to forget about foreign service and study for a Ph.D. in Arabic. This was the first time I had heard that one could specialize in Arabic Studies for a Ph.D. degree.

I had by now finished my graduate studies in Modern European History at Georgetown and was completing a Master of Arts thesis on Lebanon between the two world wars. My graduate studies at Georgetown included courses with Professor Louis Mercier, among them one on American Humanism. Mercier was teaching there after his retirement from Harvard, where he had known Irving Babbitt, about whom he later wrote. It was through Mercier that I was introduced, in another course, to the *Summa theologiae* of St. Thomas Aquinas and learned that Jacques Maritain, the great Thomist philosopher, was teaching at Princeton.

I enrolled at Princeton the following year, 1949, where I studied the History of the Arabs, the Persian and Turkish languages, and taught Levantine colloquial Arabic. In preparation for studying at Princeton I had read, during the previous summer, Philip Hitti's book, *History of the Arabs*, then in its ninth edition. I had been attracted to Princeton to study under Professor Hitti, who had done much to establish Arabic studies in the United States; I was also attracted to the University's excellent collection of Arabic manuscripts. But as there were no students at the time sufficiently prepared in Arabic, I found myself assisting in teaching the language to my own classmates and disappointed by the lack of formal work on a level dealing with the manuscript sources of Islamic history.

The full course-load in my Department at Princeton, not to mention assistance in the teaching of Arabic, precluded official registration for Maritain's course on Moral Philosophy, but I obtained his permission to audit it. Maritain gave his course once a week, in the afternoon; it consisted of two parts: a lecture and a seminar. Between the two periods there was a break during which he took coffee with us in the Student Union. It was during one of these breaks that Maritain learned of my disappointment and suggested I work with his friend, Professor Louis Massignon, in Paris.

My decision to specialize in Arabic and Islamic studies had taken a long time to develop. Before the Second World War, a knowledge of Arabic seemed to have next to no value in the United States. Those who knew it and could speak it were the Old Folks; the younger generation was thoroughly Americanized. There was no need for Arabic, and little more for French, though the Christian Brothers in high school had seemed to consider it a significant accomplishment. I realized that I had some knowledge which my friends and classmates did not, but it had no ready market of which I was aware. Some months after my return from Lebanon to Detroit, there occurred the first in a series of fortuitous events which, individually, had no special significance, but which occurring as they did at greatly separated intervals of time eventually all connected with my years in Lebanon and helped to steer me in the direction of scholarship in Arabic and Islamic Studies.

The first occurred one afternoon in 1937, between morning classes in high school English and work at the store, I decided to while away some of the time at the public library, a block or two off Woodward Avenue in the heart of the downtown district in Detroit. I had already been to the library a few times but had not gone into the large reading room on the ground floor. It was lined with books on shelves across the walls, with tables and chairs provided for the reading public. As my eyes ran across the titles of books, they came to rest on one that belonged to another world, a title as altogether out of place as would have been a carob tree on Woodward Avenue: "A Grammar of the Arabic Language," it said, "by W. Wright." It was in two volumes, one on morphology, another on syntax, and the pages were replete with the terminology of grammar printed in Arabic next to their English equivalents. I could not believe my eyes. What was a book on Arabic grammar doing in an American library? And just as puzzling, what on earth did English have to do with Arabic? In my hometown Arabic was simply the private language of the old folks on Congress Street!

My first impulse was to see whether the author knew what he was talking about. How was I then to know that this was the Arabist William Wright, the editor of the *Kamil* of al-Mubarrad, and that this he accomplished, if memory serves, at the age of twenty-one! Indeed the book was excellent and treated the subject in the very terms in which I had learned it in Lebanon. The editors of the third edition, de Goeje and Robertson Smith, had made use of the very grammar which had been my textbook, the *Bahth al-matalib* of Jurmanus Farhat, the Maronite Bishop of Aleppo, who, as I later learned, was a scholar of the eighteenth century, some of whose manuscripts have come down to us, preserved in libraries of the East and West, among them the Garrett Collection of Princeton.

The librarian in charge of the reading room, who had by this time spotted me, came to ask if I needed any assistance. I had been looking to see what other treasures were kept in this unusual library, what other surprises I could find. I asked her who could be interested in books on Arabic grammar, and why did the library have so many books of modern Arabic literature. She told me that they were for the benefit of the large Syrian community of Detroit. (The term Lebanese was not yet in use in those early days.) She was surprised that I could read Arabic; the usual run of her readers was composed of persons long past their teens.

It was time for me to go to work. As the trolley made its way towards the store on the west side, near Cass Avenue, the question that kept coming back was, "Why would readers of English be interested in Arabic grammar?" It was strange, fascinating that one could learn Arabic through English. One thing was certain: Arabic was an important language. Why else would its grammar be of interest to English readers? I could not imagine how or why this came to be. But just as French and Arabic had come together for me, a similar connection was beginning to be made with English.

My second encounter with Arabic came long after the memory of William Wright's *Arabic Grammar* had receded into the past. It was after graduation from Michigan in 1947. I had gone to Washington to study for a career in foreign service; but by the time I graduated from Georgetown University's School of Foreign Service, I had decided to change course and go in for a university teaching career. I had come to realize that I loved teaching and that I apparently had some talent for it. While still at Michigan I had enjoyed tutoring some students in French, including, in the summer of '46, a Yale student from Grosse Pointe, Michigan. In Washington, on hearing that the School of Advanced International Studies needed someone to teach Arabic, I applied for and was given the job. In this first institutional teaching experience I had four students, all of whom were older than I, highly intelligent, and holders of government posts. The experience of teaching older students gave me much needed confidence; age had not all the importance I had assigned to it in the learning process.

It was after completing the academic year 1949–50 at Princeton that I transferred to the University of Paris on the advice of Jacques Maritain. By the time I got to Paris, I had only five or six months left of the GI Bill, which was, however, extended to the end of the year. After that, my studies and research abroad continued to be financed by fellowships.

Arrival in Paris was well in advance of the Fall Term. I had time to find an apartment for my wife and two children and to become acquainted with the great city before they joined me at the end of November. The Paris of 1950 was calmer than that of '45. Having shed a good deal of ignorance at the Universities of Michigan, Georgetown, and Princeton, I felt well equipped to make use of some of what the City of Light had to offer. What struck me most on visiting the bookstores was the wealth of their wares on Oriental Studies. The *librairies* of the Left Bank were overflowing with books on medieval and modern Islam, such as I had never imagined possible in the field of Arabic and Islamic studies. I was astonished at their number and the variety of their subjects. Fortunately, meals were very inexpensive at that time, leaving some room for making a serious start on a personal library. One could eat well for the equivalent of one dollar (three hundred and fifty old francs) or for two and a half dollars if one wanted a sumptuous meal. Two bookstores in particular best served my field: Maisonneuve at 148 Boulevard St. Germain (no longer there) and Adrien-Maisonneuve at 11 Rue St. Sulpice (still prosperous). My first acquisition was R. Dozy's *Supplément aux dictionnaires arabes*. By the time I left Paris for Cairo I had two crates of books to transport besides the family's baggage.

The year I had spent out of school in Lebanon due to lack of funds had taught me to teach myself; necessity converted me into an autodidact years before I learned the meaning of the term, or the fact that the Arab-Muslim world of humanism was long familiar with the self-taught man. Nor did I know then of the existence of books that taught one how to learn. Later at Michigan, in psychology courses, I came across books on the psychology of learning and, while browsing in the university library, I happened upon Jules Payot's *Education of the Will*, in English translation, and later, in Paris, obtained a second-hand copy of the French original at the bookstore of Joseph Vrin, near the Sorbonne. Written for French students at the turn of the twentieth century, it still had much to say to the contemporary student. While at Georgetown, I bought Mortimer Adler's *How to Read a Book* and, many years later, when I could afford it, the multi-volume *Great Books of Western Civilization* with Adler's *Syntopicon* and the introductory volume by Robert Hutchins, his colleague of the Chicago period. In Paris I came across Sertillange's *La vie intellectuelle*, just published and displayed in the window of one of the bookstores, a guide to the life of scholarship. It was in this book that I came across the sixteen precepts of St. Thomas Aquinas for students.

From this time on, self-teaching consisted not only in the habit of reading but also of writing. Adler was right to say that by learning how to read we also learn how to write. With Sertillange one learns that to be productive in scholarship, one has to adopt the scholarly way of life, with its tools and its habits of work, with its need for concentration and meditation, applied regularly. Much later it occurred to me that, although we as Americans were rather lackadaisical about our education in America, especially in primary and secondary education, and in the college of the pre-World War II years (with its gentleman's grade of C), we were incontestably dead serious about our professional sports. Thus the motivated American student, who is well acquainted with sports and athletes and who wishes to lead a life of scholarship has only to take as his role model the athlete with his motivation and single-mindedness; for the true scholar is simply an intellectual athlete. Lucky is the student who comes across such athletes on his way in search of learning.

♦ ♦ ♦

As noted before, it was through Jacques Maritain that I met Louis Massignon, and through them both that I met Louis Gardet and visited with him often in Paris and other parts of France. Maritain had advised me to see Olivier Lacombe to whom he also wrote telling him of my coming to Paris. Massignon, assuming that I would study Islam from the discipline of philosophy, advised me to make a thorough study of Greek and Latin and to see Maurice de Gandillac, professor of philosophy at the Sorbonne, to discuss a possible thesis in Islamic philosophy. Simply meeting these great scholars and speaking with them in their homes and private libraries was an eye opener. Paying them each a visit brought home to me the realization that an important key to the intellectual life was a personal library.

What struck me first and foremost in Paris was the institutional set up. Here the professor took on the doctoral candidate as his personal responsibility, whereas in the American university, it was the doctoral committee, headed by a chairman, where the responsibility is diffused. In America the student's choice of where to study usually falls on the institution; the prestige of the university stands high above that of the professor, who is the university's employee. For example, Harvard's notion that the professor is an "officer" of the university is interesting and rather flattering, but American law sees the professor for what he has become, the institution's employee. On the other hand, in Paris, as in the rest of Europe, the professor was *de jure* a civil servant; the medieval tradition, not altogether dead, made him *de facto* a real force in the student's prosecution of studies leading to the doctorate. To register for a thesis a student had first to interest a *professeur en Sorbonne* to be his sponsor, that is, to take him on as a candidate for the doctorate. Two such professors were needed: one for the *thèse principale* and another for the *thèse complémentaire*. Two theses had to be accepted and registered at the Sorbonne, at which time the student became a bona fide candidate for the degree. It took me the better part of the first year to accomplish this task, during which time, and later, I attended courses at the Ecole Nationale des Langues Orientales Vivantes, with Henri Massé and Claude Cahen; at the Ecole Pratique des Hautes Etudes, with Louis Massignon, Régis Blachère, and Maurice Lombard; and at the Collège de France, with Louis Massignon and, later, Henri Laoust, in addition to attending lectures by visiting scholars (one by Sir Hamilton Gibb, then of Oxford) and listening to the series of broadcast lectures on Arabic literature by Lévi-Provençal.

As Massignon was not a Sorbonne professor and the doctorate was granted solely by the Sorbonne, I asked Professor Lévi-Provençal to accept my candidacy for the doctorate as director of the *principale* and Professor Blachère as director of the *complémentaire*. The latter accepted, but the former, seeing what the subject of my thesis would be, suggested I seek the acceptance of Professor Henri Laoust, who was then—before his appointment to the prestigious Collège de France—professor at the University of Lyon half of the year and Director of the Institut Français de Damas the other half. Massignon, who had suggested I work on the Hanbalite theologian and jurisconsult Ibn 'Aqil, was highly in favor of Laoust, whose scholarly work inaugurated the serious study of the Hanbalite movement in Islamic history. But the delegation of my candidacy to Laoust had to come from a professor at the Sorbonne, not the Collège de France, hence the need for Levi-Provençal's transfer of the responsibility to Laoust and the latter's acceptance.

On learning that Laoust was back at Lyon, I contacted him by phone and paid him a visit at his home in the nearby town of St. Cyr au Mont d'Or. I had read and studied most of what he had written, his works on the Salafiya movement and its Syrian representative Rashid Rida and especially his *Les idées sociales et politiques d'Ibn Taimiya*. I had already outlined the chapters of this work, together with those of Massignon's *La Passion d'al-Hallaj*. It was in

Laoust's work on Ibn Taimiya and his writings on the Salafiya movement, together with Massignon's references to the Hanbalites in his *Passion*, that I saw the interest there would be in studying Ibn 'Aqil, a Muslim intellectual *sui generis*, of a period two centuries earlier than that of Ibn Taimiya. All of these Muslim intellectuals belonged to the same line of development in Traditionalist Islamic thought. Laoust, after a long discussion (to me worth a dozen seminars) agreed to direct my thesis and, although he preferred at first that I work on Abu Ya'la, who was the first to organize the Hanbalite school of thought in the eleventh century, he later agreed that I could concentrate on Ibn 'Aqil.

Throughout the decade of the 1950s I met with Laoust whenever I had the chance. But meetings were not easy to arrange. It seemed that when I was in Paris, he was in Damascus; and when I was in the Muslim world, he was at the University of Lyon. He invited me to stay at the Institute in Damascus while I was studying and microfilming manuscripts at the Zahiriya Library. It was here that I met Nikita Elisséeff, Secretary General of the Institute and author of the monumental work on Nur ad-Din Zanki, and Dominique and Janine Sourdel, who became longtime friends and colleagues and who collaborated with me on the International Colloquia of La Napoule and later at Morigny. Laoust had also to make yearly visits to Paris for administrative purposes connected with his Institute, at which time we met either where he was staying or at the Café de la Paix, next to the Opéra, where we took coffee and sat for an hour discussing my progress. When he was appointed to the Collège de France, we would meet in his office. When I was well along the way of finishing the redaction of the thesis, he suggested I see him every two weeks with what I had written. In this way he read it section by section, marked the parts he thought particularly good with a "B" (for "bon"), and discussed some parts of it with me.

It was by now evident that my studies had become focused on Islamic religious history. The transition to this subject occurred over the years, influenced by the men I had met at Georgetown, Princeton, and Paris. In Paris I was influenced by Massignon's personality and his work on the mystic Hallaj and by Laoust's work on Ibn Taimiya—the connection between Hallaj and the Hanbalites in general, Ibn 'Aqil's veneration of this great mystic, and Ibn Taimiya's high regard for Ibn 'Aqil. At Georgetown, as already mentioned,

Louis Mercier had encouraged me to read St. Thomas Aquinas, at a time when there was in the States a resurgence of interest in Catholic thought, this fired by the earlier Catholic intellectual revival in France at the turn of the century. The impetus had been given by Pope Leo XIII and his foundation of the Academy of St. Thomas Aquinas at the University of Louvain in the last part of the nineteenth century. It was through Louis Mercier that I first came in contact with the writings of Jacques Maritain and Etienne Gilson; then later, on reading the *Introduction à la théologie musulmane* of Gardet and Anawati, the work of other French Thomists, among them Chenu and Mandonnet.

After meeting Massignon, the die was cast, and I was soon plunged deep into my first reading *en masse* of Islamic medieval works. My principal sources for these materials were Massignon's personal library, the library of the Ecole des Langues Orientales, and the Bibliothèque Nationale. Massignon allowed me frequent use of his library. He would have me sit in a room next to his *cabinet de travail*, at a tapestry-covered table, on which he placed the books he put at my disposal. On other visits, when I came to consult him on problems I had come across, he would give me generously of his time.

When I mentioned that of all Ibn 'Aqil's works only a few are known to exist, he suggested I look for them in libraries of the Muslim world. When I complained that none of the extant works of Ibn 'Aqil were in print, he said I would have to work on the manuscript copies and to extract his ideas and those of his contemporaries from works in which they were quoted. When I said that there were no indexes in the printed Arabic books to carry out such research, he would tell me to scan the pages and that one had to put up with much tedious reading before chancing upon a pearl. I realized that he was not telling me anything that he himself had not done, as for example in his *Passion*, in his *Textes édits et inédits*, and in the compilation of his *Bibliographie Hallagienne*. I also had meetings with Massignon in Cairo where he came frequently. I remember once having a meeting with him in a taxi. We discussed my progress on Ibn 'Aqil between Cairo and Heliopolis, where he dropped me off at my apartment and continued on his way to visit the tomb of a Muslim friend.

What I missed most as an American student in Paris was the facility of access to books. At Princeton there was the new Firestone Library, with its cubicles for students next to the bookshelves relating to one's field of study.

Whenever one needed books, one had only to step out and reach for them. Once a student familiarized himself with his sections of the library, he had no need to look up the call numbers in the card catalogue. The books he chose for his work stayed in his cubicle until he had finished with them. The time saved for study was something I had taken for granted. I became fully conscious of the convenience it afforded only when I had to make use of the Bibliothèque Nationale in Paris. Of course, the Bibliothèque was not a university library; it was the counterpart of the Library of Congress. As a public library, it required that certain preliminaries be attended to before one could accede to the books. One needed photographs for an application and an identity card; in the morning there was a queue waiting to get in; and the number of books one could have at one time was restricted. Once the identity card was obtained, the whole process from queue to books could take as much as an hour or more. It often happened that the book or books could not be found, or they were checked out by someone else, or they were in the bindery, in which case one left the library and went in search for them elsewhere. And this was Paris, not a small university town, and although it had the best means of city transportation in Europe, a lot of time was consumed on buses and in the Métro; and one did a lot of walking, not a particularly American sport.

I soon learned that for me the Bibliothèque was best used for manuscripts. These had not yet been moved to another building in the compound, on an upper floor, to the left of the entrance on Rue Richelieu. The manuscripts were still on the second floor of the main building Bibliothèque Nationale when I had the good fortune of making the acquaintance of the noted latinist medievalist Mlle Marie-Therèse d'Alverny. We often met in Massignon's seminar, in the Section of Religious Studies at the Ecole Pratique des Hautes Etudes. She graciously facilitated access to the manuscripts beyond the restricted number for one sitting. Another scholar who was of great help to me, in those early days and thereafter, was George Vajda, one of the first persons Massignon suggested I see. I finally did most of my studying in the library of the Ecole des Langues Orientales, at 2 Rue de Lille. (The library is still there, though the Ecole has moved a great distance away.) Two rooms were set aside with reference books where one could sit and work quietly. The interesting thing about the library's card catalogue was that one could find not only the titles of books but also those of articles in reprints from journals. In France a scholarly contribution was no less a contribution for being an article; this could be seen in the way the contribution was cited in a footnote or in a bibliography: whether book or article, it was always cited in italics.

The American student simply had to learn how to get around, losing as little time as possible. Maritain had warned me that I would have to learn how to use the *système D* (from the verb *se débrouiller*), to beat the system by getting around it, to shift for oneself. But that was easier said than done, at least for a "spoiled" American student where the "system" in his last university was deliberately set up to make things easy for him. It would take some time before I caught on to the system. Those first months in Paris, and in the town of Le Vesinet on the Saint Lazare line of Saint Germain, were months of sheer frustration, almost on a daily basis, not only with respect to problems pertaining to studies but also in setting up house for wife and children in a country that had only recently thrown off the yoke of military occupation and come out of the war years: no supermarkets and very little by way of products facilitating homemaking for an American wife with a small child and a baby. This, and the difficulties relating to libraries and the use of books, not to mention the weeks of red tape needed to get a visa for residence beyond the first three months, taught us how to cope. But in spite of all the inconvenience, living in France in those difficult post-war years was definitely well worth the effort.

Massignon lent me many of the books I needed. Among the first of these were Ibn al-Jauzi's *Muntazam*, a history of Baghdad, and two *Who's Who*s of the Hanbalite school of religious thought: Ibn Abi Ya'la's *Tabaqat al-hanabila* and Ibn Rajab's continuation of it, the *Dhail 'ala Tabaqat al-hanabila*, which had just been published by Laoust and Sami Dahan at the French Institute of Damascus.

During those years I developed my own style of work. I began to outline the political events of each year of Ibn 'Aqil's lifetime, including a generation or so before his birth and a like period after his death. I used Ibn al-Jauzi's *Muntazam* and later supplemented this with every historical and biographical source I could find in print or in manuscript covering the same period. From the *Who's Who*s I made a card for every person listed, including a complete list of his works, extant or inextant, with which I then familiarized myself, so that I could later at least recognize the title if I came across it in a handlist when in the Muslim world searching for manuscripts. In addition, after investing in

Brockelmann's *Geschichte der arabischen Literatur,* I made cards for each writer of the period that concerned me, together with all the titles of works in print and in manuscript. With this background, I considered that I had sufficient information to begin my research in depth.

This preparation was made with a view to gathering all the information possible on Ibn 'Aqil and his times, his teachers, and his students, covering a period of a century and a half in the eleventh and the twelfth centuries in Baghdad. In the beginning, I could not be sure if any of his works were complete. The Garrett Collection of the Firestone Library at Princeton had a copy of his *al-Wadih fi usul al-fiqh.* A microfilm of this work was brought to me in Paris by a colleague from Princeton, Herbert Bodman, now professor at the University of North Carolina, who was en route to Cairo. This was the third volume of the work. There were two other copies in the National Library of Damascus, which, as luck would have it, were volumes one and two, completing the work. It further turned out that all three volumes were in the hand of the same copyist. (I am now in process of correcting the proofs for the first of eight volumes of the *Wadih,* to be published by the German Institute in Beirut.) I later found two other complete works of Ibn 'Aqil, not mentioned by Brockelmann; the rest of his listed works were either incomplete or lost.

The information provided by secondary works on the eleventh century was very limited; and what there was turned out to be, in many important instances, at variance with the primary sources as I read them, especially as they related to the political and socio-religious history of the period. The more I learned about Ibn 'Aqil, the less he seemed to fit into the picture which the secondary sources had painted of eleventh-century Baghdad. When I left Paris for Cairo and Heliopolis, I began to collect a library of printed works and of manuscripts in microfilm, gathered from bookstores and libraries, notably from the Egyptian National Library and the library of Azhar University in Cairo, from Alexandria, from Damascus and Aleppo, and from the libraries of Istanbul (e.g., Aya Sofia, Topkapı Sarayı, Koprulu, Beyazit Umumi, Murat Molla, Suleimaniye) and of Anatolia (e.g., Bursa, Konya, Kutahya, Izmir, Manissa). Kaiseri and Diyarbakir, at the time, were off limits for military reasons, I was told.

When not reading manuscripts, much time was spent making the acquaintance of bookshops and their owners, often highly knowledgeable and always hospitable, sipping coffee with them and discussing authors and books and buying when the buying was good. One dealer, from whom I bought some valuable books long out of print, was the Damascene al-Qasibati ("The Manufacturer of Hose"), whose books were in a large high-ceilinged room in the rear of the shop, beyond the machines for making socks. In Cairo, my main supplier was Nagib Khangi, whose father had edited al-Khatib al-Baghdadi's *Tarikh Baghdad* and whose brother Sami was one of the buyers involved with acquisitions for the manuscript collection that was to become the Chester Beatty Library in Dublin.

In Abbassieh, near Cairo, I had the good fortune of working in the library of the Dominican Monastery, the Director of whose Institut Dominicain d'Etudes Orientales was Père G. C. Anawati, close friend of Louis Gardet and co-author with him of the excellent *Introduction à la théologie musulmane*, a comparative study of Islamic and Christian theological thought, previously mentioned. I had already met Father Anawati on his visit to Princeton in 1949. Jacques Maritain informed me and a classmate, James Kritzeck, author of *Peter the Venerable and Islam*, of Father Anawati's imminent visit, giving us a letter of introduction to the learned Dominican priest who became a good friend. Father Anawati was of the greatest help in Cairo and has continued his friendship, not only with me, but also with many other American students, including some of my own.

By the end of the academic year of 1953, having by now exhausted the GI Bill funds and four years of graduate fellowships, it was time to think of going back home to the States, to find a job in order to support a family and keep up acquisitions for my personal library. By this time we had three children. I wrote letters from Heliopolis soliciting a teaching post at three universities. Before leaving Princeton, Professor George C. Cameron had asked me to come on a visit to the University of Michigan, where he had been brought from the University of Chicago to start a Department of Near Eastern Studies. After spending some time with him and with a number of professors from other Departments, some of whom had been my professors, Cameron asked if I had decided to stay or go on to Paris. I said that I did not feel I was ready to teach at Michigan but would like to do so after my studies at the University of Paris. It was now time to write to him from Heliopolis, to let him know that I was ready. He responded with an offer I was pleased to accept.

The trip home from Cairo was arranged on a Norwegian freighter. I was advised to travel by freighter because of the library I had collected, consisting at the time of twelve crates. Although the accommodations were all first class and very spacious, they cost less than usual, and the books were placed in some corner of the hold where there was plenty of room and, to our surprise and appreciation, there was no extra charge. The freighter had living quarters for only twelve passengers; exceeding that limit would have required the presence of a physician on board. We had to make an unscheduled stop at Malta in order to allow a sick passenger to disembark to be operated on for appendicitis. Family members met us in Boston with a trailer for baggage and books, and we made a leisurely trip to Michigan. A month later, we had moved to Ann Arbor and teaching began soon afterwards in the Summer Term of 1953.

I was far from the point of beginning to write the thesis. A great many manuscript sources and Arabic books had been collected, and many boxes of 3-by-5 inch cards had been filled and classified, but no writing had been done. I therefore had two major concerns: to keep up the research and to prepare lectures for my classes. There was no connection between the two activities. The students were not prepared to work directly on the Arabic sources. This was not Paris. France had a long tradition in the fields of Arabic and Islamic studies. We in the U.S., on the other hand, had hardly begun. The aftermath of the Second World War was the starting point of the new venture in the States. In the early days, there were virtually no American-born professors who were recognized scholars in the field; these had to be brought in from abroad.

I soon began to research and publish studies which would serve to fill the gaps in the picture of eleventh-century Baghdad, studies which, because of their specific nature could not be part of the thesis itself but would enhance my knowledge of the Baghdad of Ibn 'Aqil. Two colleagues and friends asked me to write articles for the journals with which they were connected. Professor George Mendenhall, as editor of the *Journal of the American Oriental Society*, published my first article on the Mazyadids of Hilla. Storm Rice, a Professor of the History of Art from the University of London then visiting at the University of Michigan, suggested I do something for the *Bulletin of the School of Oriental and African Studies*, to which I sent the *Diary* of Ibn al-Banna'. There were other such invitations, and I always used them to further my understanding of religious movements in Baghdad in classical Islam. Whenever I was asked to give a lecture I did so with the intention of preparing it for publication.

As regards the *Diary*, it was while going through the more than 150 collectanea (*majami'*) of Arabic manuscript works in the National Library of Damascus that I came across some folios with the mention of Ibn 'Aqil's name. On closer reading I realized that I had a diary of some thirty folios covering fourteen months of a crucial period in Ibn 'Aqil's life. The fragment belonged to a diary of much greater length, covering four decades or so of Baghdad's history, but which was lost except for this fragment. It was the autograph of Ibn al-Banna', an author who knew Ibn 'Aqil but was unsympathetic to his cause and complained of the opposition supporting him. The private nature of the diary, in which the diarist allowed himself to write things he would not have written if they were meant for public scrutiny, was of the greatest help in introducing me to the inner workings of the Traditionalist movement, and especially of the Hanbalite school of thought to which both the diarist and Ibn 'Aqil belonged. The illegible hand of the diarist made the task a forbidding one. "*C'est un chien de texte!*" was Professor Blachère's remark when I showed him a couple of plates. But in spite of the difficulty of deciphering the manuscript, I needed to know what was locked up in those pages, especially on Ibn 'Aqil. It took three summer months to decipher them.

The *Diary*, the only extant such work in medieval Islam, brought home to me the extent of the loss to history of Baghdad's day-to-day life during one of Islam's pivotal periods. The loss was further dramatized when I discovered that Ibn an-Naj-jar had made use of over thirty-five such diaries (none of which is extant) in writing his biographical history of Baghdad as a continuation of the fourteen-volume work of al-Khatib al-Baghdadi. Another significant example of such loss of documentation is the intellectual journal of Ibn 'Aqil. It is here that he consigned thoughts that occurred to him, excerpts from his readings, things that he had heard from "the mouths" of his contemporaries, and reports of disputations in which he had participated or at which he had been present. He wrote over a period of what I believe to be some fifty years, and of all this labor, reportedly some two hundred volumes, the only part extant is the manuscript of Paris (Fonds arabe, no. 787), covering some four-to-six months, printed in 735 printed pages of my two-volume edition.

In order the better to understand Ibn 'Aqil and to place him in the context of his period, I had first to deal with his formative years. Much had been written about education in Islam and on the Madrasa Nizamiya in Baghdad, but there was almost nothing in this literature which could explain the character of Ibn 'Aqil's education. We have an excellent idea of the education of intellectuals in the medieval Christian West; but our knowledge concerning the *formation* of their Muslim counterparts was far from satisfactory. Moreover, I could find nothing in the Arabic sources to justify either the alleged objectives of the Nizamiya madrasa-college of Baghdad, the basis of its foundation, or its supposed curriculum. I had therefore to make a study of the colleges, their curriculum and personnel, in the Baghdad of Ibn 'Aqil's lifetime. That study made me realize that institutional history was closely involved with both the political and socio-religious history of the period, a realization that led to studies in that direction in the years that followed.

Meanwhile, besides editing his intellectual journal, the *Kitab al-Funun*, at the suggestion of Massignon, I was also preparing the edition of Ibn 'Aqil's magnum opus on legal theory and methodology, the *Wadih*, the only one of his major works that has come down to us complete. However, both the Princeton manuscript and one of the two Damacene manuscripts, constituting two-thirds of the only copy of this great work, had suffered extensive damage. In the process of transcribing the entire text for publication, I was under a strong impression that it was somehow familiar to me; yet there could be no doubt that I was reading the text for the very first time. It was not until I had finished the transcription of the text (over 1500 pages in my handwriting) and concentrated on re-reading the text that I was struck with a sudden realization that the structure of Ibn 'Aqil's *Wadih* was practically identical with that of the *Summa Theologiae* of St. Thomas Aquinas. On collating the basic unit of each of the two works, that is, the *fasl* of the *Wadih* with the *articulus* of the *Summa* (the Arabic *fasl* and the Latin *articulus* have the same meaning), I found that not only was the similitude remarkable but also the essential technical terms were identical; these were translations from the classical Arabic into medieval Latin.

The two main strands of influence on the formation of my own intellect were now on the verge of coming together. They were decisively linked in my next undertaking. I was still involved in trying to match Ibn 'Aqil's fields of knowledge with the curriculum of formal higher learning in Baghdad. The curriculum of the college did not encompass Ibn 'Aqil's fields. So when my friend Professor W. Montgomery Watt asked me to write a book on Islamic education, I concentrated on the college for two reasons: first, because our present knowledge was not such as to justify a general survey work on the subject, and second, because the college in the eleventh century was obviously Islam's institution of higher learning par excellence.

It was evident that many fields of knowledge, not represented in the college curriculum, were learned by other means: private teaching, tutoring, self-teaching. Ibn 'Aqil studied philosophical theology (*kalam*) in secret under two masters of the Mu'tazilite school of theological thought, which was considered unorthodox. When discovered, he was still under the protection of his patron, Abu Mansur b. Yusuf, a wealthy Hanbalite merchant whose power and influence made him a confidant of the Caliph. After his patron's death, he was forced into hiding. The college curriculum clearly did not include philosophy or philosophical theology nor the exact sciences, only computation which served the needs of the Islamic law of inheritance; otherwise, Ibn 'Aqil would not have had to resort to clandestine or private studies of these subjects.

Law in Islam had long ago become a science, as shown by Joseph Schacht in his *Origins of Muhammadan Jurisprudence*. By Ibn 'Aqil's day, the discipline had developed a method of disputation which, in the hands of Ibn 'Aqil, had reached the point of perfection as an art. It was this method that was dubbed in the Christian West some centuries later, the "scholastic method." Ibn 'Aqil called it "the method of disputation" (*tariqat an-nazar*). In my book on medieval Islamic education, *The Rise of Colleges*, I was able to tie Ibn 'Aqil's method of disputation with Aquinas' scholastic method.

Thus Ibn 'Aqil was a *scholastic*, as evidenced in his *Wadih* and in his *Funun*; and the latter work made it clear that he was a *humanist* too. This realization, however, was not to dawn on me until later, when I planned to write a brief study on physicians in Islam. A colleague in Chinese studies, who specialized in the history of science and had read *The Rise of Colleges*, suggested I write another book dealing with the sciences. I at first suggested that such a study would best be done by scholars of that field but later felt that I could at least deal with the physicians, regarding whose education I had read most of the available sources. On taking up these physicians once again, I was reminded that a significant number of them were poets and writers in addition to being physicians. Also, their presence in the courts of caliphs, sultans, and prime ministers was due not only to their knowledge and practice of medicine but also, and in some cases more importantly, for their knowledge of the humanistic fields of classical Arabic, highly prized at these courts, whether in Baghdad, Damascus, Cairo, or Cordova.

This study sent me back to early Islamic history and medieval European history in a search for the roots of the humanist movement. I remembered having read something on early European humanism, a long time back, as background for the study of American humanism under Louis Mercier at Georgetown University. I also found that the roots of the literary humanist movement go back as far as the second century of Islam (the eighth of our era), in the humanistic literary fields of *adab* literature, the *ulum al-adab*. A few years later these researches resulted in the publication of *The Rise of Humanism*. Again, the two strains of thought, Christian and Muslim, converge in my own work.

A great part of the history of the medieval Christian West from the latter part of the tenth century to the latter part of the fourteenth is tied up with Islam. It is to be hoped that a new generation of medievalists will some day explore this interrelationship involving the world cultures of the Mediterranean. There are vast mines of comparative historical data in this area of scholarship, the veins of which have hardly been tapped. They are there to be mined by young scholars with open minds, ready to follow the lead of the sources. It is to be hoped that some day scholars of history will be spared the burden of a strong tradition of Eurocentrism, resting heavily on their shoulders. European civilization is the heir of many influences, a number of which have been studied and brought to light, but essential Islamic elements have been summarily denied or ignored, as though they could somehow be made to disappear. But psychological attitudes are not the sole obstacles. There is also the language of classical Arabic that must be learned, besides at least one of the other languages involved: Latin, Greek, and Hebrew. As for the sources, there is need to make available the manuscripts themselves, not only catalogues or lists of libraries containing them.

Besides the obstacles to Islamic scholarship caused by the considerable loss of manuscripts suffered during calamities of a physical or political nature, the most dramatic and devastating being the Mongol invasion of Baghdad, another difficulty in the study of Islamic history is the percentage of printed works in relation to what remains in manuscript. These have been estimated to be as high as one to three million. A fair estimate of what has been printed would be about twenty percent, a distinct improvement over the situation as it existed in mid-twentieth century, when ten percent would have been a generous estimate, an improvement due in large measure to Arab and Muslim scholars who have given generously of their time to make new sources available. The high percentage of works still in manuscript puts a heavy burden on the historian who finds himself in the position of having to do the work of the philologist as well. Moreover, the dearth of available texts puts interested social scientists working in the modern period at the risk of drawing conclusions on the basis of insufficient documentation, unless they too do the work of the philologist, assuming their mastery of the language, in order to make use of all the available documents in manuscript as well as in print when working in the pre-modern period.

Until recently we had no way of knowing the startling similarity between the intellectual history of classical Islam and that of the Christian West. This is a rather recent development due to the high quality of medievalist latinist scholarship since the late nineteenth century, with such studies as those of Denifle, Rashdall, Grabmann, and Haskins. Before the stage could be set for the comparative study of the intellectual history of both civilizations, we have had to become knowledgeable about institutions of higher learning in classical Islam; this effort is still in process and some of that knowledge is beginning to become available. But the process of replacing received opinions is a very slow one; it will be some time before this step forward can be made. It will happen when new generations of young scholars, resisting the inculcation of old attitudes and relying on their independent research, equipped with tools adequate to the tasks at hand and minds free to explore the primary sources, come to their own conclusions.

As regards Islamic studies in the U.S., in the nearly half century that has passed since those early days, there has been a very remarkable change. America now has its own first-class scholars in the field, working together with colleagues of foreign countries in the many great universities of the U.S., teaching, publishing, advancing our knowledge, and producing scholars for the generations to come. If our public elementary and secondary education these days is, with a few exceptions, mediocre, a great many of our American universities, on the other hand, are among the very best in the world. The primary concern now is whether our excellent young scholars in this field can be integrated into the various disciplines in our schools of arts and sciences and whether the high quality of linguistic preparation can be sustained at a time when departments that offer Arabic and Islamic studies are beginning to languish and even disappear from the scene. The outlook at present is not encouraging, what with the lingering economic recession exacerbating the problem.

The field of Arabic and Islamic studies has its obstacles; but it is a vast and almost virgin field awaiting its cultivators, and its harvests promise to yield riches in historical data that will broaden our knowledge of both world civilizations, the Christian West as well as the Islamic East and West, and in the process throw light on the Byzantine, Jewish, and Judeo-Arabic intellectual cultures of the Middle Ages.

Now that I have come to the end of this autobiographical note, which has gone on longer than I had anticipated, I am brought once again to wonder, as I have on odd occasions before, just what it was that led me to a life of learning. My father came from a long line of proud mason-builders, who also owned land and lived from its harvests. My mother came from folk who were landowning farmers and immigrants to the Western hemisphere. She had travelled to Columbia at the age of fifteen and spent two years there with her brothers. She spoke fluent Spanish; I remember her speaking with Hispanics we once knew in Detroit. Transplanted from the "old country," the early Syro-Lebanese immigrants of Detroit were mostly small merchants or workers in the automobile factories, as was my father, who, before that, had worked in Lexington, Kentucky, preparing tombstones with names and dates inscribed.

None of my friends in Detroit went to college either before or after the war. It would therefore seem that my orientation towards the intellectual life was a combination of factors that had little to do with my early years in Detroit: factors such as the army experience, which set a value on the knowledge of foreign languages; the subsequent GI Bill, facilitating higher education; the role models I had among the learned men I met in the pursuit of learning, the living tradition of their scholarship and their love for the truth; my mother's encouragement and insistence on the importance of knowledge; and, perhaps not least of all, the initial success in overcoming the traumatic first year of Arabic and French and the discovery of the pleasure of self-teaching in that year without school in Lebanon during the Depression after the "Certificat d'Etudes Primaires Elémentaires."

CHAPTER 8

Vignettes—Bits
and Pieces

Don Peretz

During World War II, when I was an interpreter of Japanese with the Military Government in Okinawa, I never expected that within a few months of my army discharge in March of 1946 I would shift directions and be headed for the Middle East. (I've heard that at least two other Middle East specialists were also trained in Japanese by the U.S. armed forces during World War II.)

When I returned from Okinawa to New York the Palestine problem had thrust itself into American newspaper headlines and was a major issue before the newly formed United Nations; my interests and emotions were torn between the Far East and the Middle East. As I began to read about a new set of terms that was appearing in the media—Palestine Mandate, Zionism, Arab Nationalism, the Holy Land, Haganah, Irgun, the Mufti—my interest was piqued.

My emotions were stirred because my father, a lifelong Zionist, was born in Palestine and claimed ancestry in the Holy Land going back to the expulsion of Jews from Spain nearly five hundred years ago. With a large family in Palestine—aunts, uncles, and cousins by the dozens—I was tempted to at least visit. Although the family had lived for several generations in Jerusalem, my grandfather left the Old City in the 1890s to become the *mukhtar* (village leader, or contact with government) of Beer Tuvia and Gadera, two new Jewish settlements in the south. As a result of his position, he was imprisoned in

Damascus by the Ottoman authorities during World War I despite the fact that he had once served as a secretary to the *Vali* (governor) of Jerusalem. Furthermore, the authorities were suspicious because at that time (1916) my father had been working with Aaron Aharonson, suspected by the Turks of being a British agent. My father fled to Egypt on an American destroyer and from there immigrated to the U.S. Grandfather kept a diary while in the Damascus prison, but no one has been able to read it because it is written in a sort of code devised from a mixture of Turkish, Arabic, Hebrew, and Ladino.

I was much attracted by discussions about the possibilities of compromise in Palestine between Jews and Arabs focusing on "binationalism," a concept that was being offered by a small but influential group of Jews living in the country. They included the world renowned philosopher Martin Buber and the President of the Hebrew University in Jerusalem, Dr. Judah Magnes.

I decided to go to Palestine and see for myself what was happening in the country and to meet the binationalists. Since there was an opportunity to study at the Hebrew University in Jerusalem where Magnes was president, I used my army educational benefits (GI Bill) to enroll and to provide my living expenses in Jerusalem. The day I arrived the King David Hotel was blown up by the Irgun, an auspicious beginning of a two-year stay which was to be full of similar "excitement."

In 1946 the Hebrew University was considerably smaller in area and numbers than it is today. The campus was concentrated in a few buildings on Mount Scopus, with a view to the east of the Dead Sea and the Judean hills. The west overlooked Jerusalem's walled Old City with its scores of ancient monuments and sacred shrines. I believe that there were not more than a thousand or so students at the time. The dozen or two Americans, the first "large" group to attend the university after World War II, lived in pensions on what was then the outskirts of "new" Jerusalem. (Within the next twenty years what had been "outskirts" in 1946–47 came close to the center of the city. After the Six Day War in June 1967 the borders were extended even further to include not only the Arab sectors but several Arab villages that had never been part of Jerusalem.)

In the few remaining months before civil war between Palestinian Jews and Arabs erupted we were able to attend classes on Mount Scopus, but the tension was palpable and it was increasingly difficult to concentrate on academic affairs. Furthermore, at that time all classes were in Hebrew; the university had not yet begun its special programs for foreign students. Not only was it difficult for a beginner in the language to follow lectures, but many professors—from Germany, Poland, Romania, Hungary, and Britain—had their own peculiar versions of the language so that even Sabra students found it difficult if not impossible to follow. While I gained little "book learning" during this period, I made many personal contacts with academicians at the university who introduced me to my first scholarly study of the Middle East. At the time—1946–47—there were few academic or *scholarly* publications in English devoted to the Middle East, perhaps not more than a few dozen. They included books such as George Antonius's *The Arab Awakening*, Philip Hitti's *History of the Arabs*, Albert Hourani's *Syria and Lebanon*, and a few on Palestine, including Paul Hanna's *British Policy in Palestine* and Nevil Barbour's *Nisi Dominus*. There were several biographies and autobiographies of interest by former British officials, journalists, and long-time residents of the area, such as those by Frederick Kisch, John Marlow, or Vincent Sheean. Scholarly periodicals such as *The Middle East Journal* or the *International Journal of Middle East Studies*; had not yet begun publication. This was the eve of a tidal wave of books, articles, monographs, and pamphlets that were to deluge academia within the next few years. The term "Middle East specialist" was brand new; their number could probably be counted in the dozens rather than hundreds, or thousands as indicated by recent membership rolls of the Middle East Studies Association and similar organizations. The term "Orientalist" was still honorable, and those who generally indulged in study or research on the region tended to come from or begin with a background in the ancient Middle East.

My mentor and closest advisor was Dr. Alfred Bonné, an economist who had come from Germany before the war and wrote some of the first insightful analyses of possibilities for economic development of the region. *The Economic Development of the Middle East*, published in 1943, was perhaps his best known work; it was one of the few in English dealing with regional economics available at the time. Although Bonné worked for the Jewish Agency for Palestine, he, like several other professors at the university, was much concerned about the growing dangers of violent confrontation between Palestinian Arabs and Jews. While many of them did not overtly endorse the binational ideas of

Magnes and Buber, they often sympathized with attitudes and concerns that gave rise to the binational idea.

As tensions and violence in Jerusalem mounted day by day classes at the university became increasingly sporadic. Larger numbers of students were absent, especially men who were off at underground military training. Some of the Americans joined the locals in preparing for military service, others continued attending classes intermittently as long as they lasted, several decided to leave the country, and a few used the opportunity to risk travel or undertake "independent study" regimes of their own.

I happened to meet the NBC Middle East correspondent John Donovan at a cocktail party for Americans and convinced him that he needed a local "stringer" to keep informed of what was happening in the Jewish community. He was convinced that he should hire me when I gave him advance information about the union of Ha-Shomer Ha-Zair and Achdut Avoda in the new Mapam party. This was enough to get me a press card from the British Mandatory Public Information Office (PIO) and started me on a career as a foreign correspondent.

By this time the university was for all practical purposes closed because the bus line connecting it with the Jewish parts of Jerusalem ran through an Arab sector, then considered hostile if not outright dangerous. Thus I spent the next year or so as the local stringer for John Donovan. Although Jewish and Arab sectors of Jerusalem were becoming more and more isolated from each other, withdrawing behind barbed wire enclosures, Jewish and Arab correspondents and local stringers still drank at the bar, had lunch together, and exchanged jokes and experiences within the confines of the British controlled sector of the city, especially at the principal journalist hang-out, the old PIO in the new section of Jerusalem not far from the King David Hotel. (The British sector too was surrounded by barbed wire since the mandatory authorities decided to take precautions against the growing number of Jewish terrorist attacks on their civilian and security authorities.)

There I had my first opportunity to meet and talk with Palestinian Arabs, many of whom were later to become well-known figures, such as Abu Said Aburish, the long-time stringer for *Time* magazine. (His son, Said K. Aburish, recently published an excellent book, *Children of Bethany: The Story of a Palestinian Family.*) Many if not most of the famous war correspondents of the day, such as Robert Capa, Homer Bigart, George Polk, Claire Hollingsworth, and I. F. Stone, were in and out of Palestine during the next two years. Palestine had replaced the battlefronts of World War II as the star attraction for Western media.

My first big "scoop" was in February, 1947 when I took a "short-cut" from the Jewish sector to the YMCA in the British Zone through the Mamilla cemetery, then considered a no-man's land between the British, Arab, and Jewish parts of new Jerusalem. While crossing through the cemetery I was stopped for interrogation by an armed group of Arabs. Not satisfied with my press credentials they decided to take me to a nearby cafe for further questioning. Eventually we ended up at the headquarters of the Arab national movement within the walls of the Old City, which was totally controlled by Palestinian Arab forces. Until then no one had asked if I was Jewish, but when I acknowledged that fact, the leaders at HQ decided to try me for espionage. The trial was relatively short—only a few hours—but in the course of questioning we entered into a political discussion in which I expressed my admiration for Dr. Magnes. This seemed to make an impression on my judges, who observed that if all Jews were like Magnes, there would be no conflict between the two peoples.

Eventually I was declared innocent and escorted back to the YMCA. My escort was Said Jundi, a leader of the Palestinian Arab fighters and also a well-known local football player. He claimed to have many Jewish friends, including a Yemenite girlfriend to whom he smuggled food during the siege of the Jewish sector. We became friends and met often at the YMCA, until the British left and all contact was severed between Jewish and Arab Jerusalem. (Rumor had it that Jundi crossed into Jordan and was later involved in the assassination of King Abdullah.) Donovan even had us broadcast to the U.S. together as a human interest story about Jewish-Arab relations. Neither Jewish nor Arab officials were particularly pleased that the incident was broadcast throughout the world. By then the fighting was seen by both sides as a life-or-death struggle in which neither wanted to acknowledge the humanity of the other. Although Donovan was praised for the story by NBC authorities in New York, he soon received a cable from David Sarnoff demanding that he now "get story of Jew saving Arab" to demonstrate that the network was "even-handed."

When the story was printed on a full page of the *Palestine Post*, predecessor of today's *Jerusalem Post*, Dr. Magnes asked me to visit him, first at the university, then at home. Although my account of the trial and the reaction of these "vicious" nationalists to his name warmed his heart, he already had become embittered by the course of events. Binationalism seemed to be dead. Partition of the country, he prophesied, would lead to disaster and years of conflict. Now there was little that could be done. Even his partner in binationalism, Ha-Shomer Ha-Zair, had abandoned the idea of a Jewish-Arab state after the November 1947 UN partition resolution. A few others were not quite so pessimistic. A small group continued to meet at Buber's home and I was invited to these meetings. But by the end of the year their numbers seemed so small, the participants so aged, and their discussion at such a lofty philosophic level that Magnes's pessimism seemed justified.

By mid 1948 we began to be aware of the mass exodus of Arabs from the new Jewish state; this was especially evident in the former Arab sections of Jerusalem captured by the various Jewish, and later Israeli, armed forces. What was happening to them? Where were they "disappearing" to? I wrote of my concern to Clarence Pickett, head of the American Friends Service Committee, or AFSC (the Quaker organization in Philadelphia), suggesting that the Friends, because of their long record of work with refugees, become involved.

After the first cease-fire in the war that broke out between Israel and the surrounding Arab states in May 1948, I left Jerusalem, returned to the U.S., and learned that AFSC was about to organize a refugee relief team to work in Israel/Palestine. A decision was taken to establish a large AFSC unit to work with the several hundred thousand refugees in Gaza and a smaller unit to work with refugees in Israel. I was selected to work as a volunteer with the Israel team headquartered in the Old City of Acre. Both AFSC teams were subsidiary to the UN Relief for Palestine Refugees, which was later to become UN-RWA (United Nations Relief and Works Agency for Palestine Refugees in the Middle East), the refugee agency that has worked with Palestine refugees for the past forty years. At that time there were still a few thousand Jewish refugees who had fled from one part of the country to another as a result of the war. The Government of Israel quickly accepted responsibility for them, leaving to the UN and voluntary agencies care of Palestinian Arabs.

During most of 1949 I was an AFSC, or "Quaker," volunteer traversing the Arab villages of northern Israel, mostly distributing UN relief supplies to Arabs who had fled from one part of the country to another. Our task was complicated because many Arabs, not yet called Palestinians, had infiltrated back to their homes in Israel "illegally" from across the new state's borders, mostly from southern Lebanon. At times the government overlooked these transgressions, but they frequently were ordered not to provide such "infiltrators" with food lest we encourage a mass return.

AFSC was eager to get out of the ration distribution business and turned its attention toward projects intended to foster better relations between Jews and Arabs. One project was establishment of a community center within the Old City walls of Acre; but it was almost impossible to get Jews from New Acre to participate with Old Acre. The two communities were separated by Acre's walls and it was difficult to persuade more than a handful of either Arabs or Jews to meet on common ground.

While serving as a volunteer with AFSC, I was able to continue my journalistic career, with occasional articles for the newly created *United Nations World* magazine. Robert Capa was a collaborator on one of my articles—he supplied the photos and I the text. After nine or ten months working in the villages of Galilee, I decided that my interest in the Middle East, particularly the Arab-Israel conflict, necessitated a more thorough academic background and discipline, so I again returned to the U.S., this time as a student at Columbia University.

In 1950 Columbia had no organized and integrated Middle East program, thus I became a graduate student in Public Law and Government, taking only a few Middle East courses, most of them taught by Professor J. C. Hurewitz, who was beginning his long career with the University. Most of my courses were those prerequisite to obtaining first an M.A. then a Ph.D. in what we now call political science. The courses with Jay Hurewitz were rigorous; he was not an easy teacher, paying close attention to detail, both in substance and in style. However his seminars were excellent preparation for any student who intended to undertake advanced research or graduate work. I learned more about research methods, style, sources, techniques, and preparation from him than from any other teacher in my total academic career.

By 1950 there still was a dearth of full-length books dealing with the Middle East, but the number was gradually beginning to increase. It was still small enough so that a scholar could hope to purchase most of them, unlike today when only a major university library can afford to acquire every new volume dealing with the region. Because so few books had been published and the several periodicals or magazines devoted to the Middle East were not yet underway, official government and other documents were still principal research instruments. Professor Hurewitz introduced students in his seminar to analysis of United Nations documents, at the time one of the most useful tools for political scientists. We also learned that judicious appraisal of the area's press as a basic source.

Professor Hurewitz's first book, *The Struggle for Palestine* (published in 1950 by W. W. Norton), was an excellent model for those of us contemplating a Ph.D. thesis. The seven pages of books listed in its bibliography probably included most volumes available at the time, not only on the Palestine question but on the rest of the Middle East as well. The list included scholarly works, such as those by Hitti and Hourani mentioned above, Lenczowski on Iran, Ireland on Iraq, and Twitchell on Saudi Arabia, and also many propaganda, ideological, or biographical items that could not be considered truly scholarly works. (In addition to the seven pages of books there were also some twenty pages of other items, such as official and unofficial documents and correspondence of individuals and organizations.) In 1949–50 the number of books available was so small that a professor could ask an advanced student to become familiar with most works dealing with the contemporary Middle East.

After finishing my master's and all Ph.D. work but the dissertation, I found a respite from academia at the Voice of America (then in New York City), where I worked for a year as a Middle East Media Evaluator. The task of our office was to determine the impact, if any, of the VOA on listeners throughout the world. The method of doing this from New York was to analyze listeners' letters, reports from embassies, any references to VOA in foreign media, and chats with anyone who happened to be passing through the office from some overseas visit. I can't say that I was ever able to determine the impact of the Voice in the Middle East, but the assignment broadened my horizons somewhat as I became familiar with a wide range of new sources and learned something about how government bureaucracy works. By the end of the year the opportunity arose for me to begin work on my Ph.D. thesis, which I decided would be on Israel's policy toward the Arab refugee problem. I applied for and received one of the first Ford Foundation foreign area studies research grants.

After resigning from VOA, I spent the next year and a half in the Middle East gathering the material for my dissertation, which was to become the first book-length study in English of the refugee problem and of the Arab minority in Israel.

Before settling down in Israel for extended research, I spent a month or two in Egypt and Lebanon attempting to obtain Arab perspectives on the refugee problem. My reception in both Cairo and Beirut was rather cool; neither Egypt nor Lebanon had yet begun to welcome Jewish visitors, especially one who was attempting to pry into so delicate and controversial an issue as the Palestine refugees. Although officials at the old Arab League headquarters in Cairo were hostile, I had the good fortune to run into a reporter for a Muslim Brotherhood newspaper at the League offices. Mahmud el-Kabir approached one day after seeing me rebuffed and volunteered to assist. "I see you are being unfairly treated," he explained. "I don't believe that just because someone is Jewish he should be so ill-treated. We should judge people by what they do, not by their religious origins."

During the course of the next few weeks in July 1953 Mahmud el-Kabir introduced me to all the leaders of the Muslim Brotherhood from Hassan al-Hodeiby to Salah el-Eshmawy, i.e., from the Supreme Guide to the leader of the opposition. During an interview with Hodeiby, he attempted to demonstrate the respect for religion possessed by Hassan al-Bana (founder of the Muslim Brotherhood) by relating how al-Bana would light the gas lamps and stoves of an elderly Jewish woman who was his neighbor each Friday evening and on Saturday because she was not permitted to undertake such activity on the sabbath. In response to my query about the Brotherhood and women, Hodeiby replied by explaining that one of his daughters was a physician, another a professor.

My Brotherhood friend also introduced me to the leaders of the new Revolutionary Command Council that had seized power in Egypt a few days earlier. In all these extended discussions about religion and politics Mohammed el-Kabir presented me as a Jewish scholar from America. Only when we vis-

ited Haj Amin al-Husseini, former Mufti of Jerusalem, did he caution me not
to mention that I was Jewish. During the interview the mufti displayed far
more hatred of the British than of Jews or Israel.

Although I had little success in Egypt gathering information about the
refugees, I was able to publish a lengthy article in Max Ascoli's now defunct
Reporter magazine about the Muslim Brotherhood, one of the first "inside"
stories about the organization that was to appear in the U.S. The article is cited in Richard Mitchell's book about the Brotherhood under my journalistic
"pseudonym," Donald Peters.

I had even less success with my refugee study in Beirut, where my presence seemed to frighten or embarrass a number of Americans affiliated with
the American University of Beirut. Since AUB was receiving financial aid
from the Ford Foundation certain Americans at the university believed that
they would be contaminated if it were discovered that the Foundation was also
assisting an American Jew interested in the volatile refugee problem. The
AUB crowd convinced that local Ford Foundation representative to give me a
"hearing" before a group of "concerned Americans" who found my presence in
Beirut too compromising. The "hearing" reminded me of my Jerusalem "trial,"
and I was "ordered" to leave the country for the good of the Foundation and
the university despite assurances from some of the AUB Arab faculty, including professors Nabih Faris and Zeine Zeine, that they did not feel threatened
by my presence. Indeed, they perceived the incident as an example of bending
over backwards to appease Arab prejudices by the American Middle East
types.

My research in Israel was fruitful and I did gather more than enough data
for my dissertation using a wide variety of sources in both Hebrew and English. These included Israeli Knesset proceedings, Supreme Court hearings
and decisions, official documents, and extensive use of cuttings from Israel's
most prominent daily newspaper, *Haaretz*. It then had a fine clipping and filing system modeled on the one at the *New York Times*. The clippings were filed
according to the categories that I most needed—such as Absentee Property,
Custodian of Absentee Property, Arab Refugees, Israeli Arabs, and Court Decisions.

While in Israel I wrote as I collected data, preparing a series of working
papers on the above categories. The working papers became chapters in my

thesis, which was later published by the Middle East Institute as *Israel and the Palestine Arabs*, my first book. These working papers were to be of far greater use as standalone papers than as chapters in a book. They were requested by the U.S. Department of State, the British Foreign Office, and the United Nations Conciliation Commission for Palestine, which was then beginning a project of refugee property evaluation. The hope at the time in American, British, and UN official circles was that resolution of the refugee problem would lead to a peace settlement between Israel and the Arab states. The question of refugee property identification, appraisal, evaluation, and compensation was critical in resolution of the refugee question; therefore it was also an issue about which both Israelis and Arabs were extremely sensitive. Dealing with the refugee question at this time was like handling TNT—neither side believed that it could be handled "safely" or objectively.

In an attempt to be objective I asked the Israel Foreign Office to go over the working papers and give me its comments. A young diplomat, who was later to become an ambassador and university president, was assigned the task. When I met with him to discuss the documents he began the conversation by remarking, "Mr. Peretz, there's nothing here but facts! You haven't shown what we're trying to do in this country!" Later, another Israeli diplomat at the UN observed, "The trouble with you is that you're trying to look at this problem like a man from Mars!"

After gathering my data and preparing the series of working papers I spent the next several months in New York revising and reworking the papers into a thesis acceptable to my advisor, Professor Hurewitz, and in preparing for the dissertation defense. Sustenance was earned by part-time teaching at a variety of institutions, including Hofstra College, Long Island University, and Hunter College, and by writing articles, some journalistic, some scholarly, which were published in *Foreign Affairs, Middle East Journal, Reporter, United Nations World, Jewish Social Studies, New Leader, Progressive, Foreign Policy Bulletin, Human Relations Area Files, Socialist Call, Christian Science Monitor, Current History, American Jewish Yearbook, International Journal, New Republic, Commonweal, New Outlook, Middle East Forum, Reconstructionist, Issues, Christian Century, Orbis, Vital Issues,* and several publications in Israel.

At the time there were only a few Middle East textbooks on the market, and publishers began to be interested in the potential of new texts dealing with the area. Middle East courses were becoming more popular as part of the growing interest in non-Western area studies. The emphasis on the non-Western world was sparked by grants available from the Ford Foundation and growing interest on the part of the U.S. government and several smaller private foundations. As more colleges and universities offered these area study courses the market expanded for area study textbooks. In 1960 or 1961 John Badeau, former President of the American University in Cairo and then President of the Near East Foundation, was approached by Henry Holt Publishers to join the fray with another text. Since he was tied up with his work at the New East Foundation, he asked me to assist him. The project began with joint authorship through weekly conferences on each chapter. However, I soon became the principal drafter, then Badeau found that he had to leave the project altogether. Although he read through the final manuscript and made many useful contributions, he declined to take any of the credit or profits from the book. The result was a textbook intended for introductory history or political science classes dealing with the region. *The Middle East Today* (1st edition 1963), as the title indicates, was originally intended to be a transitional text, but the demand was great enough to keep the book in print from 1963 until the present, through a fifth edition and some eighty thousand copies. Indicative of the turmoil in the publishing business is the book's history of publishers—from Holt to Holt, Rinehart and Winston, to Praeger, to Greenwood.

My first book, *Israel and the Palestine Arabs*, a revised version of my Ph.D. thesis, was published by the Middle East Institute in 1958 with the assistance of Bill Sands, the editor of *The Middle East Journal*. Although several other books on the Arab refugee problem and the minority in Israel were to be published within the next few years, mine was considered a basic source on these subjects since it was the first published in English. Because it contained considerable detail about Arab property in Israel, government policies for dealing with the property, and ways in which the property was absorbed, it was used by a variety of agencies and organizations as a reference work. Several governments and the UNCCP (United Nations Conciliation Commission for Palestine) were interested in the contents and invited me to consult with them on the subject.

Since I undertook my research on the Arab minority and Arab property in Israel, many new sources have become available (beginning in the late

1970s) providing material for the new Israeli "revisionist" historians such as Benny Morris, Tom Segev, and Simha Flapan. The documentation that they have worked with includes many sources that were not yet available when I worked on these subjects in 1952–53. However, the "revisionists" have often made similar if not identical observations and often reached conclusions not unlike mine. They too have been attacked for "not seeing the whole picture," "looking at the problem like men from Mars," "disregarding the other side's aggression," "giving ammunition to the enemy," and so forth.

There were also Arab critics of *Israel and the Palestine Arabs*. When the book was first published it was banned in Lebanon, probably because it discussed the very sensitive question of the ratio between Christians and Muslims in the country. The book pointed out that the influx of Muslim refugees from Palestine had thrown askew the delicate balance between the two groups which has been the basis of political representation and the constitutional system. During one of my visits an official at UNRWA thought that the ban could be lifted if I were to meet the chief censor in person. He arranged the interview and, after a cordial discussion, the censor lifted the ban. However, several weeks later, after I left the country, the ban was reimposed.

My discussion of the Arab minority in Israel appeared interesting to the American Jewish Committee and the organization invited me to present it at one of their annual meetings, which led to my employment as Middle East Consultant to AJC. While I saw my role as educative, i.e., to keep the organization honestly informed about Israel and the Middle East, some of its officers believed that my function was to give a scholarly or credible overcast to AJC positions and pronouncements on the region. These tended to be uncritical if not defensive of Israel's government policies and highly critical of Arab, American, United Nations, or any other criticism of Israel. The officers of the organization were particularly sensitive about offending Israeli officials and nearly every item published concerning the Middle East had to be checked with the Israeli embassy in Washington or the consulate general in New York. Many hours were spent in internal debates with AJC staff, which always insisted on getting the official Israeli government view before publishing. Officials from the consulate would be invited to AJC or to some "neutral" meeting place like the Harmony Club to debate the wording and nuances of nearly every pronouncement or information bulletin dealing with the Middle East.

However, the organization was adamantly independent about one issue: American Jews were Americans and Israelis were Israeli citizens. The two were not to be confused. This discussion arose at a time when several Israeli officials, particularly Prime Minister Ben Gurion, were making ambiguous statements about the identity of world Jewry with the Jewish State. The AJC sent its most prestigious leaders to Israel to discuss the ambiguity with Ben Gurion. The result was a "pact" between the organization and the State of Israel intended to clarify and emphasize the distinction between American and Israeli Jews.

One of my projects while at the AJC was to establish some personal contacts between officers and leaders of the organization with Arab officials. I naively thought that such contacts would broaden the perspectives of the membership. However, after a few such meetings the project was discarded because some in the organization and some outside feared that the leadership would be "brainwashed." It was argued that they were not well enough informed to evaluate and absorb the "propaganda" that would be fed them by direct contact with educated Arabs.

Shortly after the 1956 Suez/Sinai War word came to the Committee about the difficult conditions Jews in Arab countries were facing, and I was asked to visit the region to investigate. After several weeks in Egypt, Syria, and Lebanon I concluded that indeed Jews in both Egypt and Syria were having problems, although the situation in Lebanon at that time was tolerable. There was actually an influx of several hundred Jews from both Egypt and Syria to Lebanon, and many of them settled in Beirut.

While in the area I was asked to write a series of articles for the U.S. Socialist party's magazine, *The Call*, and arranged interviews with leaders of groups such as the Ba'ath. My scheduled interview with the Ba'athist foreign minister of Syria, Salah Bitar, was aborted when the country's security authorities told me to leave "immediately" after it was discovered that I was visiting members of the Jewish community to inquire about their status. My arrest and deportation occurred within a couple of hours; I was escorted to the border and returned to Beirut.

However, within a day the leader of the Ba'athists in Lebanon called me apologizing for the "mistake;" he offered to escort me back to Damascus for the interview with Bitar. I was impressed by the fact that Bitar was more influenced by my Socialist connection than by the transgression into the highly sensitive "Jewish question." It appeared to me that if some world renowned Socialist leader came to the Middle East he might alleviate the situation of Jews in Egypt and Syria.

Upon my return to New York, after giving my impressions to the AJC, I was asked to approach the leader of the American Socialist Party, Norman Thomas, to see if he would be willing to undertake such a mission. Thomas, seventy-five years old at the time, agreed, provided I would accompany him. He had recently become interested in the Middle East and its problems and believed that the trip would provide an opportunity to take an overall look at the region. Accordingly, we set out on a six-week visit that brought us to Egypt, Israel, Lebanon, Jordan, Syria, and Iraq. During the course of the mission we had extensive interviews with President Nasser of Egypt and several other members of the Revolutionary Command Council, King Hussein of Jordan and members of his cabinet, the leaders of the Ba'ath and its Central Committee in Damascus, and the Foreign Ministers of Lebanon, Israel, and Iraq. I was impressed by Thomas' ability to present difficult problems with candor yet without creating confrontation. We covered the gamut from the problems of minorities, including Jews, Copts, and Kurds, to economic and social development. Thomas could stand before the most potentially hostile audience, like the Ba'ath Central Committee in Damascus, warning them of the dangers in an alliance with the Soviet Union, and receive warm applause at the end of his critique. Even U.S. ambassadors received him enthusiastically, confiding that they regarded him with esteem. When Thomas presented the sensitive "Jewish Question" in a meeting we had with Salah Bitar, Akram Hourani, and Michel Aflaq, they realized that they could not hide facts from him. We can't deal with the problem directly, they stated, because it is controlled by the security services. However, they promised to work behind the scenes through the party. Bitar even claimed that in local elections he received most of the Jewish votes. Some months later, after the union of Syria and Egypt in 1958, we heard that there was a slight improvement in the plight of Damascus Jews when Egyptian Security authorities overruled orders of the Syrians.

Thomas was particularly interested in meeting leaders of the various socialist groups in the countries we visited and in the programs that they might have adopted for economic and social development of the region. However he was rather disappointed to discover that not more than one or two seemed to have more than a vague conception of socialist theory or ideology as conceived by its Western progenitors. After attending a meeting of the Arab Nationalist Movement in Beirut, where we listened to a fiery oration by one of the young lights of the organization, Thomas commented to me, "I have a hard time understanding what Arab socialism means, Don. But it seems to me that its slogan should be 'Liberty, equality, and revenge!'"

The theoretical portion of our meeting with President Nasser was not much more fruitful; however we did observe that he was deeply involved in a comparative study of social and socialist programs in both the West and non-Western worlds. On his desk there were several books and pamphlets, including Hugh Gaitskill's program for Great Britain, an account of Yugoslav development programs, and a book by or about Nehru and his governance in India. We were told that Nasser perused such literature widely and that when he found an item of interest or relevance, a team of translators was assigned to present it in Arabic within a day or two.

The most impressive of the Arab leftists we encountered was Mohammed Hadid, a leader of the National Democratic party in Iraq. He had been one of Harold Lasky's students at the London School of Economics and, according to Thomas, must have been an excellent disciple. Hadid seemed to have had both the breadth and depth of sophistication and academic background necessary to comprehend Socialism as Thomas understood it; his understanding was also tempered by the kind of humanism that characterized Norman Thomas' approach to problems. Hadid conducted us on a tour of Baghdad, through the *serifas* or shanty towns that surrounded the city. These sights and the reports of unrest throughout the country that were reported to us seemed to be harbingers of the revolution that was to erupt (July 1958) a few months after we left Iraq.

The trip sparked Thomas's interest in the Middle East, resulting in a series of articles and continuing meetings in New York with personalities involved in the region. At that time relations between the U.S. and Syria were so strained that when Foreign Minister Salah Bitar came to the annual session of the UN General Assembly he was unable to make any appointments with American officials. The only notable whose name he seemed to recognize was

Senator John Kennedy, who had spoken out in favor of Algerian self-determination some months earlier. Syrian officials seemed to have no idea with whom or how to make contacts among American notables, and they called Thomas for assistance. He arranged a wide spectrum of interviews for Bitar, including Senators Hubert Humphrey, Ralph Flanders, and some union leaders and editors. But Bitar still wanted to meet Kennedy, about whom Thomas was not very enthusiastic. I contacted one of the senator's relatives, and after some delay he agreed to arrange a meeting, provided that it was kept secret. The senator did not want it bandied about that he was meeting with an Arab official who was hostile to Israel. The meeting did take place with only three persons present—the senator, Bitar, and Kennedy's wife, who translated from French to English.

My first contact with Arab socialism was in the early 1950s when I met Kemal Jumblatt in Beirut and Michel Aflaq in Damascus. At the time streetcars still ran through Damascus, so I boarded one which took me to Aflaq's home in a poorer section of the city. His apartment was in an upper story of an old building; there were dozens of children running in and out of the place, apparently not his but nephews and nieces. Then, as in later meetings, he seemed almost humble—soft-spoken, low-keyed, and semi-apologetic in his responses. Jumblatt was much more assertive even though there always seemed to be a dreamy quality about the conversations with him. He was a tall, gaunt man who claimed to be inspired by Mahatma Gandhi; some called him the Gandhi of Lebanon—rather a misnomer considering the militancy, including use of heavy weapons by his followers in Lebanon's internal struggles. At the time so little was known about Jumblatt's Progressive Socialist Party and Aflaq's Ba'ath that the U.S. ambassadors in each capital had only the vaguest notion that they existed, to say nothing of what they represented. True, Arab socialism was then very much a fringe movement, with only a handful of practitioners. Few analysts in the early 1950s perceived that within a decade the various Arab socialist groups would attain the importance that Islamic fundamentalist movements have acquired since the 1980s.

A few months after the Middle East trip with Norman Thomas my employment at the American Jewish Committee ended. Several individuals, both staff and lay members of the organization, were not pleased with my range of contacts in the Arab world, which also seemed to disturb certain Israeli officials as well. The AJC was a mainstay of their "information" efforts in the American Jewish community and in Washington; consequently, they did not want these contacts jeopardized by too friendly associations with Arab quarters. When I was offered the downgraded status of a part-time job at the Committee, I got the message and decided to leave.

After a brief interval of teaching a Middle East course in the political science department of Vassar College, I began a twenty-eight-year stint of service with the State of New York (1962–90), the first five years at the State Education Department in Albany, the rest at the State University of New York in Binghamton.

In Albany I worked at the Education Department headquarters with Ward Morehouse. He was the Director and I the Associate Director of the Center for International Programs and Services. The task of this Center was to further the development of foreign, especially non-Western, area studies throughout the New York state education system. This was an era when the educational establishment was again awakening to the lack of knowledge about the Third World among Americans. It was the beginning of the short-lived Kennedy period, when even the Washington establishment was concerned about the myopia of American foreign policy. To compensate for the restricted vision of the Eisenhower-Dulles era, when the world was divided between Communists and anti-Communists, Kennedy seemed to recognize that between the two there was a third world with its own interests and concerns, not necessarily those of either the Soviet bloc or the West. This recognition was evident in some of Kennedy's ambassadorial appointments: John Badeau to Egypt, John Kenneth Galbraith to India, Chester Bowles as an Assistant Secretary of State. The tone set in Washington had reverberations elsewhere. The Ford Foundation, already in the Third World business, gave a number of substantial grants for developing greater emphasis on the "unknown" parts of the world.

Ward Morehouse, or rather the New York State Education Department, was one of the recipients of the Foundation's largesse. With the several hundred thousand dollars the Education Department received it was able to enlarge Morehouse's operation and to initiate a wide range of activities in New York state intended to expand knowledge about and interest in Asia, Africa, Latin America, the Middle East, and Eastern Europe.

Morehouse's mandate included the entire education system in New York, from kindergarten through graduate school, in both the public and private sectors. The responsibilities of the State Education Department in New York are extensive, perhaps more extensive than in any other state, much like a ministry of education in a large Western European nation. They include not only the formal institutions of education—schools, colleges, and universities—but also museums, libraries, and just about anything else connected with education. The Commissioner of Education, appointed by the Board of Regents (a non-salaried lay body) is also the President of the University of the State of New York, not to be confused with the State University of New York (SUNY) or New York University (NYU). (SUNY is the public system of higher education; NYU is a private institution in New York City, and the University of the State of New York comprises the entire educational system in the state under jurisdiction of the Board of Regents and the State Education Department.) Thus Ward Morehouse and our office, the Center for International Programs and Services, had entree into a wide range of educational and cultural activities.

With funds from the Ford grant in-service programs were initiated in dozens of schools throughout the state for teachers at all levels from kindergarten on up. These might include a series of seminars during the school year on Chinese literature, Japanese painting, Islamic art, history of the Middle East, or courses in "lesser known" languages, such as Chinese, Japanese, Russian, Arabic, and Portuguese. Summer institutes with similar themes and/or subjects were organized for teachers and professors at all levels in some of the state's finest area study institutions, including Cornell, Columbia, and NYU. With assistance from the U.S. Office of Education, grants were received to facilitate study abroad for teachers, either in groups or for individual research projects. Several hundred New York teachers and professors were enabled to study in the Middle East, South Asia, Latin America, and the rest of the Third World through Morehouse's efforts. Reading lists, syllabi, and model course outlines were prepared by area specialists for distribution to schools and colleges to assist in the introduction of greater emphasis on these neglected regions of the world.

Top administrators were not overlooked. Ward persuaded groups of college and university presidents to attend retreats, such as the three-day seminar at a camp in the Adirondacks where they read and discussed some of the Chinese classics. The idea was to cut these leaders off from all links with the outside world—telephones, administrative assistants, and crises—so that they could actually concentrate on something related to academic substance. It took someone like Ward to persuade them to participate in such an "outlandish" venture, and it worked. Most of them greatly enjoyed the experience and a few even continued to read the books given them during the retreats. At an equally lofty level, there were seminars for school administrators and superintendents dealing with similar subjects. On occasion we would be invited to make presentations to the Board of Regents, chairs of committees dealing with education in the state legislature, or other "important" officials who needed to be persuaded of the significance of the Center and its work.

Another of Morehouse's concerns was to bridge the gap between areas, between disciplines, and between states. Thus he was an ambassador from New York to educational establishments outside the state, resulting in collaborative projects between them and New York. One of Morehouse's greatest coups was to receive a grant in Indian rupees from the U.S. Office of Education to open a New York state educational center in New Delhi. Its purpose was to develop educational materials about Indian life, history, and culture for use in the New York state educational system. Indian educators worked with American teachers and professors to develop these materials, which were widely diffused through schools in the U.S. The New Delhi center continued for many years, until the backlog of rupees was finally exhausted and the program was ended.

Still another project, with assistance from the U.S. Office of Education, was to bring educators from Third World countries to the U.S.; many came to New York where they served for a year or two as resource people or advisors in developing materials, lecturing about their own cultures or history, and assisting in the Center.

Major attention was given to the Middle East in these efforts, leading to introduction of dozens of new courses dealing with the area at several colleges and to establishment of a couple of Middle East programs, including the one at Binghamton.

Literally scores of the two hundred-odd colleges and universities in New York state were affected by the work of the Center and much greater emphasis was placed on these "neglected" areas at the pre-college level. Questions dealing with the Third World were introduced on the New York State High School Regents Examinations, which meant that teachers had to discuss the subject in their classes and to prepare themselves to deal with parts of the world that had long been overlooked in their curricula. During the nearly five years I worked at the Education Department in Albany, I must have visited a few score colleges around the state, contacting specialists at the larger ones and arranging for them to lecture at or to organize programs at the smaller. As a result of our work, we enabled teachers and professors from the smaller out of the way colleges to participate in seminars and discussions with the country's leading experts on China, Japan, India, the Middle East, Africa, and Eastern Europe. For example, Carl Brown and Morroe Berger from Princeton came to Albany to lecture about the Middle East in seminars arranged for high school teachers.

One of the more innovative projects during my stay in Albany was an attempt to develop more direct contacts with the Black community in New York City. A group of five or six of us, including Joe Nyquist, then the Deputy Commissioner (later Commissioner of Education), was selected to spend several days in Harlem, living as well as working there. We were ensconced at the old Teresa Hotel on 125th Street, where we met with a wide range of citizens representing groups from the Black Muslims to organizations of Harlem parents. We heard suggestions, and demands, ranging from introduction of Black Nationalist curriculum to assertions from middle-class parents that their children wanted to achieve the same middle-class life styles as white children. Each evening the group would break up and our members would be invited to homes of Harlem residents—teachers, prison guards, bus conductors, and ministers. While the top layers of the Education Department were much influenced by the visit, i.e., Associate Commissioners and such, it was difficult to change attitudes among the hundreds of bureaucrats in the middle and lower levels of the vast department bureaucracy. (At the time some 2,000 officials—nearly all white—worked at the Education Department in Albany headquarters.)

Harpur College in Binghamton was among the many institutions receiving assistance from the Education Department's Center for International Programs and Services between 1962 and 1967. During this period Harpur

College was designated to become one of the SUNY system's four university centers, authorized to grant doctoral as well as bachelors and masters degrees; thus Harpur College became the undergraduate division of the new SUNY center at Binghamton. Following the current trend, with encouragement from university headquarters in Albany and funding from Ward Morehouse's Ford Foundation grant, faculty at SUNY Binghamton decided to initiate a foreign area studies program. The largest number was interested in the Middle East and several had some experience in the area. These, combined with a few whose interest was in Sudanic and Islamic Africa, formed the Program in Southwest Asian and North African Studies, since known by the acronym SWANA. Because of my interest in the Middle East, SUNY Binghamton was among the colleges I was assigned to work with. After about a year the program was underway but lacked a director. After a search of several months, the university asked if I would be interested in the task. I was eager to devote more of my time and energy to the Middle East and accepted the job, part-time teaching in the political science department and part-time directing the new SWANA program.

Since 1966–67, when I moved from Albany to Binghamton, SWANA developed into one of the better interdisciplinary area study programs in the country, with a core faculty of over a dozen and courses in departments of political science, history, anthropology, sociology, geography, economics, classics, and Middle Eastern languages. The SWANA library holdings have been ranked among the dozen best in university collections. The annual conferences on Middle East themes held at Binghamton and the work and publications of its Middle East faculty have helped to give the university visibility in the academic world—graduate students come from abroad as well as from across the U.S. to undertake advanced study in the Middle East at SUNY Binghamton.

By the early 1960s there was still no large Middle East area study organization like the ones for Asian, African, and East European studies. There was no annual assembly of Middle East specialists such as the Asian Studies Association or the African Studies Association conferences. A number of us felt that a similar organization would not only be useful but was also needed for the Middle East. In the mid-1960s we persuaded the Social Science Research Council to consider the idea and to convene a meeting in New York to discuss it. A couple of dozen or so Middle East types, several of them contributors to this book, met and the Middle East Studies Association of North America (MESA) was underway. Only a few dozen people attended the first annual meeting of MESA held at the University of Chicago in 1967. Since then MESA has become, like the Asian and African and Slavic Studies Associations, a monstrous organization whose annual conferences are attended by many hundreds if not a thousand or more. Usually space is required at a couple of hotels to accommodate those attending. In addition to its scholarly quarterly, *The International Journal of Middle East Studies*, MESA publishes a bi-annual bulletin, a newsletter, and annual conference proceedings and has published a number of studies concerning the Middle East. MESA is now on a par with the other area study organizations, and its membership is around two thousand.

Supposedly MESA is a more "purely" scholarly organization than the Middle East Institute (MEI) in Washington, D.C., organized some twenty years earlier at the initiative of several individuals who had worked in the region as diplomats, teachers, and the like. Whereas MESA and its journal are intended for academicians, MEI and its quarterly, *Middle East Journal*, aim to inform not only the academic community but also a wider audience, including business, journalists, government officials, and those with a broad interest in international affairs. MESA covers a longer time span, focusing on study of the Middle East since the rise of Islam; it also strongly emphasizes humanities in addition to social sciences; whereas the Institute focuses on the contemporary Middle East, with emphasis on political, economic, and historical developments. The activities of the two organizations do often overlap, however, as is evident in many of the topics discussed at both annual conferences and in articles in both journals. The two are not competitive, and many scholars serve on the editorial and executive boards of both organizations.

Evidence of the extent to which Middle East studies have burgeoned is the large number of specialized groups that have affiliated with MESA (about twenty); several have their annual meetings at the same time and place. They include an association of Arabic teachers; associations for Maghrib, Yemini, Central Asian, Sudan, Armenian, Afghanistan, Turkish, Iranian, and Israeli studies; and organizations of Middle East economists, librarians, numismatics, and women's studies.

One has only to peruse the program of the annual MESA meeting to see how extensive coverage of the area has become since the 1960s. So many papers are presented at the annual meetings that at times it is necessary to schedule four or more sessions simultaneously. Middle East studies has become "big business," so much so that several years ago a group of younger academicians were about to form an "alternative" MESA because of their dissatisfaction with the "establishmentarian" trends in the mother organization.

One of the more troublesome aspects of Middle Eastern studies in the U.S. is the extent to which academic study and research involving the area is often overshadowed by the Arab-Israel conflict. Frequently partisans of each side tend to make academic judgements or evaluations influenced by their perceptions of a scholar's or writer's attitudes toward the conflict. If an author is believed to be too "pro-Arab" or too "pro-Israel," his/her work is downgraded or discounted regardless of its academic merits. This cleavage has created bitter conflicts at several institutions and an undertone of animosity marks the attitudes of many toward MESA and MEI. The cleavage in attitudes crosses the political spectrum from right to left. One can find both "pros" and "antis" among those who are the most conservative on other issues as well as those who are the most radical. It even affects academic employment at some institutions, where a scholar on some aspect of the Middle East, such as Persian literature or Turkish economics, may be rejected if he is perceived to bend too far toward the Israeli or the Arab stand on "the conflict."

Another divisive issue among Middle East scholars has been the extent to which they should or should not receive assistance from or cooperate with the U.S. government. The dispute arose a few years ago when the Defense Intelligence Agency solicited area study research projects, several of which related to the Middle East. The issue was sharply debated within MESA, where some argued that too close relations between American intelligence organizations, such as DIA or the CIA, would compromise the work not only of those working with such agencies but of all scholars who desired to work abroad. Some argued that any scholar would be discredited if affiliated with a university in which one of its members was engaged in a project associated with such an agency.

These issues raise the question of "objectivity" in research, writing, and teaching about the Middle East. Some maintain that "objectivity" in dealing with the area is a chimera, unattainable because we are all so influenced by our religious, ethnic, cultural, or class origins that we cannot escape from either our conscious or subconscious preconditioning. However, we have observed that there are quite a few academicians and writers who seem to have dealt with the Middle East in a fashion that does not betray their ethnic, class, or religious roots. I believe that J. C. Hurewitz sought to attain this "objectivity" in his work and attempted to instill it in his students. Of course this irritated, even exasperated, some of his students and readers who complained that they never could find out where he stood on sensitive issues such as the Arab-Israel dispute. Those who strive for "objectivity" may often find themselves labeled by each side in any of the regional conflicts as disguised partisans of the "enemy."

An issue of similar genre is whether academicians should take overt positions on many of the political and social controversies that plague the area, such as the Arab-Israel dispute, the Iraq-Iran war, the civil war in Lebanon, or the problems of minorities (Arabs in Israel, Kurds in Iraq and Iran, Copts in Egypt). I observe that those who are often so insistent that we take strong positions on these matters usually are quite selective. Each has his/her own particular group or problem that demands the world's attention, often overlooking the many other, often similar problems that exist just across the border.

An attempt to deal with Israel in a scholarly "objective" fashion was initiated at the founding conference of the Association for Israeli Studies (AIS) held at Darmouth College in 1985. Some thirty-five scholars participated, and the first Board of Directors included academicians across a wide ideological spectrum—Peace Now sympathizers to semi-hawks. The annual conferences of this group have been among the more enlightening on problems dealing with the country, and debate has been open, frank, and often revealing. Despite the wide U.S. interest in Israel, the large number of books written about it, and the many courses offered at universities, membership in the AIS has increased at a remarkably slow rate—from the original thirty-five to just over one hundred, only a fraction of the membership in other more partisan organizations that deal with Israel.

I feel that we should be free to take positions on the moral questions that confront us, such as those in the Arab-Israel conflict, the treatment of minorities in the Middle East, social and economic inequities, and human rights. I attempt to separate my feelings and "citizen" activities on these issues from my academic work by, as I was once accused (see above), presenting "the facts." However, some of my colleagues are reluctant to reveal their personal feelings on such issues even outside their academic work and thus refrain from supporting groups that "take sides."

In matters such as this I was much influenced by Dr. Judah Magnes, former President of the Hebrew University in Jerusalem. Every few years I reread an address he gave at the opening of the Hebrew University's academic year 5708 (1947–48). It was the eve of the UN partition resolution and only a year or two after the full impact of the Holocaust was revealed to the world. The address was called "Responsibility."

> These are fateful days for the world; and the fate, too, of the House of Israel hangs in the balance. Has Judaism still the power to speak in these days of mankind's crisis?…The nations, and we Jews among them, seem to have learned but little from the suffering, poverty, moral degradation, from the myriads of the killed and liquidated and maimed of the war, nominally now ended…
>
> This use of force and violence, which now characterizes our community, is a real change in the basic structure of the Jewish society. One must go as far back as the period of the destruction of the Second Temple to find a similar phenomenon. Then, the Jewish state was nearing its end, and many justified the employment of force and violence as the sole means left to the people in its desperate struggle against the Roman tyrant. There are many, too, who, under present circumstances, justify the use of force and violence as the one possible and effective method of re-establishing the Jewish state…
>
> What I do wish to ask is, what is the duty of the man, more especially the teacher, who thinks the method of force and violence to be a savage and idolatrous belief? The question is, is there room for that man? Is it his right, or even perhaps this duty, to express an opinion which may differ from the majority decisions of official institutions? Is one to sanctify these majority decisions above every other sacred thing? More than that, is there not laid upon that man the sacred task, despite majority decisions, to warn the people, to teach, to point to its error, nay perhaps its iniquity, when it sharpens its swords, and to the destruction that may overtake the people and the land? Is there no place in our totalitarian society for those who *dissent* from the decisions of the majority, and, who, conscious of

their collective responsibility, obey the command of the conscience by lifting their voice, not for murder and destruction, Heaven forbid, but for peace and understanding among the people?

As I reread Magnes it occurs to me that since I began my career in and study of the Middle East, although much has changed, much remains the same. The Middle East is still a dangerous place, and many countries, including the United States, have dangerous policies for coping, supposedly, with dangerous situations. Now, as so often in the post World War II era, the Middle East is again in the throes of a crisis that will dramatically alter its political environment; again, as in the past—seven Arab-Israel wars, the civil war in Lebanon, the Suez Crisis, the Gulf War—most proposals for coping emphasize military solutions, or the use of force. The result of such thinking in the nearly half century since World War II is that the Middle East has become the most heavily armed Third World region, the world's major consumer of military hardware, the center of the largest armies, and, despite the end of East-West tensions, the major focus for future international warfare. Do we Middle East "specialists" or "experts" have any responsibility, not for causing these unpleasant "facts," but for attempting to alter the situation?

◆ ◆ ◆

As I look back on nearly forty-five years of involvement in the Middle East, how has the area and the study of it changed? Perhaps in summary a checklist might be useful:

- The Middle East is no longer so remote in Western, especially American, consciousness. In Carleton Coon's book *Caravan* (1951) there is a story of an American recently returned from the region who responds to a friend's question, "Where have you been?" with, "I was in the Middle East." The friend replies in puzzlement, "There is no Middle East. There's only a Middle West!" Those days are gone. Although the average American may not be able to name the countries of the Middle East, (s)he knows that the region is there.

- Middle East experts, specialists, and academicians have proliferated from a few score to several thousand; no government agency, private business, non-profit organization, or university would have difficulty in finding a knowledgeable person to undertake research, write, teach, or otherwise deal with the region. Academic institutions now graduate several dozen Middle East area study specialists each year. Newspapers have no difficulty in finding capable specialists to be correspondents in the area, banks in hiring economic experts on the Middle East, and universities in employing teachers competent in Middle East subjects. There still is a shortage of native-born Americans with language competence in Arabic, Turkish, and Persian, but we now have a large supply of naturalized American citizens available with these skills.

- Publications—books, magazines, newsletters, monographs, etc.— dealing with the Middle East have so proliferated that no single individual, even one devoting full time to the task, can keep up with the literature published about the Middle East. SUNY Binghamton's relatively modest library cannot afford to subscribe to all the English language periodical or serial literature dealing with the area, even though we now receive a few dozen such publications. When I began study of the region a new book about the Middle East or one of the countries in it appeared every few weeks. Now it seems that several are published each week, if not every day. When I started my own Middle East library it seemed possible to obtain every new English language publication. Now my fairly large personal library is overflowing merely with the books that I am asked to review.

- Although a late starter among the nationally organized area study groups, the Middle East has come into its own. Its principal area study organization, MESA, with its diverse affiliated groups, has become as well known as other area study organizations, such as the Asian, African, Latin American, and East European groups. Its meetings and the number and quality of its publications compare favorably with those of other world regions.

- Middle East studies have become accepted in American academia with credentials as legitimate as those of other areas. The number of Middle East centers and study programs compares well with those in other areas.

- Political disputes within the Middle East, such as the Arab-Israel conflict, are often reflected in Middle East academia, frequently causing bitter disputes among scholars and others in the U.S. involved with the area. At times it seems that these disputes are more intense within the borders of the U.S. than within the Middle East itself and that there is less room for diversity of ideas here than in a country such as Israel, where debate about the conflict with the Arab states or treatment of the Arab minority appears to be freer of restraints than in the U.S.

- Middle Easterners' attitudes about the perceptions of themselves and of outsiders have changed greatly during the past half century. When I began my association with the region it was difficult if not actually dangerous for an American Jew to travel in the Arab world. When Israel was established it was nearly impossible to use the same passport for travel there and in the Arab world. Now several Arab countries place no obstacles in the way of visits by American Jews or others who have Israeli markings in their travel documents. Many travel agents organize tours, which may include American Jews, to both Israel and surrounding Arab countries. Several Arab countries, including Jordan, Egypt, and Morocco, have extended official invitations to delegations of American Jews for discussions of topics that were not long ago considered taboo.

- In most of the Arab world attitudes toward Israel itself have changed. Egypt formally recognizes Israel and the blue and white flag with the star of David flies above an Israeli embassy in Cairo. There also have been numerous direct contacts between Israeli officials and those of other Arab countries—covertly between Israel and Jordan, openly between Morocco and Israel. For years Arab representatives at the UN referred to the "Tel-Aviv authorities," but few today do not recognize Israel's existence or refer to it in such evasive language. Most seem to have accepted the reality of Israel even though they refute its policies and borders. Thus scholars who once were reluctant to visit Israel for fear of jeopardizing their standing in the Arab world can now travel there without the threat of undermining their credentials in the neighboring countries.

• When I first visited the Middle East even academic institutions had to be extremely cautious about treatment of the Arab-Israel conflict, so much so that some university libraries in the region placed all books on the subject under lock and key. Students would often deface references to "Israel," "Zionism," and the like. Things have changed. Not only are such materials now freely accessible to academicians, but I have seen at universities in Beirut, Amman, and Cairo public exhibitions of books by Israeli authors on these once highly censored subjects. While debate is still greatly restricted if not actually banned on such themes in some Arab countries, there are several in which they can now be openly discussed.

• Until establishment of the state of Israel in 1948 and for a decade or two after, a major objective of diplomats involved in the Arab-Israel conflict was to persuade Arabs to negotiate openly with Zionist, then later Israeli, representatives. Arabs usually refused to participate in meetings with or to appear on the same platforms in public discussions with Zionists or Israelis. The situation was such that when Martin Buber visited the U.S. in the 1950s he asked me to help him meet Arabs in New York City. I arranged such a meeting with a student who later became an ambassador of a large Arab country. Most Israelis were eager to learn about one's direct contact with Arabs, especially with Palestinians. Often in the period before the 1960s, when I suggested to Arabs the possible benefits of direct and open meetings with Israelis, they were reluctant if not outright hostile to the idea. After 1967 the situation seems to have altered. Some official Israelis were reluctant to meet openly with representatives of Palestinian organizations, such as the PLO, for fear that these meetings would be tantamount to recognition of Palestinian political existence. While many members of Israeli peace groups and a number of Israeli doves have not hesitated to participate in such meetings, the Israeli Knesset until recently made it a criminal offense for any Israeli citizen to confer with any official of the Palestine Liberation Organization, the principal group recognized by the vast majority of Palestinians as their political representative.

While these changes have facilitated overall academic research, journalistic coverage and tourist travel within the Middle East, parts of the region are still remote in American consciousness. The better known countries of the Middle East are still along the Mediterranean coast, from Egypt up through Israel, Lebanon, and Turkey. Syria is less well known, Iraq much less, and the countries of the Arabian peninsula remain beyond the ken of most despite the influx of oilmen and business types since the "petroleum revolution" of the 1970s. Unfortunately it has taken a crisis that has brought us to the brink of war to awaken consciousness of the peninsula. And what a distorted image most American have received!

CHAPTER 9

Connections

Dankwart A. Rustow

How did I become a Middle East specialist? I guess it was three accidents that did it. The first was that my father, upon emigrating from Hitler's Germany in 1933, was offered an academic position at the newly founded University of Istanbul. Second, some years later, as my study for a Swiss school exam was interrupted by World War Two, I stumbled upon an unexpectedly easy way of learning Turkish. Lastly, just as I had finished a dissertation on Swedish politics, a chance encounter with a former teacher led me to a newly created position in political science and Near Eastern Studies at Princeton University.

The background of my father's move to Turkey was that the Turkish government, as part of Atatürk's plans for rapid Westernization, decided to close down the traditional Islamic academy, or *Darülfünun*, in Istanbul and replace it with a European-style "University of Istanbul." The details of the proposal were worked out with the advice of a Swiss consultant, the Genevan educator Albert Malche. His report suggested that, to facilitate the transition from the traditional Islamic to a Western system of higher education, a number of European professors should be recruited to train the Turkish scholars who later would staff the new university. Malche's report, submitted in May 1932, was adopted as official policy by the Turkish Ministry of Education the following winter, and by the spring of 1933 Ankara's education officials were ready to look for such foreign teachers.

At this point it happened that they connected with the first group of intellectual refugees from Nazi Germany, who, early in 1933, had formed the *Notgemeinschaft deutscher Wissenschaftler im Ausland* (Emergency Association of German Scholars Abroad) in Zurich. Switzerland was a logical stopover for political refugees escaping from Germany, but, with the closely-knit personnel structure of its cantons, it had few jobs to offer. The favorite destination for most of the anti-Nazi refugees was the United States—where the New School for Social Research in New York City was establishing its "University in Exile" and individual scholars found jobs at universities from Harvard to Berkeley. Still, the number of unemployed refugees far exceeded the jobs available in the United States or in other European countries.

The secretary of the *Notgemeinschaft* in Zurich was Dr. Philipp Schwartz, a Hungarian Jew who from 1927 to 1933 had held the position of Professor of Pathological Anatomy at the University of Frankfurt. Schwartz had heard of the Turkish government's decision to adopt Malche's plan of university reorganization, and, early in July 1933, he decided to travel by Orient Express to Istanbul and on to Ankara in the hope of placing a few of his colleagues in those new Turkish university jobs. As he arrived in Ankara, the consultation with Malche, the Turkish Minister of Education, and more than a dozen of the ministry's officials began. The Ankara officials had been wondering how to lure qualified foreign academics into being professors at Istanbul, and they were fascinated by Schwartz's report about dozens of top-rate scholars looking for jobs abroad—including such internationally renowned figures as Albert Einstein. Much of the seven-hour session was spent going over a list of proposed academic positions at the future University of Istanbul, and Schwartz, well-prepared with notes and biographical directories, suggesting two or three potential candidates for each job in question.

When Schwartz first set out on his trip to Turkey, he had hoped to place perhaps three or more of his colleagues at the new University of Istanbul; but at the end of the long session in the Ankara ministry he enthusiastically cabled the good news to his secretary in Zurich, "Not three but thirty."[1] Further details on staffing the new university with German refugees were worked out during a second visit by Schwartz in late July.

Among those thirty-odd German refugee professors who became the founders of the new University of Istanbul was Alexander Rüstow. Since the mid-1920s my father had been active as the political expert of the professional association of the German tool and dye industry, fighting the steel companies' proposals for protective tariffs on foreign steel and the pressure from the *junker* landowners' lobby for agricultural subsidies. But by the early thirties my father had become aware that Hitler's brown shirts were a far greater threat to Germany's future than the steel magnates or the *junkers*; and throughout much of 1932 he was closely involved in the last-minute desperate political maneuvers to stop Hitler's advent to power—specifically, in an attempt to form a cabinet including a broad coalition of forces from the Social Democrats on the left to conservatives on the right. When those maneuvers miscarried and Hitler assumed the chancellorship in January 1933, my father found himself on one of the first political blacklists of the Nazis' secret police. Indeed, he concluded early in 1933, "This will get worse before it gets better, and I must get out." Zurich and the *Notgemeinschaft* were his first stop abroad; the place he got out to was the Istanbul chair of Economic History and Economic Geography.[2]

I was then eight years old; and since my parents happened to be in the process of divorce, they decided to place my two sisters and myself in a German boarding school that continued its progressive education with minimal concessions to the Nazi authorities.[3] In 1936–37 I briefly visited my father and stepmother in their lovely apartment in Kadıköy on the Marmara shore of Istanbul, with its magnificent view of the skyline of the old city. This was the only time in my late childhood that I saw my father—for a period of eight months that ended all too soon, as my mother insisted that I return to Germany. But then, early in 1939, a relative who had recently been to Istanbul took me for a walk in the wooded hills near the boarding school to relay to me an important message from my father: "There will be war and you must get out."

During my 1936–37 visit to Istanbul, my father had insisted that I read Hitler's *Mein Kampf* from cover to cover and informed me in some detail of the political circumstances that prompted his emigration. Thus I well understood his message. I was only 14, but the war might last for some years, and we had to make sure that I would not be drafted into Hitler's army. When arrangements for my departure had at last been made early in December 1939, World War Two had indeed broken out. My father was temporarily in Switzerland, recovering from a major operation; and I well remember the feeling of relief with which I crossed the customs checkpoint at the Basel railroad station before changing trains to go on to Geneva.

As we settled back in Istanbul early in 1940, my father did not send me to school for what to him seemed obvious reasons. The German school of Istanbul was run by the Nazis and thus out of the question. To send me to a Turkish school did not even occur to him, for he considered his Turkish stay temporary and he had not bothered to learn Turkish. Instead, he worked out a tutoring program that would prepare me to finish my schooling in Zurich, where students who had not attended the local *lyceum* were allowed to take the final examinations for the baccalaureate as "external candidates." But after Hitler's invasion of the Balkans in the spring of 1941, it became impossible for me to travel from Turkey to Switzerland.

Instead of studying for any school degree, I spent my time reading widely, first in European history and then in German poetry. Much of this reading I did by myself and some of it in an informal study group of refugee children in the home of Erich Auerbach, a comparative literature scholar then hard at work on his book *Mimesis*.[4] I also helped my father more and more with his secretarial work, filing his extensive correspondence with refugee friends in the United States and typing the increasingly voluminous drafts of what eventually became his three-volume work *Ortsbestimmung der Gegenwart*.[5]

Early in 1942, my father suggested that I audit the lectures in Roman Law and Civil Law given by his colleague Andreas B. Schwarz, and indeed I enjoyed those lectures for their depth of erudition and breadth of intellectual perspective. I also became friendly with some of my fellow students who knew German or French (then the most common foreign language in Turkey). Schwarz's lectures, like those of my father and most refugee colleagues, were presented to the students by consecutive translation—two or three sentences by the professor in German (or in the case of Schwarz's Roman law lectures, in French), and then those same sentences repeated by the Turkish assistant.

And here, then, came the second accident: I became fascinated by this translation process and discovered it as a most convenient introduction to a new language. Since I knew what the assistant was *supposed* to say, it was easy to guess what he or she *was* saying—and soon I found myself sitting there with a dictionary and taking more notes on Turkish vocabulary than on the legal subject. By the fall of 1942, I attended the Turkish lectures of the law school class as well. Most memorable among these were the lectures in Administrative Law by Sıddık Sami Onar, an erudite scholar in the best of the late Ottoman tradition, and in Criminal Law by Tahir Taner, who managed to illustrate the most arcane points of the penal code with vivid examples from everyday life. And, of course, I had plenty of occasion to practice my Turkish with my growing circle of friends in my Law School class.

I thus decided to finish my schooling in Turkey—once again as an "external candidate" for the baccalaureate, but this time at the Lycée de Galatasaray, a prestigious school in Istanbul with a Turkish curriculum in literature and social studies and a French curriculum in math and the sciences. I found the textbooks in Turkish literature and history fascinating, and I soon did additional readings that more fully introduced me to the rhyme and meter patterns of late Ottoman poetry. But I also had to prepare for the other subjects, and thus, in the summer of 1943, I divided my time between swimming at the beach in the Moda suburb of Istanbul, flirting with girls, and boning up on French textbooks in trigonometry and introductory physics.

By August 1943 I had taken the written part of the baccalaureate exam and was ready for the final orals. Luckily, I passed the physics test, but only barely. The most enjoyable part turned out to be the oral in Turkish literature. The examiner was an elderly lady, friendly and intelligent. She must have been told I was a foreign student, because she started me off easy, asking how I would characterize the relationship between Ottoman Turkish and modern Turkish. After a moment's reflection I replied that this brought to my mind a quotation from a nineteenth-century author: "Türkçenin ecza-yı terkibi olan üç lisan sözde güya muttehid, hakkikatte zıdd-ı kâmildır." ("The three languages that are the component parts of Turkish [i.e., Turkish, Arabic, and Persian] are said to be supposedly one, but in fact are complete opposites.")

The examiner seemed impressed with my knowledge of Ottoman Turkish and with the relevance of the quotation, and the rest of the exam was passed in pleasant chitchat about nineteenth and twentieth-century authors. Only later did I find out that the scholar had been Halide Edib, a leading Turkish novelist, wife of the historian Adnan Adıvar, and faculty member of the Istanbul Girls' College, who served occasionally on the exam committees of Galatasaray. It may have been Halide Edib who mentioned my exam performance to a newspaper columnist who wrote that Turkish students would do well to follow my example in taking more interest in their Ottoman heritage.[6]

Now that I had passed the *lycée* and *olgunluk* (or "maturity") examinations that entitled one to enter the university as a registered student, I had no interest in returning to my law classes. I had become intrigued over the years with the Arabic inscriptions over the entrances of mosques and other old buildings (including the gate of the Beyazit campus of Istanbul University, which formerly had been the *Darülfünun*). Also, in the law school classes, where most students tried to take verbatim notes on the lectures, I was impressed with the fact that the older ones easily took their notes at shorthand speed in the pre-1928 Arabic script of Ottoman Turkish; whereas the younger ones, who took their notes in the Latin alphabet, had a hard time keeping up with the lecturer's pace.

Thus, my decision was easy: I would study something here in Istanbul that I might not have a chance to study later anywhere else. I therefore enrolled in the Faculty of Letters for a doctoral program with Arabic and Persian as my major and comparative literature as a minor. In comparative literature I could continue my association with Erich Auerbach, this time in studying Dante, Petrarch, and other Italian classics. The Professor of Arabic and Persian was another German refugee, Hellmut Ritter, a specialist in classical Persian poetry. Ritter had had few if any students majoring in Arabic or Persian—since those were the post-Atatürk days when the Turkish intelligentsia was on the rebound from its Ottoman-Islamic heritage and the only well-attended Arabic or Persian classes were the introductory courses that were required for any Turkish literature majors.

In our first interview, Ritter seemed glad to sign me up as a doctoral student; but, fluent in a dozen languages himself, he wanted to know what languages I knew already. I replied, with modest pride, that I could handle French, Turkish, the basics of classical Latin and Greek, and some English and Italian. Musing aloud, he said, "That's not bad for a start; but of course you must become fully fluent in Italian, because *Oriente Moderno* is the leading journal in our field. And Russian is essential because much of the best Oriental scholarship is in that language. Oh yes, and of course Danish—since the classical biography of Muhammad by Frants Buhl has never been translated into any other language."

I was stunned. Here I had come to sign up for Arabic and Persian—but just as preliminaries he wanted me to learn Italian, Russian, and Danish! Clearly Ritter was a very learned and rather whimsical scholar. He also happened to be white-haired in his early fifties—and, as I turned grey and then white at about the same age, I remembered a quote from a Persian poet that Ritter used to recite with pleasure while pointing to the top of his head: "The lamp of wisdom has driven out the darkness of youth."

While attending classes and seminars at the Istanbul Faculty of Letters, and occasionally commuting northward for private sessions in Ritter's home, I also signed up for private lessons at the Academy of Fine Arts with one of the Sultan's former calligraphers, Beşiktaşlı Hacı Nuri, to whom a friendly neighbor had introduced me. Before our first visit, our physician friend had told me that, as a pious Muslim, Hacı Nuri would not charge any fees to a young man in search of learning—nor would it be proper for me to bring him any presents of value. But, as a sign of respect, before and after each of my lessons, I must be sure to bow, kiss his hand, and touch it to my forehead.

Here, at last, I could pursue my fascination with the artistic inscriptions that I had seen on those old buildings. Once I had mastered the elementary art of writing with a reed pen, I thought, surely, those final flourishes must be done with verve and gusto! But not so. They were supposed to be done deliberately, slowly, and steadily—and one word of advice that I remember from the calligraphy teacher was his oft-repeated phrase, "Acele etme, oğlum! Acele etme!" ("Don't hurry, my son! Don't hurry!")

While I was pursuing my studies with Ritter, Auerbach, and Hacı Nuri in 1944 and 1945, I also was adding to my extensive collection of hand-copied German poetry from the Baroque to Goethe to Rilke and of Ottoman nineteenth-century poetry. But above all, as World War Two was nearing its end, it was time to make plans for the future.

My father was among the small minority of refugees who were sure that they would return to Germany. Once that cruel and messy Hitler business was finished in defeat, he reasoned, it would be high time to rebuild the country. And, indeed, by 1949, my father accepted a Professorship in Sociology at the University of Heidelberg and became actively involved in the circle of neoliberal intellectuals and politicians close to the Bonn government in the days of Adenauer and Erhard.

As for me, I had no desire to return to Germany. Rather, like most refugee teenagers in Istanbul, I hoped to get to the United States as soon as possible. I thus started taking some English lessons—one of my tutors being Lewis V. Thomas, then at Robert College in Istanbul and later a colleague in the Princeton Department of Near East Studies. And of course I avidly read among the many books in English that were on my father's bookshelves or that I could borrow from friends or libraries. It was in those days that I fell in love with the poetry of Robert Browning and Christina Rossetti.

But the most important discovery on my father's shelves turned out to be a book by his refugee friend Carl Joachim Friedrich, who had joined the Harvard Government Department and, by 1937, published *Constitutional Government and Politics*.[7] For it was in Friedrich's book that I first came across the technical term "political science." Its German equivalent of *Staatswissenschaft* (or "science of state") had a repulsively authoritarian ring—but the term "political science" to me sounded exciting, indeed fascinating.

My earliest political memories had been when, early in 1933, I returned home from third grade to find Hitler's Gestapo on their hands and knees searching through the attic of our home in suburban Berlin—and later my father's announcement that, because of the political changes in Germany, he had to go off to Turkey. In short, I had come to think of politics as a wild beast that chased your family from its home country. But, if there was such a thing as political *science*, then the beast could be tamed with the power of reason! There was no question that this was what I must study once I managed to go to the United States.

When I arrived in New York early in 1946, I enrolled at Queens College to major in political science. During the academic year I earned some money by tutoring high school children in French or Latin and, during the summers, by selling hot dogs and orange juice at a Nedicks counter and later as a junior cartographer at C. S. Hammond & Co. But I also worked intensively at my studies, enrolling for summer courses both in 1946 and 1947, and, with some advanced credits for my university courses in Turkey, managed to finish my Queens B.A. *summa cum laude* in August 1947. By the fall of 1947 I started my graduate work in political science at Yale, where I had received a fellowship and, with the help of my father's friend Arnold Wolfers, who was a professor of international relations at Yale, a teaching assistantship.

By the spring of 1949 I was finishing my graduate course work and preparing for my doctoral exams when one of my teachers told me that a new organization known as the Social Science Research Council was offering fellowships for dissertation research abroad. It sounded like a fantastic opportunity—to be paid for a full year to do research on the subject of your choice! But what topic should I choose?

There had been a lively debate among American social scientists about the Swedish economy as a constructive combination of capitalism and socialism—stimulated largely by Marquis Childs' book *Sweden: The Middle Way*.[8] But there was little if any information about the political system behind that economic synthesis, and Swedish seemed close enough to German and English that I should have no difficulty in learning the language. Thus I decided to submit a research project on the Swedish political party system. In this way my wife and I were able to spend the academic year 1949-50 in Sweden and then make a brief visit to Heidelberg, where my father was just starting to teach after his return from sixteen years in Turkey.

While finishing my doctoral work at Yale, I took my first job—at Oglethorpe University in the suburbs of Atlanta, Georgia. It was not a well-known college, but the pay was excellent by the standards of the day, and, although I was still completing my dissertation, my title was Associate Professor of Citizenship.

This brief tour of duty in the South helped me overcome some typical Northern prejudices. The President of the college, Dr. Philip Weltner, had taken that job a year earlier after resigning as Chancellor of the University of Georgia when Governor Herman Talmadge vetoed his decision to start admitting Blacks to the graduate division of that institution. At Oglethorpe I found that the only colleagues with anti-Black prejudices were Northerners who had drifted South—whereas the colleagues most dedicated to racial equality were Southerners who had decided to stay so as to help transform the South.

But it turned out that the college was in financial difficulties. Having heard that the Ford Foundation had set up a program of "Faculty Development Grants" for teachers at small colleges, President Weltner suggested—indeed, virtually gave me a clear directive—to apply for such a grant. The topic I proposed was a systematic comparison of interdisciplinary teaching programs in the social sciences. On receiving the grant, my wife and I moved back to New Haven. From there I frequently commuted to Wesleyan University in Middletown, Connecticut, which offered one of those interdisciplinary social science programs, and also took longer trips to become acquainted with inter-disciplinary programs at such leading universities as Chicago and Minnesota.

And then the third and decisive accident occurred. One day in New Haven, on the steps of the Graduate School, I ran into my former Yale teacher Klaus Knorr, who, after some chitchat, asked if I were still interested in the Near East. I said I wasn't really. I had done my dissertation on Swedish politics and was currently working on a comparison of interdisciplinary teaching programs in the social sciences. Comparative politics was the field I planned to work in. "But," I added, "why do you ask?" "You see," was his answer, "Princeton University is developing a program in Near East studies, and they are looking for a staff member to develop Near Eastern politics as one of the sub-fields."

I immediately changed my stance, saying that, of course, I was very much interested in the Near East. As he knew, I was fluent in Turkish and also had a basic knowledge of Arabic and Persian; and, yes, I certainly would be interested in being considered for that position at Princeton.

The Princeton offer came in due course. The arrangement was that for the first year I would assist in the teaching of courses in such fields as comparative politics and political theory but would also spend some time improving my knowledge of Arabic. The second year I would be on paid research leave in the Near East, and during the third year I would start offering a new course in Near East politics.

In the initial negotiations the Princeton department chairman indicated that he and his colleagues had been impressed with the quality of my dissertation and asked whether I had any plans to publish it. This, I felt, gave me an opportunity to negotiate—having enjoyed the art of *pazarlık* (or "haggling") that I had learned in dealing with the fruit and vegetable vendors of Istanbul. Thus I said that I would love to spend the summer rewriting the dissertation into a publishable book, but I would have to find financial support before doing so. In response, Princeton did offer me such a summer grant, and some years later the dissertation was published by Princeton's own university press, under the title *The Politics of Compromise: A Study of Parties and Cabinet Government in Sweden* (1955).

As I started my political science teaching at Princeton in 1952–53 I also audited Arabic classes, first at the intermediate level with Farhat Ziadeh and R. Bayly Winder and then at the advanced level with Philip K. Hitti, who was then the head of Princeton's Near Eastern studies program. The shift from the intermediate to the advanced level occurred after a friendly disagreement with Bayly about which of a half-dozen types of accusative a certain word in the day's text represented. At the end of our discussion, he promised to research the matter further; the following week he announced that I had been right and, after class, suggested that I transfer to Hitti's course. One of the fellow students in Hitti's class turned out to be Malcolm H. Kerr, who was finishing his undergraduate work at Princeton but, having grown up in Beirut, took Arabic at the doctoral level.

One of the high points of that first year at Princeton was a conference entitled "The Near East: Social Dynamics and Cultural Setting" that brought together most of the small group of historians and social scientists then working in that field. There I met J. C. Hurewitz for the first time. He greeted me warmly, saying how delighted he was that I had decided to work on Near Eastern politics—which, in the past, had been such a lonely field that you could barely see the next scholar on the distant horizon.

In 1953–54 I decided to spend my "research year" mostly in Turkey, although I also took a brief and fascinating trip to Israel, then still in its nascent, idealistic phase, followed by a pleasant summer near Beirut, at a time when Lebanon was still an oasis of commercial and political freedom. This was followed by a second research year in Turkey in 1958–59, this time with side trips to Israel, Iraq, Iran, and Lebanon.

One memorable experience on my first trip to Israel was a tour of the Galilee region for which my guide was a colonel in the army who happened to be an acquaintance of my father-in-law. Israel at the time was preparing to tap the waters of the upper Jordan for a major irrigation pipeline, a plan to which Syria, on the opposite side of the river, staunchly objected. The Syrians had little need of the water themselves, and, indeed, considering the steep southern slope of the Golan Heights, would have had much difficulty pumping it into their territory. Still, to strengthen their international law case against Israel, they had begun to dig a small canal to tap the waters of the Jordan on its Eastern shore—but, as my guide took much pride in pointing out, they had planned the job so badly that they first had dug the canal uphill! A highlight of a later visit to Israel was a longish off-the-record interview with Golda Meir, then foreign minister in the Labor party cabinet.

Amidst these travels through many other countries, Turkey remained the logical focus for my detailed research in Middle East politics. Just before I had left Turkey for the United States in 1945, President İsmet İnönü had decided to relax the political controls of the benevolent one-party dictatorship he had inherited from Atatürk. Those also happened to be the days when I started reading the daily newspapers, and I had been impressed with how the better dailies, such as Ahmet Emin Yalman's *Vatan* and Hüseyin Cahit Yalçın's *Tanin*, were systematically broadening their freedom of expression. In the meantime, Turkey in 1950 had had its first fully free multiparty election, resulting in a landslide victory for Adnan Menderes' Democratic Party and casting İnönü in the new role of leader of the parliamentary opposition.

On arriving in Ankara in September 1953, I found that, after an absence from Turkey of almost eight years, it took me a couple of months to get my command of the language back to its former level. But then, reading widely on politics and recent history and engaged in a busy social life and in interviews with political figures, I found that my Turkish improved to a level of near-native fluency.

I also found that several of the friends I had met at the Istanbul Law School in 1942–44 were now teaching at the Ankara Political Science Faculty. And many of that growing circle of old and new friends also were active in politics—first mostly in the Democratic Party, but then, as Menderes drifted toward authoritarianism, in the Republican People's Party and other opposition groups. The most prominent academic politicians among those old law school classmates turned out to be Turhan Feyzioğlu, who was a constitutional law professor in the 1950s, a minister in various Republican People's Party cabinets in the 1960s, and founder of the "Reliance Party" in 1967, and Turan Güneş, who was one of the founders of the Freedom Party in 1955, joined the Republicans in the 1960s, and became foreign minister at the height of the Cyprus crisis in 1974. Others with whom I became close friends were Aydın Yalçın, an economist at the Ankara Political Science Faculty and founder of the conservative weekly *Forum*, and his wife Nilüfer Yalçın, who by the 1960s became a political correspondent and columnist for the Ankara daily *Milliyet*.

In my research on current politics, I soon developed a reliable interviewing technique. Whenever possible, I would begin my round of interviews with people in the opposition camp. They had more free time, were eager for foreign contacts, and were glad to give me their detailed views on any current political controversies or scandals. Next, when interviewing prominent government officials, I would indicate to them that I was familiar with the political situation; and, if they proved reluctant to go beyond their party's public-relations line, I would, with mock innocence, refer to the information gathered from the opposition by remarking casually, "But your critics say that the government is mishandling this, or guilty of that. What do *YOU* have to say on this subject?"

At the beginning of each interview I would assure my interlocutors that I was not a journalist and that none of what they were about to tell me would get into the press. For the same reason, I took no notes, although I would jot down the highlights of the interview as soon as I got home or, after the most important interviews, as soon as I could rush to the nearest coffee house. I also decided to conduct my interviews in Turkish, so as to get the actual flavor of the current debate. The only difficulty I had with this came in my initial interview with Süleyman Demirel, who later was to become prime minister seven times but whom I first met when he was an aspiring politician in the Justice Party in the early 1960s. I made contact with him through a political officer at the U.S. Embassy who knew him in his capacity as a former Eisenhower Fellow, and we made a lunch date in the Kızılay district of Ankara. As usual, I started talking in Turkish, but, obviously eager to emphasize his American connection, Demirel insisted on speaking English. Thus, over drinks, soup, and main course the conversation continued bilingually, I in Turkish, he in English. But finally, as we started dessert, he lapsed into Turkish, and thus we continued in Turkish over dessert and coffee. When I last met Demirel as the major opposition leader in the late 1980s, he asked me with a smile whether, this time, we should speak English or Turkish—obviously recalling our first encounter; and, even though his English had substantially improved over the years, I said politely that we could do it either way but that I would prefer Turkish.

Continuing my pattern of interviewing opposition and government officials during briefer visits from the 1960s to the 1990s, I realized that occasionally I might, within the same week, have detailed political conversations with
such diverse political leaders as Turgut Özal, Süleyman Demirel, Erdal İnönü,
or Bülent Ecevit, some of whom were barely on speaking terms with each other, thus allowing me to form a much more complete picture of the Turkish political scene than the participants themselves might have.

In my two longer stays in the 1950s I divided my time between research
on contemporary politics and on Turkey's transition from empire to republic
in the period from 1918 to 1923. In that earlier context, I particularly enjoyed
my detailed interviews about the origins of the Turkish republic with some
surviving leaders of the War of Independence, such as Ali Fuad Cebesoy and
Rauf Orbay, and with Tevfik Bıyıklıoğlu, who had been Atatürk's aide-de-
camp in the early days of the Republic and at the time Atatürk prepared and
delivered his famous Six-Day Speech in 1927.

In requesting the interview with Cebesoy, who had been one of the leading commanders under Atatürk in the War of Independence, I had sent him
a copy of a review of the first volume of his memoirs, which I had published
in the *Middle East Journal*.[9] When he ushered me into his living room, he
pointed to another gentleman whom he introduced only as "Rauf Bey"—and
it took me some time to realize this was Rauf Orbay, another prominent leader
of the War of Independence and early Republic periods. I was a bit shy about
approaching Bıyıklıoğlu, but when I finally reached him on the phone, he said
happily, "Oh! I have heard so much about you and your research project, and
I certainly was hoping to hear from you!"

But the real highlight among my interviews was a meeting with former
President İnönü, kindly arranged by his son-in-law, the journalist Metin Tok-
er. Since İnönü was hard of hearing, he invited me to sit on a sofa right next
to him, and throughout the interview we virtually sat elbow to elbow. I began
our conversation by asking him about the background of his crucial announcement on May 19, 1945, that, now that the democracies had won the world
war, the time had come for Turkey to take more seriously the populist principles of Atatürk's revolution. This announcement had soon been followed by
more freedom for the press and the formation of opposition parties; and it had
come at a time when Turkey was under heavy pressure from Moscow to cede

to the Soviets several of its Eastern provinces and allow "joint" naval control of its Straits—all this some two years before the proclamation of the Truman Doctrine. I had therefore assumed that İnönü's shift toward democracy was in part prompted by a desire for better relations with Washington. But when I asked him what role foreign policy considerations had played in his decision, İnönü's reaction at first was indignant, "All that slander that is spread about me, as if I had been swimming with the stream…You have told me yourself, Professor, that there was much internal pressure, wartime shortages—and, of course, the populist principles of the War of Independence." Then he caught his breath, relaxed, and added with a smile, "But suppose I had been swimming with the stream—that, too, is a virtue, is it not?"

Toward the end, I asked him whether he had anticipated that the opposition would win its massive victory in 1950. Once more he became indignant, "I never expected to see so much ingratitude!" ("Bu kadar nankörlük göreceğimi hic beklemezdim.") In reflecting on the conversation later, it seemed obvious to me that most observers would readily have predicted the electoral defeat of the Republican People's Party after twenty-seven years of one-party rule. But it also occurred to me how far İnönü himself, as a benevolent dictator surrounded entirely by careerist politicians and flatterers, must have been from this recognition.

Back in Princeton from my first Turkish and Middle Eastern research trip in 1954, I prepared my new course on Near East Politics, reading widely to find appropriate assignments for the students and anxiously doing much additional research on every week's lecture topic. But then, one day, I decided to relax, telling myself, "Don't worry so much. Why don't you start by telling them what you know *already*?" In dealing with the Arab-Israeli conflict, I spent some time introducing the students to the view from each side and emphasizing that the conflict was not one of right against wrong but between what each side plausibly considered its rights. I also told them that, occasionally, they might hear me expressing a political opinion of my own, but that this was not a party line; rather, I encouraged them to form their own opinions, as long as those were based on some appropriate knowledge of the facts.

In addition to my teaching at Princeton, I soon became involved in a number of other scholarly and organizational activities. In 1954–55 the Council on Foreign Relations asked me to prepare the background papers for a monthly study group on the "Defense of the Middle East"—which gave me a chance to interact with a select group of scholars, diplomats, and U.S. defense and foreign policy experts.

In 1955 T. Cuyler Young, who had succeeded Philip K. Hitti as director of the Princeton Near East Program, had been asked to chair a new Committee on the Near and Middle East, jointly sponsored by the Social Science Research Council(SSRC) and the American Council of Learned Societies(ACLS). Feeling in some need of reinforcement on the social science side, Cuyler asked me to serve as the Committee's secretary. He delicately explained that I would attend committee meetings but not have a vote, since there could not be two voting members from the same university. I said graciously that I did not mind not having a vote, as long as I could speak up occasionally when I had a relevant point to make. And I soon found that I had many other ways of contributing to the committee's work—by preparing the first drafts of the agenda and the minutes and in informal conversations with Cuyler Young and with E. Pendleton Herring, the SSRC's director, who attended most of the committee's sessions.

The committee over the years played a central role in helping to develop the field of Middle East area studies. I remember one particular item that I managed to put on our early agenda. I had found, to my surprise, that the Library of Congress was keeping boxes and boxes with thousands of Arabic books in its storage vaults uncatalogued because scholars had not agreed on any standard system of transliteration for Arabic. Here I thought the committee could make a major contribution by settling this issue. In our preliminary discussion, one committee member, Wilfred Cantwell Smith of McGill University, remarked that, of course, he "would never yield on a matter of principle, such as transliteration." So I quietly saw to it that this particular "man of principle" would not be part of the transliteration subcommittee. The most knowledgeable subcommittee member turned out to be Sir Hamilton A. R. Gibb, who had recently moved from Oxford to Harvard; and while I did not concur in all of *his* principles, I gladly yielded in the end, since it obviously was more important to resolve the issue of transliteration than to get hung up on its details.

Another important matter that the SSRC-ACLS committee took up at my suggestion was the fact that the Middle East by the 1960s was the only world region without an American scholarly association; and we thus became closely involved in founding what by 1967 became the Middle East Studies Association of North America. In the preparatory work I helped to make sure that the association would be well balanced in its composition, including social scientists, as well as linguists and historians, and specialists on Turkey, Iran, and Israel as well as Arabists.

One scene I remember vividly from the founding meeting was a seemingly endless and increasingly contentious debate about some rather trivial passage in the proposed by-laws. For some minutes I agonized, asking myself how I could help the assembled scholars get out of this impasse. If I intervened for or against the proposed bylaws amendment, I would obviously antagonize the other side; if I proposed a third solution—or an indefinite tabling—I might antagonize both; and, either way, the debate would be needlessly dragged out. But, suddenly, I had a better idea.

I rose to ask for the floor and, when recognized by the chair, proceeded to say, quietly and firmly, "Mr. Chairman, I propose that we change the name of this organization we are about to found from Middle East Studies Association to Middle East Studies Society." As I sat down without further explanation, there was a moment of puzzled silence. Then a few people throughout the room started smiling and whispering to their neighbors the acronym that had been my true intent: *MESS!* Soon there was a wave of laughter—and the previous trivial issue was dropped without further ado as we returned to the more serious part of the agenda.

One of the most stimulating experiences at Princeton was to work with Gabriel Almond, who, as chairman of the SSRC's Committee on Comparative Politics was trying to make the purview of that field truly worldwide. Traditionally the field had been limited to studies of the United States and of Europe, or, by the 1940s, contrasting descriptions of democracy vs. totalitarianism. But now Almond was arranging a series of conferences and assembling a team of scholars that would include Asia, Africa, and Latin America in a more systematic, global comparison. Thus I contributed the Near Eastern section to what became *The Politics of the Developing Areas*, edited by Almond and James S. Coleman,[10] and contributed to many other conferences and joint volumes sponsored by Almond's SSRC Committee.

The only point on which I had some reservations was the "functional-structural" terminology that Almond at a certain point decided to adapt from Talcott Parson's work in sociology. Instead, I would have much preferred to stay with plain English and with the political role of groups that had been the SSRC Committee's original focus. But in the crucial discussions among the contributors to the Almond-Coleman volume, I remained the only dissident, and rather than quit the fascinating project, I did my best to analyze Near Eastern politics according to those seven "functional" dimensions of "socialization, articulation, aggregation, communication, rule-making, rule application, and rule adjudication." Except that, after one long and intense summer that we spent at Stanford University, I could not resist venting my dissent at a "fun and farewell party" with an adaptation of a song from *Porgy and Bess*: "It ain't necessarily so; Structures and functions, Parsonian disjunctions, They ain't necessarily so...Little matrix was small, but, oh my! When it got debated, It got so inflated..."

In addition to Almond and his ambitious comparison of Third World politics from Latin America to Southeast Asia, a major intellectual influence I enjoyed was close contact with the historian Cyril E. Black, who first developed modernization as a major concept in the study of political and social change.[11] And a comparative study sponsored by Almond's committee and organized by Robert E. Ward and myself on *Political Modernization in Japan and Turkey*[12] provided a major opportunity constructively to combine those perspectives.

When I first joined the Princeton Department of Politics, I had been assured that my teaching would be half in Near East politics and half in other fields such as comparative politics, political theory, or international relations. But it turned out that the senior colleagues in those fields were involved in some intense and petty rivalries and, hence, preferred to have those courses taught by their own younger protégés rather than by an intruder from the Near East field; in sum, the non-Near East part of my Princeton teaching program never properly worked out. This became the major reason why, in 1959, I was attracted by an offer from Columbia University, which asked me to develop a new field of study to be known as "International Social Forces," which, under my aegis, became something like a comparative study of politics and society in the Third World.

For two years I also combined my teaching at Columbia with a research project at the Brookings Institution in Washington, D.C., which enabled me to take extensive research trips to Latin America, Africa, and Asia. My Brookings project eventually resulted in a book entitled *A World of Nations: Problems of Political Modernization*.[13] The research project also gave me a further chance to combine Almond's comparative perspective with Black's hypotheses of social and historical dynamics. Specifically, I attempted to compare the social and political problems of newly independent Third World countries, such as the insecure sense of nationhood and the danger of military coups; and, to my pleasant surprise, the book was to stay in print in paperback for as long as eighteen years (1967–1985).

By 1970 an offer including a lighter teaching schedule and a substantial pay increase lured me from Columbia to the City University of New York. For the first few years I divided my teaching between an undergraduate course at Brooklyn College and a graduate course at the CUNY Graduate School, but by 1979 I took over the editorship of the quarterly *Comparative Politics* and thus was able to concentrate entirely on my graduate teaching in courses such as International Political Economy; History and Philosophy of Social Science; Comparative Politics of the Middle East; International Relations of the Middle East; Debt, Development, and Democracy; and Transitions to Democracy.

This last course was an outgrowth of a research interest that had begun with a comparison of the Swedish and Turkish experiences of transitions to democracy and my attempt to formulate a number of dynamic hypotheses concerning the forces that might move an aristocratic, elitist, or dictatorial regime toward democracy. The article that I published on the subject in 1970 turned out to be widely quoted and reprinted in anthologies and foreign translations.[14] By the late 1980s I decided to make this my major research focus. As it turned out, just then most Latin American nations were headed for their transition from military dictatorship toward democracy, and soon the collapse of communism in Eastern Europe and the Soviet Union made the question of the process of transition toward democracy of even broader interest.[15]

Another research interest that I developed in my early years at CUNY was OPEC and the global politics of energy. The initial impetus came from John Licht-blau, head of the Petroleum Industry Research Foundation, who happened to be a close personal friend and, in 1970, asked me to prepare a memorandum on the "Political Prospects for Middle East Oil."[16] Encouraged to offer my best long-range estimates, I boldly predicted that half of the Middle East's oil would be nationalized by 1975 and the rest by 1980. Those forecasts at the time caused much dismay among oil executives; but, as my essay was going into page proof, Algeria in February 1971 set the first precedent of nationalization. And, a year later, the *New York Times* oil correspondent asked me teasingly whether I would not wish that the Arabs had stuck to my cautious schedule instead of forcing the pace.

Following the oil price jumps of 1973 and 1979 I found myself much in demand for lectures and consultations on global oil both in this country and abroad (from Mexico to Norway and Hong Kong). I also set to work on a book entitled *Oil and Turmoil: America Faces OPEC and the Middle East*, intended for both academic and general readers.[17]

One pleasant memory from an oil lecture trip to Mexico was a report in a local newspaper featuring my picture under a headline exclaiming, "No Todo Esta Perdido." It happened to be a period of declining oil prices at the very time when Mexico was joining the world's oil exporters. But I explained that the long-term trend, as I saw it, was that oil prices would rise through much of the 1980s—and the Mexican journalist's summary of my remarks thus was that "Not Everything Is Lost."[18]

By 1982 I organized a set of monthly dinner meetings at the CUNY Graduate School called "The Energy Forum," which over the years has developed into a leading discussion group in New York among oil and energy experts from private industry, government, and academia and has attracted prominent speakers both from the U.S. and abroad. As its name implies, each discussion at the Energy Forum is typically opened by two or three experts presenting different aspects of, or contrasting points of view on, the subject. Among those speakers over the last decade have been such outstanding personalities as Algerian Energy Minister Nordine Ait-Laoussine, M. A. Adelman of M.I.T., Theodor R. Eck of Amoco, Nobel-laureate Lawrence R. Klein, Robert Mabro of Oxford, Charles Maxwell, Edward L. Morse of *Petroleum Intelligence Weekly*, Peter Odell of Rotterdam, former US Energy Secretary James R. Schlesinger, and *New York Times* columnist Leonard Silk.

By the mid-1980s I also returned to my Turkish interests, following close-ly the political developments after the 1980–83 military coup in what would seem to be Turkey's final transition to democracy. I was particularly pleased that my book on *Turkey: America's Forgotten Ally*, appeared in paperback both in English and in Germany and Turkish translations soon after its publication by the Council on Foreign Relations (New York, 1987, 1989).[19]

It also gave me some satisfaction when a research organization in Bonn called Zentrum für Türkeistudien asked me in 1986 to join its academic advi-sory board as its only non-German member and in 1991 to chair that same group, for this gave me an opportunity to help work toward some intellectual rapprochement among the two countries that had been my home before I moved to the United States—and, incidentally, the twice-yearly trips also gave me an opportunity to visit some of my German relatives more regularly.

Among the activities that I have particularly enjoyed was organizing con-ferences (e.g., those resulting in the volumes *Philosophers and Kings: Studies in Leadership*[20] and *Comparative Political Dynamics*);[21] a number of Latin Amer-ican and European lecture tours organized by the United States Information Agency (USIA) and a series of visiting professorships abroad that I held dur-ing sabbatical and other leaves—including those at the London School of Economics (1965), the University of Sussex (1977), Heidelberg (1961), Man-nheim(1970), Trier(1976–77), and Torino(1969).

The visiting professorships were not without surprises. For example, for the Torino visiting semester I had suggested in the preliminary correspon-dence that I would conduct my seminars either in English or French but that the students should feel free to respond in Italian. However, when I arrived in Torino in May 1969, my hosts explained to me about "lo sciopero"—the stu-dent strike that had closed down the university for most of the spring. Classes would start three weeks later than scheduled. And, oh yes—the students did not really know enough French or English; so would I mind conducting my classes entirely in Italian? I took a deep breath, putting the two announce-ments together—and promptly decided that this would give me time for three weeks of intensive work to bring my Italian up to snuff.

I dashed to the bookstore, buying a grammar, a dictionary, and a current novel, and went off to Rome, where I had more contacts than in Torino. I read the newspapers intensively, listened to the radio till late at night, and in restaurants eavesdropped on other people's conversations. I also found that Italians—in contrast, say, to French people—are very encouraging to foreigners who are trying to learn their language; and a cocktail party just before returning to Torino gave me a chance to test my progress. For the first week's lectures, I prepared an almost complete outline with a dictionary; the second week, I came prepared with basic notes; and by the third week I found I could converse quite freely in my newly improved Italian.

Among the individual foreign lectures I particularly enjoyed one in Rio de Janeiro in 1966. My host, Candido Mendes, was the dean of a private law school, and in our preliminary correspondence I had suggested a variety of possible topics. Among these he had chosen "The Political Role of the Military in the Middle East"—somewhat to my surprise, since Brazil then was still struggling to overcome a spell of military rule. My host also told me that the lecture would be followed by a press conference, and he personally undertook to translate for me—perhaps to avoid any inadvertent embarrassments. My basic theme was the contrast between Arab armies losing many wars over the decades but filling the political vacuum at home by seizing power in military coups against unarmed civilians in the capital.

I had spent some time the night before thinking of questions that might be asked at the press conference—and soon the question I anticipated indeed was asked, "You have told us about the role of the military in the Middle East; how would you apply all this to Brazil?" My well prepared answer was, "As you know, I am an expert on the Middle East. All of you know so much more about Brazil than I do. I wish you would draw your own conclusions." And indeed, the following day, several Rio newspapers carried the story of my talk, one of them featuring a picture of me with an ironic smile, and the caption explaining that "Professor Rustow declines to analyze the case of Brazil, saying that it is Asia that is his specialty."[22]

Among the many conferences that I attended, I vividly remember the symposium called "Iran: Past, Present, and Future" held at Persepolis in September 1975. The meeting was sponsored by the Aspen Institute and officially hosted by Reza Shah's wife, "Her Imperial Majesty the Shahbanu." I used the occasion to ask any of the Iranian colleagues whom I met for their own views on Iran's present and future. Typically, I got two sorts of answers. Those who were secretly in opposition to the regime were saying that the government was losing its grip on the country, and hopefully there would be some major changes toward more constitutional government soon. Those on the Shah's side said that, unfortunately, the regime seemed to have no coherent plans and that the political situation was growing more and more difficult. But as soon as a second Iranian joined the conversation, both opponents and supporters quickly changed their tune to say how good the political situation was and how wisely the government was dealing with the country's political and economic problems.

The experience shocked me. The Iranian participants must all have been persons in good standing with the regime. I therefore drew several conclusions. First, the government had few genuine supporters, and even those few were very pessimistic about the regime's prospects. Second, instead of building support around a constructive program, the government was trying to keep in control by the ubiquitous use of secret police informants. Third, and obviously, the regime could not last long—except that, like many other Western observers, I mistakenly assumed that this would mean a return to the kind of progressive parliamentary government attempted by Mossadegh in the 1950s. Instead, it turned out that the political vacuum created by the Shah's secret police was so complete that the only group in a position to fill it was the Shi'ite clergy—with a network of organization well-enough established that even the Shah could not uproot it.

Other memorable experiences from trips to the Middle East were visits to Jerusalem, Cairo, and Riyadh in the 1970s and 1980s. For example, on one of my visits to Jerusalem, I was staying with my sister-in-law Lotte Salzberger, who at the time was Deputy Mayor of Jerusalem and Mayor Teddy Kollek's main contact with Jerusalem's Arab community. When I heard that she was arranging a meeting between Kollek and a prominent Arab from the West Bank, I politely asked whether I could be present at the meeting, although I promised to remain silent. Municipal elections were due shortly, and, in the past, the Arab residents of Jerusalem had consistently abstained from voting—not wanting to give implicit recognition to Israel's annexation of the Eastern part of the city. But, as Kollek and Salzberger pointed out to the Arab guest, the next municipal elections would be a very close race, which Kollek and his moderate ticket of city councilors might well lose to the alliance of Likud and ultra-orthodox parties. In short, Arab voting participation this time might make the crucial difference. The Arab guest promised that he would pass the word to his Jerusalem Arab contacts to bring out their full vote. But he added that there was one strict condition. None of this must get into the press, or else the deal was off. In due course, Kollek was indeed re-elected—and in a subsequent election four years later, it became an open secret that Jerusalem Arabs were helping to provide his majorities.

From a visit to Cairo in the early 1980s I remember the enormous overload both of the telephone and the traffic systems. I had been planning a number of interviews with some leading academics and government officials—but found that it was impossible to reach anyone by phone. And the traffic was so hopelessly congested that thousands of cars were stuck and blew their horns. Luckily, my hotel was in the center of town, and, to avoid getting stuck in this "symphonie de klaxons," I soon discovered that the best way to make appointments was to *walk* to the academic institute or government office, drop my card with the secretary, and ask her to leave a message at the hotel switchboard confirming the time of the appointment.

In arranging to apply for my Saudi visa I was asked by my Saudi contact in Washington whether I was "a cousin"—a polite way, I gathered, to find out whether I was Jewish. I explained in some detail that I was Protestant on my father's and Catholic on my mother's side—but also mentioned that my wife was Jewish and indeed that a sister-in-law was Kollek's deputy mayor in Jerusalem. I did get the visa eventually, and the highlight of my stay in Riyadh was a long interview with Prince Abdullah ibn Faisal al-Turki, who was one of the most knowledgeable oil experts in the royal family and, at the time, in charge of developing the new ports of Jubail and Yanbu.

Of particular interest among my increasing foreign contacts in the 1980s was a series of discussion meetings on current Middle Eastern problems among leading U.S. and Soviet scholars sponsored by IREX (International Research and Exchange) and held alternately in Moscow (1983 and 1988) and the U.S. (1986 and 1990), for which I became the American co-chairman. The Soviet co-chairman at first was Yevgeny M. Primakov, the leading Middle East expert at the Soviet Academy, and later his younger colleague Vitaly Naumkin. When Primakov and I first met to discuss plans for the original 1983 session, I explained to him that I thought the U.S. and the Soviet Union had genuine differences, even sharp differences, in the Middle East. But I added that there seemed to be at least one common interest: not to let a regional conflict in the Middle East escalate into a full nuclear confrontation between the superpowers. Therefore, the Middle East for Washington and Moscow was not a zero-sum game. Primakov seemed very impressed with this notion, and several times when I met him later he kept referring to this "non-zero-sum game" approach. Some years later I was pleased to learn that Primakov had become a member of Gorbachev's inner circle, advising him on the resolution of regional conflicts, notably the Iraq-Kuwait crisis of 1990-91.

◆ ◆ ◆

As I reflect on my four decades as a political scientist specializing in the Middle East, I consider myself fortunate to have entered the field at an early stage. In the 1950s, as a newcomer to an as yet undefined and unexplored academic specialty, it was natural to view the Middle East as a regional whole. It also was essential to connect one's own work with scholarship in other fields. As J. C. Hurewitz remarked to me in our first 1952 encounter, you had to try hard to see the next scholar on the horizon—and, at this time, those scholars distantly visible to the junior political scientist were likely to be not political scientists but, above all, Middle Eastern historians and specialists in literature, economics, and sociology.

Those, after all, were the days when historians such as Hamilton A. R. Gibb, Bernard Lewis, and Gustave E. von Grunebaum joined forces to work on the ambitious project of a definitive *Encyclopedia of Islam*; when contemporary events in Israel still seemed intimately linked to the earlier history of Zionism and of Judaism as a whole; when Daniel Lerner tried to apply the principles of sociological analysis of public opinion to a country such as Turkey; and when W. W. Rostow proposed his ambitious socio-political theory of economic growth.[23] And the fellow political scientists with whom it was essential to maintain contact were specialists on Europe or on other developing regions—or else on international relations in the early Cold War period.

Thus it was natural enough for me to focus my own Middle Eastern research not only on questions of contemporary politics but on the transition from the Ottoman Empire to the Turkish Republic—and, of course, I was lucky to be able to obtain personal interviews with some of the surviving key participants in those events of the decade after World War One. After such initial stimulation, I was well prepared for such later challenges as the Almond committee's proposal to compare modernization in Japan and Turkey or Cyril Black's invitation to join him in teaching his seminar on the comparative history of modernization.

But now, as the field of Middle East politics over the decades has become well established and attracted an ever-larger cohort of experts, it has also become more highly specialized. As a result, a majority of younger scholars seem to have become country specialists; and even those who transcend those narrow country limits typically concentrate on specific aspects, such as Islamic conservative movements, oil policies, or arms trading. In short, the field is crowded with specialists—and it is easy not to see the forest for the trees.

For myself, a broader, interdisciplinary orientation had long since become a habit. Interdisciplinary social science happened to be the theme of my research project when I received Princeton's invitation to develop Middle East politics as a teaching field. A quarter century later at the CUNY Graduate School I became the founding chairman of a Committee on Interdisciplinary Studies—explaining to a general faculty meeting that I saw it as our task to "transcend scholarly disciplines without losing scholarly discipline."

In the 1960s at Columbia I enjoyed my close contacts with Albert O. Hirschman, then hard at work on his empirical theory of economic development based on the experience of Brazil and other Latin American countries. At Brookings, I was glad to try to broaden my perspective on Middle Eastern politics into an empirical theory of the politics of modernization in post-colonial countries from Latin America to Southeast Asia and from questions of national identity to endemic threats of military coups. Meanwhile, I pursued my own comparison of the historic process of "Transitions to Democracy" in Sweden in the past century and in Turkey today and, in response to Lichtblau's request, set out upon my analysis of the political factors shaping the economic realities of the Middle Eastern and the global oil market.

Thus, as mentioned earlier in this memoir, I have combined over the years academic and extracurricular activities focused on the Middle East with work on more broadly comparative themes. Similarly, many of my former students at Princeton, Columbia, and CUNY, such as Philip H. Stoddard and Walter F. Weiker, have pursued scholarly careers in Middle Eastern politics or history, while others, such as Douglas E. Ashford, M. Donald Hancock, and Ezra N. Suleiman, have worked in European or, more broadly, comparative politics.[24]

I also take pride in the fact that some of the doctoral candidates whom I sponsored at Columbia or CUNY have entered a broad range of non-academic professions—that is, in a sense, left the ivory towers to reconnect with the real world. Among these I might mention John F. Mugno, a Vice President for petroleum and energy at Citibank; Yosef Goell, an editor of the *Jerusalem Post*; Susan Kaufman Purcell, Vice President of the Americas Society; and Jonathan Chanis, an expert with the first Soviet overseas bank in New York and later on the post-soviet economy with Goldman Sachs.

When I first connected with the Middle East in my adolescent years in Turkey in the early 1940s, the country still was clearly in its transition from an Ottoman-Islamic to a modern Western and European culture. One of the basic aspects of the Middle East that I have found particularly attractive is that it is truly in the middle—between Europe, Asia, and Africa; between the Mediterranean and the Indian Ocean; and between NATO, the former Soviet Empire, and the developing countries. Thus, over the years, I have come to appreciate more and more a Turkish saying that I first learned in my Istanbul days: "Münasebet lâzım, efendim; münasebet lâzım!" ("You need connections, Sir; you need connections!") And I take much pleasure in thinking that in my career as a teacher, writer, and conferencier I may have been able to trace and reinforce some of those connections.

Notes

1. Cited Horst Wildmann, *Exil und Bildungshilfe: Die deutschsprachige akademische Emigration in die Turkei nach 1933* (Bern: Herbert Lang, 1973), 56.
2. Cf. my essay, "Alexander Rüstow (1885–1963): A Biographical Sketch," in Alexander Rüstow, *Freedom and Domination: A Historical Critique of Civilization* (Princeton: Princeton University Press, 1980), xiii–xxix.
3. Cf. my essay, "Erinnerungen an die Odenwaldschule," *OSO-Nachrichten*, no. 8 (Heppenheim, Spring 1985), 14–37.

4. *Mimesis: Dargestellte Wirklichkeit in der abendländischen Literatur* (Bern: A. Francke, 1946); English translation, *Mimesis: The Representation of Reality in Western Literature* (Princeton University Press, 1953).

5. Erlenbach-Zurich: Rentsch, 1950–57; I later edited a condensed, one-volume translation entitled *Freedom and Domination, op. cit.*

6. See column by Va Nu, *Akşam* (Istanbul), 4 June 1944, 45.

7. C. J. Friedrich, *Constitutional Government and Politics: Nature and Development* (New York: Harper, 1937; 2nd ed., 1941). A later, revised edition was entitled *Constitutional Government and Democracy: Theory and Practice in Europe and America* (Boston: Ginn & Co., 1950).

8. New Haven: Yale University Press, 1939, rev. ed., 1951.

9. Vol. 10, no. 3 (Summer 1956), 325–26.

10. Princeton University Press, 1960.

11. See Black's *The Dynamics of Modernization: A Study in Comparative History.* Harper, 1966.

12. Princeton University Press, 1964.

13. Washington, D. C.: The Brookings Institution, 1967.

14. "Transitions to Democracy: Toward a Dynamic Model," *Comparative Politics,* vol. 2, no. 3 (April 1970), 337–63.

15. For an early preview of my research see "Democracy: A Global Revolution?" *Foreign Affairs,* vol. 69, no. 4 (Fall 1990), 75–91.

16. "Dependability and Dependence: Political Prospects for Middle East Oil" in *Oil Imports and the National Interest,* New York: Petroleum Industry Research Foundation, Inc., March, 1971, 21–48.

17. New York: Norton, 1982.

18. *Noticias* (Monterrey), 26 February 1983.

19. Incidentally, while the Council had selected the subtitle "America's Forgotten Ally" over my objections, the translations gave me a chance to choose my own subtitle (in German, *Die Türkei: Brücke zwischen Oriente und Okzident,* Göttingen: Vandenhoeck & Ruprecht, 1990).

20. New York: Brazillier, 1970.

21. With Kenneth Paul Erickson, New York: Harper, 1991.

22. *Jornal do Brazil* (Rio de Janeiro), 27 September 1966.

23. See Daniel Lerner, *The Passing of Traditional Society: Modernizing the Middle East* (Glencoe: Free Press, 1958); W. W. Rostow, *The Stages of Economic Growth: A Non-Communist Manifesto* (New York: Cambridge University Press, 1960).

24. Stoddard for many years edited the *Middle East Journal.* Publications by the others mentioned include: Walter F. Weiker, *The Modernization of Turkey: From Atatürk to the Present Day* (New York: Holmes & Meier, 1981); Douglas E. Ashford, *Political Change in Morocco* (Princeton: Princeton University Press, 1967), *National Development and Political Reform: Political Participation in Morocco, Tunisia, and Pakistan* (Princeton: Princeton University Press, 1967), and

The Emergence of the Welfare State (Oxford: Blackwell, 1986); M. Donald Hancock, *Sweden: The Politics of Postindustrial Change* (Hinsdale, Ill.: Dryden, 1972); and Ezra N. Suleiman, *Politics, Power, and Bureaucracy in France: The Administrative Elite* (Princeton: Princeton University Press, 1974), *Elites in French Society: The Politics of Survival* (Princeton: Princeton University Press, 1978), *Private Power and Centralization in France: The Notaires and the State* (Princeton: Princeton University Press, 1987).

CHAPTER 10

Winds Blow Where Ships Do Not Wish to Go

Farhat Ziadeh

I was meant to be a lawyer, not a college professor specializing in Arabic and Islamic studies. But the vicissitudes of World War II and the Palestine Question altered my course and set me on a new direction that I had never thought I would take.

As a matter of fact, during my high school years at the American Friends School for Boys in Ramallah, Palestine, I was bored with Arabic and the pedantic manner in which it was taught, while I was delighted with English classes to the point that I started composing English verse. The Arabic teacher, Farid Tabri of blessed memory, was a disciplinarian of the first order, a product of a German school in Jerusalem who valued discipline and decorum above enticing the young minds to the admitted beauties of Arabic. He even scolded his students not in the colloquial dialect but in highfalutin classical Arabic that was full of metaphors and ironies, to the secret delight and chuckles of his students who would repeat his phrases of scolding after class amidst hilarious laughter. It was only after graduation from school that his former students discovered in him the kind and sensitive soul that he really was. Unfortunately, though, very few of those students were sufficiently enthused by him and his discipline to specialize in Arabic studies on the college level.

After graduating from high school I was sent to the American University of Beirut to study political science in preparation for the study of law in England. In the same way that the poet in pre-Islamic times was looked upon as the defender and the spokesman of his tribe whose glory he would sing, the lawyer in early twentieth-century Middle East was viewed as the defender of his people against colonial powers. The lawyer knew the language and mentality of colonial administrators and was conversant with concepts of rights and legal remedies. He could therefore stand up to those administrators and even pound the table in court while pleading his cause, to the astonished and admiring gaze of his countrymen in the audience. The prestige of such a lawyer was immense, and some of that prestige rubbed off onto members of his family and clan. My family wanted their son to be a lawyer and to be called by the admiring public Farhat Effendi! To my half-hearted suggestion that I might want to study dentistry, my outraged peasant grandfather, who had just acquired a set of false teeth that he compared to the stone terrace walls he used to build in his fields, cried out, "Are we to revert to lining up the stones of terrace walls?" So that was that, and I was to study political science in preparation for law.

At the American University of Beirut, Freshman Arabic was part of the curriculum and it was taught that year by Professor Jibrail Jabbur. Although I approached that course with trepidation, I was soon won over by Jabbur's accounts of the escapades of the Umayyad poet 'Umar ibn Abi Rabi'ah—whom Jabbur had studied in two volumes—and his love poetry addressed to the beautiful women who visited Mecca for pilgrimage. In modern Arabic poetry, Jabbur's explanation of the meaning of the verses from Shawqi's poem about the Lebanese town of Zahleh and sung by 'Muhammad 'Abd al-Wahhab stands out so vividly in my memory, especially because I had previously repeated the verses of that song without much understanding. A new world of Arabic literature and culture opened up to me, a world so different from the pedantic Arabic of high school days. This budding interest in things Arabic was augmented in my undergraduate years by three fellow Palestinian student friends who wrote poetry and delighted in reciting it on their afternoon walks along Hamra Street, then a red sandy road flanked by cactus bushes leading from Ras Beirut westward towards the sea. The three were Sa'id al-'Isa, the late resident poet and literary critic of the Arabic service of the British Broadcasting Corporation, the late 'Abd al-Mun'im al-Rifa'i, poet and former prime minister of Jordan, and Mahmud al-Hut, poet and educator in Beirut.

Interest in Arabic culture was transformed into pride in that culture by a professor who has had an enormous influence on the cultural and national development of his students, Constantine Zurayk. Through his classes in Arab history and particularly his course on Arab science, Zurayk nurtured an admiring respect for Arab achievements and Arab contribution to world civilization. This respect for Arab culture started to counterbalance the awe I had felt toward Western culture, and I no longer looked at my cultural background as something to be apologetic about. Reading George Sarton's works on the history of science, and particularly Arabic science, assigned by Zurayk, confirmed my newly discovered pride. I even participated in the activities of the Arab students' cultural society called al-'Urwah al-Wuthqa (whose name harked back to the journal founded by Jamal al-Din al-Afghani and Muhammad 'Abduh in Paris and ultimately, of course, to the Quranic phrase found in the second chapter, al-Baqarah) and wrote articles in Arabic for its journal of the same name, including an article about the American union as a model for a union of Arab states. Zurayk, who was the faculty advisor of that society, edited that latter article and encouraged me to continue writing in Arabic.

al-'Urwah al-Wuthqa's orientation was decidedly pan-Arab. Terms such as "Arab union" and "Arabism" (*'urubah*) dominated the scene and were unquestioned like religious dogmas. Students who belonged to the Syrian Nationalist Party (PPS), which emphasized the ancient Semitic background of Syria before the Arab invasion, or to the Iraqi Society, which was formed on campus then to support the Bakr Sidqi-Hikmat Sulayman coup of 1936 in Iraq against the pan-Arabist premier Yasin al-Hashimi, were given the pejorative name *iqlimiyyun*, or parochialists, and were considered rather suspect in a vague sort of way. Even I, who like most Palestinian students supported the pan-Arab ideology, was the object of whisperings around the campus to the effect of being an "internationalist" (communist?, nihilist?) for having been the president of the International Relations Club!

This newly developed interest in Arab culture and Arab themes was to be continued in England, to which I set out to study law at the London School of Economics of the University of London and at Lincoln's Inn. The boat that I took from Haifa stopped in Beirut and Alexandria before proceeding to Naples. It was exciting to see Beirut again from the ship, but upon departing Beirut past the beautiful campus of the American University of Beirut with its many trees and red-roofed buildings, the four years I had spent there flashed through my mind. The many friendships I had formed among students and faculty and the many experiences I had had on and off campus paraded themselves anew and produced a swelling of nostalgic emotion that was hard to control.

The ship anchored in Alexandria harbor the second morning to take on a huge load of cotton bales. Passengers were told that they could go ashore during the two days that the loading process would take. I was most excited to see that great metropolis built by Alexander and to experience life in yet another Arab country, with its distinct Arabic dialect and its reputed light-hearted inhabitants. But my hopes were dashed when I presented my passport to the police, for they unceremoniously turned me back to the ship because I was an unaccompanied minor! Nothing could have been more deflating to my ego. True, I was a few months shy of that magical age of twenty-one, which supposedly turns boys into men, but I had a bachelor's degree in my pocket and I puffed on cigarettes with the air of an experienced and debonair traveler. But these were not to convince the police. My only consolation was that one other person was turned back to the ship to become my companion during the two days it took to load the ship. He was a Lebanese artist who was going to Paris to continue his study of painting. His passport described his profession as "artist." But the Egyptian police understood that to be an *artiste*, one of a breed of men and women who plied the nightclubs of the Middle East with their dances or songs and were considered by the police to be unsavory characters!

The study of law at the University of London was an inter-collegiate affair, which meant that lectures on various topics of law were given at different colleges, while tutorials were offered to a student at the college in which he was registered. Registered at the London School of Economics (LSE), I had my tutorials there and walked over to King's College for Harold Potter's lectures on torts or took a bus to University College for Herbert F. Jolowicz's lectures on Roman law and George Keaton's lectures on the law of trusts and to the School of Oriental and African Studies (SOAS) for Seymour Vesey-Fitzgerald's lectures on Palestine law. Constitutional law lectures were given at LSE by Ivor Jennings and an LSE lecturer who later went into politics delivered the lectures on contracts and criminal law. Another LSE professor, Theodore Plucknett, delivered the esoteric lectures on the history of English law. Following the declaration of war, when LSE moved to Cambridge in anticipation of an air attack on London, LSE students attended Cambridge faculty lectures and lectures given by some University of London faculty. I attended lectures on torts and international law by P. H. Winfield and Hersh Lauterpacht of the Cambridge faculty, respectively, and on legal theory and Islamic law by Jennings and Fitzgerald of the London faculty, respectively. In the case of Fitzgerald, however, it would be stretching the meaning of the word "lectures" when applied to his course on Islamic law because I was the only student Fitzgerald had and the course assumed the guise of a tutorial or a discussion session.

Compared to the relaxed atmosphere of study at the American University of Beirut, the law course in London was highly intensive and competitive. Roughly one-third of the students failed the intermediate examination at the end of the first year. Besides, London was like Beirut neither in weather nor in the pleasant camaraderie among students and the population generally. To counter the sense of estrangement and loneliness, I used what little time I had away from my studies to make contact with other Arab students from Palestine and Iraq who had formed the Arab Students Society. The only other Arab student group was from Egypt, but Egyptian students had their own club, no doubt financed by the Missions Section of the Ministry of Education. The Arab Students Society was strictly secular; its membership included Muslims, Christians, and one Iraqi Jew. It was pan-Arab in orientation and focused on the Palestine question as a problem that the British public should know more about. It held two or three mini-conferences outside London (including one at Oxford) to define Arabism and to debate the Palestine question with Zionist protagonists. Among its membership were Musa Abdullah al-Husayni, who later was implicated in the assassination of King Abdullah in Jerusalem and was hanged; 'Abd al-Rahman al-Bazzaz, who later filled Iraqi government posts and was a theoretician of Arab nationalism; 'Abd al-'Aziz al-Duri, the well-known Arab historian of Baghdad and Jordan universities; Nicola Ziadeh, the prominent historian and teacher at the American University of Beirut; 'Abd al-Ghani al-Dalli, later to become a minister in the Iraqi government and a prominent businessman in Beirut; and myself.

Members of the society, particularly al-Husayni, were very active in calling, and in preparing, for a conference of Arab students in Europe. The conference was held over the Christmas vacation at the Cité Universitaire in Brussels in the year 1938. Students from England, France, Germany, and Belgium attended. Papers the definition of Arab nationalism and on the political, social, and economic programs of a pan-Arab movement involving the Arab countries from the Atlantic to the Gulf, prepared beforehand by members of the society in England, were debated in the appropriate committees and later adopted by the plenary session. Many of the attendees, who will not be named because of lack of space, later assumed the highest positions in their respective countries. The proceedings of the conference were printed that year by al-Husayni, but unfortunately my copy was lost when I had to leave Palestine in 1948 (but one understands that Professor Tariq Ismail of Calgary will deal with that conference in a future publication).

The academic year 1938–1939 was the second year of my law program, and it was fortunate for me that the year did not end up with final examinations, which were regularly given at the end of the third and final year. The year was hectic. Chamberlain had bought time with his Munich agreement, but people expected war to break out. The British government tried to tidy things up in the Middle East in expectation of war. The Higher Arab Committee of Palestine, some of whose members had been exiled to the Seychelles by the British, were brought to London together with representatives of Arab states to attend a conference to ease the situation in Palestine. Together with some other students and representatives of Arab embassies, I met the Palestine delegation at Victoria Station but was deeply distressed by the caliber of one of its members who declared at the train platform, "Thanks be to God that we came to London and imprinted our name on History." It was as if the important thing to this nameless leader was to print his name on history, not to attempt to solve the Palestine problem!

The Arab Office in London that had been established as a center of information on Palestine was very active at this time. Interested Arab and, particularly, Palestinian students frequented this office to get news of the Middle East, to meet visiting dignitaries and diplomats, and sometimes to receive speaking assignments at clubs and church groups if the officers of the Arab Office could not meet those engagements. Dr. Izzat Tannous, the director; Mrs. Stewart Erskine, the well-known writer on the Middle East; and George Mansour, the Palestinian labor leader, constituted those officers. Their counsel and advice were always appreciated, and they helped in the molding of attitudes and orientations.

Of the Arab ambassadors in London, the most accessible to students was the Saudi ambassador, Dr. Hafiz Wahbah, an Egyptian by origin and a friend and companion of the founder of the modern kingdom, 'Abd al-'Aziz ibn Su'ud. A wonderful raconteur and scholar (he is the author of *Jazirat al-'Arab*), he always delighted visitors with his accounts about Arabia and Ibn Su'ud. I absorbed much about Arabia and its mores and customs from him.

One particular story about Ibn Su'ud opened up my eyes to the fact that repression, discrimination, and violation of human dignity can come not only from colonial powers and their functionaries but from ignorant traditional rulers as well. It seems that when Ibn Su'ud acquired a fleet of limousines, he would ride in one and insist that his close associates ride with him, but they had to sit on the floor of the car because they were not his equals so as to sit on the same level. Dr. Wahbah, quite understandably, considered that demeaning, so he would excuse himself from riding in the same car and would follow in another. Finally Ibn Su'ud realized that if he were to receive the counsel of Dr. Wahbah while riding from one place to the other, he would have to make him sit in the back seat with him. And so he did.

It was Dr. Wahbah's office that arranged for Musa al-Husayni and me to receive tickets to the visitor's gallery of the House of Commons when that body was debating the White Paper on Palestine following the London conference of 1939. While they listened to the Colonial Secretary, Mr. Malcolm MacDonald, expound on the Paper, a gentleman sitting beside us was obviously not pleased as evidenced by his demeanor. The Paper limited Jewish immigration into Palestine and restricted land sales to Jews. It suddenly dawned on us that the gentleman was none other than Chaim Weizmann, the future president of Israel, whose picture we had seen in the newspapers!

Speaking of future Israeli leaders, a future foreign minister and premier of Israel, Moshe Sharett, spoke once at the Zionist club at the London School of Economics. During the question period, I asked him whether he thought the Zionist scheme would be unjust to the Arabs. He conceded the point but said, "The justice to the Jews exceeds the injustice to the Arabs!" This doctrine of relative justice was certainly a new subjective principle in international affairs! At the end of the meeting, Sharett headed toward me to ask about my background. When told, he inquired about the principal of the Friends School in Ramallah. Sharett certainly knew Arab Palestine and possibly had more empathy to Palestinians than other Israeli leaders.

In the summer of 1939, I went to the United States to visit my father, who was working there, and some relatives. I stayed most of the time with some cousins in Brooklyn, who owned a wholesale dry goods establishment in Manhattan. The store was only a few blocks away from the offices of an Arabic newspaper, *al-Sayeh*, run by the two brothers, 'Abd al-Masih and Nadrah Haddad. These two littérateurs and poets were the daily hosts of other littérateurs and poets, some of whom, like the Haddads, were former members of the Pen League founded by the famous Arab-American poet and writer Kahlil Gibran. Among the group were the poets Nasib 'Aridah and Rashid Ayyub and the writers Dr. George Khayrallah and Habib Katibah. What a delightful group of people they were! Over cups of Turkish coffee they reviewed the news of the day, especially the news of the Arab countries, and discussed new books and publications in a very witty vein. I visited this "salon" as often as I could, and my budding love for Arabic poetry and letters was deepened. Once, those assembled toyed with the idea of each composing on a card (coll. Arabic: *kart*; pl.: *krute*) a single verse with specified rhyme and meter. Then we collected the cards and read them aloud to see whether the poem composed of these verses made sense. Naturally, the result was hilarious and completely nonsensical. So one member dubbed the poem *qasidah 'a-krute*, which could mean "a poem on cards" or in a more risque vein "a pimpish poem."

Next to *al-Sayeh* offices was an office of an Arab-American organization called the Arab League headed by Fu'ad Shatara, a Palestinian medical doctor and surgeon, and directed by Habib Katibah, a writer of Syrian origin. On Labor Day of 1939 it held a *mahrajan*, or open-air festival, in Flint, Michigan at the farm of Tom Mansour, a successful businessman originally from Nazareth, Palestine. Several people were invited to address the festival, including Fu'ad Mufarrij, a former instructor of political science at the American University of Beirut and a rising nationalist leader in Lebanon and Syria; Fakhri al-Shaykh, an Iraqi graduate student at Columbia University; 'Abd al-Majid 'Abbas, an Iraqi scholar who had just obtained his Ph.D. from the University of Chicago, and myself.

Mufarrij, al-Shaykh, and I set out from New York for Flint, and later for Dearborn, in a small car of ancient vintage belonging to al-Shaykh. The enthusiasm generated by the speeches of the young scholars and the hospitality of the hosts in Flint and Dearborn seemed at the time to overshadow and dull the news of the outbreak of World War II. But a decision had to be made as to whether I could return to England to finish my studies. I therefore left my two companions and joined 'Abbas in an equally ancient but bigger car which was heading for New York in order to consult my cousins as to what to do. Three days later the news reached New York of the death of Mufarrij and al-Shaykh in a car accident on their way to Chicago. The excruciating news of their death, added to the somewhat guilty feeling I had for not being with my two companions at the time of their death and the uncertainty of travel to England, was most unsettling. Finally, some of my friends wrote to say that LSE had moved to Cambridge and that classes had resumed. By the time I arranged for passage to Genoa on an Italian ship (Italy was non-belligerent then) and made my way to England by train and ferry, the first term of the academic year was almost over, and I was admitted to classes only by a special petition due to the circumstances of the war.

At Cambridge I joined my friends al-Husayni, al-Duri, and al-Dalli at a boarding house on 1 West Road, west of King's College. Although the setting was beautiful, the winter was especially cold and the only heat available was from those gas heaters with meters fed with shillings. (One wonders whether the Industrial Revolution did indeed begin in England!) To add to the discomfort, a few weeks after my arrival the British government decreed that all aliens were to observe a curfew from 6:00 p.m. until the morning of the second day. My protestations that I was a "friendly alien," and in fact a holder of a passport inscribed "British Passport—Palestine," were of no avail since Palestine, being a mandated territory, was not officially part of the British Empire so as to enable its citizens to claim British citizenship and to escape the curfew. The almost nightly visit of the German Messerschmits with their pulsating drone seeking the airfields next to Cambridge were not especially conducive to study. Still, the final examinations were approaching and study had to be undertaken in earnest. Immediately after the examinations, al-Husayni, who was reading history, and I left for London to find a way to return to Palestine.

It was during this stay in London that I was first introduced to the teaching of Arabic. While waiting to make travel plans to Lisbon, a neutral port, and then to Palestine, I was asked by Bernard Lewis, whom I had met through al-Husayni and al-Duri, his pupils at SOAS, to assist him in teaching Arabic to a group of British officers destined for the Middle East. Although no syllabus or any plan of study was available and the teaching involved both "Syrian" colloquial and modern classical in an ad hoc arrangement, I thoroughly enjoyed the teaching sessions. I did not know then that the teaching of the Arabic language, literature, and culture would form a goodly part of a future academic career. But first things must come first, and a career in law in Palestine was the primary target. It is true that I had not had the time to sit for the final examination at the Bar, but that could wait until the end of the war. Accordingly, al-Husayni and I set out by train to Liverpool, where we spent a harrowing night at a hotel near the port because of bombing runs made by German planes and boarded the British ship Avoceta for Lisbon. The voyage took almost two weeks because the ship had to sail in a convoy around Ireland and well into the Atlantic, zigzagging all the time to avoid German submarine torpedoes, and then make a dash eastward for Lisbon.

Arrangements were made in Lisbon to board a Yugoslav ship bound for the eastern Mediterranean, stopping first in Italy. But before sailing, Italy declared war and the shipping company would not allow us to board the ship because we were considered British subjects holding British passports and might be held as prisoners of war by Italy. The irony was that England had considered us aliens for purposes of the curfew, but now we were being branded as British. Our lot was always to reap the whirlwind of this nationality!

Being stuck in Lisbon during the war was no fun. Everybody was trying to escape somewhere, and Lisbon was the gate. Al-Husayni had no choice but to travel to Berlin to be with his cousin the Mufti of Jerusalem and to work for the Palestine cause. Later he found out that the Germans were no better than the British in furthering Arab interests, and so he joined Jena University and worked for a doctorate in Islamic history. Because of family and ideological considerations, I wanted to travel to the United States, and it took me four months to obtain a visa due to the thousands of refugees forming endless lines around the U.S. Consulate.

Back in New York I thought I would further my legal training by working as a law clerk with a prominent Lebanese-American lawyer, Joseph W. Ferris, who was associated with the firm of Goldstein and Goldstein. After a few months it became clear to me that I was not being intellectually engaged with questions of law as much as with filing papers at court, delivering papers to clients, and even serving process in situations that were touchy and rather deceptive. So I left my job vowing never to practice law in New York and went to Florida to help my father in his business as a salesman and to await the end of the war to return to Palestine.

A year later, 1943, while visiting New York to find employment more suited to my academic temperament, I heard from Nabih A. Faris, the head of the Arabic Desk at the Voice of America (then in New York City) and a former instructor at Princeton University, that Dr. Philip K. Hitti of Princeton was looking for instructors to teach Arabic to U.S. soldiers enrolled in the Army Specialized Training Program (ASTP) at Princeton. A visit to Princeton, during which my previous experience as a teacher of Arabic to British officers in London for a few weeks was unduly emphasized, landed me a job as an instructor of Arabic. The other teachers were Habib Kurani, a professor and Registrar at the American University of Beirut; Jamil Barudi, who later became a Saudi Arabian delegate to the United Nations; Goro Deeb, a Ph.D. candidate in political science at Chapel Hill; Raji Dahir, an Arabic newspaperman; Peter Dughman, a Washington, D.C. lawyer; Shukri Khoury, a Boston lawyer; and Ibrahim Freiji, a Lebanese lawyer and writer. The latter three had been inducted into the armed forces but were released to teach Arabic to the troops. As can be readily perceived, the teachers had no previous training in the teaching of Arabic, but we all had a good command of it, both in its classical and colloquial forms. Word spread on the campus, however, that Professor Hitti had scoured the New Jersey waterfront for Arab sailors to teach Arabic! Perhaps it was to reassure himself about these teachers' intellectual caliber that Dean Christian Gaus accosted Dr. Habib Kurani and myself, took us to his office, and engaged us on a prolonged discussion about a host of subjects.

At that time there hardly existed a book or manual for the teaching of colloquial Arabic, or even classical Arabic for that matter, and since the Army insisted on the teaching of colloquial, lessons had to be prepared by the staff.

Professor Hitti prepared a few conversation lessons in transliteration, but after a couple of weeks a switch was made to the Arabic characters. The teaching at the various sections was uneven because the teachers differed in their zeal and innovativeness. Quite naturally this gave rise to grumbling among the soldier students and some remedial measures had to be adopted. The Army had insisted that the soldiers be taught not only the ordinary and polite conversation but also Arabic profanities and invective so that they would be aware of possible abusive speech directed against them. None of the teachers volunteered to write such a lesson, so the task fell to Professor Hitti, who must have recalled to memory curses he had heard in his youth in Lebanon some decades earlier, for the result was, in the opinion of the teachers, most amateurish!

Parallel with Arabic, Turkish was taught to a different contingent of soldiers by a group of teachers assembled for that purpose under the direction of John K. Birge, the author of *The Bektashi Order of Dervishes*. Lessons in Arabic and Turkish were supplemented with lectures and readings on the history, politics, economics, geography, and social customs of the Middle East given mostly by visiting lecturers or by the Arabic and Turkish teachers themselves. This combination of language training with courses in the social sciences of the area gave rise to the idea of area studies, which after World War II mushroomed on many campuses around the country. Professor Hitti later built upon the ASTP experience to found in Princeton the first program in Near Eastern studies in the country.

The Princeton campus during the war period looked more like a camp with soldiers and sailors from the various military programs going back and forth from the halls to classes in formation. Some enterprising students of Arabic even translated into Arabic a song that was popular at the time and was fit for a marching beat. It was most amusing to see the soldiers marching in formation and hear them repeat:

> *Hutti 'l-fard bi'l ard bint, hutti 'l-fard bi 'l ard,*
> Lay that pistol down, babe, lay that pistol down.

The intensive course in Arabic lasted for six months, at the end of which the students, on the whole, could converse in what might be called Eastern Arabic. They also could read signs and newspaper headings, but they were not

proficient in modern standard Arabic. Most students took their work seriously, and even a few made a career after the war with some aspect of the Middle
East. Among those were Morroe Berger, who became the sociologist of the
Middle East at Princeton, and Roger Davies, who later joined the State Department, served in the Middle East, became the head of the Arabic Desk at
Voice of America in the early fifties, and was appointed as ambassador to Cyprus, where he was killed in August 1974 during an attack on the embassy,
presumably by right-wing extremists.

When the first group of students departed and a new group arrived to take
their place, hopes were high that the first group would soon be sent to some
Arab country where they would use their Arabic to justify the gruelling experience of six months of intensive Arabic. But the Army in its wisdom sent
them to India, thereby causing a flood of complaints from the students to Professor Hitti and the teachers, as if they were responsible for sending them to
India! Needless to say, these complaints were not especially helpful in keeping
up the morale of the new group.

Following the departure of the second group, Professor Hitti utilized the
unexpired term of some of the teachers' contracts by having them translate
into Arabic the short version of his *History of the Arabs*, entitled *The Arabs: A
Short History*. Shukri Khoury, Ibrahim Freiji, and I undertook to do the translation. It must be said that this experience was of prime importance in my future orientation for not only did I share in the task of translation but also
looked up and became familiar with the sources that Professor Hitti depended
upon in writing his book. That was necessary in the case of the Arabic sources
so as to use the exact Arabic wording of those sources in the translation. The
translation was printed in Beirut in 1946 under the title *al-ʿArab: Tarikh Mu-
jaz*.

But the exigencies of the war situation were to re-direct me into a totally
different academic field. The cultural affairs section of the State Department
was interested in producing a book about the history of the United States in
Arabic to be distributed in the Arab World, and a contract was assigned to
Princeton to do the job. Ibrahim Freiji and I were chosen to write the book
under the supervision of Professor Hitti. In view of the fact that Freiji's English was limited then, I was to consult with the History Department, under
Joseph Strayer, and particularly with Stow Pearson about the sources and the

organization of the material and to write a first draft. Freiji, whose Arabic was superb, often would recast the sentences before turning the section over to Professor Hitti for final review. The printing was done by the American Press in Beirut under the supervision of Nabih Faris, but the publisher was Princeton University Press (1946).

But my life was still to take a different turn. The Arab-American community in the United States was becoming apprehensive about the activities of the Zionists and their influence in Congress, so at a meeting in New York in 1944, at which delegations from many parts of the country were present, it was decided to create an organization that would advocate the Arab cause, particularly in Palestine. The Arab National League, which had had a similar function, had become moribund following the death, apparently by suicide, of its director Dr. Fu'ad Shatara. The new organization, with headquarters at 120 Broadway in New York City, was called the Institute of Arab-American Affairs and its staff consisted of Professor Philip Hitti as temporary Director, Habib Katibah as Editor, Ismail Khalidi as Arabic Secretary, and myself as English Secretary. Professor Hitti, who was serving without remuneration, was more of an advisor since he could not be away from his post in Princeton. Since I lived in Princeton and commuted to work in New York, I acted as a link between the Director and the New York office. The Institute had to raise funds and to propagate the Arab cause. Toward the latter end, it published a fortnightly bulletin, which it mailed to its members, interested parties, Congressmen, and some libraries. It also published special papers. Two of the papers or pamphlets with which I was associated before leaving the Institute to go back to England following the end of the war were *Papers on Palestine*, a collection of articles by American and British authors, and *Arabic-Speaking Americans* by Katibah and Ziadeh, an account of early immigration and the activities of Arab-Americans in business and the professions. It might be noted that this was the first time that Arab-Americans were identified as such. Previously they had been referred to as Syrians or even Lebanese. Actually, the name "Arabic-Speaking" in the title of the pamphlet was a compromise, because some Lebanese associated with the newspaper *al-Hoda* in New York objected to the appellation "Arab-American," and Professor Hitti sought to pacify them.

Before leaving New York, Ismail Khalidi and I had occasion to receive the members of the newly constituted Arab Office that had been dispatched by the Palestinian leader Musa al-Alami to explain the Palestinian point of view to the American public. The delegation was headed by Ahmad al-Shuqayri, who later became the first Chairman of the Palestine Liberation Organization, and included several bright young men who were not conversant with American ways or sources of information. It fell to the Institute staff to help their colleagues in that regard. Also, the Institute acquired a new director to take the place of Professor Hitti in the person of Dr. Khalil Totah, formerly the principal of the American Friends School in Ramallah. But the efforts of the Arab and Arab-American organizations in the field of information paled in comparison with those of the Zionist establishment.

Aboard the ship back to England, I had long discussions on the Palestine problem and the Arab world with two fellow passengers, Mahmud Abu al-Fath, the owner and editor of the Egyptian newspaper *al-Masri*, and an American Jewish journalist named I. F. Stone, who was reporting then for a New York publication called *PM*. A clipping from that publication sent to me in England by Khalidi indicated that those sessions aboard the ship might have had some effect. In any case, I. F. Stone impressed me then with the liberal and humane outlook that was so characteristic of his later *Newsletter*.

London in 1945 was in a sorry state, what with the visible effects of bombing and food rationing. Because my legal studies at Lincoln's Inn had been interrupted for almost five years because of the war, I wasted no time in picking up the threads of those studies. Special attention was paid to those subjects not adequately covered at the University of London, namely, law of evidence, company law, and a special subject on the Islamic law of inheritance taught by my former Professor at the University, Seymour Vesey-Fitzgerald. Also, I had to complete the required number of terms at Lincoln's Inn by eating six dinners per term there. The food there was far superior to that served at my boarding house, and therefore I readily availed myself of it. One ritual of the dinners always amused me, though. The Benchers—prominent judges and lawyers who were members of the Inn—would walk in and stand at their special elevated table to say the grace which was invariably the same: "God preserve the King, the Church, and this Honorable Society, Amen." The welfare of the rest of humanity was no concern of theirs!

After being called to the Bar in 1946, I headed to Palestine, after an absence of nine years, to take up the legal profession for which I had prepared. But before doing so, I had to sit for the Palestine Bar examination and to undergo a period of clerkship at the office of an established lawyer. The period was normally two years, but for Barristers-at-law, it was shortened to six months. I therefore joined the law firm of Atallah and Atallah in Jerusalem and commuted from my home in Ramallah. I specifically remember the kindness of the head of the firm, Antoun Atallah, a former judge and later a foreign minister of Jordan, in discussing the legal points of his many important cases with me.

When the period of clerkship was over, I was appointed by the Chief Justice of Palestine as a magistrate for the town and district of Safad, in the Galilee, with a limited civil and criminal jurisdiction. The civil jurisdiction was limited to claims not exceeding two hundred Palestinian pounds, with no limitation on counter-claims, and the criminal jurisdiction was limited to misdemeanors, with a punishment of one year's imprisonment. The latter jurisdiction also involved conducting preliminary enquiries of felonies to determine whether there was enough evidence to commit a defendant to trial at the District Court of Haifa.

I faced these new duties with awe and a heightened sense of responsibility. At the same time I had a sense of having arrived at my professional goal. I was especially thankful that I had studied Islamic law, which continued then to be the civil code of the land, and the Ottoman land laws, which together with British ordinances, governed the rights to land in Palestine. Practically all civil cases involved these bodies of law. One important series of cases stands out in my memory. The cases involved the lands of Lake Huleh basin, which were the home of some bedouin tribes who had been on the land from time immemorial. The lands formed a part of a concession obtained by the Salaam family of Beirut from the Ottoman government to develop that area. The concession was later sold to the land development company (Keren Kayemet) of the Jewish Agency which, according to a British ordinance, would consider anybody living on the land without its permission to be guilty of criminal trespass. Accordingly trespass complaints were filed in the Magistrate Court of Safad sitting in al-Khalisa (today Kiryat Shmoneh) against many bedouin families. Conviction, according to the ordinance, would entail eviction from the land.

High-powered lawyers appeared for the two sides, Ahmad al-Shuqayri, whom the readers have met earlier, for the defendants, and A. Ben Shemesh for the plaintiff. In view of the volatile nature of the cases and their political implications, the previous magistrate had listened to some evidence for each one of the many cases and kept on postponing them to hear more testimony, thus postponing a final determination. I followed the same course until the end of the British mandate in May, 1948.

Another case which deeply exercised me was the case of the teenager Hamda. It seems that Hamda, who lived with her grandmother in al-Khalisa, was impregnated by the son of the *mukhtar* following promises of marriage which were never fulfilled. When she gave birth, unbeknownst to her grandmother, she carried the baby to the local stream and placed it Moses-like in a basket and hoped for somebody seeking drinking water or performing his ablution to pick it up. A man from the village heard the whimpering of the baby, and as he picked it up he saw Hamda a short distance away watching from behind a bush. Unfortunately the baby died from exposure and Hamda was brought to court charged with infanticide. Since the defendant was underage, the court changed the felony to a misdemeanor and proceeded to try the case, instead of committing her for trial at the District Court in Haifa. Although the facts of the case were not in dispute, it seemed unfair to send her to prison or a correction home. A cousin of hers came forward and offered to marry her, but she almost fainted when that suggestion was made. I had no way of knowing whether she hated her cousin that much or whether she was afraid he would kill her for her previous immoral action. Finally, word reached the court through the prosecutor that Chief Azzouz of the L'haib tribe would offer her protection and would allow her to live in his household together with his daughters. Accordingly she was released under his recognizance. The pity was that the police did not charge the son of the *mukhtar* for statutory rape; apparently they thought the evidence against him was not sufficient!

Apart from the myriad of cases which kept me very busy, the unsettled situation in the country on account of the Arab-Jewish conflict and the conflict of both groups with the British Mandatory Government added to my burdens. I had to take special precautions to protect myself, my court, and my staff. A maze of barbed wires protected the entrance to the court, which was located in a fortress on Mount Canaan, one of the many fortresses built by the

British Army all over Palestine and holding the name of General Tagert, who had designed them. I moved from my small hotel just below the Citadel to an apartment in the Tagert building above the court, which I shared with the District Officer (*qa'im maqam*), a Baha'i named Yazdi, and the Assistant District Commissioner, a Scotsman named Alex Sinclair. The camaraderie we shared among ourselves and with the Chief of Police, Stacy Barham, who was living in an adjoining apartment with his wife, helped to relieve the tension that was building up towards the end of 1947, especially after Britain announced its intention to withdraw from Palestine. Yet despite the precautions taken against bombing and stray bullets from the nightly firings that took place between the Jewish and Arab quarters in the town below, life-threatening incidents did take place. Stacy Barham, who one afternoon rushed with a police force to the area of 'Ayn Zaytoun outside Safad to put an end to a clash between Arabs and Jews, received a bullet wound in the shoulder, and I, while returning from my court at al-Khalisah to Safad with a British police escort in January 1948, was shot at by a Jewish ambush just outside the Jewish colony of Ayelet Hashachar. Fortunately my car was not hit. The thought did occur to me, though, that the object of the ambush was not myself personally but the existence of the British jurisdiction and administration in that area, which Jews were trying to extinguish.

That jurisdiction was not long in folding up. Preparations were made at the court for withdrawal. Stacy Barham and I supervised the burning of several bags of hashish slabs that had been held for evidence against some followers of Ahmad al-As'ad, a south-Lebanon chieftain, who had been smuggling them into Palestine. Only a sample was left with the folder of the case, which was put in the open safe of the court. Some monetary proceeds were also placed in that open safe in the hope that they would be received by a succeeding government.

In the afternoon of March 18 the Irish Guards, who had been responsible for the security of the area, evacuated the British police, the Assistant District Commissioner (ADC) Sinclair, the Jewish District Officer Kahana, and myself down the road to al-Ja'unah (Rosh Pina), where the group spent the night at the Irish Guards' camp. On the following day Sinclair, Kahana, and I were put on a personnel carrier and driven through Tiberius, while we three lay flat on our backs to avoid any stray bullets being fired in the town. It was certainly comical to see the representatives of the British Empire, with all its glory, flat on their backs! Sinclair's car, a sports MG, was towed behind the personnel carrier to Nazareth, where Kahana was placed in a police car to be taken to Haifa and where Sinclair and I spent the night. Sinclair stayed at the house of District Commissioner Evans, a cold and inhospitable man who did not even have the decency to inquire about my welfare, accommodation, or travel plans. Accommodation was arranged with difficulty at a local hotel that had been jammed to capacity with Germans who had fled their two prosperous agricultural colonies west of Nazareth for fear of the Haganah. It was understood that they would be permanently resettled in South Africa.

On the morrow, Sinclair and I rode in Sinclair's MG sports car and headed for Nablus, to which he had been assigned as an ADC pending British evacuation of the country. Since the sun was shining in the morning, the top of the car was put down, but later it started raining and the top went back up. As we approached Nablus, Sinclair stopped to put the top down again, although it was still raining. To my protests Sinclair explained irritably that it was not appropriate nor seemly for a British governor to sneak into town completely covered up in a low-lying car! Once in Nablus, I took a taxi to my home in Ramallah and my service with the Palestine Government came to an end.

Several factors at this stage helped to fashion my plans and to make me opt for an academic career in the United States. A career in law when the country was undergoing such a severe upheaval with uncertainty as to the future government was out of the question. To be sure, I made an attempt, with Aziz Shehadeh, a prominent Ramallah lawyer, and Anwar Nuseibeh, a barrister and future defense minister of Jordan, to set up a temporary court at the Ramallah municipal building following the British withdrawal, in order to have a semblance of authority in the area, but the arrival of Jordan's Arab Legion and the fact that Nuseibeh was wounded by gunfire from West Jerusalem on his way back to his home in East Jerusalem put an end to that effort. Another factor was that the family income from my father's orange grove north of Tel Aviv near the village of Telmond was in jeopardy because no member of the family could reach the orange grove on account of fear of attack. A third factor was that my father, who had returned to Palestine from the United States in 1946, died on his way back to the United States in March 1948 when a Pan Am plane crashed at Shannon, Ireland en route to New York, making me the sole guardian of my teenage sisters, who had to be protected from advancing Jewish soldiers and irregulars. The clinching factor was that, in answer to an inquiry, a letter arrived from Professor Hitti inviting me to teach Arabic at Princeton during the Fall of 1948. So I, and a month later my sisters, found my way through Jordan, Syria, and Lebanon to the United States to start a new life here.

During my three or four years of absence from Princeton, great changes had overtaken the Department of Oriental Languages and Literature, as it was called then. Whereas before it had consisted only of Professor Hitti and the semi-retired professor of Sanskrit, Ernest Bender, it now boasted two more professorships, one in Turkish, occupied by Livingston Wright, and one in Persian, occupied by T. Cuyler Young. In addition, two instructorships or lectureships were created in Arabic and Turkish, one filled by myself and the other by Lewis V. Thomas. Professor Hitti, benefiting from the war experience of the Army Specialized Training Program, was on the way to creating an integrated program in Near Eastern Studies. For the social science part of the program, he later arranged with the appropriate departments to appoint a sociologist, Morroe Berger, and a political scientist, Dankwart Rustow. Berger had been a student in the ASTP and Rustow had studied Turkish while residing in Turkey before and during the war, but both continued studying Arabic in my classes. Early changes in the staff included the appointment of L.V. Thomas as an assistant professor of Turkish and Turkish history following the untimely death of Livingston Wright and the appointment of R. Bayly Winder as an instructor in Arabic. In 1950 I became a part-time lecturer in Arabic as I had gotten married and needed a second job to support my family, including my sisters, who went to high school in Princeton. I joined the Arabic Desk of Voice of America in New York, first as a scriptwriter and later as an editor.

My first year at Princeton was spent in teaching and in preparing a little primer entitled *Arabic Primer* (Princeton University Press, 1949). The field of Arabic teaching in the U.S. had been completely devoid of any graded teaching materials. The only book available was a chrestomathy prepared under the auspices of the American Council of Learned Societies, but it was not suitable for a beginning class. The primer represented, therefore, the first attempt to answer that need. The first few lessons were devoted to the mechanics of Arabic writing. Later lessons afforded the instructor the chance to deduce the simple rules of syntax and morphology. The gradation involved presenting nominal sentences before verbal ones, sound verbs before weak verbs, the perfect before the imperfect, the active before the passive, etc. Later lessons consisted of simple selections from Arabic literature, old and new. The first generations of students of Arabic at Princeton and elsewhere learned their Arabic through that little primer.

It was not long, though, before it became apparent that students were in need of a full-fledged grammar of modern Arabic constructed on the same graded principles, employing words of high frequency and presenting complete tables of paradigms. I therefore embarked on such a project. Later, when R. Bayly Winder joined the faculty, we collaborated in producing a mimeographed version of *An Introduction to Modern Arabic*, which was later amended and published in hard cover by Princeton University Press in 1957. Due to the fact that I was working for the Voice of America during the four years of its writing, the working sessions had to be conducted at night. Few collaborative efforts could have been as happy due, in large measure, to the jovial personality of Bayly, may he rest in peace. The book is still going strong and has sold more than 25,000 copies.

The period 1950–1954 that I spent as an employee of the Voice of America afforded me the chance to make new friendships, to develop the art of popularizing knowledge and information, and to train myself to speak extemporaneously in classical Arabic while sticking to the rules of syntax and final inflection. The first head of the Arabic Desk was Archibald Roosevelt, whose memoirs have been recently published. Roger Davies, whom the readers met before, headed the desk at a later period. Of the more outstanding members with a literary reputation were Isa K. Sabbagh, an eloquent broadcaster with a golden voice who had established his reputation at the British Broadcasting Corporation in London, and Dr. Ahmad Zaki Abu Shady, the well-known Egyptian poet and founder of the Apollo literary group. The literary and political discussions with all these colleagues was most edifying to me.

Aside from the occasional original piece, like a political commentary, a book review, or a literary program, most of the output in the nature of news, commentaries, and features was fed by the central desk and translated or adapted for broadcast. The routine nature of the work was at one time made much more lively by a conference which I was delegated to cover and for which I was designated the information officer. The conference, entitled "Colloquium on Islamic Culture in Its Relation to the Contemporary World," was held in September 1953 at Princeton University and the Library of Congress in Washington. A large number of Muslim and American scholars attended. The Director was Bayard Dodge, the former president of the American University of Beirut, and most of the funds were provided by the United States Information Agency. The topics covered literature, history, education, social reform, law, and philosophy. Aside from the Princeton faculty, many first generation scholars familiar to American students of the Middle East attended. Among them were John Badeau, Carleton Coon, Kenneth Cragg, Richard Ettinghausen, Nabih Faris, Richard Frye, Halil Inalcik, Majid Khadduri, Fazlur Rahman, Franz Rosenthal, Wilfred Cantwell Smith, and Gustave von Grunebaum. The papers and discussions were published in two books, *Colloquium on Islamic Culture* (Princeton University Press, 1953) and M. Khalafallah, ed., *al-Thaqafah al-Islamiyah wa-al-Hayah al-Mu'asirah* (Cairo, 1956), as well as articles in the *Middle East Journal* and *The Muslim World*. At a session at the Library of Congress in Washington, F. S. C. Northrop, Sterling Professor of Philosophy and Law at Yale Law School, addressed the conference on legal philosophy. Since several delegates from the Arab world did not understand English, I was asked to sit in a translation booth behind the stage and, out of sight, to translate for those delegates through their earphones. Not only was the subject too esoteric to be conveyed to them in an extemporaneous translation, but the speaker kept on pacing to and fro on the stage, sometimes within and sometimes beyond the capacity of the stationary microphone to pick him up and transmit his words to the translation booth. I literally sweated in my booth in the effort to make sense of what was being said, but I finally gave up and blurted out in Arabic, "I cannot follow what this man is saying, and I am sure you do not either. I will therefore, cease this translation now but will attempt to give you a lucid summation at the end." A few chuckles, I was told later, emanated from those delegates to the surprise of other delegates listening to the English original!

In 1954 the Voice of America operations were scheduled to be transferred from New York to Washington, so I had to decide whether to move my family to Washington or accept a tenure-track assistant professorship at Princeton

University with a 40 percent cut in salary. It was definitely in keeping with my academic nature and preference that I chose the latter course. Professor Hitti had just retired and the chairmanship of the Oriental Languages and Literature Department devolved upon T. Cuyler Young, who was aptly described as a shepherd of scholars. His wise and gracious leadership created a congenial atmosphere within which faculty and students could best pursue their goals of study, teaching, and research. Graduates of the Department and associated departments in a decade or so became later leaders in the field of Middle Eastern Studies on campuses all over the country. Names that come to mind are Rifaat Abou-El-Haj, Ibrahim Abu-Lughod, Eqbal Ahmad, Peter Bechtold, Herbert Bodman, Edmund Burke, Richard Chambers, William Cleveland, Daniel Crecelius, Richard Debs, Martin Dickson, Caesar Farah, Oleg Grabar, Nicholas Heer, Norman Itzkowitz, John Joseph, James Kritzeck, Robert Landen, K. Allin Luther, Jon Mandaville, Michel Mazzaoui, William Millward, Richard Mitchell, Willard Oxtoby, David Partington, Frank Peters, Howard Reed, Donald Reid, George Scanlon, Stuart Schaar, Stanford Shaw, Philip Stoddard, Peter Sugar, Bernard Weiss, John Williams, and John Woods. In addition to teaching Arabic, I introduced new courses in Islamic law and Islamic institutions and pursued my research. Within that period, I edited and translated Subhi Mahmassani's *Falsafat al-Tashri' fi al-Islam* [The Philosophy of Jurisprudence in Islam] (Leiden, 1961), wrote *A Reader in Modern Literary Arabic* (Princeton, 1964), and prepared the manuscript for *Lawyers, the Rule of Law and Liberalism in Modern Egypt* (Hoover Institution, Stanford, 1968). The *Reader*, which is still being used in this country and abroad, was republished in 1981 by the University of Washington Press.

Teaching at Princeton continued to be pleasant and congenial. I was granted tenure in 1958 and continued to enjoy my students and colleagues. But a few years later, the interdisciplinary program in Near Eastern studies was split from the Department and was placed under a separate administration from outside the Department. The result was under-the-surface friction and competition between the two bodies that gave rise to gossip and backbiting. The promotion of a colleague was held up primarily because of interference from outside the Department, and the chairman seemed to have lost the independence and control that he had maintained. In that charged atmosphere, two of the tenured faculty resigned. Bayly Winder went in 1966 to New York

University to establish a department of Near Eastern Languages and an inter-disciplinary program in Near Eastern studies, and I went to the University of Washington in Seattle to do the same there.

The switch from a comparatively small and private university where I had no administrative responsibility to a large state university, which had charged me with establishing a Near East program and eventually a department of Near Eastern languages, was most challenging. Initially my colleague, Nicholas Heer, who had preceded me to Seattle, and I were placed in the Department of Classics on the assumption that the classical civilizations and the Near Eastern civilizations shared the same geographical area and background. In the following couple of years, appointments were made in Persian, Turkish, Hebrew, and ancient Near Eastern civilization. Appointments were also made in the Departments of History and Political Science, in addition to a pre-existing position in Balkan and Near Eastern history filled by Peter Sugar. Thus a viable Near Eastern program was created following the Princeton model. Courses had to be developed, degrees had to be worked out, and a library had to be built up. Within four years, the program reached a point where a separate department was thought advisable, so the umbilical cord with Classics was cut with thanks to that department and its far-sighted chairman, John McDiarmid, who had nurtured the program since its beginning.

With the benefit of hindsight, it can be safely said that it was a mistake to copy the Princeton program of having many specialized courses in the languages and civilization of the Near East to service the degree candidates in that field, with only a couple of general courses for interested undergraduates. At a private university, once a discipline is established, a sufficient number of faculty members are appointed to cover its various aspects with not much emphasis laid on the number of student credit hours (SCH). But at a public university, such as the University of Washington, the dean would always be conscious of SCH, and the various committees of the state legislature would always examine the records to "cut out the fat" and save money. I remember how I used to squirm at meetings of departmental chairmen when the Dean would produce his statistics once a year to show that the Near East Department was 1.64 of formula whereas the English Department was .68 of formula, meaning that the faculty of the Near East Department is .64 above entitlement, and the faculty of the English Department was .32 below. The

Dean would then look at me and say, "The English Department is really supporting you!" Of course explanations would follow that it was not fair to make a comparison between these two departments and that a meaningful comparison would be with another Near East Department at a comparable institution. If the Dean was sympathetic, he would accept the explanation and consider the shortfall in the SCH as a fact of life, or he might even agree to a higher designation of beginning language courses to raise the number of SCH to a respectable level. But deans change often and the same process of harassment would start all over again when a new dean was appointed!

One other point to keep in mind is that departments at these universities compete for funds and are not deterred in their avaricious behavior by an ideal of collegiality or loyalty to humanities on the whole. At one time, when the Department of Near Eastern Languages was being reviewed for possible elimination, humanistic departments not only raised no objections but even supported the Dean in that endeavor, hoping to receive new faculty positions as a result of that attempted elimination. Even members of certain humanistic departments served on a committee appointed by the Dean which proceeded to recommend elimination without bothering to interview the Chairman of the Department! Fortunately, a university-wide committee, after a thorough review, recommended the continuation of the Department with some reorganization.

The lesson to be learned from this experience is that at a university such as the University of Washington, the Near East is considered too far away and, therefore, tangential. Where emphasis is laid on the Pacific-rim countries, and where some elements are not enthusiastic about the presentation of Arab and Islamic culture in a favorable light, extra efforts should be made not to expose the department to criticism on account of insufficient SCH. Hence, it would be advisable in a situation such as this to start a program with a fair number of general courses on the Near East or to repeat one or two courses in every quarter to generate a strong base of SCH that would give the department enough credit and allow it to create specialized degree courses. Such a course of action would undoubtedly put a heavy burden on the faculty, but once the general courses are well mapped out and the faculty as a whole participate in them, the extra load can be managed. This way the department can have its own small number of students on the undergraduate and graduate levels and still enjoy a reputation of viability and service to the university.

Another legacy of the Princeton model that did not sit well with some elements of the university and the community at large was the emphasis laid on ancient Near Eastern culture and Biblical Hebrew as a foundation for the medieval Islamic culture and other Near Eastern cultures. A position in that field was one of the early positions created in the Department. To be sure, a position in modern Hebrew was also secured from the dean for a few years, but when Washington state was passing through an economic crunch, the dean took away one of these positions. After consultations with the chairmen of the Department of History and the Comparative Religion Program, it was decided to make a temporary appointment in ancient Near Eastern culture and Biblical Hebrew with a teaching assistant teaching modern Hebrew. But Jewish Studies on the campus and several faculty members interested primarily in the affairs of modern Israel pressed for making the remaining position a modern Hebrew one, and finally the dean went along with that trend. A colleague at some other campus pointed out that the traditional ancient Near Eastern studies, as understood in European and American universities, are giving way on several campuses because of similar pressures, either to modern Hebrew studies or to a type of ideological scholarship that tries constantly to connect Biblical studies to modern Israeli life, without any reference as to what transpired in between.

Developing both a department of Near Eastern languages and civilization and a Near East Center, with support from the Department of Education for center and fellowship funds, in addition to developing and teaching almost a full load of courses, took a toll on my capacity to pursue my interests in research. A project I started while at Princeton involving an edition of al-Khassaf's *Adab al-Qadi* with a commentary by al-Jassas was set aside for several years until I was able in 1972 to get a leave of absence for six months in Cairo to finish a large part of it. The work was published by the American University in Cairo Press in 1979. A similar leave in 1977 enabled me to finish a manuscript of a book entitled *Property Law in the Arab World: Real Rights*. It was published in London by Graham and Trotman in 1979 as well.

A course introduced by me at Princeton for the first time and continued at the University of Washington was Islamic law. There will be an occasion later when the importance of Islamic law will be delineated. For now it is of interest to note that this course at the University of Washington fitted rather well with the desire of the U.S. Department of Education to establish close relations between the language and area programs and the professional schools. The course was cross-listed at the Law School, I was made an adjunct professor of law, and many law students wrote interesting papers comparing certain doctrines of Islamic law with similar doctrines in the Common Law. After my retirement my position was filled by Aron Zysow, a scholar of the Near East and an accomplished lawyer, who continued to offer the same course at the Law School.

Teaching and caring for students continued to occupy an equally high place with research in my estimation. It was gratifying to see graduates of the Department filling professorship positions at the University of Tennessee, McGill University, and Portland State University. What was not gratifying, and indeed saddening, was that teaching at what are called research universities did not count for much, compared with research, in the evaluation of faculty. Two of the Department's best teachers resigned their tenured positions partly because of the pressure to publish. Their value as excellent teachers outweighed by far any article that they might have written on an obscure subject. But the system demanded publications, and they elected not to be caught up in the system! One is glad, though, that universities nowadays are giving more recognition to teaching in the evaluation process.

At the University of Washington there were two set retirement dates, one for purposes of administration and the other for teaching. It was assumed that at the age of sixty-five a professor holding an administrative position like that of a chairman of a department or a director of a center becomes semi-senile and should not be trusted with budgets and weighty administrative decisions. His mild senility, however, could be tolerated if he were to impose it only on the minds of students but not on fellow administrators, so he would be relieved of his administrative position but would be allowed to teach for five more years. At seventy senility becomes total, and he would be allowed to teach only those evening extension courses attended by housewives and school teachers seeking extra credit for higher pay. But these latter groups would not know the difference between the hallucinations of senility and a very learned discourse!

Having given up my duties as Chairman of the Department and Director of the Near East Center, I was looking forward to five years of teaching and research unencumbered by administrative duties. But colleagues at other universities saw in my relinquishing of administrative duties at the university an opportunity to saddle me with the directorship of an inter-university program. The Center for Arabic Study Abroad (CASA), which had been ably run by Ernest McCarus of the University of Michigan, was in need of a new home and director, and the Selection Committee for that purpose directed several persuasive appeals to me to take up the charge. CASA, as is well known, trains American students in advanced Arabic at the American University in Cairo and raises funds from Federal and private sources for that purpose. The opportunity of participating in this endeavor to train students, and even some faculty, in the skills of reading, writing, and speaking Arabic at a fairly advanced level persuaded me to accept the offer. The added bonus of traveling to Cairo twice a year to supervise and evaluate the program certainly figured in accepting this responsibility, especially since I had several friends in Cairo and always felt the need to travel to the Arab world to revitalize my interest in it. Having served as director for six years, I now look back with fond memories to the friendships made with the students, teachers, and administrators and to the efforts made to improve the program and to place it on a solid financial foundation. I am glad that the directorship is now in the hands of Gerald Lampe of Johns Hopkins School of Advanced International Studies, who is known for his enthusiastic and energetic support of the study of Arabic in this country. The numerous graduates of CASA, who by now exceed seven hundred, filling important positions on university campuses, in government, and in private industry and foundations, attest to the unprecedented success of this program.

With the approach of my final retirement from teaching in June 1987, my colleagues at the University of Washington, and particularly Charlotte Albright, Jere Bacharach, and Nicholas Heer, called for an international conference on Islamic law to mark the occasion. The three-day conference was attended by prominent scholars of Islamic law from this country, Canada, and the United Kingdom. The papers were later edited by Nicholas Heer and published under the title of *Islamic Law and Jurisprudence* (University of Washington Press, 1990). Also to mark the occasion, a fund in my name was created at

the University of Washington by many friends, former students, and colleagues for the publication of scholarly works in Arabic and Islamic studies.
Three books have already been supported by this fund, which will continue to
receive funds and to support publications.

As can be seen, I have been interested in both Arabic language and literature and Islamic law. Mahmoud Al-Batal, who wrote a much-appreciated
note in Arabic about me in the *Newsletter* of the American Association of
Teachers of Arabic, suggested facetiously that my interest in the two disciplines might produce a personality split! I am happy to report that such a split
has not, as yet, taken place and that I am able to present some coherent and
integrated remarks about these two disciplines as they have developed in the
United States.

As mentioned earlier, the teaching of Arabic in the United States followed a traditional method suited for philology, where the instructor would
introduce an easy classical text and start explaining the morphology of words
and the syntax all at once. I remember Professor Hitti starting his first-year
students of Arabic with the first chapter of the Qur'an. Prepositions, nouns,
verbs, and case endings were explained as they would appear in the text in an
inductive method that was hoped would round out the knowledge of grammar
for the student. Readings in the various genres of classical Arabic literature
from the chrestomathy of the American Council of Learned Societies would
follow at a plodding pace, where almost every word was to be looked up in a
dictionary and every sentence was to be grammatically analyzed in class. The
aim was the understanding of the text, and therefore it sufficed to make a
translation from Arabic into English with no attention paid to really learning
Arabic through a translation from English into Arabic or through practicing
writing and aural-oral comprehension and speaking. Some improvements
were effected through the controlled texts of Ziadeh and Winder, mentioned
earlier, and *Elementary Modern Standard Arabic* and *Intermediate Modern Standard Arabic* by Peter F. Abboud et al., but the field still needs considerable improvement in the aural-oral approach. The efforts being made by many
colleagues in this regard, particularly at the Center for Arabic Study Abroad
in Cairo, the Middlebury Summer School, and the proficiency approach being
propagated at the University of Pennsylvania, are to be applauded.

In most of these efforts the primary goal has been the mastery of modern standard Arabic. There was a time when modern descriptive linguists associated with the Foreign Service Institute advocated the study of the colloquial language first as a basis for the study of the modern standard and the classical varieties on the assumption that it was the natural way to acquire a language. But there has developed an agreement among linguists and non-linguists alike that the emphasis should be placed first on modern Standard Arabic because of several factors, chief among which was the non-availability of the appropriate milieu in the U.S. for the continued augmentation of the colloquial.

In any case the standards of language proficiency among students have risen tremendously in recent years. I remember an instance when a Ph.D. candidate defending his dissertation at Princeton could not write the title of his dissertation in Arabic. Today, graduates of the Center for Arabic Study Abroad can converse in Arabic, read novels, and write a respectable letter! Proficiency in Arabic might not have reached that of German or French in our universities, but with the introduction of Arabic into high schools in some parts of the country, a similar standard might not be far in coming.

Proficiency in language has not yet led to the strengthening of the old philological concerns of the early Near Eastern departments that followed the philological traditions of Europe. Those concerns embraced language and literature, history, religion, and thought. Much emphasis was placed on the establishment of texts, through the editing of manuscripts, and the explication of those texts. Although that tradition has not entirely died and appointments are still being made in that field, most appointments nowadays are made in disciplines that are separate from philology. Historians go to the history departments, political scientists to the political science departments, religious specialists to departments of religion, and so forth. Even in the special preserve of Near Eastern departments, namely language and literature, there have been some centrifugal tendencies that threaten the philological core. Specialists in language are now descriptive linguists who fit more in a linguistics department than in a department devoted to philology, and specialists in literature are now specialists in critical theory who fit more in a department of comparative literature. Young faculty members are now more conversant with Chomsky and Lord and Parry and with structuralists and post structuralists, modernists, and post modernists, than they are with Tabari, Yaqut, and Ibn Khaldun!

The field of Islamic law has had a phenomenal rise. The United States lagged behind Europe in this discipline until about the middle of this century. German scholars were interested in it academically while British, French, and Italian scholars were interested in its practical application in overseas possessions. Professors Joseph Schacht of Columbia University and Majid Khadduri of Johns Hopkins did much in propagating it. Still interest in it in the early sixties was not overwhelming. I remember that it took a lot of persuasion to convince the chairman of the Department of Oriental Languages at Princeton to introduce a course in Islamic law at the graduate level; to have introduced such a course on the undergraduate level, given Princeton's zealousness in controlling the number of its undergraduate courses, was simply impossible.

Today, many major centers of Near Eastern studies offer courses in Islamic law. Professors J. N. D. Anderson and the late N. J. Coulson of the University of London often came to this country as visiting professors of Islamic law. Conferences on Islamic law and jurisprudence have been held at many centers, and international conferences sponsored by the Social Science Research Council have been held at European locations. The enthusiastic call for the application of Islamic law in several Islamic countries and the concomitant interest in the practical application of this law moved several law schools in the United States to introduce Islamic law into their curricula. The number of scholars with an Islamic law specialty among the members of the Middle East Studies Association exceeds twenty, not counting those scholars interested only in jurisprudence (*usul*). A few among these who are also trained in Western law appear occasionally as expert witnesses in cases touching upon Islamic law as applied in the Middle East. University and commercial presses in this country and England started to canvass for books on the subject, and a goodly number have been published ranging in quality from the excellent to those written in haste to satisfy a rising interest, especially among Muslims resident in Europe and North America.

Islamic law, furthermore, has come to be studied by students and scholars in order to understand the spirit of Islam. Professor Schacht was right in saying in the "Introductory" to his *An Introduction to Islamic Law*, that "Islamic law is the epitome of Islamic thought, the most typical manifestation of the Islamic way of life, the core and kernel of Islam itself."

Several questions of Islamic law still need to be explored. Although a few scholars are presently working on some areas of jurisprudence, (*usul*) the field needs more extensive treatment. This is particularly true of the jurisprudence of minority groups such as the Shi'ites. For that matter, the positive law of Shi'ites needs further elaboration. Another area of study that should yield good results concerning the development of law through the centuries is the collection and study of *fatawa* works. Such studies should prove that the law has not been as static and rigid as it has been assumed to be. In addition, *fatawa* works should increase our knowledge about social and economic issues throughout the ages and provide a most credible source for historians. A third area is that of descriptive law, or the law of procedure and evidence. In recent years, a few works on *Adab al-Qadi* have been published, but save for one or two articles on the subject, the whole field of procedure and evidence, which is so important for the protection of individual rights, needs a thorough treatment. Related to this is the question of conflict of laws as between the different jurisdictions representing different schools of law, and the relation between *muftis* and *qadis*. Finally, a number of works on Islamic law are still in manuscript and need to be edited. It is true that scholars in the Arab world have in the past few decades produced excellent editions of important works. But a number remain, and some manuscripts are yet to be discovered. A useful task is making lists from these edited works and manuscipts of technical terms together with their explanation in English in easily understood terms.

These few remarks are to be understood as a part of my experience in pursuing the twin disciplines of Arabic language and literature and Islamic law. They should not in any way be understood to be a discourse about the state of the art relative to both of them. Such a discourse, although very desirable, was not attempted here.

In the beginning of this essay, the Arabic verse declared that winds blow where sailing ships do not wish to go. It must be said, though, that the trip was most enjoyable, replete with physical and mental adventures, satisfying and self-fulfilling.

Contributors

Pierre Cachia (1921–). Pierre Cachia was born a British subject in Fayyum, Egypt. He attended French, Italian, Egyptian, and American schools in Egypt and was graduated B.A. (with distinction) from the American University in Cairo in 1942. After war service with the British Eighth Army in Libya, Tunisia, Sicily, Italy, and Austria, he returned to the American University as a teacher from 1946 to 1949. He obtained a Ph.D. from the University of Edinburgh in 1951 and taught there until 1975, when he was appointed as chair of the Department of Arabic Language and Literature at Columbia University. He became Professor Emeritus in 1991 and spent the following year as a Fellow of the Woodrow Wilson International Center for Scholars.

Pierre Cachia has published eight books, of which the most important are *Taha Husayn: His Place in the Egyptian Literary Renaissance; Popular Narrative Ballads of Modern Egypt;* and *An Overview of Modern Arabic Literature.* He has contributed to various encyclopedias and other works of references, as well as to professional journals. He is a co-founder and joint editor of the *Journal of Arabic Literature,* a member of the Maltese Academy, and a member of the Standing Panel of Experts on Arabic in the University of London.

Albert Hourani (1915–93). Albert Hourani was the second son of Lebanese Arab parents who migrated to Manchester, England, where he received his early education. He took a B.A. degree from Magdalen College, Oxford, then enjoyed over a decade of first-hand experience of Middle Eastern affairs as an instructor at the American University of Beirut, as a political analyst, and then as an advisor to the Arab Office, which was established to present the Palestinian case to the world after World War II.

In 1948 he returned to Oxford to pursue the D. Phil. and was invited to become the university's first lecturer in the history of the modern Middle East. A decade later, he was appointed the founding Director of the Middle East Centre newly established at St. Anthony's College. He was often a Visiting Professor at American universities, most notably at Harvard; the University of Chicago, where he was given an honorary degree in 1991; and the University of Pennsylvania. Upon retirement, he was named Emeritus Fellow at St. Antony's College and, in 1990, he was awarded the CBE (Commander of the British Empire).

His books include *Arabic Thought in the Liberal Age, Europe and the Middle East, The Emergence of the Modern Middle East*, and, most recently, *A History of the Arab Peoples*.

J. C. Hurewitz (1914–). Professor of Government Emeritus at Columbia University, J. C. Hurewitz received the B.A. in philosophy from Trinity College and the M.A. and Ph.D. in government from Columbia. He taught at Columbia from 1950 to 1985, directing its Middle East Institute from 1971 to 1984.

He was a senior analyst on the Near East for the Office of Strategic Services (1943–45) and the U.S. Department of State (1945–46); a political advisor to the U.S. Cabinet Committee on Palestine (1946); a political affairs officer in the Department of Security Council Affairs of the UN Secretariat (1949–50); and later a consultant to the departments of State and Defense, the Rand Corporation, the Stanford Research Institute, and the Congressional Office of Technology Assessment.

Hurewitz was a founding member of the Near and Middle East Committee of the Social Science Research Council; founding fellow of the Middle East Studies Association and the American Institute on Iranian Studies; and governing board member of the Middle East Institute (Washington), the American Research Center in Egypt, the American Research Institute on Turkey, and the Center for Arabic Study Abroad. He organized major international conferences on Middle East studies in liberal arts colleges, Soviet-American rivalry in the Middle East, American-French relations in the Middle East and North Africa, the Middle East and the crisis among industrial states, and world energy. He was an advisory editor of *The Middle East Journal* from its creation in 1947 to 1981.

His principal works include *The Struggle for Palestine*; *Middle East Dilemmas: The Background of United States Policy*; *Diplomacy in the Near and Middle East* (2 vols.); *Middle East Politics: The Military Dimension*; and *The Middle East and North Africa in World Politics* (2 vols.).

Halil Inalcik (1916–). Halil Inalcik is Professor Emeritus of History at the University of Chicago. Born in Istanbul, his father an immigrant from Crimea and his mother from Turkey, he received all of his formal education in Turkey, completing his Ph.D. at the University of Ankara in 1942 with a thesis entitled "Tanzimat and the Bulgarian Question."

He was a Professor of Ottoman History at the University of Ankara from 1952 until 1972, when he joined the History Department of the University of Chicago, where he continued to teach until his retirement in 1986. He also held visiting appointments at Columbia (1953–54), Princeton (1967, 1990–92), University of Pennsylvania (1967), and Harvard (1993). He is currently Professor of Ottoman History at Bilkent University in Ankara.

He has been a member of the Turkish Historical Society since 1947, the American Academy of Arts and Sciences since 1984, an honorary member of the Royal Asiatic Society, and a corresponding member of the Royal Historical Society (London). He has received honorary degrees from Bogaziçi University (Istanbul), the University of Athens, and Hebrew University of Jerusalem. He was co-editor with Tibor Halasi-Kun of *Archivum Ottomanicum* until 1974 and is co-editor of *Journal of Ottoman Studies* (Istanbul) and of Vol. V of *A History of Scientific and Cultural History of Mankind*, prepared by UNESCO. His publications include *The Ottoman Empire: The Classical Age, 1300–1600*; *The Ottoman Empire: Conquest, Organization and Economy*; *Studies in Ottoman Social and Economic History*; and *The Middle East and the Balkans Under the Ottoman Empire*.

Charles Issawi (1916–). Charles Issawi is Bayard Dodge Professor in Near Eastern Studies, Emeritus, Princeton University. Born in Cairo of Syrian parents, he was educated at Victoria College, Alexandria, and Magdalen College, Oxford. Most of his working life has been spent in academia, but he also worked for several years in various governmental organizations: Ministry of Finance, Cairo (1937–38); National (Central) Bank of Egypt (1938–43); and United Nations, New York (1948–55).

He began his teaching career at the American University of Beirut (1943–47), where he taught economics and political science. While at the UN he was a Visiting Lecturer at Harvard in 1950 and at Columbia from 1951 to 1955. In 1955 he joined Columbia full-time, in the Department of Economics, where he became Ragnar Nurkse Professor, and the Middle East Institute, serving as Director from 1962 to 1964. In 1975 he joined Princeton University, where he taught until his retirement in 1986. He was Visiting Professor in Economics at New York University from 1986 to 1991. He received the Giorgio Levi della Vida medal in 1985.

Charles Issawi was Vice President of the Middle East Studies Association in 1968 and President in 1973 and was President of the Middle East Economic Association from 1978 to 1982. He has served on the Editorial Board of many journals and publications and as consultant to the FAO and UN.

He is the author of more than a dozen books, including documentary economic histories of Iran, Turkey, the Fertile Crescent, and the Arab countries and *An Economic History of the Middle East and North Africa since 1800*. Other writings include three books on Egypt, two on oil, a volume of essays (*The Arab Legacy*), two volumes of essays in Arabic, a translation of selections from Ibn Khaldun, and (his favorite) a book of aphorisms (*Issawi's Laws of Social Motion*).

George Makdisi (1920–). George Makdisi is Professor Emeritus of Arabic and Islamic Studies at the University of Pennsylvania. He was born in Detroit, Michigan of Syro-Lebanese parentage. His early schooling began in the U.S., but he attended public schools and lived in Lebanon between the ages of ten and seventeen. He completed high school in Detroit and graduated from the University of Michigan following four years of service in the U.S. Army during World War II. He holds a second bachelor's degree from the

Georgetown University School of Foreign Service, a master's from George-town, a Docteur ès-lettres degree from the Sorbonne, and an honorary Doc-tor of Humane Letters from Georgetown University.

He began his teaching career at the School for Advanced Studies in 1947 and returned to teaching in 1953 at the University of Michigan. Primary aca-demic appointments have been at Harvard University from 1959 until 1973 and the University of Pennsylvania from 1973 until his retirement in 1990.

George Makdisi was the recipient of Guggenheim Fellowships in 1958 and 1968. He has been president of the American Association of Teachers of Arabic (1963–66), the Middle East Studies Association (1976–77), and the American Oriental Society (1987–88). In 1969 he was named to the Chaire d'Etat of the Collège de France, for which he gave a series of lectures on L'Islam Hanbalisant. In 1993 he was awarded the Giorgio Levi Della Vida Award for Excellence in Islamic Studies. He is also an honorary member of the Société Asiatique.

Major publications include *Ibn 'Aqil et la resurgence de l'Islam traditionaliste au XIᵉ siècle de l'Hégire*; *The Rise of Colleges*; *The Rise of Humanism: With Special Reference to Scholasticism*; *History and Politics in Eleventh-Century Baghdad*; and *Religion, Law and Learning in Classical Islam*.

Ernest N. McCarus (1922–). Ernest McCarus, born in Charleston, West Virginia, graduated from Charleston High School in 1939. He served in the Army of the United States from December 1942 to June 1947, with assign-ments to Signal Intelligence in Washington, D.C. and in Korea. He attended the University of Michigan, receiving a B.A. with Distinction in Japanese Language (and election to Phi Beta Kappa), an M.A. in Spanish Language, and a Ph.D. in Linguistics.

He joined the Department of Near Eastern Studies of the University of Michigan as instructor of Arabic and Kurdish Linguistics in 1956, was pro-moted to Associate Professor in 1960, and became Professor in 1967. He served as chairman of that department (1969 to 1977) and as Director of the Center for Middle Eastern and North African Studies (1983–92).

He served in the United States Foreign Service as Director of the Foreign Service Institute of Arabic Language and Area Studies at the American Em-bassy in Beirut (1958–60), was Director of the Center for Arabic Study

Abroad (1974–83), and Director of the Program for Inter-Institutional Collaboration in Area Studies at the University of Michigan (1988–93). He has been president of the Michigan Linguistic Society, the American Association of Teachers of Arabic, and the Arabic Linguistic Society. His publications concern primarily Kurdish language analysis and instruction and Arabic instruction, semantics, and metrics.

Don Peretz (1922–). Don Peretz is Professor Emeritus of Political Science at SUNY-Binghamton. He held the position of professor at SUNY-Binghamton between 1966 and 1992 and served as Director of its Southwest Asian-North African Program from 1966 to 1976. Before coming to SUNY, he taught at Williams, Vassar, Hunter, Long Island, Dropsie, and Hofstra Universities and was Associate Director of the Center for International Programs and Services for the New York State Education Department (1962–66). He received his Ph.D. from Columbia University in 1955.

During World War II Don Peretz was a Japanese interpreter for the U.S. Army in Okinawa; after the war he was a foreign correspondent for the National Broadcasting Company and *United Nations World* and a representative of the American Friends Service Committee with the UN Relief for Palestine Refugees (UNRPR).

Don Peretz is a member of the Council on Foreign Relations, the Institute for Strategic Studies, the National Press Club, and the Middle East Studies Association of North America and is a former Fellow of the Middle East Institute. He serves on the Board of Advisory Editors of the *Middle East Journal* and is a member of the Editorial Board of S*hofar: Interdisciplinary Journal of Jewish Studies*. In 1992 he was a Visiting Fellow in the Jennings Randolph Program for International Peace, U.S. Institute of Peace. Major publications include *The Middle East Today* (6th edition 1993), *Government and Politics of Israel, Intifada—The Palestinian Uprising, Israel and the Palestine Arabs*, and articles in *Foreign Affairs, Middle East Journal, Nation, New Republic, Christianity in Crisis, Jewish Social Studies, Jewish Frontier, Christian Century, Orbis, World and I, Wilson Quarterly, Current History*, and others.

Dankwart A. Rustow (1924–). Dankwart A. Rustow is Distinguished Professor of Political Science and Sociology at the Graduate School of the City

University of New York, where he also is editor of the quarterly *Comparative Politics* and chairman of The Energy Forum, a monthly discussion group of business experts. He has served as Vice President of the Middle East Studies Association (1969–70) and of the American Political Science Association (1973–74) and as co-chairman of the biennial U.S.-Soviet Symposium on the Contemporary Middle East (1983–90).

Dankwart Rustow received his early education in his native Germany and in Turkey. He received his Olgunluk degree from Galatasaray (Istanbul, 1943), his B.A. from Queens College (1947), and his Ph.D. from Yale (1951). Before joining the CUNY faculty he taught at Princeton (1952–59) and Columbia (1959–70) and served as a senior researcher at the Brookings Institution in Washington, D.C. (1961–63).

His publications include *Comparative Political Dynamics: Global Research Perspectives* (1991, ed. with K. P. Erickson); *Turkey: America's Forgotten Ally* (1987, also in German and Turkish translation); *Oil and Turmoil: America Faces OPEC and the Middle East* (1982); *Philosophers and Kings: Studies in Leadership* (ed., 1970); *A World of Nations: Problems of Political Modernization* (1967); and *The Politics of Compromise: A Study of Parties and Cabinet Government in Sweden* (1955). His articles on contemporary history and politics have appeared in scholarly and general publications, including *Foreign Affairs, Foreign Policy, Daedalus, Yale Review, The American Scholar, World Politics, The Encyclopedia of Islam, The New Leader, The New York Times, The Wall Street Journal,* and *The Times Literary Supplement*—as well as in translation into Danish, French, Italian, Thai, and Turkish.

Farhat J. Ziadeh (1917–). Farhat J. Ziadeh was born in Ramallah, Palestine. He was educated at the American Friends Boys School in Ramallah and the American University of Beirut. In 1937 he traveled to London to study law at the University of London and Lincoln's Inn, where he was called to the Bar—after the interruption of the war years—in 1946.

During the war he taught Arabic and lectured on the Middle East in the Army Specialized Training Program at Princeton University and co-authored a book in Arabic on American History for distribution to Middle Eastern libraries.

In 1946 he joined a law firm in Jerusalem and later served as a magistrate for Northern Galilee. The Arab-Israeli war and the loss of the family income from an orange grove in Israel brought him back to the United States, where he taught Arabic at Princeton and worked in New York as an editor for the Arabic Desk of the Voice of America for four years before finally devoting himself completely to teaching Arabic and Islamics at Princeton. In 1966 he was called to the University of Washington to organize the interdisciplinary program in Near Eastern Studies and the Department of Near Eastern Languages and Civilization and taught there until his retirement in 1987. On the occasion of his retirement he was honored by an international conference on Islamic law, which resulted in a *festschrift* on Islamic Law and Jurisprudence, edited by Nicholas Heer. He served one year as President of the Middle East Studies Association, one year as President of the American Association of Teachers of Arabic, and six years as Director of the Center for Arabic Study Abroad.

His publications include *An Introduction to Modern Arabic* (with R. B. Winder); *Lawyers, the Rule of Law, and Liberalism in Modern Egypt*; *Property Law in the Arab World*; and the edition of al-Khassaf's *Adab al-Qadi*.

Index